Delayed Transitional Justice

This book addresses the issue of the timing of transitional justice policies in countries that had negotiated transitions from authoritarianism to democracy.

Why are transitional justice measures often being implemented decades after the events they refer to? More specifically, what combination of factors leads to the implementation of transitional justice policies at certain moments in time? And, what explains countries' different choices and trajectories? To address these questions, this book pursues a comparative analysis of three cases: comparing a case of 'robust' implementation of transitional justice measures (Uruguay), a case where only victim-centered measures were approved (Spain), and a case that sits in between these two (Brazil). Through an in-depth empirical analysis of these specific country-cases, and focusing on seven different transitional justice initiatives, the book identifies the determinants behind delayed transitional justice policies and explains why such policies are more robust in some settings than in others. In doing so, it provides a holistic account of post-transitional justice outcomes, offering more general conclusions and insights about the study of the drivers of transitional justice.

This book will appeal to scholars and students of transitional justice in politics, law, and sociology, as well as to policymakers involved in the implementation and administration of transitional justice measures.

Mariana S. Mendes is a post-doctoral researcher at the Mercator Forum for Migration and Democracy, Institute of Political Science, Technical University Dresden, Germany.

Part of the TRANSITIONAL JUSTICE series

Series editor
Kieran McEvoy, Queen's University Belfast, UK

for information about the series and details of previous and forthcoming titles, see https://www.routledge.com/Transitional-Justice/book-series/TRANJ

A GlassHouse book

Delayed Transitional Justice

Lessons from Spain, Brazil, and Uruguay

Mariana S. Mendes

Routledge
Taylor & Francis Group
a GlassHouse Book

First published 2024
by Routledge
4 Park Square, Milton Park, Abingdon, Oxon OX14 4RN

and by Routledge
605 Third Avenue, New York, NY 10158

Routledge is an imprint of the Taylor & Francis Group, an informa business

a GlassHouse book

British Library Cataloguing-in-Publication Data
A catalogue record for this book is available from the British Library

ISBN: 978-1-032-31836-3 (hbk)
ISBN: 978-1-032-31839-4 (pbk)
ISBN: 978-1-003-31160-7 (ebk)

DOI: 10.4324/9781003311607

Typeset in Sabon
by Deanta Global Publishing Services, Chennai, India

Contents

Acknowledgments *vii*

Introduction 1

PART I
Conceptual and theoretical framework **11**

1 Definition and operationalization of transitional justice: The Transitional Justice Scale 13

2 Theoretical framework: A holistic approach to delayed transitional justice 22

PART II
Transitional justice trajectories in context **43**

3 Spain: From deliberate forgetting to limited acknowledgment 45

4 Uruguay: From blockage to criminal accountability 110

5 Brazil: From a marginal issue to the 'right to truth' 159

PART III
Comparative analysis **209**

6 Making sense of the timing of transitional justice 211

7 Making sense of differences in countries' trajectories 229

Conclusion 243

Annex *251*
Index *253*

Acknowledgments

My deepest gratitude goes to all of those who were part of this research when agreeing to provide me with some of the time, insights, knowledge, and personal stories in the interviews I conducted in Brazil, Uruguay, and Spain. A particular mention goes to those who, despite their limited resources, continue to use their voice and best efforts to achieve forms of accountability for past wrongs.

I am eternally indebted to the Foundation for Science and Technology, Portugal, and to the European University Institute for financing my doctoral studies and therefore, having made this work possible. When I initiated this project, my home country was still plunged in a deep economic crisis, and a significant part of its youth could only dream of an opportunity like the one I was about to get, which adds to my sense of responsibility and appreciation.

I also want to thank my doctoral supervisor, Donatella della Porta, for having given me the opportunity to pursue a PhD in a place like no other as well as for her trust and support.

All those who provided me with feedback on this manuscript and who have supported me along this (very long) way should feel acknowledged too. The list is too long to include here and would probably turn into a nostalgic journey throughout my Florentine years, when I was lucky enough to meet a good number of young academics who manage the feat of being bright, kind, and fun, all at the same time. I do have to mention, however, Manès Weisskircher and Kristina Chmelar, because without their 'push' this book would probably never have seen the light of day.

Finally, the last word always goes to family. There are countless things I am grateful for, but at top of that list is my family's support and the fact that Dennis is now part of it. This book is dedicated to them.

Introduction

At the time of his death in December 2006, Augusto Pinochet had just been put under house arrest for his involvement in the 'Caravans of Death' case, an episode dating back to 1973 when an army death squad tortured and killed more than 70 Chilean political prisoners. Though he would continue as commander-in-chief of the Chilean Army up until 1998, becoming a 'senator-for-life' thenceforth, Pinochet would spend the final years of his life fighting the successive legal cases opened against him in Chile and abroad. At the same time as his death, but on the other side of the globe, the government of Cambodia had just agreed with the United Nations to establish the so-called Khmer Rouge Tribunal, charged with bringing to justice the senior leaders of a regime responsible for the genocide of about 25% of the country's population some 30 years before. Meanwhile, in Poland, the parliament was preparing to pass a series of amendments leading to a radical expansion of lustration legislation, a mechanism widely used in Eastern Europe to screen, exclude, or limit the access of former Communist agents to public office. This was one year before the Spanish parliament approved the so-called Law on Historical Memory, the first legislative initiative in Spain formally condemning Franco's regime and recognizing the victims of violence – all 30 years after Spain's transition to democracy. Brazil would take until 2011 to approve a state-sponsored investigatory commission – the *National Truth Commission* – on the most serious violations of human rights committed during the 1964–1985 dictatorship. This list of examples could go on indefinitely, speaking vividly about the spread of efforts to address problematic historical periods or, to use a term that non-coincidentally was coined in Germany, engage in *Vergangenheitsbewältigung* ('coming to terms with the past'). On the one hand, it is most intriguing that all these efforts take place decades after the events they refer to. This goes against Huntington's (1991: 228) prediction that public interest in justice rapidly erodes over time or O'Donnell and Schmitter's (1986: 29) assertion that time attenuates the bitterness of memories and those involved will be forgotten. On the other hand, not all of them are examples of criminal accountability; some, in fact, speak to the variety of methods that can be used to address a violent past. This

DOI: 10.4324/9781003311607-1

book constitutes an effort first, to explain the *timing* of this kind of initiative and second, to account for cross-country differences in the choice of diverse ways of 'dealing with the past'. Specifically, it focuses on three cases that hold the similarity of having had a 'negotiated' transition to democracy but that differ in their trajectories later on: Spain, Brazil, and Uruguay.

Why focus on timing?

The range of possible institutional measures meant to tackle past violations of human rights and provide some form of redress to the victims of a dictatorial regime and/or a war has become a field of scholarship of its own, commonly known as *Transitional Justice* (TJ). It was initially labeled as such given the prominence of the topic in 'transition periods' – from a dictatorship to a democracy or from a war to a period of peace – and because it was born following the widespread turn to democratic regimes in Europe and in the Americas during the so-called third wave of democratization in the 1970s and 1980s. At the time, practitioners and scholars were confronted with how to find some measure of justice for victims of repressive state apparatuses, whether to punish those responsible, and how to balance moral imperatives with the desire for political stability (Orentlicher 1991; Zalaquett 1992; Arthur 2009). Even though TJ was initially defined as justice in times of political transition (as in the founding works of Kritz [1995] and Teitel [2000]), the expectation that transitional settlements would lay to rest accountability issues is no longer the norm today, as more and more scholars underline that its study extends far beyond what are considered transition periods[1] (Elster 2006; Roth-Arriaza 2006; Aguilar 2008; Collins 2010; Skaar et al. 2016).

Jon Elster (2006: 6) distinguishes between (a) *immediate* transitional justice, (b) *protracted* transitional justice, when the process starts immediately after the transition but goes on for a long time, (c) *second-wave* transitional justice, when processes are initiated and concluded and after a long period of latency, new proceedings are undertaken, and (d) *postponed* transitional justice, when the first actions take place many years after the transition. There are various reasons to expect *immediate* and *protracted* to be the rule and *postponed* to be the exception. Memories of the period of violations become less vivid, investigation of the abuses becomes more difficult, perpetrators grow old and die, victims and families of the victims move on, public interest diminishes, and the past becomes mostly an issue for historians to deal with. Moreover, if is it true, as Méndez (1997) suggests, that new democracies are impelled to draw a thick line under the past to boost their credentials as radical departures from the past, then the use of TJ measures as a regime-legitimation device naturally makes most sense during the foundational stages of a new regime. Elster (2004: 77) himself says that the closest he has come to a 'law' on transitional justice is that the intensity of the demand for retribution decreases with time, though he goes on to add that 'even here, we find that counteracting mechanisms may keep memory and resentment alive for a century or more'. Indeed, and as the examples mentioned earlier demonstrate, there is plenty of empirical evidence attesting to instances of *postponed* justice. This analytical puzzle forms the starting point of this book: *why engage with violations of the past regime so long after they occurred? Why now, when victims and perpetrators are old or even dead?*

Why focus on negotiated transitions to democracy?

Though the Transitional Justice field still lacks strong theoretical foundations, much of the initial literature was inspired by the political constraints the transition period could pose for the concretization of accountability measures, as challenges to the previous elites could prove destabilizing for the newly founded regime. Indeed, a characteristic common to many transitions is the 'omnipresent fear that a coup will be attempted and succeed' (O'Donnell and Schmitter 1986: 25). A fundamental and generally accepted hypothesis – dating back to classics such as O'Donnell and Schmitter's *Transitions from Authoritarian Rule* (1986) or Huntington's *The Third Wave* (1991) – is that prosecution and punishment are more likely to happen when the old elites have been overthrown and replaced than when they get to negotiate the terms of the transition. The type of transition – ranging from negotiated transitions (voluntary ending of the regime) to ruptured ones (regime collapse)[2] – is seen as symptomatic of the balance of power between old and new elites and therefore, of how much room there will be for the former's rule to be challenged during the transition period (Huyse 1995; Sutter 1995; Barahona de Brito et al. 2001; Elster 2006). 'The more a transition entails the defeat of the old authoritarian elite and repressors, the wider is the scope for truth and justice policies' (Barahona de Brito et al. 2001: 11). In Huntington's words (1991, 228), justice is a function of political power – 'officials of strong authoritarian regimes that voluntarily ended themselves were not prosecuted; officials of weak authoritarian regimes that collapsed were punished, if they were promptly prosecuted by the new democratic government'.

Indeed, this hypothesis holds true for a large number of cases (Olsen et al. 2010: 156). While the collapse of the regime in Greece and Argentina gave way to trials of the military *juntas*, in countries such as Brazil or Uruguay, a controlled transition – in which the military stepped down voluntarily and retained great autonomy – came with the enactment of amnesty laws that retroactively foreclosed the possibility of criminal liability. While in the first set of cases, the collapse of the regime was accompanied by its widespread delegitimization, creating room for accountability initiatives, in the second, the risk of instability and the eventual loyalty to negotiated agreements prevented the enactment of robust TJ measures.[3] Therefore, much of the empirical variation between cases of *immediate* TJ and *postponed* TJ is likely to be accounted for based on the transition type/relative power hypothesis. While it is true that 'ruptured' transitions are also not risk-free, the incentives to use TJ measures as a means to draw a thick line under the past and to boost the credentials of the newly funded regime are much greater.

This is why this book will focus on contexts of negotiated transitions to democracy only, where *postponed* TJ is more likely and where variation in TJ trajectories later on cannot be reduced to the transition type variable. If it is true that in these cases, the type of transition is already an integral part of the answer to why there were no TJ measures during the transition period, this does not fully account for why they are enacted later on. The gradual disappearance of the conditions that prevented the implementation of TJ measures during the transition period – the reversal of an unfavorable balance of power or the disappearance of the perceived risk of instability – certainly provides a more favorable context, but it falls short of a sufficient explanation for *why*, *when*, and *which kind* of transitional justice measures are approved. If this were the case, one would expect to see the resolute implementation of TJ measures as soon as new elites take over and a potentially favorable balance of power is observed. In practice, progress tends to be slow and uneven, and to vary across countries with similarly stable democratic regimes.

The cases

This study deals with the cases of Spain, Brazil, and Uruguay because these countries hold a number of important similarities. Besides (a) having had a negotiated transition to democracy, (b) they have all transitioned from an authoritarian regime that carried out systematic and violent repression during at least part of the dictatorial period and (c) they have successfully achieved what is generally perceived as a consolidated democratic regime. The latter is important because functioning democratic and rule-of-law systems are critical to the ability of countries to implement transitional justice, while in semi-authoritarian states, the chances are that TJ is either not implemented or put to perverse political uses (Fletcher et al. 2009; Vinjamuri and Snyder 2015: 317). In addition, they all transitioned to democracy during the early stages of the so-called 'third wave of democratization' (1975–1985). This is an ideal period of study, not only because the analysis of *postponed* TJ requires that a considerable amount of time has passed, but also because temporal nearness among cases allows me to keep features of the international environment constant and conveniently restricts my selection pool to Latin America and Southern Europe. This time period also corresponds to the TJ 'norm emergence' period, that is, to the moment in which TJ practices began to be enacted but were still not commonplace (Sikkink 2011). While Spain is the only case in Southern Europe where the transition to democracy was negotiated (in contrast to Portugal and Greece), there are various examples in Latin America in the first half of the 1980s: Brazil, Uruguay, Ecuador, Honduras, and Peru. I decided to restrict the analysis to the former two because Ecuador, Honduras, and Peru did not experience an actual transition to a state respectful of classical political rights, as a pattern of authoritarian human right abuses against political opponents continued afterwards, thus complicating the comparative analysis of TJ trajectories.

This sample is small enough to allow an in-depth analysis of each case but also sufficient to provide significant variation in TJ paths. In fact, Spain, Brazil, and Uruguay all have different records when it comes to the application of TJ policies. While they all experienced negotiated transition to democracy where TJ measures were either seen as inconceivable or hazardous, Uruguay has nowadays gone as far as to convict various high-profile agents of the dictatorship, whereas Brazil and Spain have kept their amnesty laws intact. Brazil instead created a 'Truth Commission' in 2011/12, an investigatory body with an important public acknowledgment function, which could be somewhat equated to the 2001 Peace Commission in Uruguay. Spain, on the other hand, has restricted itself mostly to victim-centered measures of the reparatory type, something on which both Brazil and Uruguay also have a record (though not necessarily with the same degree of comprehensiveness) (Table 1.1). In short, although all three countries constitute what Vinjamuri and Snyder (2015) define as 'easy cases' – where democratic institutions, fairly developed legal systems, and a free civil society make the success of TJ policies likely – the reality is that there is still much variation to be accounted for. This makes it all the more pertinent to go beyond the question of what explains TJ measures to the question of variation in TJ choices and paths.

Table I.1 Most significant transitional justice measures (1990–2020)

Country-(transition year)	*First step*	*Second step*	*Third step*
Spain (1977)	1990 Law 4/1990 (reparations)	2007 Law 52/2007 (Historical Memory Law)	
Uruguay (1985)	2000 Peace Commission	2005 Executive's 'loophole approach' to the amnesty law	2011 Law 18.831 (derogation of the amnesty law)
Brazil (1985)	1995 Law 9.140/95 (reparations)	2011 Law 12.528 National Truth Commission	

Design and methods

An in-depth case-oriented analysis is, at a first stage, crucial to understand the unfolding of transitional justice trajectories over time for each of the three countries. Close attention is paid to the sequence of relevant events and actors for each case in order to draw descriptive and possibly explanatory inferences. In particular, and in order to answer the first question of interest – *what leads to the implementation of TJ measures at certain moments in time?* – careful and thick analysis of the moment leading up to the adoption of specific TJ policies is needed in order to identify relevant actors, interactions, and possible motivations, as well as potentially relevant contextual changes. The individual cases under study are, then, the various instances of TJ measures in Table I.1 (seven in total), and the main method of analysis consists of detailed description of relevant events previous to the implementation of the specific measure under study.

The analysis of these specific critical junctures – the moments preceding policy formulation – will be embedded in a broader historical analysis of TJ trajectories for each of the three country-cases, as this is essential in order to tackle the second question of interest: *what, from a comparative perspective, explains different transitional justice paths and outcomes?* In accordance with Mill's method of difference, the study of the historical evolution of the relationship of state institutions and key actors with their recent past, across three country-cases with different final outcomes, is expected to bring to the fore key dissimilarities, which will shed light on the reasons why Uruguay managed to go further than Spain in its TJ policies and why, roughly speaking, Brazil appears to be mid-way between the two. A comparative analysis that is *historical* appears essential, since, following a historical institutionalist approach, I deem that the choices made during early stages have a cumulative and enduring impact, leading to the establishment of ideas and preferences that generate self-reinforcing and path-dependent processes (Capoccia and Kelemen 2007). To put it simply, previous approaches towards the political treatment of the past, from the moment of their inception, matter in understanding later approaches, an argument I will develop and substantiate later on.

For these purposes, different types of data are triangulated. First of all, I draw heavily on the existing country-cases literature. Although few studies have focused on the specific set of questions I am asking, there is valuable country-specific literature that has helped me to reconstruct in detail the transitional justice trajectories of each country. Secondly, I have conducted about 50 expert and elite interviews in all three countries during the period 2015–2018. These comprise (a) policymakers who were part of or close to the policy circles responsible for TJ-related legislation, (b) individuals engaged in civil society initiatives that issued TJ claims, and (c) academics who are country experts. These were semi-structured interviews, adapted to the different profiles of the interviewees. They were essential in allowing a greater familiarization with the debates, having actual perspectives 'from the field', and providing rich details and points of view. The full list of interviewees, discriminated by country and category, is available in the Annex. In addition, I also resort to the analysis of primary documents, most notably legislation that falls into the scope of transitional justice, parliamentary initiatives and debates, judicial decisions, and party-associated publications. The most important TJ legislation as well as party programs were scanned in all cases. Lastly, I used media sources when lacking a detailed context on a specific event or when assessing the public salience of an issue.

It is in the exhaustive combination of all these different methods that this work finds its methodological strength. The combination of different sources allowed me to obtain the necessary fine-grained knowledge, which is of essence in building a thick narrative, focused not only on the description of relevant moments or events but also on the analysis of the possible factors leading to the specific outcomes under study. Obviously, some TJ choices/policies received greater coverage than others, and therefore, the level of detail is not the same for each case. I attempt to be as transparent as possible in terms of the limitations found as well as the various (and often confounding) factors that appear in each moment.

Plan of the book

This manuscript is structured in three parts. In Part I, I introduce the conceptual and theoretical framework this work relies upon. First, I make clear how transitional justice is defined and operationalized. Secondly, I lay down expectations regarding the determinants of (variation in) delayed transitional justice, namely, (a) which type of factors I will look for when accounting for the timing of implementation and why, and (b) how cross-country variation will be approached. Part II of the book is constituted by 'country chapters', that is, in-depth analyses of the transitional justice trajectories of each individual country, relying heavily on thick description but also on detailed analysis of the reasons behind the (lack of) treatment of the past during the transition period and the implementation of TJ measures later on. Case-study chapters are organized identically so as to facilitate inter-case comparison later on. I start by contextualizing each case, looking at its history, the characteristics of political repression, and the political context of the transition to democracy, because these are fundamental in understanding where they come from. I also focus on how violations of the past regime were approached during the transition period and the reasons why this was so, as I deem that the ways in which the past was approached during earlier periods have an impact on its later treatment. I then move to the analysis of transitional justice trajectories later on, in a chronological fashion, focusing on the events and relevant actors behind the implementation of TJ measures. Finally, Part III puts the three countries under a comparative light, summarizing the main findings and providing more direct answers to the main questions under study. It is divided into two chapters, each tackling a different question: Chapter 6 provides answers to the question of *timing* of TJ implementation (also shedding light on the reasons behind the *kinds* of TJ policies chosen and their *sequencing*), while Chapter 7 focuses on the potentially relevant factors that account for cross-country differences.

Notes

1 Renowned scholars of transitions from authoritarian rule like O'Donnell and Schmitter (1986: 5) define 'transition' as the 'interval between one political regime and another', which stops at the moment that a new regime is installed, being 'delimited on the one side by the launching of the process of dissolution of the authoritarian regime and, on the other, by the installation of some form of democracy'. It is debatable whether the transition actually ends with the first democratic elections, but it relatively safe to assume that after two regular free and fair elections, one can already speak of a *post-transition period*.

2 The classification of regime transitions into two broad types – negotiated versus ruptured – can obviously be met with the criticism of being too simplistic or reductionist. However, there is a strong qualitative difference between regime transitions that were set in motion and were (at least partially) controlled by agents of the former regime and those in which those same agents were forced to step down or flee, which makes this distinction a warranted one.

3 This hypothesis is stronger in cases where the military is directly implicated in the violations of the previous regime and where the risk of instability comes from a military insurgency. It is no coincidence that the strongest critiques to Huntington's theory come from scholars of Eastern Europe, where there was no military threat.

References

Aguilar, Paloma. 2008. 'Transitional or Post-transitional Justice? Recent Developments in the Spanish Case.' *South European Society and Politics* 13, no. 4: 417–433.

Arthur, Paige. 2009. 'How 'Transitions' Reshaped Human Rights: A Conceptual History of Transitional Justice.' *Human Rights Quarterly* 31: 321–367.

Barahona de Brito, Alexandra, Carmen González-Enríquez and Paloma Aguilar, eds. 2001. *The Politics of Memory: Transitional Justice in Democratizing Societies*. Oxford: Oxford University Press.

Capoccia, Giovanni and Daniel R. Kelemen. 2007. 'The Study of Critical Junctures. Theory, Narrative, and Counterfactuals in Historical Institutionalism.' *World Politics* 59: 341–369.

Collins, Cath. 2010. *Post-Transitional Justice: Human Rights Trials in Chile and El Salvador*. University Park: Pennsylvania State University Press.

Elster, Jon. 2004. *Closing the Books. Transitional Justice in Historical Perspective*. Cambridge: Cambridge University Press.

Elster, Jon. 2006. *Retribution and Reparation in the Transition to Democracy*. Cambridge: Cambridge University Press.

Fletcher, Laurel, Harvey Weinstein, and Jamie Rowen. 2009. 'Context, Timing and the Dynamics of Transitional Justice: A Historical Perspective.' *Human Rights Quarterly* 31: 163–220.

Huntington, Samuel P. 1991. *The Third Wave: Democratization in the Late Twentieth Century*. Norman: University of Oklahoma Press.

Huyse, Luc. 1995. 'Justice after Transition: On the Choices Successor Elites Make in Dealing with the Past.' *Law & Social Inquiry* 20, no. 1: 51–78.

Kritz, Neil J., ed. 1995. *Transitional Justice: How Emerging Democracies Reckon with Former Regimes*. Washington, DC: United States Institute of Peace Press.

Méndez, Juan E. 1997. 'Accountability for Past Abuses.' *Human Rights Quarterly* 19, no. 2: 255–282.

O'Donnell, Guillermo and Philippe Schmitter. 1986. *Transitions from Authoritarian Rule. Tentative Conclusions about Uncertain Democracies*. Baltimore: Johns Hopkins University Press.

Olsen, Tricia D., Leigh A. Payne, and Andrew G. Reiter. 2010. *Transitional Justice in Balance: Comparing Processes, Weighing Efficacy*. Washington, DC: United States Institute of Peace Press.

Orentlicher, Diane F. 1991. 'Settling Accounts: The Duty to Prosecute Human Rights Violations of a Prior Regime.' *The Yale Law Journal* 100, no. 8: 2537–2615.

Roth-Arriaza, Naomi. 2006. 'The New Landscape of Transitional Justice.' In *Transitional Justice in the Twenty-First Century: Beyond Truth versus Justice*, edited by Naomi Roth-Arriaza and Javier Mariezcurrena, 1–16. Cambridge: Cambridge University Press.

Sikkink, Kathryn. 2011. *The Justice Cascade: How Human Rights Prosecutions are changing world politics*. New York: W. W. Norton.

Skaar, Elin, Jemima García-Godos, and Cath Collins, eds. 2016. *Transitional Justice in Latin America: The Uneven Road from Impunity Towards Accountability*. Abingdon: Routledge.

Sutter, Daniel. 1995. 'Settling Old Scores. Potholes along the Transition from Authoritarian Rule.' *Journal of Conflict Resolution* 39, no. 1: 110–128.

Teitel, Ruti G. 2000. *Transitional Justice*. New York: Oxford University Press.

Vinjamuri, Leslie and Jack Snyder. 2015. 'Law and Politics in Transitional Justice.' *Annual Review of Political Science* 18: 303–327.

Zalaquett, José. 1992. 'Balancing Ethical Imperatives and Potical Constraints: The Dilemma of New Democracies Confronting Past Human Rights Violations.' *Hastings Law Journal* 43, no. 6: 1425–1438.

Part I

Conceptual and theoretical framework

Chapter 1

Definition and operationalization of transitional justice

The Transitional Justice Scale

The existing literature is not always clear and rigorous when it comes to the definition and operationalization of transitional justice. Debates revolve around the kind of mechanisms or measures that should be included under the TJ heading, what its goals are or should be, and whether the concept is suitable at all. The field is often vaguely taken as the set of mechanisms to 'deal with the past' or inversely, restrictively identified with one single mechanism. As Roth-Arriaza (2006: 2) puts it,

> transitional justice can be broadly or narrowly defined. At its broadest, it involves anything that a society devises in order to deal with a legacy of conflict and/or widespread human rights violations, from changes in criminal codes to those in high school textbooks, from the creation of memorials, museums, and days of mourning to police and court reform, to tackling the distributional inequality that underlie conflict.

This contrast with the field's initial stages, when TJ referred to the dilemmas involved in achieving accountability for past abuses during transitions from authoritarianism to democracy, being narrowly identified with criminal prosecutions and at times, with state-led investigatory commissions. Since then, the field has become a victim of its own popularity and is nowadays often used to include broad issues and agendas, to the point that it has been criticized for having been transformed into a 'non-field' that has become 'all things to all people' (Bell 2009).

Part of this is a result of its enthusiastic adoption among policy circles involved in post-conflict settings. This is visible in the ambitious definition given by the *International Center for Transitional Justice* (2009), which defines TJ as a 'response to systematic or widespread violation of human rights [which] seeks recognition for victims and promotion of possibilities for peace, reconciliation and democracy'. Academics are often more agnostic about the goals and potential of transitional justice policies. Vinjamuri and Snyder (2015: 305), relying on various definitions used in academic circles, succinctly define it as 'the set of institutions, policies, and practices to deal with atrocities

DOI: 10.4324/9781003311607-3

and major politically motivated human rights violations in the process, anticipation, or aftermath of regime change or violent conflict'. They do not explicitly mention its goals, but they are usually related to producing accountability – which Skaar et al. (2016: 4) define as 'an explicit acknowledgment by the state that grave human rights violations have taken place and that the state was involved in or responsible for them'. Recognizing the victims as bearers of equal rights and rectifying their sense of wrong is implicitly or explicitly assumed as the main purpose of accountability. TJ's relationship to broader and more ambitious goals – such as peace, reconciliation, and democracy – is instead (rightly) taken as an empirical question, which has been subject to some debate and not yet conclusive evidence (Thoms et al. 2010).

The concept's suitability has also been put under scrutiny, namely, whether it should be differentiated from ordinary justice at all or whether it makes sense to apply it to non-transition periods or to speak of *transitional* when analyzing TJ mechanisms in non-transition settings (Posner and Vermuele 2004; Bell 2009). Winter (2013) has gone against these views. He contends that forms of redress in established democracies still deserve to be put under the 'transitional justice heading' given (a) the similarities of practices/measures, (b) the trans-regime context, (c) and the political legitimating function they still perform, something that, he argues, is part of *transitional* politics, given the normative transformation in the way grievous wrongdoing is dealt with when implementing TJ policies.

Indeed, if anything, a framework different from ordinary justice makes sense, given that when speaking of transitional justice, we are referring to a concrete political period and to measures that imply a rejection of a certain political order (and the legitimation of a different one). The object of transitional justice is also specific: mass violations of human rights, which are not individual and isolated acts but committed in a systematic manner. The targets of criminal accountability measures are also particular, as they invariably include state agents (those who are most supposed to protect human rights in the first place). It could moreover be argued that because victims are numerous, accountability and redress are not individual-focused procedures but perform a societal/ collective function. All of this is largely independent of the period of time in which TJ measures are implemented, which is why I consider that it still makes sense to speak of transitional justice in non-transition periods. Authors who have similarly focused on instances of *delayed* TJ have simply proposed to use the term *post-transitional justice* to refer to the reintroduction of the issue of past violations (and how to address them) on the agenda and concomitant revisiting of transition-era settlements (Collins 2010; Raimundo 2012).

That said, we are still left with the issue that when it comes to specifying what transitional justice is actually about, the term tends to be overly restricted or poorly defined, which is why authors such as Grodsky (2009) have argued that a new methodological and more rigorous approach is needed. In the following, I offer one possible avenue for operationalizing and categorizing TJ measures, an important step for any rigorous cross-national evaluation of TJ trajectories. My classification has a few similarities to the one proposed by Grodsky (2009, 2010), but also important differences, in that it aims to be at the same time more systematic and open-ended. In an attempt to balance the need for good operationalization with the wish to avoid a rigid and pre-defined 'one-size-fits-all' approach, I first opt to categorize TJ measures according to their most proximate target – (a) victims, (b) the broader society, and (c) agents of the former regime. To be clear, the category of victims is here meant to encompass those who suffer varied types of human rights violations, that is, those who, usually for political reasons, 'disappeared', were murdered, tortured, unlawfully detained, dismissed from their jobs, or forced into exile. Families of a direct victim of serious crimes are also victims as per international jurisprudence. Classifying TJ measures according to their most proximate target, rather than specific TJ policies, has the obvious advantage that such policies do not have to be defined a priori and that any other potentially relevant measures can be included later. In the following, I give various examples of TJ measures that fall into these three categories and explain why my empirical analysis of TJ trajectories considers only some of them. I then proceed to explain why it makes sense to operationalize these measures in the form of a 'Transitional Justice Scale', which will be used throughout this work to assess how far countries have gone in their transitional justice trajectories.

Victim-centered policies typically consist of what has been broadly defined as reparations, usually in the form of monetary compensations for the damage suffered. Restitution and rehabilitation procedures are commonly considered to fall into the category of reparations, the first being understood as steps to restore the victim to the original situation before the violations were committed (restitution of property, employment, computation of retirement pensions so as to include years of prison, etc.) and the second traditionally referring to the provision of medical and psychological assistance to victims. Not all measures that fall into the 'reparation' category have the same qualitative value, though. Measures that simply aim at giving back to the victims the rights they were stripped of during the previous regime, or that aim at putting them on an equal footing to other citizens (usually of the restitution type), are more of a basic obligation of any democratic state than an attempt at producing accountability and rectifying the victims' sense of wrong. This, together with practical considerations, is the reason why, when speaking of *significant* transitional justice steps in each of the case-studies, I do not include restitution-type procedures but focus on the most important reparation measures instead.

Though often not taken as a transitional justice measure, the search, recovery, and identification of the remains of those who went missing is an important victim-centered aspect of 'dealing with the past'. This is, in fact, a top priority for family members, as the case-studies will show. Giving the victims a proper burial is not only a fundamental step in the mourning process for the families but also a basic recognition of the victim's human dignity, which is why such measures should be included in victim-centered types of policies. This is in line with Kovras (2017), who makes a plea for the inclusion of exhumations as a TJ mechanism and who highlights that a stage of 'forensic truth' is often the first step in transitional justice efforts, sometimes opening the door to 'broader forms of truth'.

As for the second category of TJ measures, i.e., measures targeted at the broader society – or, to put it differently, aimed at producing public awareness and acknowledgment – the most renowned have been what are often called 'truth commissions', state-sanctioned investigatory bodies meant to gather and compile systematic evidence of the country's past record in terms of human rights violations and possibly unravel large patterns of conduct, producing a final public report and sometimes involving acknowledgment ceremonies. Publicly visible apologies or other forms of public recognition of wrongdoing are also a form of acknowledgment. Memorialization initiatives (including museums, the creation of memorials, changes in street names, etc.) and changes in high school textbooks also fall into this category. However, as it would be unmanageable to collect data on all of those types of initiatives, the case-study analysis will be restricted only to the most important public acknowledgment measures, judging on the basis of their visibility (public impact) and comprehensiveness.

Finally, when it comes to procedures targeted at the agents of former regimes, they can go all the way from processes of vetting or purges up to trials of the ones responsible for human rights abuses. Vetting and purges refer to removal from public office based on either prior individual conduct or simply prior affiliation. These were measures more systematically used in Eastern and Central Europe, where the efforts at de-communization took this particular form (known as *lustration*), something that is related to the particular type of repressive methods (based on widespread informant networks and an active secret police) (Grodsky 2010: 58–74). In other contexts, including the ones under study, the absence of vetting policies does not necessarily imply there was absolute continuity in personnel, but it makes it unfeasible to attempt to trace the individual fate of those involved in the dictatorship's repressive apparatus,[1] which is why the case-study analysis will be restricted to criminal accountability proceedings.

While at first sight these measures might have little in common with each other, they all contribute to the same general purposes of producing accountability, implicitly or explicitly condemning a violent past, and providing some form of recognition and redress for the victims, which explains why I include them in the 'TJ package'.[2] This is not an exhaustive list, however, and the advantage of this target-based classification system is precisely that additional measures can be easily incorporated a posteriori.

It is logical to think that the greater the institutional effort to confront a violent past, the more likely the implementation of various types of TJ measures is. Even if the specific TJ measures may vary from context to context, it is expected that a comprehensive effort to deal with a violent past will in some way or another target the three types of actors mentioned earlier, based on the fundamental moral premises that (a) victims should be recognized, (b) societies should be aware of their recent history, and (c) perpetrators should be condemned. A holistic approach to TJ is, in fact, commonly defended in policy circles as the most desirable one, since the various TJ mechanisms are said to complement and reinforce each other, working better together than in isolation. This is because while prosecutions send a strong signal to society, they also carry a greater risk of being viewed as a form of scapegoating or political revenge when unaccompanied by other initiatives; in the same vein, public acknowledgment policies in isolation from other measures can be interpreted as 'mere words' with little or no consequences, while reparations alone will likely be perceived as an attempt to buy the victims' silence (International Center for Transitional Justice 2009).

In practice, though, TJ policies do not tend to be implemented at the same time (particularly in sensitive contexts such as the ones under study), nor are they perceived to be of equal value in the extent to which they contribute to the general purpose of accountability. In fact, their perceived importance in fulfilling the goals of TJ is proportional to their degree of riskiness, that is, the more relevance they are granted in the literature, the more controversial and difficult their implementation seems to be. Take criminal prosecutions. Because the greatest obstacle to TJ usually lies in the opposition of those who represented or allied with the previous regime, criminal procedures targeted at them will logically be the most sensitive measure. Legalist/retributive theoretical and normative approaches, however, naturally defend criminal punishment as the only genuine form of justice and thus, the optimal method for dealing with past crimes (Vinjamuri and Snyder 2004; Aukerman 2002). Even those who argue for non-prosecution alternatives generally do it out of concern for political stability and concede the desirability of prosecution (Aukerman 2002: 40). Its benefits in terms of trust in the rule of law (demonstrating that all are liable under the same law), deterrence of future abuses, honoring the victims, and establishing the wrongfulness of past crimes are commonly deemed to be superior to those of other TJ mechanisms (Vinjamuri and Snyder 2004). In addition to this, it is often the preferred policy option for the victims, too.[3]

In the practical impossibility of conducting trials, though, measures directed at public acknowledgment of the events tend to be considered a second-best option in fostering the goals of honoring the victims and producing some form of accountability. Victims themselves have often underlined the importance that public recognition carries for them, perceived as superior to other forms of reparation (Magarrell 2007: 2). 'Truth commissions' have been particularly praised for their capacity to produce public acknowledgment and help in the construction of a historical narrative that takes victims and human rights violations seriously. The distinction between *knowledge* and *acknowledgment* is important here – and this is why state-sanctioned investigatory mechanisms have been defended as an addition to the work of historians, who produce the former but not the latter. Acknowledgment, in the words of Thomas Nagel, is 'what happens and can only happen to knowledge when it becomes officially sanctioned, when it is made part of the public cognitive scene' (quoted in Weschler 1990: 4). Michael Ignatieff (1996: 111) has famously stated that truth commissions can 'reduce the number of lies that can circulate unchallenged in public discourse'. Nevertheless, the greater room for politicization of this kind of mechanism (when compared with trials) and their inability to produce the same kind or degree of accountability means that they occupy more of a middle ground in their relative importance.

Victim-centered policies, on the other hand, are the most innocuous ones. Though they are surely indispensable in any comprehensive TJ package and have the value of focusing directly on victims, they are perhaps the most fragile mechanism when implemented alone. The fact that reparatory mechanisms have been the least researched in the transitional justice literature already tells a great deal about their perceived importance. It is often argued that reparatory steps should be taken together with policies that foster public acknowledgment, given that their implementation alone generally acquires less public visibility than other measures and particularly in the case of monetary reparations, risks being seen by victims/families as a 'silencing measure' or 'blood money' rather than a sincere form of condemnation of past events (although this may well depend on the previous degree of economic marginalization of the victims [Robins, 2011]). As Minow (1998: 93) notes, monetary measures are hardly a remedy for non-monetary harms and risk trivializing suffering. Together with public recognition measures, though, they do have the potential to turn words into deeds.

To judge how far a country has gone in 'dealing with its past', it is, then, fair to assess how much and how far it has moved from the least to the most robust measures – that is, from victim-centered to perpetrator-focused ones – along what I denominate the 'Transitional Justice Scale' (Figure 1.1). Robustness here is understood in terms of the extent to which these measures contribute to the overall goals of TJ. This hierarchy is quite implicit in most

Figure 1.1 Transitional Justice Scale.

of the literature, but to the best of my knowledge, has not been spelled out and operationalized as such thus far. This scale is similar to Grodsky's (2010) 'transitional justice spectrum' in two ways, since it also organizes TJ mechanisms along a continuum that proceeds from restorative-type measures to retributive ones and similarly, broadly reflects an incremental degree of risk and severity (going from most lenient to harshest measures), since each step up the ladder involves the implementation of a more provocative or threatening policy with respect to the members of the old regime (Grodsky 2010: 39). However, it also has two main differences from Grodsky's scale. The first is that rather than proposing a specific set of measures, it is more open-ended, focusing on targets (rather than specific policies) and thus, leaving the door open for the inclusion of other measures. The second is the addition that this classification makes sense not only from the point of view of empirical expectations in terms of degree of riskiness/conflict but also from a normative perspective, since this ladder equally reflects an unacknowledged but very much present hierarchization of TJ measures in terms of their perceived importance to the overall goals of TJ.

It should be made clear that this scale is first and foremost a way of categorizing TJ measures and of operationalizing the 'robustness' of countries' efforts in implementing TJ policies. This is an important step for a comparative evaluation of the different countries' TJ trajectories, as it provides specific grounds on which to base the 'hierarchization' of the three case-studies – Uruguay being the country that went the furthest on the TJ scale, as it implemented all three types of measures, Brazil standing mid-way, because it has established quite robust victim-centered and public acknowledgment measures, and Spain lagging the furthest behind, because it has enacted mostly victim-centered measures only. It should be acknowledged, however, that this is only a coarse measure, since the simple recording of the presence or absence of certain measures does not tell us much about the *quality* of each measure.

While this scale is not strictly meant to be an empirical representation of the sequence in which societies implement TJ measures – in theory, any type of measure can be implemented first – it should come as no surprise to see the least antagonistic or least risky measures being implemented first, particularly in delicate political contexts such as the one under study. After a negotiated transition, in which amnesty laws and political concerns prevent the implementation of TJ measures or simply render them unthinkable, the window of opportunity for TJ steps will only gradually and slowly open up, and it is likely that policymakers will have a preference for less risky or less conflictual measures first. Similarly, TJ advocacy groups (most notably relatives) are strategic in their demands and often adapt to the perceived opportunities. Once some measures are in place, new demands for further steps can then more realistically be made, building on previous steps. This is very similar to Kovras' (2017: 13) observation that 'truth recovery' processes are driven by a logic of 'peeling the onion', in which every layer is connected to a previous one, and new demands are based on strategic (legal and political) precedents, creating a form of path dependence.

In sum, while the transitional justice scale is first and foremost a way of turning the abstract concept of 'transitional justice' into a concrete and observable set of policies, in practice, it might also reflect an empirical reality in terms of the sequencing of TJ measures. However, it does not tell us a lot about our two main variables of interest – timing and cross-country variation – which is what the next section attempts to do.

Notes

1 The dissolution of repressive institutions naturally implied the relocation of their members or their early retirement. However, lack of data on this, together with the absence of any active, systematic, or consistent policy effort, invalidates its inclusion in the empirical analysis.

2 I consider that (1) amnesty laws and (2) institutional reforms fall outside this scope, and therefore, I do not include them as transitional justice measures. Amnesties – a word that comes from the ancient Greek *amnestia*, meaning forgetfulness or oblivion, and nowadays used to refer to official legal measures towards pardoning and prospectively barring criminal prosecution against individuals involved in political crimes (Lessa and Payne 2012) – are often considered a TJ mechanism in normative-free/pragmatic accounts of TJ for their usefulness in neutralizing opponents and securing a stable transition. However, they do not produce accountability, nor do they provide any form of redress to the victims, and therefore, are at odds with commonly accepted definitions of TJ. As for institutional reforms, they are not always considered to fall within the umbrella of TJ. This is because the purpose of reforming institutions generally goes well beyond the purposes of TJ. Building an accountable and democratic state apparatus will necessarily involve institutional reforms that tend to be forward-looking rather than backward-looking, in contrast to other TJ measures. In fact, they are better suited as an independent variable, since institutional reforms – take the judiciary as an example – are certainly an important condition for the implementation of TJ measures.

3 The view that criminal prosecution is the most 'robust' TJ measure can certainly be a matter of debate. However, such measures are more debatable in the case of post-conflict societies than post-dictatorial ones (given that individualizing guilt can prove more problematic in the former, and because in poorer societies, the top priority might be to address the inegalitarian power structures that were at the basis of a civil conflict). Ultimately, the best means to address past violence is context-dependent, and a combination of various types of mechanisms is surely a better formula. However, the benefits of criminal prosecutions are still numerous, and in societies where Western-style understandings of justice predominate and which have transitioned from authoritarian rule – where violence is more restricted and directed towards political opponents – criminal accountability usually emerges as the preferred option for the victims.

References

Aukerman, Miriam. 2002. 'Extraordinary Evil, Ordinary Crime: A Framework for Understanding Transitional Justice.' *Harvard Human Rights Journal* 15: 39–97.

Bell, Christine. 2009. 'Transitional Justice, Interdisciplinarity and the State of the "Field" or "Non-Field".' *The International Journal of Transitional Justice* 3: 5–27.

Collins, Cath. 2010. *Post-Transitional Justice: Human Rights Trials in Chile and El Salvador*. University Park: Pennsylvania State University Press.

Grodsky, Brian. 2009. 'Re-Ordering Justice: Towards a New Methodological Approach to Studying Transitional Justice.' *Journal of Peace Research* 46, no. 6: 819–837.

Grodsky, Brian. 2010. *The Costs of Justice. How New Leaders Respond to Previous Rights Abuses*. Notre Dame: University of Notre Dame Press.

Ignatieff, Michael. 1996. 'Articles of Faith.' *Index on Censorship* 25, no. 5: 110–122.

International Center for Transitional Justice. 2009. 'What is Transitional Justice?' Accessed May 1, 2016. https://www.ictj.org/sites/default/files/ICTJ-Global-Transitional-Justice-2009-English.pdf.

Kovras, Iosif. 2017. *Grassroots Activism and the Evolution of Transitional Justice. The Families of the Disappeared*. Cambridge: Cambridge University Press.

Magarrell, Lisa. 2007. 'Reparations in Theory and Practice.' International Center for Transitional Justice. Accessed May 15, 2016. https://www.ictj.org/sites/default/files/ICTJ-Global-Reparations-Practice-2007-English.pdf.

Minow, Martha. 1998. *Between Vengeance and Forgiveness: Facing History after Genocide and Mass Violence*. Boston: Beacon Press.

Posner, Eric A. and Adrian Vermuele. 2004. 'Transitional Justice as Ordinary Justice.' *Harvard Law Review* 117: 761–825.

Raimundo, Filipa. 2012. 'Post-Transitional Justice? Spain, Poland and Portugal in Comparative Perspective.' PhD diss., European University Institute.

Robins, Simon. 2011. 'Towards Victim-Centered Transitional Justice: Understanding the Needs of Families of teh Disappeared in Postconflict Nepal.' *The International Journal of Transitional Justice* 5: 75–98.

Roth-Arriaza, Naomi. 2006. 'The New Landscape of Transitional Justice.' In *Transitional Justice in the Twenty-First Century: Beyond Truth Versus Justice*, edited by Naomi Roth-Arriaza and and Javier Mariezcurrena, 1–16. Cambridge: Cambridge University Press.

Skaar, Elin, Jemima García-Godos and Cath Collins, eds. 2016. *Transitional Justice in Latin America – The Uneven Road from Impunity Towards Accountability*. Abingdon: Routledge.

Thoms, Oskar, James Ron and Roland Paris. 2010. 'State-Level Effects of Transitional Justice: What do We Know?' *The International Journal of Transitional Justice* 4: 329–354.

Vinjamuri, Leslie and Jack Snyder. 2004. 'Advocacy and Scholarship in the Study of International War Crime Tribunals and Transitional Justice.' *Annual Review of Political Science* 7: 345–362.

Vinjamuri, Leslie and Jack Snyder. 2015. 'Law and Politics in Transitional Justice.' *Annual Review of Political Science* 18: 303–327.

Weschler, Lawrence. 1990. *A Miracle, A Universe. Settling Accounts with Torturers*. Chicago and London: The University of Chicago Press.

Winter, Stephen. 2013. 'Towards a Unified Theory of Transitional Justice.' *The International Journal of Transitional Justice* 7: 224–244.

Chapter 2

Theoretical framework

A holistic approach to delayed transitional justice

Few longitudinal studies have been carried out to explain why, when, and how societies revisit transitional justice (TJ) settlements (Kovras 2017: 4). Though there is a burgeoning literature on transitional justice, there is little theorization and comparative empirical analysis when it comes to the timing (the *when*) and transitional justice trajectories (*which kind* and if several, *in what sequence*). A good deal has been written on the *why* – or what determines the implementation of TJ measures – but a large part of the literature has focused on single TJ mechanisms (most notably criminal accountability), single countries, or static/snapshot pictures of TJ in time. Among the studies that do provide a comparative in-depth empirical analysis, many attempt to account for variation in TJ policies in countries that exhibit great contextual differences to begin with, thus pointing to explanatory variables that are obviously important, such as the strength of a country's democratic and judicial institutions, levels of security or stability, or the type of transition to democracy.

This is not to say that a great deal cannot be learnt from the extant literature on TJ. In fact, studies that speak of the determinants of TJ naturally have the potential to speak about timing too if, for example, conditions that are deemed favorable to TJ implementation became available only at a certain point in time. In general terms, the literature can be categorized according to the relative emphasis it puts on certain types of factors (Table 2.1). A typical divide, common in fact to all the social sciences, is the one between accounts that focus on actors' agency and those that privilege structural/environment-type factors instead (Vinjamuri and Snyder 2015). The constraints imposed on actors by the political realities of the transition period or the transnational diffusion of a TJ norm in recent decades are the most commonly emphasized features of the latter type. Perhaps even more conspicuous than this divide is the difference in relative importance given to different types of actors, i.e., the tendency to privilege one set of actors over others (political actors, advocacy groups or victims' groups, judicial actors, etc.). The relative importance of the different spheres in which they operate – domestic sphere versus international/transnational sphere – is another common divide.

DOI: 10.4324/9781003311607-4

Table 2.1 Types of explanations commonly emphasized in the TJ literature

	Structures	*Agents*
International / transnational sphere	Diffusion of a TJ norm; 'justice cascade'; deepening of liberal norms.	International courts; international organizations; transnational activist networks; foreign states, etc.
Domestic sphere	Institutional factors; political environment; normative environment; public opinion, etc.	Political actors; judicial actors; the military; civil society, victims' groups, etc.

These different emphases are in part a natural outcome of differences in the objects of study, that is, the specific countries and TJ mechanisms under analysis. To give a few examples, literature that has focused on post-Communist states – where the use of lustration mechanisms is common – has naturally privileged approaches that focus on the strategic considerations of political actors, as lustration policies affect the permanence/removal of public officials and are thus prone to politically motivated use (Welsh 1996; Nalepa 2010; Grodsky 2008). Instead, studies that have focused on criminal accountability put much emphasis on the role of legal mobilization by private accountability actors and/or the institutional features that facilitate legal action (Collins 2010; Skaar 2011; Sikkink 2011; Kim 2012; Michel and Sikkink 2013; González-Ocantos 2014). This, however, also depends on the specific cases under study, as there are settings, most notably in the former Yugoslavia or Africa, where external pressures from the 'international community' or the International Criminal Court (ICC) are more important than domestic legal activism.

While this obviously means that specific answers are inevitably tied to the context and object of study, Table 2.1 nonetheless has the heuristic value of providing some relevant categories to think of TJ and its determinants for different case-studies. With that in mind, this study constitutes an attempt at providing a holistic approach, where both the agents of TJ and the environment in which they operate are considered. Having said that, different research questions and objects of study beg for different emphases or at least, different starting points.

As mentioned before, research that has focused on transition periods has put much emphasis on the structural constraints imposed by the political environment (even if also recognizing that the convictions of political actors matter too [Pion-Berlin 1994]). In contrast, it is safe to assume that actors will have more leeway for action once fears of upsetting the transition process vanish and democracy becomes 'the only game in town'. In the absence of obvious structural constraints – or in the presence of a relatively more favorable environment – TJ policies in normal times are not radically different from other policy areas in that they can be approached and explained via the actions of policy and norm entrepreneurs. Authors who have focused on post-transition settings, such as Collins (2010) and Raimundo (2012), seem to share this view, judging by the former's emphasis on private accountability and civil society actors and the latter's focus on political elites and parties. A parsimonious way to think of the plethora of possible actors involved is to conceptualize them in terms of 'supply' and 'demand' – i.e., TJ policymakers, on the one hand, and the various sources of pressure pushing for (or against) TJ measures, on the other hand. Rather than prioritizing a set of actors ex-ante, my research aims instead to assess their relative importance for each of the TJ policies under study. Hopefully, this will constitute a welcome addition to a literature that tends to privilege one over the other.

This is to say that when approaching the first research question – concerned with the *timing* of implementation of specific TJ measures – my focus will be primarily on the actors that are responsible for such measures, directly (decision-making actors) as well as indirectly (pressure-making actors). This does not imply that answers will come down to actors only, as I will attempt to trace the various factors influencing them. In any case, the proximate focus on the *timing* of implementation of TJ measures is based on the assumption that there are specific contextual features of that point in time that speak for why those measures were put forward then. This may be the appearance of new sources of pressure, but also of new decision-makers with positive TJ preferences, or events that raise the salience of TJ issues and thus influence the actors involved.

That said, if the *specific timing* of implementation is best approached via a study of the actions of policy and norm entrepreneurs, no answer to the overall puzzle of delayed implementation is complete without taking into consideration that, for cases of negotiated transitions to democracy in particular, the overall political environment has become more favorable over time. In fact, this is true at both the domestic and the transnational level. On the one hand, it is obvious that the progressive consolidation of democracy and the gradual disappearance of a military threat at the domestic level contribute to the significant reduction of major obstacles to TJ measures. On the other hand, significant changes in the international or transnational normative environment have occurred in the past few decades, thanks to the diffusion and consolidation of a 'transitional justice norm'. The ideas that states ought to confront a problematic past, that heads of state should be held accountable for past state violence, and that victims deserve justice and reparation – in essence, what the TJ norm is about – is quite recent in world-historical time and as developed in the following, has consolidated itself at the same time as the countries under study went from young to more consolidated democracies. The ways in which this norm penetrated into the domestic sphere of the three countries under study, backed up the cause of

'TJ norm entrepreneurs', and eventually influenced TJ steps is thus a relevant dimension to which this work will also pay attention. However, as the decision to make use of TJ principles and transform them into specific policies is ultimately in the hands of domestic decision-making actors, an actor-centered approach will be privileged, whereas the concrete ways in which the TJ norm influenced them will be subject to empirical enquiry.

But if an actor-centered approach appears more suitable for a research question dealing with the *timing* of a specific policy, this is the less the case for the second research question, focused on comparing the various countries' overall trajectories and explaining the different extents through which they moved along the TJ scale. Granted, there are likely cross-country differences in terms of the strength of pressure-making actors and/or the extent to which decision-makers are open or favorable to TJ claims. However, an actor-centered approach does not tell us much about why this is the case, i.e., where the differences in strength, preferences, or for that matter, behavior and perceptions come from. In this sense, my analysis aims to go one step deeper and place actors within their specific historical context. This is not to assume a deterministic course, but rather, to emphasize that individuals or groups do not act in a vacuum and are *influenced* by contextual features that *help* account for their choices. This is partially the reason why each country study starts with a 'historical contextualization' section – exploring in particular the context of political repression and its characteristics – as well as an in-depth analysis of the transition period, investigating the historical evolution of each country's relationship with past violence since 'moment zero'. On the one hand, this is a means of incorporating additional structural factors that the existing literature has highlighted when accounting for differences in TJ outcomes, such as the degree and characteristics of political repression. On the other hand, this allows me to explore the ways in which the question of 'how to deal with the past regime's crimes' was dealt with from early on, at the moment in which it was perhaps most pressing (i.e., the transition period). This is important because, assuming that TJ policies can be seen as part of an overall 'TJ trajectory' and that trajectories are path-dependent, earlier approaches towards the treatment of the past will have an influence over future approaches. I thus follow 'path-dependence' approaches in the basic idea that history matters and that earlier choices condition future paths.

More specifically, I borrow the notion of 'memory regimes' from Bernhard and Kubik (2014) – which they define as the dominant pattern of memory politics in reference to the past dictatorship – to argue that the characteristics of the 'memory regime' at its early stages are important in understanding later trajectories. To put it differently, actors' views are shaped or conditioned by the different 'memory regimes' in which they have been embedded. This is relevant in the context of the cases under scrutiny here, because even though all the regime transitions were negotiated, they actually differed considerably in how political and social agents approached the violations of the outgoing regime during the transition period. As explained in more detail later, I categorize memory regimes into 'conflictual' and 'unified' ones and make the innovative argument that the former facilitate the adoption of more robust TJ measures later on, while the latter constrain them. I also attempt to explain where the different 'memory regimes' come from, pointing to some important structural differences that the comparative TJ literature has highlighted, such as the characteristics of repression and the country's democratic tradition.

All in all, by combining a focus on actors when tackling the question of *timing* and on the evolution of the 'memory environment' in which they are embedded when thinking of different TJ outcomes, this manuscript has the overall ambition of providing a holistic view of the determinants of TJ trajectories in the cases of Spain, Brazil, and Uruguay. In what follows, I will go into greater detail on the various dimensions outlined previously. First, focusing on the issue of *delayed* implementation, I will say a bit more about relevant (structural) changes in the political and normative environment that have opened up opportunities for the treatment of the past once democracy was the 'only game in town', focusing in particular on the diffusion and consolidation of a transitional justice norm at the transnational level. Secondly, I will focus on demand and supply dynamics and make the case that they should be approached jointly, outlining three possible scenarios that account for the implementation of TJ measures at specific moments in time. Finally, when focusing on the comparative analysis of country differences, I will develop at greater length why the concept of 'memory regimes' is useful and I will make a summary of the factors (or variables) that the existing literature has highlighted when accounting for TJ outcomes, explaining why and how these factors will be taken into consideration in order to understand both the type of memory regime enacted and differences in TJ outcomes.

Delayed transitional justice: A changing political and normative environment

If the passage of time might impact TJ processes negatively because of diminishing public interest, less vivid memories, or increased difficulties in investigating past events, all three case-studies under examination prove that these assertations are largely mistaken. Offsetting these potential negative impacts is the fact that – at least for cases of negotiated transitions occurring during the early stages of the third wave of democratization – the general political and normative environment, at both domestic and transnational level, has become more propitious towards the implementation of TJ steps. This is particularly the case when contrasting political and normative conditions in recent times with the period of transition to democracy. Table 2.2 summarizes the two most important structural factors that – even though insufficient to

Table 2.2 Relevant structural transformations facilitating the adoption of TJ measures in a post-transition period (for cases of negotiated transitions in the 1970s–1980s)

	Transition period	*Post-transition period*
Domestic sphere	Delicate political context	Consolidated democracies
Transnational sphere	Early emergence period of the TJ norm	Consolidation of a TJ norm

fully account for *timing* and TJ trajectories – can be said to have contributed to open up the 'opportunity structure' for the implementation of TJ measures in a post-transition setting.

The first is the most obvious and has to do with the consolidation of democracy (and the concomitant normalization of civil–military relations), in opposition to a delicate transition context, where incoming political groups have to weigh a potential desire for retribution against the risk of upsetting the transition process. While this is true for all transitions to democracy, it is more acute in cases of negotiated transitions where the outgoing sectors have not been ousted but retain a position of greater relative power. It is sufficient to think of the 1981 coup d'état attempt in Spain (four years after the 1977 general elections), when 200 paramilitary men stormed the Spanish parliament and held its deputies hostage, to realize that what appears today as a secure path towards a consolidated democracy was in no circumstance the case or perceived as such at the time. Each country chapter will cover the political conditions of the transition period in depth (and how that affected the way the past was [or was not] approached back then), and therefore, this factor does not need to be further developed here. Suffice it to say that the progressive consolidation of democracy and the gradual disappearance of the risk to regime stability naturally provide for a more favorable domestic environment for TJ steps later on when compared with the transition period.

The second factor, instead, relates to the evolution of the transitional justice norm at the transnational level and its consolidation in recent decades, that is, after the countries under study transitioned to democracy. The period of the third wave of democratization is, instead, best described as a period of 'norm emergence', when TJ practices occurred here and there but had not yet achieved broad acceptance and the internationally recognized status of today. It is, in reality, not far-fetched to argue that the appearance of what we would today consider TJ measures in the early stages of the third wave of democratization (such as in Portugal and Greece in the mid-1970s) was not so much because they were perceived as an ethical means to redress past wrongs but because the collapse of the regimes created incentives for such policies. As the authoritarian regimes were overthrown and suffered a major legitimacy crisis (in both Portugal and Greece due to military debacles abroad), strong demands for punishment emerged. These, however, were not so much about accountability as they were a call for old-style political trials resembling the ancient cries of 'death to the King' (Sikkink 2011: 33).

In her influential work, Sikkink (2011) focuses on the evolution of the norm of individual criminal accountability for human rights violations in particular and shows how the prosecution of heads of state went from something virtually unimaginable to an increasing common trend in world politics, a development she refers to as the 'justice cascade'. The most dramatic breakthroughs in this regard occurred throughout the 1990s, with the creation of UN-sponsored international tribunals, the drafting of the Rome Statute giving origin to the ICC, and the arrest of General Pinochet in London in 1998 after an extradition request from a Spanish judge, following the principle of universal jurisdiction enshrined in the 1984 Convention Against Torture. Sikkink attributes particular importance to the case of Argentina as an early instigator of the accountability norm – with the creation of an investigative commission in 1983 and the Trials of the Juntas in 1985 – something she connects to a vibrant domestic human rights movement and its insertion and network capacity within the international human rights scene. Even though Olsen et al. (2010: 97–108) find that the 'justice cascade' is overstated in statistical terms, they nonetheless recognize that there is a discernible increase in the domestic and international demand for justice, with new actors, venues, and justice mechanisms. Spatial and temporal clustering patterns in human rights prosecutions support the idea of a 'diffusion effect', particularly among culturally similar countries (Kim 2012).

One can, however, speak more broadly about the transnational diffusion of a 'transitional justice culture', as Golob (2010) does. She defines it as a set of beliefs, practices, and norms with an overtly didactic nature, grounded in the rejection of impunity, confrontation of the past, state accountability, and social inclusion of the victims (Golob 2010: 7). This relatively new 'culture' – which now ties the quality of transitions to democracy to the process of accountability for the crimes of the past regime – is said to be capable of affecting both the domestic and international legitimacy of the state (Golob 2010: 14). Key actors in this regard are human rights non-governmental organizations (NGOs), international lawyers and judges, international courts, institutions such as the United Nations, as well as victims' groups. The radical expansion in the number and impact of such advocacy networks over the past two decades or so has done much to promote the normative view that acknowledging and redressing past wrongs is a moral necessity, to the point that some speak of a 'global movement for historical justice', concerned not only with the recent past but also with more distant injustices, such as slavery or colonialism (Neumann and Thompson 2015). Subotic (2012: 107) goes as far as to state that TJ is no longer simply a norm but has become firmly established as a 'paradigm of the rule of law'.

This development has, in turn, to be placed within the broader 'human rights revolution', that is, the turn to the protection of individual rights as a core moral principle, including individual protection against the state. Though the 1948 Universal Declaration of Human Rights is often seen as a founding moment, it is only later that the language of human rights begins to resonate with a broader community of people. Moyn (2010) convincingly argues that as understood today, human rights took shape throughout the 1970s thanks to a growing human rights movement – including the rise to prominence of Amnesty International, awarded the Nobel Peace Prize in 1977 – and to key political actors – most notably Jimmy Carter – who moved the human rights rhetoric to the forefront of world politics. The consolidation of the human rights regime is, however, only more evident throughout the 1990s, with the UN operating more freely after the end of the Cold War and with a denser network of human rights NGOs benefiting from the possibilities opened by technological advancements and greater mobility.

This is all to make the point that the international normative environment has changed considerably in the last few decades, namely, when it comes to general expectations towards states' treatment of past human rights violations. While in the early stages of the third wave of democratization, the TJ norm was not readily available, today there is a well-developed normative framework that is not only relevant to understanding TJ expectations placed upon new democracies but can contribute to open opportunities for new TJ steps in consolidated ones. The mechanisms through which this norm penetrates into the domestic sphere are multiple, ranging from the way in which it backs up the cause of domestic activists to more direct pressures from international institutions on domestic governments.

This is not to say, however, that its impact is automatic or that the strengthening of this norm is without contestation. To the (by now dominant) view that the past should be remembered and that victims have the right to public recognition, there is a counterview that forgetting a difficult past is the best means for a society to move forward and avoid conflict. Those who sympathize with this view problematize the possibility of arriving at a fair and single collective memory of contentious events and emphasize that history should be left in the hands of professional historians. Transitional justice advocates will instead politicize the role that public institutions inevitably have in shaping 'collective memory' and their duty to facilitate avenues for society to know and recognize the victims' sense of wrong. To the deontological argument that there is an intrinsic moral duty towards victims of abuses and society at large, they will moreover add the consequentialist claim that TJ has a positive impact in fostering a human rights culture and avoiding future repetitions. While this can turn into a lengthy discussion, the point here is simply to underline that this is not an entirely contestation-free debate, but that the consolidation of the *transitional justice* field has been decisively accompanied by the strengthening of the normative view that remembering past violations is a moral necessity.

Therefore, if a more favorable normative environment at the international and transnational level is an important structural change to have in mind – which can also be seen here as contributing to a more favorable 'opportunity structure' – it is still the case that global norms are filtered through domestic actors and institutions in a process that is far from conflict-free. As Golob (2010: 16) eloquently describes, global norms are not the result of the revolutionary overthrow of outdated norms but play out in the domestic realm through iterative, contentious, and evolutionary processes in which the home state remains the objective. Thus, when studying the timing of implementation of TJ policies and the shape these policies have taken in the three domestic contexts under study, I will first focus on the actors responsible for their conception and from there, attempt to trace the various factors motivating them in that particular direction. These might well include dynamics that reflect the influence of the TJ norm, but this question will be left for empirical investigation.

The timing of transitional justice measures: the role of supply and demand

Whereas the abovementioned structural features contribute to explaining why the political environment has become progressively more favorable in a post-transition setting, they cannot tell the whole story. As argued earlier, the enactment of TJ measures long after the transition period must be taken as the product of not only the disappearance of the conditions that made them unwise during the transition period, but also specific contextual features of the post-transition period, including social and political actors with an intentional TJ-related project. In fact, speaking of prohibitive conditions during the transition assumes that TJ policies were in the minds of decision-makers back then – and that it was only the external political environment that prevented them from putting such measures forward – when this was not necessarily the case. I thus start from the assumption that the specific timing of implementation of a TJ policy can be best explained via the action of policy entrepreneurs and that an investigation of the supply and demand dynamics is necessary when approaching this question.

To be sure, this is far from a novel approach, as most authors recognize there are both demand and supply factors at hand in the implementation of TJ policies. Nonetheless, it is quite striking that there is often a tendency to focus on one over the other. In his seminal work, Pion-Berlin (1994) is skeptical about the influence of mass pressures while arguing that 'the personal experiences, convictions, and priorities of a head of state influence policy-making' and that 'how political leaders assess the political costs, benefits, and risks involved in a decision invariably influence their choice of policy instruments'. This is similar to Grodsky's (2008, 2010) more recent work, which puts much emphasis on the strategic considerations of those who run the country, arguing that they weigh their favorable pre-formed preferences against costs and benefits and pursue their preferred policies when these pose minimal risk (or are seen as politically advantageous) and do not interfere with the provision of public goods. In contrast, Lessa et al. (2014) identify widespread agreement in the literature on factors such as the role of civil society demand and international pressure in the pursuit of accountability.

Kovras' work (2017: 233–234), focused on post-transition efforts, is one of the most recent examples of studies that put the emphasis on the 'courageous efforts of the relatives of the missing in shaping contemporary human rights norms and transitional justice practices' and their ability 'to keep the issue central on the political agenda'.

Implicitly, this tendency reflects a broader divide in the political science discipline between elite-based approaches – focused on the ideology, interests, and agency of political actors – and non-elite-based ones – focused on social movements, interest groups, or general public opinion. In this particular study, there are good reasons to expect both supply and demand factors to be at play, and therefore, rather than privileging one factor ex-ante, this study puts them to the test and asks questions such as: under what configuration of the two are TJ policies enacted? Which of the two played the most part? Is a combination of both always necessary? What can they say about the kind of TJ policy decision-making actors decide to implement?

As my main concern rests with *timing*, particular emphasis will be given to the significant *changes* in supply and demand occurring shortly before the decision to enact a TJ policy. In this sense, three possible scenarios can be foreseen: (1) a change in supply (in the absence of a change in demand), (2) a change in demand (in the absence of a change in supply), (3) a concomitant change in supply and demand.

1. In scenario 1 (*change in supply*), the most significant event is a change in power where new heads of state/ governments take over and commit to TJ policies out of a pre-established preference. Here, a previously non-favorable executive appears to be the main reason why TJ measures were not implemented before. Preferences can be assessed via previous postures, party programs, and the 'quality' of the specific measure (since low-quality measures are unlikely to reflect a strong preference). However, this does not mean that there are no sources of pressure keeping preference 'alive', but only that *timing* seems to be best explained by a change in office holders.
2. In scenario 2 (*change in demand*), the most significant event prior to policy implementation is new sources of demand/pressure. Pressure can originate either directly from pressure-making actors (ranging from civil society groups up to transnational and international actors) or from events – such as the discovery of bodies, military confessions, or a condemnation by an international court. These events can, in turn, boost the 'pressure potential' of non-state actors, increase the salience of the topic, and influence decision-makers. In this scenario, new sources of pressure arise when an executive had been in power before (i.e., when there is no change in supply), thus substantiating the fact that this is the factor that deserves the most credit. However, none of this means that receptive decision-makers are not a necessary condition for policy implementation, only that new pressures were needed for them to act.

3. In scenario 3 (*change in supply and demand*), there are both new political actors and new sources of pressure at play, and both are equally necessary to understand the timing of policy implementation. This is different from the first scenario (and similar to the second) because TJ policies are not necessarily the result of a pre-established preference but are best explained by new sources of pressure. It is, however, distinct from the second scenario (and similar to the first) in that a shift in power was necessary for pressures to have an effect.

Even though it is possible to conceive of these different scenarios, there are good reasons to expect a variable degree of demand and supply factors to be always at play. On the one hand, it is difficult to imagine decision-making actors taking a TJ step purely out of preference without any sort of agenda-setting pressures they can point at in order to justify their actions. On the other hand, pressure obviously works best when sympathetic political actors are in power. This is especially the case for policies that do not provide obvious electoral returns, and TJ policies in a post-transition setting are most likely among these, as they tend to remain a key concern only for small groups, most notably victims and their families.

In fact, because TJ measures are intimately linked to a politically and ideologically laden view of the country's past political history – vexing for those sectors that were sympathetic to the previous regime and gratifying for those who were part of the political opposition to the dictatorship – TJ measures are usually expected to be enacted by the same political sectors that congregate those who were part of the opposition to the dictatorship or who are direct descendants of the victims of the dictatorship's repressive apparatus (Grodsky 2008, 2010; Raimundo 2012). This is the case for left-wing groups in right-wing dictatorships, such as the ones under study (but it is likely the opposite for left-wing dictatorships). This does not mean that other political sectors will not find incentives to implement TJ policies, but this will only be the case when there are clear strategic gains (Nalepa 2010).

All that has been said so far assumes that the timing of policy implementation is best explained by some varying combination of supply and demand factors, in particular (a) decision-makers' own preferences and (b) sources of pressure pushing for TJ steps. Nevertheless, this is not all there is on a decision-maker's plate when equating the implementation of TJ measures and in particular, the type of TJ measures to be implemented. Deterring them from taking TJ steps or moving further along the TJ scale are, obviously, the perceived costs associated with such measures, namely, the degree of political conflict they are expected to generate. Besides the usual costs that come with most policies (e.g., financial costs), TJ measures will rarely be free of political conflict, especially with the sectors that were sympathetic or ambivalent towards the previous regime – most notably the military, but also conservative political sectors and the conservative media. This is particularly the case for negotiated transitions to democracy, given that these sectors did not go through the same process of 'delegitimation' that they would have otherwise gone through in a 'clean break' setting (especially if TJ measures are implemented early on, as these further contribute to delegitimizing them). There will always be dissenting voices arguing that the past should be left in the past, that it is a matter for historians and not politicians, that it should not consume limited state resources and attention, or that it is a revenge-based exercise, to mention only some of the most commonly used arguments.

Therefore, assuming that policymakers are rational actors who weight perceived benefits or incentives against potential costs, it is expected that the latter will be factored in not only in the decision to take TJ steps but particularly in the choice of policy instruments. As different types of TJ policy produce very different degrees of conflict (as per the TJ scale), I do not expect to see policymakers opt for the most conflictual measures (i.e., perpetrator-centered measures) unless they are faced with strong incentives to do so (e.g., strong demand). Conversely, victim-centered measures tend to be perceived as the least costly and therefore might be the preferred option in contexts where decision-makers wish to avoid conflict and/or do not perceive sufficient incentives to go further. In other words, a study of supply and demand dynamics is important to understand not only *timing* but also the *kind* of TJ policy instrument chosen.

Though none of these dimensions is easily measurable – and they will invariably depend on a qualitative assessment of the cases at hand – the chapters on specific countries will provide rich narratives that will allow a strong empirical basis for the comparative analysis performed in the final chapters. Each case-study will go in detail in tracing the demand and supply forces behind each significant TJ step, attempting to weight in their relative influence and providing clues as to what is ultimately motivating decision-making actors. The results of the case-studies will be synthesized and put into direct comparison in Chapter 6.

A note on the judiciary

All that has been said so far refers to political actors and not to judicial ones. While it is the case that the judiciary can have an active and important role in pushing forward criminal accountability measures, my task is facilitated by the fact that the executive (sometimes with the support of the legislative) was the key actor for all the TJ policies under study, with the courts playing little role. Even in the Uruguayan case, where there were a few criminal convictions, the initiation of prosecutions was dependent on the green light of the executive, in accordance with the text of the country's amnesty law. In Spain and Brazil, the judiciary has limited itself to upholding the amnesty law in the few times it was confronted with the issue, in both cases throwing the ball at the legislature when stating that it would be the job of the parliament to outlaw the amnesty provisions. This does not mean that judicial actors did not play any role in pushing the accountability issue forward (for instance, a few civil actions in Brazil allowed for the recognition of damages or ordered the military and the state to facilitate access to information), but these were isolated steps that, rather than justifying the inclusion of the judiciary as a separate TJ-making actor, will be taken as part of the agenda-setting/pressure-building momentum.

This does not imply that the reasons why the judiciary has not taken a more active stance are not worthy of empirical enquiry. In practice, however, this would be the equivalent of asking why the judiciary has followed the law, the answer being perhaps self-evident. Criminal prosecutions for events that occurred decades ago not only imply challenging the countries' amnesty laws but often go against two cornerstones of criminal law – (1) statutory limitations, that is, prescription periods; and (2) the legality principle, including the non-retroactivity of law (prohibiting criminal sanctions for actions that were not typified as crime at the time they were committed, which can be the case for 'forced disappearances').

While the Argentinian or Chilean cases have shown that judges can overcome such obstacles based on creative arguments, often derived from international human rights law, this is a controversial move that requires a fundamental shift in legal culture, away from a formalistic/positivist legal philosophy and towards a view of the courts as '*justice* engineers' rather than 'legal administrators' (Golob 2010; González-Ocantos 2016). It is therefore more instructive to ask what allowed this shift in cases such as Argentina than to ask why a formalistic legal culture is still predominant in other cases. While a detailed answer is outside the scope of this work, it suffices to say that Argentina benefited from a combination of favorable conditions that are hardly replicable elsewhere: (a) its 1994 Constitution grants wholesale constitutional status to human rights treaties; (b) it has an exceptionally strong pro-accountability movement, which, similarly to Chile, has engaged in sustained and publicly visible litigation for decades; (c) its networks of support involve professionalized legal teams that, through events like seminars and workshops, have promoted what González-Ocantos (2016) defines as 'pedagogical interventions' inside the judiciary, fostering the necessary legal–ideational change needed for a transformation of the legal culture; (d) litigation agents have decisively benefited from a favorable political environment, being able to go as far as to promote the replacement of recalcitrant judges through, for example, strategies of 'naming and shaming' for their association with the dictatorship (González-Ocantos 2016). In turn, developments in Argentina cannot be disconnected from broader structural factors such as the type of transition to democracy and the exceptionally high levels of political repression, conducted largely extrajudicially (and therefore not implicating the country's judicial system).

As we will see, most of the conditions described here were largely absent in Brazil and Spain. The judiciary of both countries continues to be described as conservative and highly formalistic in this regard, which is unsurprising in the absence of a strong social and political environment demanding criminal accountability for the dictatorship's crimes. Although the levels of favorability of political decision-making actors do not have to go hand in hand with those inside the judiciary, the support of the former makes a great difference. This was arguably key in fostering the prosecutorial momentum in Argentina, where the Congress passed a law in 2003 declaring the amnesty laws null and void. Political support was hardly independent of the strength of the pro-accountability movement, which was in turn ultimately responsible for what Collins (2010: 218) defines as a cumulative and attritional case-by-case litigation approach that brought the issue to the courts in the first place. This is yet another reason to begin by focusing on the broader social and political environment.

Variation in transitional justice trajectories: the role of memory regimes

If the first research question deals with single TJ policies individually and the drivers behind their implementation at specific moments in time, the second is focused on cross-country differences in how far they went on the TJ scale, looking at each country's TJ trajectory and putting them against one another. Why did Uruguay implement all sorts of TJ mechanisms and go as far as to put former heads of state in jail? Why were TJ policies relatively timid in Spain, and why does Brazil stand mid-way between the two? A logical upshot of what was said earlier is that when it comes to answering this question, differences in factors such as the overall level of demand or the distinct preferences of decision-makers are important. However, this does not tell us much about where these come from and the specificities of the historical, normative, and cultural context in which domestic actors are embedded.

As argued earlier, actors do not act in a vacuum, and different contexts shape the players themselves, the options perceived, the choices made from among them, and the outcomes (Jasper 2004, 5). Affecting the understandings and perceptions of what is desirable (i.e., preferences) and what is possible (i.e., the TJ options on the table and the perceived costs involved) are not only present circumstances but also how the issue at hand has been dealt with before. Particularly in the case of political parties' representatives, it is expected that the preferences for TJ policies in a post-transition setting will be conditioned by what their previous postures were, out of either genuine preference or rhetorical entrapment. Assuming that one can think analytically about TJ as part of an overall 'TJ trajectory' that starts during the transition period and that follows a path-dependent pattern – and knowing that the issue of 'how to approach the violations of the past regime' was not dealt with in the same way everywhere during the transition period – I deem that TJ trajectories later on are conditioned by the prior dominant approach toward the political treatment of the past, that is, the 'memory regime' that has been put in place in each domestic context. This is to say that when tracing a TJ trajectory, relevant actors in different countries are not departing from the same baseline, and to understand their present predicaments, it is necessary to look at where they came from. As the period of transition from dictatorship to democracy is the moment zero of a memory regime, it is crucial in setting and defining its contours and therefore deserves particular attention. The existence of a particular regime is expected to place the country in a specific TJ path-dependent course within which actors will (re-)act, influencing their perceived room for action, expectations, and eventual choices later on.

Bernhard and Kubik (2014: 16–18) distinguish three types of memory regimes – *fractured*, *pillarized*, and *unified* – essentially dependent on how political actors position themselves towards the past. Fractured memory regimes are populated by 'memory warriors', who construe a sharp line between 'us' and 'them', between a 'true' version of the past and others. Pillarized regimes refer to settings where competing versions of the past are widely accepted ('we agree to disagree'), whereas in unified regimes, there is an agreement over the approach towards the past, either because it is consensually seen or because politicizing the past is perceived as too costly. The authors do not make a clear distinction between versions of the past (in terms of content) and approaches towards the past (in terms of form), and sometimes it is unclear whether they mean one or the other. For the sake of clarity and simplicity, my definition refers to the latter – whether the past should be a political object or not (a proxy for whether TJ measures should be implemented or not). I summarize them into two ideal-types: (1) a conflictual regime, where relevant political and social actors see the past as an object of political contention, and some of them push for TJ measures; (2) a unified regime, where there is a dominant and more or less consensual approach towards the treatment of the past among relevant political and social actors, which can entail either (a) the more or less consensual implementation of TJ measures or (b) an explicit or implicit consensus to avoid the politicization of the past ('to leave the past behind'). In the context of negotiated transitions and in the period of 'TJ norm emergence', the latter is naturally the most expected sub-type of unified regime. This does not mean that dissenting voices are entirely absent, but only that they are mostly unheard.

If the type of transition to democracy tends to correlate with the implementation of TJ measures, it might not say much about the type of memory regime to expect. The depoliticization of the past might be an integral part of the content of elite negotiations, but social and political actors outside the negotiation table might well strive to put the dictatorship's crimes under the public eye. Indeed, and as will become clear from the in-depth analysis of the cases in hand, there is much variation in the extent to which the violent practices of the dictatorial regime became a politicized and salient issue during the transition period, depending (most proximately) on the mobilization capacity of the victims/families, their networks of support, and the decision of relevant political actors to endorse their claims (in other words, demand and supply factors). While Uruguay comes close to a perfect example of a conflictual memory regime, where criminal accountability for the dictatorship's crimes became the flagship issue of the left, Spain is the prototype of a unified regime, where a consensual elite agreement to leave divisions behind went virtually unchallenged. Even though a referendum in Uruguay would dictate that the amnesty law was to be kept, the fact that it was a highly salient, divisive, and politicized issue sets the Uruguayan case on a different course. In Spain and Brazil, instead, legal provisions covering the crimes of state agents were either entirely unnoticed by most or taken as a natural counterpart, in a setting where the prosecution of members of the past regime was simply perceived as inconceivable.

Therefore, actors who enter the memory field later on operate in very different environments depending on the type of memory regime they are embedded in. In a conflictual one – where the idea has been planted and has become an object of social and political contention in the past – expectations are that future political and social actors who have an already consolidated preference on the issue will reintroduce the topic into the political agenda once there is a perceived window of opportunity to do so. Although this is by no means automatic, past conflict on an unresolved issue lays the ground for future conflict when the particular constraints that prevented its resolution in the past have changed, when committed political actors take office, when memory actors (i.e., TJ norm entrepreneurs) do not give up their fight, or when certain events produce salience-increasing effects. The reappearance of the issue in the public and political agenda in these contexts does not come as a surprise, especially if social actors continue to mobilize around the issue and are capable of pressuring a previously committed actor to follow up on its words once in office.

On the other hand, in unified memory regimes, where there was a consensus to 'leave the past behind', new political actors will hardly wish to radically reverse the previous state of affairs, not only because this can prove a costly business but also because radical breaks might simply appear inconceivable, disproportionate, or out of sync with reality. This is the more so if the memory regime is perceived not only as a by-product of the process of regime change but also as an integral part of the successful transformation of the regime and the concomitant redefinition of collective identities, as in Spain. The transition 'reconciliation ethos' – which to some extent, was present in Brazil too – is thus an impediment to the adoption of overtly conflictive postures later on. Even if the memory regime undergoes changes (e.g., new sources of pressure), responses will likely be more moderate than in the regimes that have always been conflictual. In sum, preferences, actions, and rhetoric are conditioned by past postures. Even if present incentives and expectations lead political actors to take steps that have not been taken before, those steps are likely to be based on ideas that have gained a certain social traction before, rather than positions that will be generally perceived as radical.

In this sense, my general expectation in terms of the *sequencing* of TJ measures is that political actors in a post-transition setting will first opt for the type of measure that is more in accordance with the type of memory regime they have been embedded in. TJ measures that face the least opposition, that

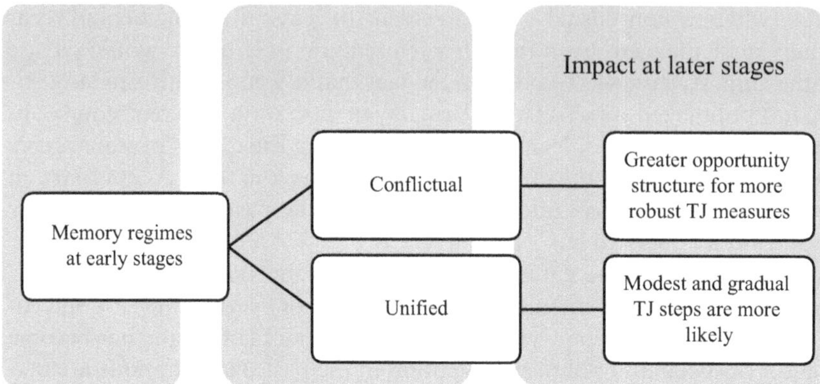

Figure 2.1 Types of memory regimes and their influence at a post-transition stage.

are the least visible, and that are more directly focused on victims, such as reparations, are more likely to rank among the first preferred options in unified memory regimes. In conflictual ones, instead, visibility is more of a desirable goal, given that political actors will want to be seen as responsive to the existing demands, likely centered on justice. Responding to visible demands for justice with reparations might be taken as an insult in conflictual memory settings, whereas the enactment of reparation policies in unified regimes will provide a response to a small and low-key demand for some form of historical justice without necessarily transforming the memory regime into a conflictual one. This does not mean a unified regime stays so forever, as memory activists might find mobilization opportunities that were missing before, and new political actors might endorse different perspectives or perceive new benefits. However, it is unlikely that these will be strong enough to provoke radical breaks, and a moderate and gradual step-by-step approach will probably be preferred (Figure 2.1).

Where do different 'memory regimes' come from?

The type of memory regime developed during the transition period is most directly dependent on the mobilization capacity of the victims/ families, their networks of support, and most importantly, the decision of relevant political actors to endorse TJ claims so as to make them visible and politicized. But, why do social and political actors find the strength to mobilize around TJ-related issues in some contexts and not in others? In other words, what explains the different forms that memory regimes can take and as an extension, cross-country differences in TJ outcomes?

Though contingency should be allowed when assessing actors' preferences and behavior – particularly at a political time in which interactions, strategies, and outcomes are in flux and are highly indeterminate (O'Donnell and Schmitter 1986) – there are cross-country differences that can help provide answers to these questions. The existing large-N literature has used a good number of different variables when attempting to account for variation in the implementation of TJ measures. Olsen et al. (2010) did a good job in summarizing them, dividing them into (a) authoritarian regime factors (regime duration, degree of repression, timing of transition since the height of repression, type of leadership of the regime), (b) transition factors (type of transition, background of new leaders, democratic past, strength of civil society), (c) economic constraints on TJ, and (d) international influence.

Though these factors were used to explain differences in TJ outcomes, they can also serve to account for variation in memory regimes, since a conflictual regime is a necessary condition for the implementation of robust TJ measures, whereas a consensual depoliticization of the past in a unified regime like the ones under study is a guarantee that no significant steps will be taken. In fact, the factors that the literature has pointed at are usually thought through (even if only implicitly) in terms of the impact that they have on the willingness and capacity of social and political actors to make TJ a politicized and salient issue (and thus establish a 'conflictual memory regime'). To give an example, when correlating the degree of repression with TJ measures, the underlying assumption is that the higher the level of atrocities, the greater the demand for accountability, and thus, the higher the likelihood that TJ measures will be implemented.

Not all factors carry the same explanatory weight, though. In their statistical analysis, Olsen et al. (2010) find that among the variables they consider in the first two sets of factors, only the (1) type of transition and (2) democratic history are correlated with the use of trials and truth commissions at a statistically significant level. This does not mean other factors are not relevant in specific cases, and this is why I will take the whole pool of factors into consideration, though with modifications, adjusted to my best knowledge of the three cases at hand. In Table 2.3, I take the list of factors used by Olsen et al. (2010) and explain why and how they will be taken into consideration when accounting for variation in the memory regimes of Uruguay, Brazil, and Spain in Chapter 7.

I will come back to this list in Chapter 7 and provide further details on how these potentially relevant variables can help explain variation in memory regimes and TJ trajectories. While some of these factors have straightforward answers (such as 'regime duration' and 'democratic past'), others require further exploration. This is particularly the case for (a) the characteristics of repression, (b) the transition's political context, and (c) international influences. This is part of the reason why I start each case-study chapter with a contextualization section, exploring in particular the patterns of repression and the transition's general political context. I then look in detail at the political treatment of the violations of the outgoing regime during the transition stage, so as to substantiate my claims on each country's memory regime,

Table 2.3 List of potentially relevant factors in accounting for TJ outcomes

Authoritarian regime factors	
Regime duration	The (unconfirmed) expectation is that countries with longer authoritarian regimes will be less likely to implement TJ measures, as the regime was more institutionalized, authoritarian legacies remain, civil society is weaker, and democratic forces are more willing to accommodate authoritarian forces. Because there is significant variation in the three countries under analysis, this variable is included in the list of potentially relevant factors.
Degree of repression	Findings in the literature are contradictory, but it is logical to predict that the greater the degree of repression, the higher the demand for accountability. Even though, at first impression, the cases at hand would not fit expectations in this regard (as repression levels were higher in Spain), there are other repression-related variables that should be taken into account, including (a) the type/context of violence (e.g., the context of civil war in Spain); (b) the type of repressive methods (disappearances, murders, imprisonments); and (c) the previous history of state repression.
Timing of transition since the height of repression	This is another potentially important repression-related variable. The underlying expectation is that the more time has passed since the height of repression, the less significant are demands for retribution.
Leadership of the old regime	There is not enough variation in the type of leadership of the old regime to make it a variable worth considering (the assumption is that more 'personalistic' regimes will make robust TJ measures easier).
Transition factors	
The political context of the transition	Even though there is no variation in the type of transition, there is more to the transition context than a binary categorization of the type of transition. The perceptions of risk, the strength of political parties, and the concrete political challenges were not everywhere the same. In particular, the political context in which each country's amnesty law was approved can tell a great deal about the memory regime.
New leaders with a human rights background	None of the new leaders at the time (including left-wing leaders) had such a background and thus this variable will not be included.
Democratic past	The underlying assumption is that, contrary to authoritarian regimes that have long been entrenched (regime duration variable), countries with a strong democratic history will have an easier time restoring their political and legal systems and their governments will enjoy greater legitimacy, enabling them to stand up to the authoritarian regime. This is a potentially relevant variable for the countries under study.

(*Continued*)

Table 2.3 (Continued)

Strength of civil society / Ethnic fractionalization	The variable 'ethnic fractionalization' is not applicable to the cases at hand. The strength of civil society *per se* is also not a good indicator given that this bears no direct relationship with TJ demands (e.g. despite a strong civil society, TJ demands in Brazil were restricted to a small group of families). What is most relevant is, obviously, the strength of TJ demands. However, this is very *proximate* to the variable of interest here – the form of the memory regime – given that strong demands for TJ necessarily make for a conflictual memory regime. In fact, most other variables in this list are supposed to help account for the strength of social demands too.
Economic constraints on TJ	
Economic costs	There is not enough variation in the level of economic development between the three countries to make it a variable worth taking into consideration. Plus, contrary to expectations, the most developed country (Spain) has taken the fewest steps.
International influence	
International influence	International influence can be thought of in terms of the work of international advocacy networks, norm diffusion, and contagion or learning from the experience of neighboring countries. This is a potentially relevant variable, though it might be precocious to speak of norm diffusion at the early stages of the third wave of democratization. As the TJ norm was at a nascent stage at the time, and judging by the role Argentina played in this regard, this appears as a relevant variable in accounting for Uruguay's conflictual regime given the cultural affinity with Argentina, together with the countries' shared experience in terms of repression.

providing context-bound tentative explanations for why and in what ways the past became, or did not become, an object of contention. These explanations will be systematized and put under a comparative lens in Chapter 7 when trying to make sense of cross-country variation in TJ trajectories and outcomes.

References

Bernhard, Michael and Jan Kubik, eds. 2014. *Twenty Years After Communism. The Politics of Memory and Commemoration*. New York: Oxford University Press.

Collins, Cath. 2010. *Post-Transitional Justice: Human Rights Trials in Chile and El Salvador*. University Park: Pennsylvania State University Press.

Golob, Stephanie R. 2010. 'Evolution or Revolution? Transitional Justice Culture Across Borders.' Working paper, Instituto de Políticas y Bienes Públicos (IPP), CCHS-CSIC, no. 3.

González-Ocantos, Ezequiel A. 2014. 'Persuade Them or Oust Them: Crafting Judicial Change and Transitional Justice in Argentina.' *Comparative Politics* 46, no. 4: 479–498.

González-Ocantos, Ezequiel A. 2016. *Shifting Legal Visions: Judicial Change and Human Rights Trials in Latin America.* New York: Cambridge University Press.

Grodsky, Brian. 2008. 'Weighing the Costs of Accountability: The Role of Institutional Incentives in Pursuing Transitional Justice.' *Journal of Human Rights* 7, no. 4: 353–375.

Grodsky, Brian. 2010. *The Costs of Justice. How New Leaders Respond to Previous Rights Abuses.* Notre Dame: University of Notre Dame Press.

Jasper, James. 2004. 'A Strategic Approach to Collective Action: Looking for Agency in Social-Movement Choices.' *Mobilization: An International Journal* 9, no. 1: 1–16.

Kim, Hun Joon. 2012. 'Structural determinants of human rights prosecutions after democratic transition.' *Journal of Peace Research* 49, no. 2: 305–320.

Kovras, Iosif. 2017. *Grassroots Activism and the Evolution of Transitional Justice. The families of the Disappeared.* Cambridge: Cambridge University Press.

Lessa, Francesca, Tricia Olsen, Leigh Payne, Gabriela Pereira and Andrew Reiter. 2014. 'Overcoming Impunity: Pathways to Accountability in Latin America.' *The International Journal of Transitional Justice* 8: 75–98.

Michel, Verónica and Kathryn Sikkink. 2013. 'Human Rights Prosecutions and the Participation of Victims in Latin America.' *Law and Society Review* 47, no. 4: 873–907.

Moyn, Samuel. 2010. *The Last Utopia: Human Rights in History.* Cambridge, MA: Harvard University Press.

Nalepa, Monika. 2010. *Skeletons in the Closet. Transitional Justice in Post-Communist Europe.* Cambridge: Cambridge University Press.

Neumann, Klaus and Janna Thompson, eds. 2015. *Historical Justice and Memory.* Madison, WI: University of Wisconsin Press.

O'Donnell, Guillermo and Philippe Schmitter. 1986. *Transitions from Authoritarian Rule. Tentative Conclusions about Uncertain Democracies.* Baltimore: Johns Hopkins University Press.

Olsen, Tricia D., Leigh A. Payne and Andrew G. Reiter. 2010. *Transitional Justice in Balance: Comparing Processes, Weighing Efficacy.* Washington, DC: United States Institute of Peace Press.

Pion-Berlin, David. 1994. 'To Prosecute or to Pardon? Human Rights Decisions in the Latin American Southern Cone.' *Human Rights Quarterly* 16, no. 1: 105–130.

Raimundo, Filipa. 2012. 'Post-Transitional Justice? Spain, Poland and Portugal in comparative perspective.' PhD diss., European University Institute.

Sikkink, Kathryn. 2011. *The Justice Cascade: How Human Rights Prosecutions are Changing World Politics.* New York: W. W. Norton.

Skaar, Elin. 2011. *Judicial Independence and Human Rights in Latin America: Violations, Politics, and Prosecution.* New York: Palgrave Macmillan.

Subotic, Jelena. 2012. 'The Transformation of International Transitional Justice Advocacy.' *The International Journal of Transitional Justice* 6: 106–125.

Vinjamuri, Leslie and Jack Snyder. 2015. 'Law and Politics in Transitional Justice.' *Annual Review of Political Science* 18: 303–327.

Welsh, Helga A. 1996. 'Dealing with the Communist Past: Central and East European Experiences after 1990.' *Europe-Asia Studies* 48: 413–428.

Part II

Transitional justice trajectories in context

Chapter 3

Spain

From deliberate forgetting to limited acknowledgment

Out of the cases under examination, Spain is the one where the implementation of transitional justice (TJ) measures has proven the most difficult. In fact, it was not until the twenty-first century that its recent past became an object of political debate, culminating in the approval of what became known as the Law on Historical Memory (Law 52/2007 of 26 December). Prior to this, only (timid) rehabilitation and reparation measures had been enacted, in accordance with the transition's reconciliation policy and the tacit decision not to instrumentalize past divisions (the so-called 'pact of silence'). This 'consensual memory regime' lasted until the conservative Popular Party took over (1996–2004) and was most obviously shaken by the adoption of Law 52/2007, an initiative that despite the unprecedented degree of symbolism, made Spain advance only modestly in the transitional justice scale. To speak of transitional justice in Spain is therefore to speak mostly of its absence, with the added difficulty involved in accounting for non-events over a long period of time. This chapter attempts to answer two main questions: (1) why were there no significant transitional justice measures (besides partial rehabilitation and reparations ones) prior to the 2000s? In other words, why did Spain develop a 'consensual memory regime' and keep it for so long? and (2) what changed in the 2000s, leading to the approval of Law 52/2007? By looking at the trajectory of the Spanish state's relationship with its past from a historical, political, and social point of view, various cues will also be given as to why Spain has not (yet) advanced more significantly on the TJ scale.

Unlike Uruguay, where a 'pacted' transition imposed clear limits on existing accountability demands, in Spain, neither the democratic opposition nor civil society showed any visible interest in revisiting the past. If political circumstances did indeed look prohibitive during the transition period (1975–1977/1982[1]), the lack of any significant initiative during the following 20 years – a large part of which comprised left-wing governments (1982–1996) – makes the Spanish case particularly puzzling. If Spain can be put in parallel with Brazil when it comes to unfavorable political circumstances and the absence of visible TJ demands, it stands out for the fact that not only was there no possibility/interest in revisiting the past, but there was actually an

DOI: 10.4324/9781003311607-6

active concern with drawing a line under it. In the name of reconciliation, social peace, and ultimately a successful transition, political elites agreed that the transition constituted a re-foundational moment in which past conflicts were to be left behind and a new historical stage inaugurated. The left was notoriously keen on embracing this discourse, which raises legitimate questions as to why it did so after more than three decades of authoritarian repression over part of its members.

Various explanations have been put forward in the existing literature. I will follow Encarnación (2014) in dividing them between (1) explanations of the psycho-political type, based on the trauma and memories of the Civil War experience, and (2) explanations focused on the balance of power and sensitive context of the transition period. Far from mutually exclusive, these two types actually make most sense together. On the one hand, left-wing forces were pushed towards a posture of compromise in a setting where reformist sectors *within* the regime had the upper hand and where various destabilizing elements made the road to democracy all but certain. Out of the three country-cases under study, Spain is the one that most struggled with political violence during the transition and with the menace of a coup d'état, which alone are sufficient reasons to understand why no one wished to 'rock the boat'. On the other hand, the emphasis on reconciliation, consensus, and moderation – though carrying instrumental benefits – cannot be properly understood without taking into consideration a history of war and fratricidal ideological divisions. I argue, however, that the desire to 'overcome past divisions' had less to do with feelings of collective guilt over the war than with the pragmatic wish to build an integrated and all-inclusive democratic polity.

The perceived success of the transition was such that the 'Spanish transition model' became a source of admiration both domestically and abroad (Alonso and Muro 2011: 1–3). This was, for many, the confirmation that a strategy of moderation worked, namely, when it came to the non-politicization of the past. The idea that this was an important step in securing coexistence and stability became the 'dominant frame' for the years to come, at the same time that Spanish elites were thoroughly focused on a forward-looking project of modernization and consolidation of democracy. This, together with the absence of positive sources of pressure (at a time in which the TJ norm was not yet available in Spain), contributes towards accounting for why it would take a new generation for the so-called 'pact of silence' to be broken. The turning point at the social level occurred only in the early 2000s, when the exhumation efforts of a few individuals ignited a series of follow-up social initiatives related to the 'recovery of historical memory'. This was at the same time that international and domestic political dynamics were contributing to bring the past to the political scene, namely (a) the Pinochet indictment by a Spanish judge in 1998 and (b) the rule of the right-wing Popular Party, a party whose historical links to Francoism could be used as a 'political shaming tool' by the opposition.

The growing visibility of related topics in the public scene, the exhumations effort, the co-optation of the topic by small left-wing parties, and the fact that the socialist minority government of 2004 needed the parliamentary support of radical left parties all contributed to a process that culminated in the approval of Law 52/2007 (known as the Historical Memory Law) recognizing and amplifying rights and establishing measures in favor of those who had suffered persecution or violence throughout the Civil War and the dictatorship. While in practice it is a largely victim-centered law that only timidly goes beyond the reparatory dimension of TJ, its language, its symbolism, and the parliamentary and public debate generated by it were unparalleled and far-reaching in a country where political institutions had turned a blind eye to the issue until then.

The degree of controversy sparked by the introduction of the topic on the political agenda, more than 65 years after the end of the Civil War and 30 years past Franco's death, revealed the extent to which Spanish elites are still unable to agree on a harmonized view of the Civil War and Francoism. In fact, what proved to be particularly conflictual was not so much the specific measures but the historical interpretations that they implicitly carried. If the same could be said of other contexts, this seems to be particularly accentuated in the Spanish case. Besides the added complexity of having a dictatorship that was the result of a civil war whose origins are still debated today, resuscitating past issues also amounted to questioning the legitimacy of the founding moment of Spain's peaceful and democratic coexistence – the transition – highly cherished by the generation that lived through it. While virtually no one would take seriously the argument that questioning the past today would endanger Spain's democracy, to speak of the transition's moral cop-out – i.e., its oblivion of those who had fought against Franco and his regime – is to taint the image of what had been highly regarded as a major success. As one of the most significant and transformative historical periods in Spain's recent past – and unlike a long previous history of conflicts – the Spanish transition came to acquire the status of a quasi-'founding myth', a moment in which the country decided to break with a divisive history and give birth to the modern and European Spain of today. This is one of the main reasons why Spain has progressed so little and so slowly when it comes to transitional justice measures – although there are relevant recent changes that will be explored at the end of this chapter.

Contextualization

Political disputes were not an uncommon phenomenon in Spanish history. Throughout the nineteenth, century continuous cycles of political instability shook Spanish political life to the core – including three civil wars and various military uprisings. It was only with the founding of the so-called Restauration period (1874–1931) – when an artificial system of party rotation was established – that the country experienced relative stability. The system would, however, undergo a deep crisis in its last years (~1915–1923), culminating in the 1923 coup d'état and the instauration of the Primo de Rivera dictatorship

(1923–1930). This would turn out to be a deeply unpopular regime, which eventually lost the backing of its allies, including the military. Delegitimized, the Spanish king was forced into exile after Republican parties took over some of the most important urban centers in the 1931 municipal elections.

The proclamation of the Spanish Second Republic (1931–1936) would bring radical changes to Spain's political life. This still constitutes a controversial historical period in Spanish collective memory, often described by its supporters as an utterly progressive regime and by its critics as excessively radical and antagonistic. On the one hand, the 1931 Constitution promoted major innovations in the protection of what are today considered fundamental rights (women's suffrage, divorce, free and obligatory education for all, etc.). On the other, its drastic stance towards many fracturing themes – in particular, church–state relations – produced powerful enemies. Agrarian reform, labor relations, military reform, and Catalonia's Statute of Autonomy were some of the other dividing themes, all in the context of economic crisis. Political polarization and fragmentation would be the norm throughout this period, resulting in unstable governments. A revolutionary strike movement took place in 1934, promoted or endorsed by a radicalized Socialist Party and labor unions. Although rapidly suppressed in most of the country, a full-scale insurgency came to life in the Asturias mining area, with miners taking control of several towns and establishing 'revolutionary councils'. This was the most violent episode of the Second Republic and for some, a prelude of the upcoming civil war. Anticlerical violence reached disquieting levels, and the revolt's brutal suppression by the army resulted in a few thousand deaths and many more arrests. It was, however, the election of the Popular Front in February 1936 – a loose coalition of left-wing Republicans from various political persuasions – that made the alarm bells ring more decisively among right-wing sectors and sections within the military, who promptly started organizing the coup d'état that would take place five months later. The ongoing destabilization provoked by strikes, land seizures, and violent squads of various political persuasions provided the coup plotters with the right pretext to 'reestablish order' and granted them the support of the Church and much of the conservative, business, and landowning elites.

The 17 July 1936 insurrection against the Spanish Second Republic led to a bloody three-year long civil war fought, roughly speaking, between those who stayed loyal to the Republic and those who sided with the rebels, the so-called Nationalists. Whereas the former suffered from bitter internal divisions, the latter proved more disciplined and organized, assisted by better-prepared sections of the army and more robust sources of international support (Mussolini's Italy and Nazi Germany). Republicans, on the other hand, had fewer resources and were forced to depend on the Soviet Union's help after Western powers refused to help. This led to an exponential growth of the presence of the Communist Party throughout the war. Communists, together with factions of the Socialist Party and moderate Republicans, were wary of the bottom-up anarchist revolution that had taken over large parts of the Republican area in 1936. This was one (though not the only) source of infighting that handicapped the Republican side.

Characteristics of repression

Described at various times as an ideological, a religious, or a class conflict, the Spanish Civil War is said to have gone down in history for the dehumanization of the adversary and the horrific violence generated (Casanova and Andrés 2014: 168). On top of the 150,000 or 200,000 men who died in the battlefield, it is the high number of civilians who died extrajudicially behind battle lines that makes Paul Preston go as far as to speak of the 'Spanish holocaust' (Preston 2012). Although numbers remain problematic, recent research suggests that the total number of victims of repression is at least equal to the number of military deaths (Juliá 1999; Payne 2012; Preston 2012). By now, it is also known that the death toll in the zone controlled by military rebels was higher than in the Republican-controlled areas. While the number of those murdered in the Republican zone is known to be around 50,000, the calculation of numbers of victims of rebel violence has faced more obstacles (Juliá 1999; Preston 2012). Nevertheless, it is estimated that this number varies between 100,000 and 150,000, making Nationalist repression about two to three times greater. This difference is nowadays explained by some historians as the result of the deliberate war plan of the rebels to destroy the adversary through mass murder and terror (Preston 2012; Casanova and Andrés 2014). This is not to say that repression and retribution were less cruel in places where the military uprising was initially unsuccessful. Anticlerical violence, in particular, did much damage to the image of the Republic.

The end of the war on 1 April 1939 did not signal the end of political persecution, though. From then onwards, violence was mostly one-sided and vertical,[2] as the newly installed dictatorship intended to eradicate what was left of the pro-Republic establishment. Rather than a policy of pardon or reconciliation, prosecution and punishment of the vanquished ensured a new period of mass executions, imprisonment, and forced labor, particularly harsh in the immediate years after the war. Estimates for the number of postwar executions in the following decade vary between a minimal figure of 28,000 (Payne 2012: 245) and 50,000 (Casanova and Andrés 2014: 220). This comes on top of the hundreds of thousands sent to prison or labor camps, where hunger, diseases, and maltreatment were common. The proportionate prison population would return to prewar levels only during the 1950s (Payne 2012: 247). The population exodus was also significant, with almost half a million people leaving the country in 1939, though the majority would return in the following months, leaving a net permanent migration of approximately 170,000 (Payne 2012, 245).

In addition, the regime was successful in establishing a system of collaboration where informants of all kinds, out of either fear or retribution, ensured that Spain was being effectively cleansed of the 'red scum' (Fox 2010, 36).

Stigmatization against anyone associated with the 'reds' forced many to move or to shut themselves up in silence. Institutionalized discrimination translated into jobs, pensions, health care, and all sorts of benefits being granted to those who had fought or sympathized with the Nationalists and refused or taken away from those considered politically or religiously unreliable. Assets and property were confiscated. Exhuming, mourning, or commemorating anyone who had died at the hands of Nationalist troops was unthinkable, while sites of remembrance celebrating the Nationalist uprising and honoring those who had perished for its cause were widespread. This explains why the calculation of the number of Republican-associated victims has been more difficult.

Although political dissent was repressed throughout the 36 years of Franco's dictatorial rule (1939–1975), the kind and degree of brutality of the post–Civil War period (1939–1945) were unmatched. The successful elimination and silencing of any remaining opposition meant that a disciplined and fearful populace would not create much trouble in the upcoming decades. The ferocious repression of the war and postwar years and its contrast with a largely peaceful period in the next decades has meant that historians are still nowadays concentrating their efforts on quantifying the death toll of the earlier period. Statistics on Franco's repression during the regime's peaceful years are significantly more difficult to come across. Portal González (2014) has summarized the challenges in attempting to compile information on this, namely, in terms of access to archives, organization of existing information, and data protection laws.

In an attempt to compile a list of people who were sentenced to death between 1952 and 1975, the author comes up with a minimum number of 70 people (Portal González 2014). The majority (54 out of 70) were convicted during the 1950s, usually involving cases of aggravated murder. Among those, there were at least 15 'maquis', members of the guerrilla group who survived the war (a number that is not greater only because by 1952 the movement had been largely wiped out). Portal González also attempts to collect the names of those who died as a result of police violence without a previous judicial procedure in the period 1952–1975, being able to gather information on 59 cases, 47 of them concentrated in the years 1970–1975, when protest and unrest grew.

Juan José del Águila's (2001) study on the Court of Public Order, which dealt with most political crimes (created at the end of 1963, partially replacing military tribunals and the then suppressed Special Court for the Repression of Freemasonry and Communism), shows that between 1964 and 1976, there were a total of 8,943 people indicted, resulting in 3,798 sentences, 74% of which involved criminal convictions (Águila 2001: 245–260). Tellingly, one of the reasons why this court was created was to show a legal face that court-martials lacked. This was clear in the 1963 execution of Julian Grimau, a leader of the Communist Party and the last person to be executed for crimes committed during the war. Despite the appearance of legality, his case created great international pressure and embarrassment for the regime.

Ironically, it is after Franco's death in 1975 that lethal political violence becomes most intense. Demystifying the image of a peaceful transition, Mariano Sanchéz Soler (2010) points to 591 deaths between 1975 and 1983. This includes 54 victims of police repression, 51 people who fell as a result of conflicts between the police and armed groups, and 8 who died in police custody. It should be noted, however, that the majority were actually victims of non-state violence, coming most prominently from ETA – responsible for 344 deaths in this period – and also other violent groups (51 victims of the far-left group GRAPO and 49 killed by extreme right-wing groups). This adds to the Spanish transition a climate of political violence that should not be ignored when assessing the elite's preferences for moderation and reconciliation.

As tragic as all these deaths are, there is an obvious quantitative difference in the scale of repression between the hundreds of thousands killed during the war, the tens of thousands in the postwar years, and the few hundreds who perished as a result of institutionally sponsored violence throughout the following decades of dictatorship. There are various reasons why the uneven temporal distribution of repression – in the context of a civil war and a particularly lengthy dictatorship (1939–1977) – is important. To start with, the fact that the bulk of the dictatorship's repression is concentrated in the period that follows the Civil War and that violence is selected against the 'defeated' camp meant that the civil war logic of neutralization of the adversary prevailed. Franco's worst repressive period could therefore be associated with the 'excesses' of the fratricidal collective tragedy that constituted the Civil War, an argument that serves to exculpate Francoist repression.

This is the more so because the transition to a democratic regime would be initiated only three decades later, at a time in which the new generations considered this period to be 'historical past' and its interpretations distorted by 36 years of Franco's indoctrination. It should be kept in mind that research on the true extent of Franco's repression was not possible during the dictatorship and that Franco's regime had more than enough space and time to establish its own version of history, largely anchored in the vilification of the 'reds' and the chaos they had allegedly plunged Spain into. In this, Franco counted on the active support of the Catholic Church, a prime socialization vehicle, which never ceased to remember its almost 7,000 clergy martyrs. The length of the dictatorship necessarily meant that a new generation had reached its adult years without directly recollecting the horrors of Francoism's first decade. According to Aguilar (2008a: 175), 73% of elected parliamentarians in 1977 were less than 49 years old and therefore, too young to recall the worst period of violations. The so-called 'sons of war' generation had lived their key socialization years under Franco, and most of what they knew about Spain's recent past was filtered through the dictatorship's schooling system and controlled media. This is not to say that Franco's narratives were uncritically appropriated but rather, that they left an imprint, as is shown by the prevalent associations between 'the II Republic and chaos' and 'Franco and peace/order' (Molinero 2006: 241–243). In this, one has to consider that the 'sons of war' generation witnessed the devastating economic, social, and psychological consequences of the conflict during the 1940s and 1950s, and its contrast with the last 15 years of the dictatorship, a period of rapid economic growth and modernization.

Temporal changes in the quantitative distribution of repression were also accompanied by changes in the type of repression, as extrajudicial executions and the use of the death penalty for the gravest crimes became a lot less common over time. In the late stages of the dictatorship, the crackdown on dissent and protest activity more often involved sanctions and imprisonment rather than outright killing. This is important, because while in other countries, activism comes mostly from families of the 'disappeared' – who still carried the hope of finding their loved ones – in Spain, the families of those extrajudicially executed could not realistically hope to find anything but skeletons in the 1970s.

On top of this, if it is true that there was a recrudescence of repression in the last stages of the regime, it is first of all not comparable to the postwar period; secondly, it is unevenly distributed geographically, as it is concentrated in the Basque Country; and thirdly, it is not an exclusive top-down phenomenon. Before Franco's death, ETA had already claimed more than 45 victims in the period 1960–1975, including the prime minister Carrero Blanco in 1973, meant to be Franco's successor (Powell 2014: 43). ETA's actions prompted a violent cycle of provocation and retaliation involving both state forces and other extreme groups (Encarnación 2014: 65). Police repression was more intense in the Basque Country, not only because of ETA but also because it was the area with the most social unrest and radicalization. The reasons why this is important are twofold: first, and in a similar vein to the civil war logic, it blurs the responsibility of the police for disproportionate use of force, particularly in cases where terrorist suspects were allegedly involved; secondly, it strongly reinforced the calls for peace and reconciliation, which in Spain's transition was the equivalent of 'leaving the past behind'. Moreover, because political violence was more intense after Franco's death, these deaths were hardly associated directly with the dictatorial regime.

The transition's political context

Spain's transition has been commonly described as the paradigmatic case of a pacted transition or as the 'very model of the modern elite-settlement' (Linz and Stepan 1996; Higley and Gunther 1992). In exchange for the release of political prisoners, the highly contested legalization of the Communist Party (still seen by the military as an archenemy) or the dissolution of Francoist institutions, left-wing opposition parties accepted the monarchy, the transformation of Franco's elites into 'democrats', a postponement of the process of territorial devolution, and less progressive economic and social policies than they wished for (Maraval and Santamaría 1986: 83–84). The 1977 Moncloa Pact on economic reforms and the drafting and approval of the

Spanish Constitution in 1978 became the definitive embodiment of the so-called 'politics of consensus' (Gunther 2011). Restraint and compromise became the dominant characteristics of the 'Spanish transition model', which became a source of admiration both domestically and abroad (Alonso and Muro 2011: 1–3).

This general overview hides, however, what was a more complex, bumpy, and in no way previously predictable road towards democracy. Generally speaking, the success of the transition was far from assured, given how delicate the political context was, namely, in terms of mounting terrorist violence, the restlessness of some sections of the military, the context of economic crisis, not to mention the divisive institutional challenges Spain was set to face – such as the establishment of a constitutional monarchy, the transformation of church–state relations, and the most explosive of all, a new model of territorial organization. This sensitive context, together with the historical lessons taken from the Second Republic experience, contributed to the general spirit of moderation and compromise that is said to characterize this period. Note that unlike Uruguay, the orchestrators of the Spanish transition did not have a living memory of a stable democratic experience in their country.

To be sure, there were a number of structural conditions that supported the move towards democracy, namely, a favorable international environment, with Portugal and Greece already on the road to democracy and the European Community offering a powerful incentive to political and economic elites in Spain. Pressure and protest from below had, moreover, given evidence of the public's desire for political change. Working-class opposition had increased substantially between the 1960s and the transition period. This was the more so after Franco's death from old age in November 1975, with the workers' movement greatly intensifying the number of strikes in the early months of 1976. This was an additional element contributing to the regime's sense of crisis, the other fundamental one being intra-regime dynamics, most notably divisions within competing Francoist elites (Share 1986; Preston 1986).

Indeed, it is at the elite level that one can begin to understand the initial stages of the process of transition to democracy. After a failed intent at *apertura* (opening) under the leadership of Carlos Arias Navarro (November 1975 – July 1976), which satisfied neither the hardliners nor the progressive factions of the regime, the so-called reformists (*reformistas*) took over and embarked on a quite extraordinary 'political operation' that would seemingly do the impossible: set Spain on the road towards democracy while convincing hardliners and reform skeptics (with important positions in state institutions and the military) to approve this move. The first great obstacle to the reformist sectors was therefore the resistance *within* the regime itself and not the pressure of the left-wing democratic opposition. Only after securing the support of the skeptics within the regime in a first stage (July 1976 – December 1976) did the so-called reformists proceed to negotiate with the democratic opposition ahead of the democratic elections that were to take place in June 1977.

King Juan Carlos, who had been handpicked by Franco to be his successor, is generally credited with initiating the process of change and entrusting the young and charismatic Adolfo Suárez with this task. Suárez's impeccable Francoist credentials meant that no one initially suspected the extent of his transformative intentions. Nominated in July 1976 as prime minister, he was quick to initiate a series of contacts with a wide range of political sectors in order to prepare the ground for his reform plans. This culminated in the submission of a Law on Political Reform to the Francoist *Cortes* in November 1976, officially presented as an amendment to the Fundamental Laws of the regime, though in practice contravening much of their spirit and opening the door to democratic elections. Suárez's public speeches at the time made it more or less clear that the historical choice the *Cortes* were facing was between opening the democratic road via legal means in an orderly and controlled manner or leaving the door open for social conflict (Linz and Stepan 1996: 94). The (unfulfilled) promise not to legalize the Communist Party, amendments to the initially proposed electoral system (favoring right-wing forces), and promises of future positions of influence to individual members of the *Cortes* are all said to have been important in securing votes (Share 1986; Preston 1986). The submission of the Law on Political Reform to a referendum in December 1976 and its approval by 94% of the electorate (with a 78% turnout) invaluably strengthened Suárez's position and put Spain on the path to democracy.

In light of this, it is hardly surprising that the opposition to the regime – most notably the Spanish Communist Party (PCE) and the Spanish Socialist Workers' Party (PSOE) – came to adopt a posture of compromise despite the initial calls for a *ruptura* (break with the regime). Notwithstanding the dilemma that a transition controlled by an authoritarian regime initially posed for them, the willingness to negotiate was ultimately a result of the recognition of their lack of capacity to force a more pronounced change in regime type. On the one hand, the opposition was fragmented and had little control over labor unrest, lacking the capacity to lead mobilizations of sufficient magnitude and endurance (Share 1986; Fishman 1989). On the other hand, as the regime continued to benefit from the undivided loyalty of the state's coercive apparatus, chances were that a bottom-up effort could turn violent and endanger the transition process. Since the successful establishment of a democratic regime was the opposition's primary goal (after more than three decades of clandestinity), Suárez's shortcut to democracy naturally offered incentives.

While rhetorically, it remained critical of a transition conducted from within, the opposition gradually moderated its stance, particularly after the popular approval of Suárez's reform in December 1976 and his demonstrated willingness to enter into dialogue with the opposition. Important in this regard was also Suárez's unremitting commitment to his 'legal reformist' program despite the wave of terrorist attacks that shook Spain in early 1977. In a cycle of action and reaction, right- and left-wing terrorist activity increased after the December referendum and reached a peak at the end of January. In Madrid alone, during the so-called 'Black Week' (23–28 January), two students, five Communist lawyers, and five policemen were murdered (Maraval and Santamaría 1986: 84). Fearing that these constituted explicit attempts at derailing the undergoing political transformation process, both the opposition and the government were cautious to avoid polarization, urging calm and reiterating their commitment to the transition towards democracy (Share 1986: 122–123). This further inclined the left to moderate its aspirations. Its basic demands at this stage comprised the dissolution of Francoist institutions, the recovery of democratic freedoms, and amnesty for all political prisoners. These were partially and gradually met by Suárez before the June 1977 elections, starting with the dissolution of the Tribunal of Public Order in January, the first wave of legalization of political parties in early February, the legalization of trade unions together with the establishment of the right to strike in March, and the dismantling of the *Movimiento* (Franco's single party) and the *Sindicatos Verticales* (state-controlled labor unions) during the Spring. Suárez's most audacious decision was the unexpected legalization of the Communist Party in April, a move that provoked much hostility within Francoist and military circles. In what were becoming typical behind-doors negotiations, Suárez held a long meeting with the Communist leader Santiago Carrillo beforehand, in which a possible agreement was made. Though the Communists had already given clear signs of moderation, nowhere was their 'submission' more symbolically visible than in their first legal meeting in April, when the party accepted the monarchy and appeared with the official Spanish flag, renouncing the Republican one.

In addition, one should not underestimate the extent to which the opposition reacted to public opinion clues. Writing on the Socialist Party in particular, Share (1985: 89) points out that the PSOE elites realized that a maximalist rhetoric would alienate the bulk of the electorate, which, as opinion research showed, was mostly located in the center-left of the political spectrum, for which the PSOE had to compete with a well-organized and surprisingly moderate Communist Party. Besides the evident public support for Suárez's reform program, the fact that working-class agitation had not spilled over into the 'great national action' that the Communists had hoped for was a sign that there was a silent majority hoping for a non-turbulent move towards democracy. This is in line with public opinion surveys from 1976, which showed that 'peace' was by far the political value that Spaniards cherished the most (36% said so in 1976, followed by 27% who emphasized 'justice' and only 6% who prioritized 'democracy') (López Pintor 1981: 22). The results of the first Spanish general elections (June 1977) were the confirmation that a moderate strategy was electorally profitable. The unexpectedly good results of the PSOE (29.4% of the vote) meant that it had no incentives left to oppose the way the process of change was being conducted. Moreover, the victory of the center-right party Union of the Democratic Center (UCD) of Adolfo Suárez (34.6%) confirmed the public's endorsement of his project and the general desire for moderation. The poor electoral scores of both the Communist Party and the People's Alliance (an ex-Francoist right-wing coalition), on the other hand, were largely interpreted as a repudiation of past solutions.

It should be kept in mind that even though the 15 June elections inaugurated a new stage in the transition process, in no way did they signify a definitive transition to democracy. Persistent terrorist attacks, the agitation of the military, the economic crisis, the institutionalization of regional autonomies, and the upcoming constitutional negotiations were heavy stones that still had to be taken out of the way. All of these factors, together with the fact that Suárez's UCD did not reach an absolute majority, further extended and intensified the strategy of compromise and pact-making between the various political forces. This was most clear in the so-called Moncloa Pacts (October 1977) – when parties agreed to share the burden for the economic reform package involving austerity measures – and even more so in the so-called 'Constitution of Consensus', the product of long face-to-face negotiations behind closed doors.

The fragility of the process was put in evidence by signs of anti-democratic ferment within the army, a problem that would not cease to grow until 1981, at the same time as ETA escalated its activity. Besides often targeting military forces directly, ETA's defense of everything the military abhorred the most (Marxism and separatism) made it a natural archenemy. Talks among top military elites about a possible coup d'état had been known at least since September 1977, with one major coup plot uncovered in the fall of 1978 (*Operación Galaxia*). Lieutenant Colonel Antonio Tejero and others were condemned to a mere seven months' sentence in prison by military courts, only to attempt another more dramatic coup on 23 February 1981, when the entire Spanish parliament was taken hostage for several hours in a powerful demonstration of how fragile the democratic system still was. The televised condemnation of King Juan Carlos (to whom many within the military showed deference) and the consequent inability of the plotters to convince a majority within the military to join in the effort dictated the failure of the coup attempt, not without first shocking most Spaniards and sending a powerful warning sign to the political class.

The transition's unified memory regime: the emphasis on reconciliation

The above-mentioned political scenario already tells us a great deal about why there were no calls for accountability regarding the dictatorship's crimes. In addition, there are two domestic contextual features particular to the Spanish case that place it in a more complex level of analysis and add to the reasons why there were neither political nor civil society calls for transitional justice or, in other words, why Spain's memory regime was unified. The first has to do with the context of civil war that gave birth to the dictatorship, which not only makes issues of liability more problematic but also leaves a traumatic imprint that is said to have influenced the overall posture of moderation and reconciliation. While in theory, one could disentangle the Civil War from the dictatorship and focus on demands for retribution for the former, this is impossible in the Spanish case, as in practice, the two periods have been conflated everywhere (including in transitional justice–related legislation), showing the extent to which Franco's regime is perceived as an extension of the war. The second complicating factor is that we are speaking of a violent transition context, where violence was far from being an exclusive top-down affair and where, besides a left–right ideological confrontation, there was a salient center–periphery cleavage at stake. This, I argue, made it all the more pertinent for the political class to put an emphasis on moderation and reconciliation.

Indeed, to zoom into the transition process in Spain is to realize that not only were there virtually no calls for retribution, but there was instead a generally accepted call for reconciliation and peaceful coexistence. This has to be understood in light of the perpetuation of the division between the winners and the defeated of the Civil War for over 40 years and the fact that the transition was bringing back left and right to the political arena after such a long interregnum. Moderation and compromise were most obviously a result of the balance of power and the context of the time, but the emphasis on reconciliation and rejection of past divisions cannot be dissociated from the previous history of fratricidal conflict. Although it is trivially asserted today that amnesty (or forgiving) does not necessarily entail amnesia (or forgetting), reconciliation seems to have been broadly interpreted by the political elite as the equivalent of 'forgetting' or, to put it in a more concrete and perhaps more accurate way, avoiding any political and moral engagement with the past. Nowhere was this posture so clear as during the parliamentary debate on the 1977 Amnesty Law:

> How could we reconcile, we that have killed each other, if we do not erase this past once and for all? (...) Amnesty is a national and democratic policy, the only capable of sealing off a past of civil wars and crusades. We want to seal off a stage and open a different one.
>
> (Communist Party Representative – Amnesty Law debate, 14 October 1977)

This has led many to speak of a 'pact of silence' or a 'pact of forgetting' that allegedly explains why, during the transition and for the years to come, there were neither robust transitional justice measures nor symbolic ones such as the condemnation of the dictatorship or a memorial to the victims of the regime (Encarnación 2014: 2). Although there was never any formal 'pact', the 1977 Amnesty Law (Law 46/1977) is said to be the backbone of the so-called 'pact of forgetting'. The parliamentary debate on this law denotes, indeed, the general desire of the political elites to leave a tragic past behind and to inaugurate a new historical stage in Spain's history, as we will see later.

Quite some ink has already been spilled on the possible reasons for why the left committed to what in Spanish is commonly termed *hacer borrón y cuenta nueva* (wiping the slate clean) despite having been disproportionately affected by Francoist repression. Existing explanations can be grouped into two broad types, which are in no way mutually exclusive: (1) those that emphasize the politically constrained environment of the transition; and (2) explanations of the psycho-political type focused on the impact of Civil War memories, which –via either trauma, feelings of shared left–right responsibilities, and/or political learning – prompted the desire not to touch a divisive past (Encarnación 2014).

The first type is obvious once one is familiar with Spain's transition context, namely, the fact that reformist sectors of the regime had the upper hand in the negotiation process and that threats coming from both the military and terrorist activity could jeopardize this process, making the calls for reconciliation all the more pertinent. In other words, the left had no political margin to make TJ demands that went beyond the most urgent and necessary restitution measures, such as freedom for political prisoners and devolution of rights to those who had been deprived of them for political motives. The fact that it was willing to make great compromises on issues that had been of historical importance – such as republicanism – already tells us a good deal about its willingness to avoid conflict. Take the testimony of a trade union leader at the time, who later became a PSOE high representative:

> The transition was carefully set, we were very afraid of a coup (…) and there was a strong wave of ETA terrorism, killing military men, therefore the thin equilibrium of a pacted transition – which felt very uncertain – prompted everyone to be prudent (…). Maybe we mistook pardon for forgetting, but it was an intelligent decision of the Spanish people. What mattered was embracing democracy, achieving freedom (…)
>
> (Interview SP12)

The second type of explanation – psycho-political, focused on the impact of the memories of the Civil War – has also deserved a good deal of attention. Paloma Aguilar (2002, 2008a) has been the frontrunner in this regard, arguing that the war trauma and the fear of repetition of a similar conflict, together with feelings of 'collective guilt', prompted political actors to learn from an excessively radical and divisive past and fostered not only conciliatory and moderate attitudes but also the more or less tacit decision to 'leave the past behind'. A similar argument to the one of 'collective guilt', but with a realist twist to it, is the one that the past constitutes a source of embarrassment for the Spanish left, given its problematic and painful history during the 1930s (Encarnación 2014: 58–59). This is the case not only because of its share of responsibility for political killings during the war – the so-called 'red terror' – but also because the left can be associated with the levels of radicalization and instability experienced during the Second Republic.

Whether it was via trauma, political learning, or guilt, the fact is that few analysts would deny that the breakdown of the Second Republic and the Civil War experience had weight in the choices and discourses of the transition's elites. This, in turn, is often said to be associated with the dominant cognitive representations of the Civil War at the time. Contrary to the black-and-white interpretation that Franco initially promoted, the image that emerged during the transition was one painted in 'shades of grey', in which all sides practiced unjustifiable levels of violence in the fratricidal collective tragedy that constituted the Civil War (Aguilar 2002: 132–134; Juliá 2006: 38–41). Regardless of who had committed the most crimes or with what intent, the dominant feeling was one of senseless suffering and devastation (Edles 1998). The image of 'two Spains' predisposed to savage discord – which was already a common motif in Spain's historiography before Franco heightened it – was implicit in these representations (Preston 1990: 30 in Davis 2005: 876). Even those sectors who rejected Franco's explanations about the origins of the war accepted that radical confrontation had characterized the Second Republic and that inexcusable violence was produced in the Republican area too (Molinero 2010, 45). Though pro-accountability sectors nowadays point towards Franco's greatest responsibilities – by initiating the 1936 coup d'état and victimizing a larger number of people – this is still a controversial posture in Spain, given how widespread the image of two-sided unjustifiable violence is.

The left's relationship with the past

If there is no doubt that the image of a divisive past was in the mind of political elites at the time, it is also the case that readings of history are mediated by the context in which they are made and in the case of political actors, constrained by political considerations. This is to say that rather than two independent types of explanations, the weight and shape of psycho-political factors is best understood within the particular context of the transition. In fact, there are good reasons to think that Civil War memories not only shaped *but were also shaped by* the dynamics of a transition occurring under challenging circumstances (Fishman 2011: 22). In other words, the fact that Civil War divisions could be drawn upon in order to justify and encourage a position of moderation/negotiation – which was desirable in light of the political circumstances – is an additional part of the story. It is surely not accidental that readings of the past were congruent with the aims of the transition's crafters – to achieve a quick and peaceful transformation to a democratic regime in the presence of various disturbing elements. Civil War divisions were publicly evoked *only* as long as they testified to the tragic results excessive political confrontation and radicalization could bring (and never to discuss other issues, such as their use and perpetuation by the authoritarian regime). On the one hand, they served well the posture of moderation of the left, after advocating for a *ruptura* but having to accept a transition led from within instead. On the other hand, they served the reform-minded sectors of the regime, who could claim that Civil War divisions had been overcome, therefore tackling the reticence of the non-reformist sectors to bring the left back to the political game and proving Franco's myth of 'Spain's ungovernability' wrong. In this way, and in the absence of a crisis of regime failure, Franco's legitimacy formula could be undercut and a new source of legitimacy created – based on the break with the perpetuation of divisions promoted by Franco, and thus, proving the authoritarian regime obsolete (Fishman 2011).

More generally, and thinking counterfactually, it is plausible to assume that if the macropolitical context had been different, political readings of Spain's past history would have been distinct too. Had the Franco regime suffered a debacle similar to the colonial wars in Portugal, the Falkland war in Argentina, or the Cyprus episode in Greece, dominant representations of the past would probably not have been the same. In the same way as everywhere in Europe, where representations of Nazi resistance were emphasized over collaborationist ones – as Nazism was militarily and morally defeated – Franco's crimes could hypothetically have been emphasized over the Civil War and the Second Republic's problematic history had the balance of forces been different. To be sure, calls for reconciliation and the concession of amnesties will always be part of postwar scenarios where there is a commitment to building an all-inclusive and democratic polity, regardless of the macropolitical context. However, these are not incompatible with retribution measures for the highest chains of command or for the most serious violations, or with the scenario of a reconciliatory stance towards the Civil War and a policy of condemnation of the dictatorship, even if only symbolically. That these options were *not an option* in Spain is certainly more in line with the delicate political context than with the interpretations the left held of the country's recent history.

Proof of this is the fact that the depiction of the Civil War in pre-1977 party documents is not as 'grey' as suggested earlier. In fact, *El Socialista* – the organ of the Socialist Party executive committee – commonly depicts the Civil War as a struggle for freedom against fascism. It shows little restraint in classifying the dictatorship as a 'murderous fascist regime' (*El Socialista* 1974a). The Civil War trauma seems to be more about the fact that 'by force of arms, popular sovereignty was taken away from the people, consigning them to terror and obscurantism' (*El Socialista* 1976). Interestingly, it goes as far as to speak of justice for the people mistreated and oppressed by the Francoist regime:

> [W]e cannot ever forget the responsibilities of those that during so many years oppressed the people. We do not want vengeance, only the strict

> application of justice. We cannot speak of pardon for torturers and for those who were tortured, as if the latter were criminals. (XIII Congress – Summary of the Report of the Executive Committee on the Spanish situation and the party policy.)
>
> (*El Socialista* 1974b)

As Barrutia (2006) demonstrates, the evolution of PSOE's posture went hand in hand with the party's strategic position on alliances, negotiation, and political competition. The more the transition balance tended towards Suárez's reformist program, and the more the PSOE was confident in its role as a left-wing protagonist, the more the Socialists abandoned maximalist positions (Barrutia 2006). This is not to say that the history of past divisions did not play an important role in the adoption of reconciliation postures. However, speaking of the direct impact of Civil War memories on the decisions to adopt a posture of compromise and avoid a concrete or symbolic engagement with the past is to claim a direct association between variables that have been decisively filtered through a political context that encouraged moderation in the first place.

The case of the PSOE is different from the Communists, who had already officially adopted a reconciliation stance as early as 1956. The reasons for this also appear to be largely pragmatic, as the party leaders recognized that the emergence of a 'liberal bourgeois opposition' coming from previous bases of support of the regime was an opportunity for 'an agreement on the fight against the dictatorship among political forces that twenty years before had fought on opposite sides' (Ibárruri et al. 1960: 257). According to the party's official declaration on 'national reconciliation' in 1956, it was also a recognition that maintaining Civil War divisions made less and less sense in a changing context, which included 'a new generation that did not live the war' and whose concerns are now related to 'freedom, popular sovereignty and economic development'.[3]

The case of the 1977 Amnesty Law

Importantly, a significant part of the arguments of the 'psycho-political' type draw from the 1977 Amnesty Law and the concomitant parliamentary debate. As mentioned, this law was portrayed as the embodiment of 'wiping the slate clean' and is therefore one of the few actual occasions on which political representatives speak of how the past should (not) be approached. Some of the most notorious quotes do seem to imply a sense of shared responsibilities and learning from the past:

> Because it must be remembered, even if – as I would wish – for the last time, that here sitting together there are people who have militated on

> different sides, people who hated and fought against each other. (…) It is not worth invoking bloodshed because there has been bloodshed on both sides.
>
> (Catalan and Basque Minorities representative – parliamentary debate of the Amnesty Law, 14 October 1977)

> This holds the uncontested value of being an amnesty on which almost all political forces of this room show the will to bury a sad past for Spain's history and build a different one on different grounds, overcoming the divisions that the Spanish people have suffered over the last forty years.
>
> (Socialist Party Representative – parliamentary debate of the Amnesty Law, 14 October 1977)

This debate has, however, to be put in a context in which the release of prisoners condemned for 'blood crimes' was at stake. Although the 1977 Amnesty Law acquired a high degree of symbolism – not least because it was debated in a newly inaugurated democratic parliament in which left and right were sitting together for the first time in four decades – the fact is that other pardons and amnesty decrees had already been approved throughout 1975 and 1976 and had released the majority of political prisoners (Aguilar 2008a: 288–291). What the October 1977 law did, in reality, was extend the scope of application of the 30 July 1976 amnesty (Royal Law Decree 10/1976), which covered only political prisoners who had 'not endangered or injured the life and integrity of other people'. The 1977 Amnesty Law, instead, covered 'all acts committed with a political intention, regardless of their consequences', that is, violent crimes. Many believe this was a required step for the pacification of the Basque Country and eventually, the end of terrorist attack. Amnesty for *all* political prisoners was one, if not the main, popular demand in the Basque Country at the time.

Since pardoning 'terrorist crimes' was a sensitive topic among conservative sectors, the discourse on reconciliation, forgiving, and forgetting had, obviously, one instrumental dimension that arguably went beyond feelings of trauma or collective guilt for a war in which many had not been involved. Even though the war experience was often invoked during the parliamentary debate, the actual relationship of the 1977 Amnesty Law with Civil War–related crimes is far from straightforward. If one considers the most relevant effect of the law – the extinction of criminal responsibility – it actually does not appear to have a clear impact in Civil War–related situations, since there were no war prisoners left in Spanish jails by 1977, and the statutes of limitations would have already applied by then (meaning Civil War crimes would have prescribed).

That the left insisted on portraying the Amnesty Law as a symbolic and definitive closure of all past divisions – and that the People's Alliance was against it and called for 'a strict application of law and justice' – is quite revealing of which kind of crimes were at stake. To invoke the end of Civil War divisions, on top of all the other symbolic benefits, was therefore also suitable in the release of political prisoners accused of 'blood crimes'. It is telling that it was the representative of the Catalan and Basque minorities who, during the parliamentary debate, emphasized the need for the amnesty to be 'a forgetting from everybody to everybody'. It seems clear in his speech that when speaking of 'both sides', he is not referring only to the Civil War: 'we cannot talk about terrorism, because there has been terrorism on both sides, because if terrorism is the imposition of a policy of terror, the state has done it too'.

In fact, the 1977 Law was indeed directed at 'both sides', but rather than the contenders in the Civil War, the Law granted an explicit amnesty both to 'all acts committed with a political intention' and to 'offenses committed by officials and law enforcement agents against the exercise of people's rights' as well as offenses 'that resulted from the investigation and prosecution of the acts included in this law' (art. 2 §e and §f). Oddly, these provisions seem to have escaped everyone's attention at the time, as they did not merit any consideration either by parliamentary representatives or by the media. Though little is known about the negotiations behind the Amnesty Law text, nothing indicates that the inclusion of a provision covering state agents was an object of controversy, and there is evidence that the main dispute referred instead to the limits of the amnesty for military personnel (Aguilar 2008a: 293–294). The fact that this seems to have escaped everyone's attention and that it was the release of the remaining prisoners that became the trademark of this law is also quite telling of the extent to which abuses committed by state agents were not generally put in the same moral baseline as terrorist acts and were not perceived as something that could have even been discussed. To put it plainly, how could the left oppose an amnesty for state agents when it demanded an amnesty for what at the time were considered the most ignominious acts?

In sum, if the 1977 Amnesty Law has symbolically put victors and vanquished of the Civil War on an equal footing (Aguilar 2008a: 297), in practice, it only equates terrorist crimes with police wrongdoings (Juliá 2007). This complex game between the law's intended symbolic breadth and its concrete scope of application ought to be considered when using this law and its debate in parliament to extract conclusions on the feelings of political representatives towards the country's history. This is not to say that the opposition was not genuinely interested in a great solemn act symbolizing the end of past divisions, but the reasons for this had to do not only with war memories but also with the symbolic intent of overcoming all other major sources of division in Spain, the regional–nationalist cleavage being a prominent one.

The Socialist period of 'memory consensus' (1982–1996): restitution amidst institutional silence

While little could be expected from the elected government of 1977 – led by the newly formed Union of the Democratic Center of Adolfo Suárez, whose ranks were filled with senior Francoist civil servants – the subsequent turn of the electorate to the left in 1982 and the four consecutive terms of the PSOE in power could have provided a window of opportunity for concrete transitional justice steps. While it is true that the PSOE took over only one year after the failed 1981 coup d'état, it is also the case that by the time it left power in 1996, democracy was fully consolidated and the military under civilian control. In practice, though, Felipe González's governments did little more than give continuity to the reparation procedures initiated by Suárez, enacting (at a slow and gradual pace) a whole body of legislation aimed first, at complementing the procedures foreseen in the 1977 Amnesty Law and second, at granting social/economic assistance to those who had fought in the Civil War (or to their families in the case of death). These were essentially restitution-type measures in the sense that they aimed, above all, at 'overcoming and repairing the discriminatory situations established as a consequence of the civil war' (as stated in Law 18/1984), that is, at integrating the defeated of the Civil War as equal citizens, granting them the same rights that those who had fought on Franco's side already benefited from (note that this is different from compensations for a recognized harm). No one opposed these measures, given the 'spirit of reconciliation' of the transition and the incompatibility of Franco's discriminatory system with the new democratic polity.[4]

It was not until 1990 that reparatory measures went beyond restitution and rehabilitation procedures (mostly for Civil War–related situations) and foresaw compensations for the dictatorship's political prisoners. The 1990 State General Budget Law (Law 4/1990), on its 18th additional provision, established a financial compensation for those imprisoned 'as a consequence of the circumstances contemplated in the Amnesty Law 46/1977', or their spouse in the case of death, though it had two important caveats: it only applied to those who had spent more than three years in prison and to cases where the recipient was more than 65 years old by the end of 1990.[5] The number of requests was unexpectedly high, with a total of 103,000 people applying for compensation, out of which 60,479 were accepted.[6]

It is worth noting that there had been previous resistance by the ruling party to establishing a compensation scheme, judging by the fact that at least two parliamentary law proposals on the same subject had already been put forward before and been either ignored or rejected.[7] When justifying its rejection, the PSOE representative argued, among other things, that it would be impossible to repair every situation, which would make it unjust to repair some, mentioning also that unlike other compensatory schemes in Europe, the Spanish context was different, since there was not a 'radical rupture' with the past but rather, 'a process of transition to democracy, praised and admired all over the world, but which had its own consequences' (DSCD, Num. 118, 7 June 1988).

The reticence of the PSOE – and the insistence of small left-wing parties (especially the Communists) – is perhaps linked to the parties' own past experiences: while the PSOE suffered mostly from the Civil War and the exile experience, its internal opposition after the Civil War was feeble, unlike the Communists, who had by far the largest quota of political prisoners. The fact that the PSOE and the Communists never held much affinity for each other (to put it mildly) helps explain why unlike the Uruguayan case, the collectives of ex-prisoners had no obvious links to the ruling party. The Communist Party, on the other hand, had explicit connections to what was one of the few organized collectives of political prisoners – the Association of Anti-Francoist Ex-Prisoners and Politically Persecuted (AERPA) – whose members were for the most part militants of the party (though the association declared itself as non-partisan). AERPA was initially formed in 1965 and legalized in 1979, having as one of its aims 'the moral, political and economic reparation of those who fought for freedom and democracy'. Law 18/1984 and the subsequent 18th additional provision of Law 4/1990 were, for the AERPA, a recognition of their struggle and persistence (Lara 2013).

Legislators seemed to be well aware of the presence of such groups. Law 18/1984 – the only one to focus on the economic needs of ex-political prisoners prior to the 1990 provision (recognizing years of prison as years of work for social security effects) – made explicit in its text that it 'satisfied the demands of political parties and associations of ex-prisoners'. The same possibly holds true for the decision of the ruling party to incorporate an amendment on compensation for political prisoners into the 1990 State Budget Law, though there is no evidence of this, as very little is known about AERPA, and the issue seems to have failed to attract media attention at the time. The fact is that the approval of this law, in June 1990, occurred after yet another parliamentary proposition on the matter by the group that included the Communists (*Izquierda Unida – Iniciativa per Catalunya* [IU-IC]), in March 1990 (BOCG, B-31-1, 21 March 1990). Their willingness not to let the issue die out possibly influenced the ruling party, with one PSOE representative later confirming that the party decided to consider such an option in response to the proposition put forward by IU-IC and to the 50th anniversary of the end of the Civil War in the previous year (DSCD, Plenary Session, No. 58, 25 September 1990, p. 2789).

Despite being the measure that most evidently established a compensation for a recognizable damage, the language of Law 4/1990 was, like the reparation measures approved before, strikingly apolitical. Its text did not carry anything resembling a moral or symbolic recognition of the unjust character of the imprisonments, let alone any mention of the dictatorial regime responsible for them (thus failing to meet what is one of the basic expected standards when assessing the *quality* of reparation programs). The fact that the issue did not deserve a law of its own, appearing instead as a provision in the State General Budget Law, is evidence of the desire to keep it a low-key issue (being criticized by IU-IC as a strategy to avoid discussion and publicization).

The only exceptions to this general silence during González's terms in office (1982–1996) were the timid mentioning of the political prisoners' 'fight for freedom' in Law 18/1984 and more openly, the recognition of what the International Brigades had done 'in the name of freedom and democracy' in Royal Decree 39/1996 (Aguilar 2008a: 422). The latter measure – on the concession of Spanish nationality to those who were part of the International Brigades – was, indeed, the only one that carried what came closest to a clear message of symbolic recognition. As with Law 18/1984, this was an outcome of social demands. The socialist spokesperson stated that it was a response to the Association of Friends of the International Brigades (AABI), even while declaring his 'utmost satisfaction' with the defense of this proposition (DSCD, Plenary Session, No. 186, 28 November 1995, p. 9876). AABI had been created shortly before in order to push for this initiative and to plan a large tribute to the Brigades on their 60th anniversary in 1996 (having amongst its founders AERPA's president). Over 300 members of the International Brigades visited Spain at the time, receiving official tributes at the local, regional, and state level, in what was the first public recognition event of this type.[8]

In short, González's governments enacted some reparatory measures over time – which falsifies the common perception that in Spain there were no transitional justice measures whatsoever – but as Alicia Gil Gil (2012) puts it, it still constitutes a case of 'partial rehabilitation with [almost] total oblivion'. Those partially rehabilitating measures were meant to overcome inequalities but did not entail any significant engagement with the past or almost any moral or symbolic recognition of the individuals involved. A good example of this was the absence of any official commemoration on the 50th anniversary of the Civil War's onset in 1986. On this occasion, the government issued a written declaration in which it stated that the Civil War should not be commemorated because of its fratricidal character. It further wrote that:

> Spain has repeatedly demonstrated its willingness to forget the wounds opened by the civil war as well as its will to live in a regime based on tolerance and coexistence, in which the memory of the war is, in any case, a stimulus to peace and understanding among all Spanish people. (…) The government expresses its desire that the 50 anniversary of the civil war seals once and for all the reconciliation of the Spanish and its irreversible integration into the hopeful project that started with the establishment of democracy.
>
> (National Government's Declaration on the Occasion of the 50 Anniversary of the Start of the Civil War, 18 July 1986)

This clearly shows that the premises on which the transition's unified memory regime was based were dominant also during González's terms in office. Spain's democratic period is equated with peace, tolerance, coexistence, and reconciliation. The idea that the defense of those values requires 'forgetting the wounds' of the past is quite explicit.

Accounting for institutional silence

If one had to summarize the broad goals of this first period of socialist governance (1982–1996), these would be consolidation of democracy and modernization. The PSOE came to power only one year after the failed coup d'état, and thus, the consolidation of democracy, with normalized civil–military relations, was a top priority. Modernization, including an extensive program of economic reform and integration into Europe, was also a keystone of socialist policy. Antagonizing the military or implementing a strategy different from the transition's premises was not at all what the Socialists had in mind. The posture of moderation and compromise had proved successful (and electorally profitable), and the PSOE had no intention of challenging that. Nowhere was its moderation strategy more visible than in the radical transformation of the party itself, which went from being one of the most radicalized socialist parties in Europe prior to 1977 to one of the most conservative by 1982 (Share 1986: 185).

Felipe González himself, the general secretary of the PSOE from 1974 to 1997 and Spain's prime minister from 1982 to 1996, is considered one of the key actors of the transition and therefore, one of the figures who came to represent its consensus-building spirit. Though this was not the Socialists' initial preferred policy, González recognized that it was imposed on them by the circumstances and that it benefited Spanish society as a whole (quoted in Nash 1983: 41). He was the one who supervised and often pushed for the radical transformation the PSOE went through in the transition years, including the much-disputed move to drop references to Marxism from party programs. This was, first of all, a result of electoral considerations, but also an outcome of the will to consolidate what was still seen as a fragile democracy. The 1981 coup attempt and the uncovering of another coup plot scheduled for the eve of the expected 1982 electoral victory were powerful reminders of that. Plus, the serious internal crisis of the ruling UCD (whose demise was already anticipated in the 1982 elections) could be interpreted as leaving a power vacuum, enhancing the PSOE's desire to appear as a responsible party, capable of safeguarding democracy (Share 1985, 1986). In this sense, the 1982 elections were far from an opportunity to implement a radical socialist policy, but rather, the continuation of a strategy of gradual and cautious transformation that the PSOE had already committed to when becoming an active part of the transition's consensual approach.

When it comes to the treatment of the past, breaking with the transition's premises was never even an option on the table. Democratic consolidation was equated with peaceful coexistence, and as seen before, the latter came to be interpreted as being best achieved if past divisions were left behind. González himself made clear later on that the primordial goals of democratic coexistence seemed incompatible with 'digging into the past' and that prudence was recommended if the peaceful coexistence premises on which the transition was based were not to be jeopardized:

> In accordance with the limits that we thought we had, we wanted to overcome the past without touching the old ashes, under which sparks still flew. We faced the great challenges that had threated our coexistence during a century and a half. (...) We tried to reconfigure the 'we' fundamental to democratic coexistence.
>
> (González Márquez 2001)

González also made explicit that he did not wish to upset the military, revealing that General Gutiérrez Mellado had advised him, shortly before his coming to power, not to dig into the Civil War issue because 'under the ashes, there is still burning ember; Please wait until people like me disappear to discuss these issues again' (quoted in Zaguirre 2001). His decision not to commemorate the 50th anniversary of the Civil War in 1986, he said, was the result of this.

If one takes González's words for granted, the decision to perpetuate the 'pact of forgetting' seems therefore a result of a posture of conflict avoidance in light of the potential costs for democratic consolidation. Moreover, it must be said that González's governments had to continue dealing with some of the major sources of conflict in Spanish society, which made them keen on retaining the consensus-driven approach that the previous administration had successfully employed. Writing in 1990, Pérez-Díaz (1990: 20) notes how the main business of politics since the transition had consisted of pacts and agreements among competing forces, namely, with regional political elites (which have helped channel regional nationalist conflicts) as well as with social actors (e.g., unions, businesses), in the effort to support sweeping economic reforms and reduce the level of conflict. For the author, this was part of a larger institutional and cultural effort to 'invent' a new identity and tradition: that of a democratic Spain (as opposed to the Francoist Spain), which this time around is 'modern' and 'Europeanized'. Others have argued along similar lines, speaking of PSOE's ambitious project of national identity building, aimed at debunking the conservative–catholic–culturally homogeneous image of Spain, and reimagining it instead as a modern, forward-looking, multicultural European state (Encarnación 2014: 88). The 'pact of forgetting' is seen as instrumental in this regard, as it repressed the very same things that made Spain look backwards, providing the government with something of a clean slate on which to project a new vision of Spain (Encarnación 2014;

Balfour and Quiroga 2007). If anything, Spain's recent past seemed to be more a source of embarrassment than a source of pride (Faber 2005: 211). Indeed, the more successful the project of democratic consolidation proved, the more reasons there were to take pride in the transition's rejection of the past. The declarations of the president of congress (PSOE) on the commemoration of the 10th anniversary of the 1978 Constitution illustrate this:

> It is no small matter to see the consolidation of liberties and democracy in light of a consensus in which the compromise of everyone broke with the negative consequences of past constitutions that had been at the service of some against others.
>
> (DSCD, Num. 157, 6 December 1988, p. 9424).

When asked about the (lack of) treatment of the past during this period, representatives of the PSOE invariably argue that frames and priorities were different at the time (Interviews SP9, SP10, SP11, SP12). The dominant mindset in regard to the past was the one adopted during the transition, based on reconciliation and mutual pardon (Interviews SP10 and SP12), and the political agenda was thoroughly forward-looking, focused upon modernization and the economic advancement of Spain (Interviews SP10 and SP11). What today is known as transitional justice – or as 'historical memory' in Spain – was simply 'not a topic which was present' (Interview SP10). In the words of one representative, 'no one would raise this topic, there were no petitions, no social or parliamentary initiatives; the amnesty law did what we thought had to be done' (Interview SP9). Indeed, everything that has been mentioned so far neglects one important variable: the fact that the PSOE not only induced but also seemed to reflect the 'mood of the time'. To put it crudely, why would it open up a possible Pandora's box for which there were no public pressures? Why would it create an issue that was not generally perceived as a political issue?

The absence of civil society demands

Not only were there no significant social pressures for TJ measures up until the 2000s, but the general perception seemed to equate with the political elites' stance that those issues were better left untouched (Interview SP2). A survey from 1991 revealed that 68% of respondents agreed with the sentence: 'what occurred in the civil war was so terrible that it is best to forget than to talk about it' (Aguilar 2006: 300). For some, this is interpreted as a result of Spanish people's general desire for stability and fear of another confrontation (Aguilar 2006), while for others, the general perception was that the war belonged in history and that Francoism was residual and therefore, simply not conceived as an object of public policy (Julià 2006: 58). But rather than delving into the reasons affecting the general public, what is most relevant is to understand the silence of the segment of the population that could have a personal interest in TJ, that is, those directly affected by Francoist repression, from whom TJ-related demands were most likely to come. In-depth and methodologically sound work on this issue is non-existent – and frankly, quite difficult to conduct – and therefore, the following arguments are explorative.

There is, however, one reason that comes up time and again when speaking to anyone involved in the recent wave of exhumations and who is familiar with the stories of the relatives involved: the fear and trauma of the old generations, greatly aggravated by the 1981 coup d'état (Interviews SP1, SP2, SP3, SP5).[9] Fear of another conflict, of the capacity of the military to derail the transition process, or simply of retaliation by right-wing squads might seem exaggerated in retrospect, but this was not experienced in the same way by many of those who had living memories of repression and who had learnt to live with trauma, and often silence, for decades. Those who participated in the recent exhumation process speak of the endurance of a regime of silence, fear, self-censorship, shame, and humiliation among the Civil War defeated, which often affected or blocked intergenerational transmission (Férrandiz 2007, 2008; Labanyi 2009; Serrano-Moreno 2012; Río Sánchez 2008). A founding member of the Association for the Recovery of Historical Memory (*Asociación para la Recuperación de la Memoria Histórica* [ARMH]) (created in 2000), for example, retells how old people still often show frightened behavior, such as speaking in whispers (Interview SP3). Note that this is a phenomenon specific to the older generations with a living memory of the worst repressive period.

The impact of the 1981 coup d'état on the revival of such fears is confirmed by data on exhumations. Contrary to the recent wave of exhumations (2000–today), there was a first wave during the transition period, which did not get media attention at the time (with the exception of one controversial magazine[10]), and whose details scholars are only starting to find out now. The background to this is that in line with Franco's policy of commemorating exclusively those victimized by Republicans, only these bodies were recovered and granted a proper funeral, whereas tens of thousands of Republican bodies were left in unmarked graves (whose approximate location was often known by locals), a situation that the newly founded democracy did not address. Geographically concentrated in certain regions and executed with rudimentary means, this first wave of exhumations was entirely treated as a local and private family affair.

Aguilar (2017) compiles information on three of the autonomous communities most active in this regard and shows that the number of exhumations drops drastically from 1981 onwards. Her study also shows the importance of a different type of factor: the existence of external networks of support. The Navarra example is particularly telling, given that the exhumation effort was more thorough in this province and benefited from one exceptional source of support – a sector of engaged and well-organized parish priests

– something that is explained by the distinct background and stance of a sector of the church in Navarra (Aguilar 2017). In the same way as positive sources of support matter, Davis (2015) shows, in a different study (conducted in the Catalan city of Santa Coloma de Gramenet), that counter-pressures are important too. He claims that local initiatives of remembrance were thwarted by far-right militants and unreformed institutions (police, judiciary, civil governors) who failed to cooperate and who ultimately led to the demobilization of interested local sectors (Davis 2015).

Incipient studies such as these two naturally raise the question of whether the apparent absence of civil society demand was actually not, in part, a result of the absence of networks of support. While it is the case that the 1981 coup d'état was the ultimate reminder of risk – and surely was a major factor in the reinforcement of a regime of fear – this was probably not experienced in the same way by everyone, and there were various potential actors who could have constituted positive sources of support over the following years and did not (from the media to the church to political parties). This, in turn, is intimately linked to the dominant 'memory regime' of the time – put forward during the transition and reinforced by its success – based on the premises that the past is better 'left behind' and that the transition period inaugurated a stage of reconciliation in which there should be no room for divisive behavior that could trouble the construction of a unified Spain. The fact that all dominant elites embraced this discourse left the 'political opportunity structure' closed. Many of those involved in the family-led exhumation movement today have pointed in a similar direction, referring to the perception that nothing could be done given the generalized lack of interest or silence on the past, the lack of public spaces for the articulation of war memories, as well as the absence of political and cultural frameworks that helped the defeated construct their memories and see or affirm themselves as victims (Férrandiz 2007, 2008; Labanyi 2009; Interview SP7). All of these tap into the idea that the absence of networks of support and of a favorable political opportunity structure contributed to the absence of civil society demands.

Of particular importance here is naturally the role of the two dominant left-wing parties and the fact that they fully embraced the transition's reconciliation rhetoric.[11] This left any potential dissidents without a political interlocutor. This is no small matter when considering that they were precisely the ones who were disproportionately affected by repression, which would make them the natural vehicles for channeling TJ-type demands. Instead, there is evidence that the leadership of the two parties considered that encouraging exhumations would be interpreted as revengeful, possibly jeopardizing the tacit pact of reconciliation (Aguilar and Ferrándiz 2016: 3; Aguilar 2017:, 414). If this was their stance on what is possibly one of the least controversial TJ measures – the recovery of a relative's body – it is easy to imagine how inconceivable more robust forms of TJ were.

All that has been said naturally raises the question of whether it was civil society silence that drove elite silence (as suggested earlier) or the other way around, a question that seems spurious and virtually unanswerable, as this is likely a dynamic and mutually reinforcing process. Moreover, both elites and civil society are embedded within the same context, and thus, the extent to which they are affected by the same factors should not be ignored. But if much has been said about the overall political context and its effect on the elites, there are also inhibiting structural and contextual factors that motivate and help account for the absence of TJ demands. I highlight two, which I consider fundamental: (1) the Civil War factor together with the temporal distribution of repression in the context of a lengthy dictatorship; and (2) the absence of an international transitional justice regime at the time, or what Golob (2010) calls 'transitional justice culture'. The reason why the latter is important is because scholars (including myself) might be setting the bar too high for a transition in which the international norm of accountability for state agents had not yet reached a 'tipping point', meaning that forms of transitional justice were simply not expected or even conceived as a possibility in the context of a negotiated transition.

The first factor has already been explored. The fact that the bulk of the most serious abuses occurred during the war and the postwar period means that the identification of a clear victim–perpetrator relationship is more complex than in the context of a dictatorship, raising arguments about shared responsibilities. This, in turn, might dilute the sense of victimhood of those affected by violence. This is the more so in the context of a particularly lengthy dictatorship, in which Franco had more than enough time to apply 'victors' justice' and spread fear and propaganda. The families of the 'reds' had been silenced and stigmatized for more than four decades before the transition to democracy. Unlike the families of the 'disappeared' in Latin America, they generally knew what the fate of their loved ones had been and did not have the same sense of urgency or possibly the same sense of victimization, since killings in a war context are, to an extent, to be expected. Though these are, of course, gross and tentative generalizations, it is common to hear of cases where new generations had been told to keep silent or were actually spared any details on the families' past (Férrandiz 2007, 2008; Labanyi 2009; Serrano-Moreno 2012; Río Sánchez 2008). The passage of such a long period of time between the worst repressive period and the transition also meant that the newest generations had no direct recollection of the worst events. A top-down negotiated transition, which put an emphasis on 'forgive and forget', was hardly seen as an opportunity to reverse a long-lasting state of affairs, particularly when the right-wing threat was still looming.

This, however, concerns the victims of the worst period of repression and not the victims of the subsequent stages of Francoism. There are good reasons to focus on those, given the changes in the quantitative distribution of repression as well as in the type of repression over the course of the dictatorship. As other cases have shown, families of the disappeared or assassinated will have a greater mobilization impetus than those who were imprisoned for political motives and later released, something naturally associated with the gravity of the crime. Moreover, it is common for anti-Francoist activists to see themselves as protagonists (or even heroes) rather than victims, leaving sentiments of injustice to the private sphere, compensated by what is considered the best possible achievement in the public sphere – a democratic regime in which they could finally participate (Molinero 2010: 43).

This, in turn, touches upon an issue that the recent development of a 'transitional justice culture' has helped to imbue – the construction of a sense of victimhood and the feeling of entitlement to certain rights as a result – a 'culture' that was not available in Spain either during the transition or during the 1980s. This goes in the direction of Blakeley's (2005: 45) argument that a framework of international human rights norms was far from consolidated then, and many of its features were not yet available or widespread, such as a well-established network of human rights non-governmental organizations or some of the mechanisms that are part of TJ nowadays. Encarnación (2014: 104) quickly dismisses Blakeley's arguments based on the 'experience of transitional justice in Portugal and Greece, whose transitions virtually coincided with Spain's'. Encarnación is, however, turning a blind eye to the crucial difference that these were non-negotiated transitions in which there were incentives for the condemnation and punishment of the past regime and its members. The sudden loss of their power position and the popular mobilizations that accompanied that process were accompanied by calls for their punishment, as this was not only a viable but also a legitimacy-enhancing endeavor. However, the Portuguese and Greek transitions did not take place in a world-historical time where the punishment of agents of the past regime was seen as a moral duty towards the victims or where the public accounting of their crimes was perceived as a requirement for the construction of a robust democracy. The language of transitional justice – centered on the respect for human rights and the moral responsibility towards victims – was not what the Portuguese and Greek experiences were about. Whereas measures to distance new regimes from the past one were a welcomed benefit (rather than a duty) in such instances of regime collapse, they were nowhere to be expected in contexts of negotiated transitions in the 1970s or 1980s.

The demise of Spain's consensual memory regime: the resurgence of the past in the parliamentary scene

It has become a commonplace to speak of the 'break of the pact of forgetting' (Davis 2005) or Spain's 'memory boom' (Boyd 2008). Manifestations of this have occurred in every sphere of public life in the early 2000s, from political institutions to civil society associations, from academia to the cultural production industry. There is, however, little consensus as to what sparked this resurgence of interest in Spain's past. Various events coincide in time, which complicates the task of disentangling multiple dynamics occurring at the political, social, cultural, and international level.

At the civil society level, the creation of the ARMH at the end of the year 2000 is considered a milestone. Its efforts to locate and open mass graves started to attract considerable media attention throughout 2002 and 2003, when its exhumation activities took off. Its creation did much to popularize the term 'historical memory', which was later used in popular and journalistic circles to coin Law 52/2007 as the Law on Historical Memory. At the cultural level, this period coincided with a wave of novels, memoirs, television programs, films, documentaries, exhibitions, and historical studies on Francoism and the Civil War (Faber 2005; Gálvez Biesca 2006). The fact that a lot of these activities overlapped with important anniversaries – 60 years of the end of the Spanish Civil War in 1999, 25 years of the death of Francisco Franco in 2000, or the 25th anniversary of the first democratic elections in 2002 – is often highlighted (Blakeley 2005). In addition, demographic and generational dynamics are commonly considered an important factor (Blakeley 2005; Aguilar 2006; Sumalla 2011). The rationale behind this is either that there was a sense of urgency in dealing with this topic, because the most directly concerned generation was dying out from old age, and/or that new generations were free from the fears and inhibitions of the older generations.

At the political level, if it is true that the topic captured the government's attention only during the PSOE's 2004-2008 term, attentive observers would not fail to notice the outburst of parliamentary initiatives proposed in the previous legislature (2000–2004) by the left-wing opposition at a time when the right-wing *Partido Popular* (PP) was in power. Figures 3.1 and 3.2 compile information on a total of 76 parliamentary initiatives on matters related to the Civil War and Franco's regime during the sixth and seventh legislatures (1996–2004). Note that the large majority (71 out of 76) are motions (rather than bills), non-binding instruments serving to urge the government to take action and to make explicit the position of the parliament (something that makes them more prone to fall on deaf ears, together with their high numbers). Figure 3.1 shows their evolution over time, confirming that it was during the PP's second legislature (2000–2004) that these topics gained more prominence.

Figure 3.2 shows which parliamentary groups were more active in this regard. The majority of initiatives came from the United Left (*Izquierda Unida* [IU]), which comprises the Communist Party, and the Mixed Group (*Grupo Mixto* [GMX]), an ad hoc parliamentary unit formed by parties unable to constitute their own parliamentary group. The parties within the Mixed Group more active in the matter were left-wing groups representing the Basque and Catalan regions – Basque Solidarity (*Eusko Alkartasuna* [EA]), Initiative for Catalonia Greens (*Iniciativa per Catalunya Verds* [ICV]),

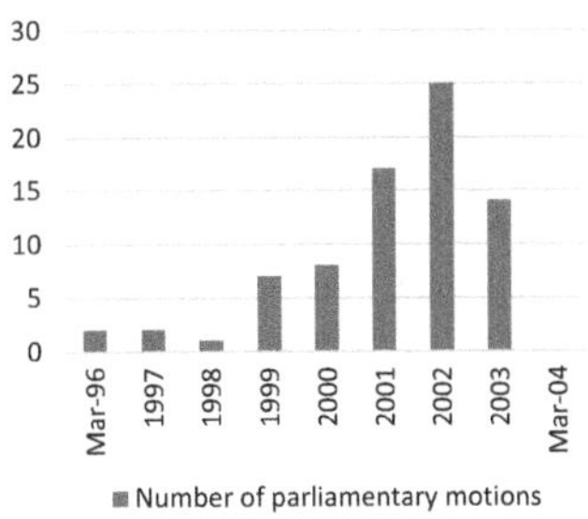

Figure 3.1 Distribution over time.

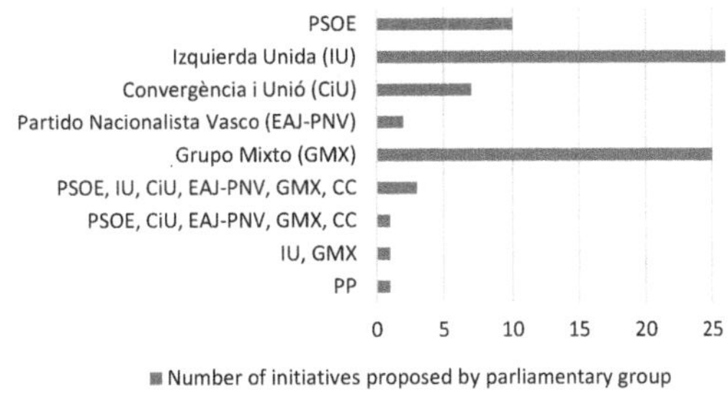

Figure 3.2 Distribution according to parliamentary proponent.

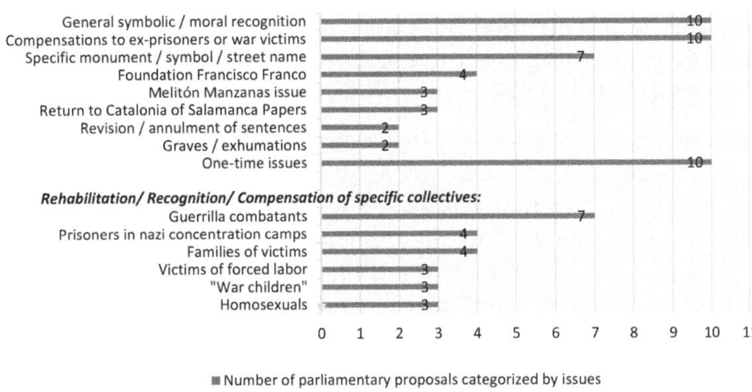

Figure 3.3 Distribution according to subject matter.

Parliamentary initiatives on issues related to the Civil War and Franco's regime during the VI and VII legislatures (Mar. 1996 – Mar. 2004).

and Republican Left of Catalonia (*Esquerra Republicana de Catalunya* [ERC]). This is a good indicator of the vehicles through which issues entered the Congress of Deputies. On the one hand, given its history of opposition to the dictatorship, the Communist Party is the one that has most direct links to those who are the object of compensation and/or recognition. On the other hand, civil society initiatives often have a greater capacity to have their demands heard at the regional level. In fact, it is common to find that some of the issues brought up in the Congress of Deputies are already part of the agenda of some regional parliaments. Though this is not exclusive to the Basque and Catalan regions, it is unsurprising to find parties from these regions pushing for issues related to the past, given their distinct sense of grievance (related to the suppression of regional nationalisms during the dictatorship) and the crucial role of memory discourses in identity politics.

Figure 3.3 categorizes each initiative according to the specific issue under discussion. Some are circumstantial and respond to specific events taking place at the time. This is the case of the backlash against the award given to Melitón Manzanas for being an ETA victim but a well-known police torturer under Franco; or the motions that referred to ex-prisoners in concentration camps, which were in part a response to the fact that Germany and Austria were at the time taking measures to compensate those subject to forced labor in concentration camps, measures that could potentially include the Spanish citizens who were sent there.[12] Many of the other initiatives, however, do raise the question of why they were being brought up at this moment in time.

Parliamentary initiatives on issues related to the Civil War and Franco's regime during the sixth and seventh legislatures (March 1996 – March 2004)

When it comes to accounting for the resurgence of the past in the political debate in particular, there are two dominant lines of explanation in the existing literature. The first has to do with changes in the international environment and in particular, the influence of the Pinochet affair (Davis 2005; Encarnación 2014; Blakeley 2005; Golob 2008). The second is instead related to internal political dynamics, particularly the election of the PP with an absolute majority in 2000 and the opposition's use of the past as an instrumental political weapon (Humlebaek 2004, 2010; Aguilar 2006; Julià 2009). To these I add a third one, related to civil society dynamics. Though the associative movement was only incipient at this stage, their demands often set the agenda. In the following, I explore each of these three factors.

The Pinochet affair

The Pinochet affair is said to have had an impact in Spain first and foremost due to the direct involvement of the Spanish judge Baltasar Garzón, who indicted Pinochet in October 1998, asking for his extradition to Spain. This was one of the first times the principle of universal jurisdiction[13] had been invoked, resulting in Pinochet's arrest in London on 17 October 1998. The involvement of the Spanish magistrate put the Spanish government under the spotlight, with the Chilean president considering it an illegitimate interference in Chile's domestic affairs and accusing Spain of 'showing signs of poor memory', given that it had not dealt with its past either (*El País* 1998).

Authors like Davis (2005: 869) and Encarnación (2014: 133) argue that this case struck a chord in Spain, reminding the political class and the public of Spain's unresolved past. In the words of Davis (2005:, 870), the 'whole affair seems to have resensitized Spain to the limitations of its own transition to democracy and created a new environment and space for the articulation of histories and memories hitherto suppressed'.

These authors base their arguments on the repercussions of the case in Spain, the willingness of the opposition to use the PP's uncomfortable position as evidence of the government's protection of a dictator, and the parallels that were established between Spain and Chile's recent history. Davis (2005: 869), however, recognizes that 'such a hypothesis can hardly be proven', and there is indeed the possibility these authors exaggerate the impact of the Pinochet affair. They draw heavily on Malamud's (2003) study of public opinion's reactions to the Pinochet case, using some of the quotes he extracted from the Spanish press, including a line by a political commentator stating that 'Pinochet's arrest is the vicarious dream of a historical impossibility, that of Franco being arrested in bed' or the reaction of a socialist spokesman who accused the government of adopting a 'pro-Franco ideological attitude'. However, as Malamud (2003: 159) himself notes, accusations of somebody being pro-Franco had already been frequently used in political language and in the press.

That being said, it is nonetheless striking that there is an obvious temporal coincidence between the Pinochet affair and the change in political institutions' relationship with Spain's past. The best piece of evidence in this regard is that the Committee of Foreign Affairs of the Spanish Congress condemned the 1936 coup d'état for the first time on 14 September 1999, the same day that this Committee debated the position of the Spanish government towards the Pinochet affair (DSCD, Comisión Asuntos Exteriores, No. 743, 14 September 1999). It should be said that this was not a highly symbolic or impactful gesture, consisting of a simple motion (*proposición no de ley*) approved in a committee meant to mark the commemoration of the 60th anniversary of the Spanish exile. The direct motivation behind this proposition was, according to the speeches of various political representatives, a visit of a Congress delegation to Mexico in which members of Congress were surprised to find out that the Spanish exile was being commemorated there (one of the main exile destinations), contrary to what was happening in Spain. It is, nonetheless, significant that the motion condemns the military uprising of 1936 and goes as far as to speak of a 'fascist military coup against the legal republican regime', sparking a debate with the PP, who opposed this formulation. This was right after the same committee had debated various issues related to the Pinochet affair. During this debate, a representative of the Basque Nationalist Party (PNV), Iñaki Anasagasti, mentioned that he 'personally regrets (...) that Francisco Franco was not in the same situation as Pinochet is now'.

There is, however, nothing in the debate that explicitly connects the Pinochet affair to the motion that condemns the 1936 coup, which was in fact presented at the end of May, before the opposition requested a debate on the Pinochet affair. Nevertheless, the fact that the tone of the motion constituted quite a radical departure from past propositions suggests there was a transformative event behind it. The PP representative fittingly points out that a proposition signaling the commemoration of the exile did not need to entail judgments on the causes of the Civil War. That the opposition chose to do so for the first time in 1999 – at the same time as it was trying to extract political capital from its position in favor of the extradition of Pinochet to Spain – is probably not a coincidence. There are several reasons why this might be so. On the one hand, Spanish public opinion was largely in favor of the extradition of Pinochet, thus signaling to the opposition that they could obtain political gains from politicizing Spain's own past. As the legitimate heirs of the opposition to Franco, they could appropriate this case for their own benefit. On the other hand, the PP's ambiguous position towards the Pinochet case could be conveniently used to stigmatize the PP, a strategy reinforced by the use of Spain's own past.

Note, still, that the Pinochet affair constitutes more of a background factor that opened up the political space to bring the past to the fore, an opening that was more immediately motivated by the opportunity the opposition saw in making political use of the past. In fact, when looking at the media debate and the declarations of the members of the opposition following the motion's discussion, no parallel with Pinochet was ever drawn. Instead, members of the opposition took the opportunity to state that the PP 'is the heir of the old right-wing and therefore unable to condemn the military coup' (PSOE representative) or that the PP's reaction puts in evidence its 'connections with the dark francoist past' (IU representative) (*El País* 1999). Tellingly, everyone seemed more concerned with the refusal of the PP to endorse the said motion than with the fact that it was actually approved (as the PP had no absolute majority, and all other parties endorsed it).

The idea that the Pinochet case was more of a background factor is reinforced by my interviews with political representatives. None of them mentioned the Pinochet debate when asked about the renewed willingness of the opposition to bring the past to the fore of the political debate. When a representative in the Foreign Affairs Committee at the time (present during both the Pinochet discussion and the motion on the commemoration of exile) was explicitly asked about a possible effect, he stated that 'the Pinochet case had no influence, maybe it provided more of an indirect support' (Interview SP13). Instead, he insisted on his frustration with the governing party, emphasizing the unwillingness of the PP to make concessions and to 'turn the page on the civil war'.

The past as part of the opposition's strategy

Resorting to symbolic aspects of the past in the political debate – particularly in cases where different political groups can be associated with past factions – is a relatively common practice, meant either to demarcate political fields or to delegitimize the opponent (Kovras and Loizides 2011; Igreja 2008). This is the more so in competitive settings, where those who can benefit from an instrumentalization of the past have their relative position in the political game jeopardized, resorting to all the political instruments available to extract political capital. It is in this light that Julià (2009: 6) and Aguilar (2006: 283) interpret the practice of instrumentalization of the past in the political debate in Spain, pointing out that the first time this occurred was in the electoral campaign of 1993, when the PSOE feared losing its long-held majority to the PP and used references to the past to discredit the opponent.

Following this logic, it is for many an obvious non-coincidence that the opposition started to make a more explicit use of the past when the PP cast a dominant shadow over Spanish politics (Humlebaek 2004, 2010; Aguilar 2006; Río Sánchez 2008; Julià 2009). For Humlebaek (2004: 164), this was a win-win strategy for the opposition: if it managed to force the PP to condemn Franco's regime, some of its most conservative voters would be let down; if not, it had all the tools needed to stigmatize the PP as 'francoist'.

As persuasive as this argument is, there is, however, one obvious flaw: the fact that the PP had been in power since 1996, but the opposition took until September 1999 to introduce a controversial initiative involving a value judgment on the past. When it comes to explaining the exact timing of this initiative, the Pinochet affair provides, therefore, more explanatory leverage (and so does the commemoration of the 60th anniversary of the end of the Civil War in 1999, together with the 1999 visit of the Congress delegation to Mexico). A plausible counterargument is that the timing of this initiative is not independent of the fact that the 2000 elections were approaching, and that the absolute majority of the PP could already be anticipated.

The temporal coincidence between the period in which the PP governed with an absolute majority (2000–2004) and the wave of parliamentary initiatives on the past can be understood from both an instrumentalist and an ideological perspective. From a purely instrumentalist point of view, which Julià (2009) represents best, this was simply the outcome of the fact that under an absolute majority, the PP had more free room to reject these initiatives, which allowed the opposition to elevate the tone of confrontation and politicize the PP's complicated relationship with Spain's past. From an ideological perspective, however, the more confrontational stance of the opposition in the second legislature is justified based on the contrast between the PP's attempted 'move to the center' during the first legislature and the drift towards the right in the second one. While in 1996, the PP won the elections by a 1% margin and had to make pacts with three regional nationalist parties to secure its investiture (*Convergencia i Unió* [CiU], *Partido Nacionalista Vasco* [PNV], and *Coalición Canaria* [CC]), these constraints did not apply in 2000, and its centrist image is considered to have died out. In addition, while the 1996 results gave the opposition hopes that the 1996–2000 legislature constituted a parenthesis in Spanish politics, the 2000 elections represented the definitive consolidation of the presence of a strong right-wing party. According to an academic who has closely followed this issue, the PP's absolute majority struck a chord with the left and created much restlessness within leftist and regional nationalist parties, who saw in the PP a reminiscence of the old conservative Spain and feared the permanent return of the right's hegemony (Interview SP2). He argues that the new willingness of the left to bring the past to the political scene cannot be solely the result of an attempt at shaming the PP – because everybody was well aware of its Francoist roots anyway – emphasizing instead that the use of the past served as a good counterweight to what these parties saw as an ill-fated drift towards the right in Spanish politics (Interview SP2). A PSOE representative in Congress at the time (2000–2004) similarly points out that as a reaction to the PP's leadership, left-wing parties were ready to be more radical and started to question the pacts of the transition (Interview SP10).

In addition, the fact that the PP no longer needed the parliamentary support of nationalist parties greatly increased the general tone of confrontation between the two, at a time in which the center–periphery cleavage was at the heart of Spanish politics, with ETA ending a 14-month truce at the end of 1999. Relations were particularly tense with the PNV, which had its reputation damaged by the failure of its attempt to secure a ceasefire and which had appropriated ETA's goal of achieving an independent Basque state (Muro 2008: 167–171). For the PP, moderate and radical nationalism became part of the same problem, while for the PNV, Aznar's 'tough approach' to ETA was evidence of his authoritarian tendencies. It is, therefore, not surprising that during the second legislature, the PNV was the first to bring a controversial initiative to the Congress of Deputies, pushing for the condemnation of the 1936 military uprising and adopting a strongly antagonist language, speaking of the current presence of 'sociological Francoism' (BOCG, D-123, 22 January 2001). The intention to use this motion as an instrument of delegitimization of the adversary was plainly evident, as the motion already approved in September 1999 was similar in content.

The idea of debating the past in order to tackle the rise of the right was, however, not entirely new. In December 1997, a PSOE member of parliament had already published an eloquent piece in *El País* entitled 'Speak, memory, speak' (Yañez-Barnuevo 1997). In it, he advocates for a recovery of the memory of the dictatorship as a means of 'political pedagogy for the new generations as well as to strengthen the democratic culture of the Spanish people'. He points towards a 'revival of Francoism' in various spheres and deems that those nostalgic for Franco feel emboldened since the PP came to power, criticizing the authoritarian tendencies of the ruling party. It is thus plausible to conclude that the idea of bringing the past to the fore of the political debate was already germinating in opposition circles before the PP's second legislature, receiving an important boost from events such as the Pinochet affair and the consolidation of the PP's rule in 2000.

External dynamics and the civil society impulse

Even though the willingness of the opposition to bring the past back to Spanish politics is decisively shaped by the above-mentioned context, the story would be incomplete if it were not for various external dynamics, including a growing societal interest and demands of civil society groups, who were behind several of the propositions put forward by opposition parties between 2000 and 2004. In spite of the fact that dynamics 'from below' were not so visible that they would force the issue into the parliamentary scene, the parliamentary debate over the past would not have acquired the shape and magnitude it did had it not been for specific demands and events taking place outside parliamentary doors, as several of the discussed issues would not have 'existed' in the first place if they had not been brought up by them.

An example of this is the attention given to specific collectives, such as ex-guerrilla combatants. This is an issue that IU repeatedly insisted upon in 2000 and 2001, an effort that can be traced back to a grassroots initiative born in 1997: the Archive, War and Exile Association (*Asociación Archivo, Guerra y Exilio* [AGE]). Despite receiving much less attention than the ARMH, AGE was actually the first association to speak of the need to recover the memory of Civil War–related aspects. One of the first issues it focused upon was the moral and political rehabilitation of ex-guerrilla combatants. It was behind the creation of an *Organizing Committee of Ex-guerrillas from Spain and the Exile* in May 1999, responsible for preparing a draft proposition that was then submitted to the Congress of Deputies and regional parliaments. This proposition's text is identical to the various motions submitted by IU to the Congress, and therefore, the role of the AGE is plainly evident. In an interview, an AGE founding member recounts how the association established contact with the spokespersons of various parties and how, after some failed attempts, a motion was finally approved in May 2001, something the AGE considered a victory and takes credit for (Interview SP16). Before that, various regional parliaments had already responded to AGE's calls and approved similar texts. This was a direct result of the efforts of the association to spread its message over the territory, organizing the so-called 'memory caravans' in 2000. These consisted of a sizeable representation of ex-guerrilla combatants, members of the International Brigades, and the so-called 'war children', who toured the Spanish territory, telling their stories and revealing their claims. They were received officially in regional parliaments and town halls (with the exception of Galicia and Valencia, where the PP governed). According to an AGE representative, this was part of a strategy to gather local and regional support and in this way, apply pressure at the Congress of Deputies' level (Interview SP16).

A different matter AGE took ownership of, after realizing their vulnerable and unknown situation, was that of 'war children' – children who had been sent abroad during the war for safety. Although the majority went to France, there was a contingent of a few thousand sent to the then USSR. Because members of the not yet existent AGE had visited the Spanish Center in Moscow when organizing the 1996 tribute to the International Brigades (so as to invite the Russian brigadiers), they were confronted with the precarious financial situation of the remaining 'war children', now of retirement age. This was one of the events that inspired the creation of AGE, which then deepened its contacts with this collective. As a result, AGE asked members of Congress to provide them with a dignified pension and to recognize them as victims of exile rather than simple migrants. These were demands taken up in Congress for the first time in 2003 (on three occasions), and which would be partially addressed in 2005 under Zapatero (Interview SP16).

Another issue conditioned by dynamics occurring outside the Congress of Deputies was the one of compensation and recognition of political prisoners. Because Law 4/1990 had important gaps – including the fact that it did not apply to people who had spent less than three years in jail – this was an unresolved matter. Through their contacts with Workers' Commissions, the PSOE, IU, and PNV periodically received the demands of the associations of those affected by political persecution during Francoism (Casqueiro and Díez 2002). Similarly to what was said about AGE, the president of AERPA, Gervasio Puerta, wrote in a letter to *El País* that the association has kept personal contact with the spokespeople of all the parties and that the motion under discussion at the time (on the economic and moral compensation of those imprisoned) was proposed by AERPA (Puerta 2002). Moreover, it is likely that dynamics occurring at the regional level affected the activity of the Congress of Deputies in this regard. In light of the inaction of the central government, and after a recommendation of the Spanish Ombudsman on the matter in 1996, there were various autonomous communities taking steps to cover (part of) those who had been excluded by Law 4/1990, a situation that created regional discrepancies. This was something IU noted in its motions (BOCG, Num. D-115, 22 December 2000; DSCD, Num. 139, 19 February 2002). It is likely that here, too, members of the collective concerned with this matter brought the issue to the attention of regional representatives. This was clear in the case of Catalonia, where there is evidence of interaction between the Catalan Association of Ex-Political Prisoners and representatives in the Catalan parliament (DSPC, C-414, Num. 42, 18 February 1999, p. 29).

Last but not least, the impact of the actions of the ARMH is visible from 2002 onwards. Even though it was created at the end of 2000, it was in 2002 that the ARMH definitely made it to news outlets. One reason behind this is that it dedicated itself to the emotionally charged process of exhuming mass graves, attempting to identify the bodies and restitute them to the families. This was a dormant issue in Spanish society despite the fact that Spain is one of the countries in the world with the most mass graves. What started as a one-time exhumation to recover the remains of Emilio Silva's grandfather, in October 2000, rapidly turned into an association meant to respond to the requests Silva would receive from then onwards coming from families wishing to exhume and give a proper burial to their relatives. The association took off in 2002, when it gathered the means and support to conduct exhumations more systematically, handling more than ten in 2002. At the time, its network of support was constituted by volunteers, including archeologists and forensic experts. A second reason behind the ARMH's impact is the decision of its founder to submit the Spanish case to the United Nations Working Group on Enforced or Involuntary Disappearances (under the Office of the High Commissioner for Human Rights) in the summer of 2002. When making an initial call for families to reveal the cases of their relatives so that they could be submitted to the UN, the ARMH received more than 1,000 petitions. Media coverage intensified from then onwards, speaking of 'the earth giv[ing] back its dead' (Cué 2002a), '65 years of hidden history' (EFE 2002), or 'Our disappeared' (*El País* 2002). Naturally, this reflected on the propositions presented in the Congress of Deputies in the second half of 2002, with five motions referring either to the issue of exhumations or to the rights of the families. When asked about the wave of parliamentary propositions during the PP's second legislature, a PSOE representative, in an allusion to associations like the ARMH, states that 'they were meant to respond to the requests that were arising from active associations and which demonstrated the lack of state aid' (Interview SP9).

In light of the avalanche of propositions at the time, political representatives decided to take several of those issues to the Constitutional Committee of Congress on 20 November 2002 (the anniversary of Franco's death), where the theme of exhumations and the actions of the ARMH were at the center of various interventions. There, the most significant resolution under the PP's rule was approved, honoring and granting 'moral recognition to all men and women who were victims of the Spanish Civil War as well as those who later endured repression under Franco's dictatorship' (DSCD, Comisión Constitucional, No. 625, 20 November 2002, p. 20511). Despite having already voted in favor of a few of the motions that referred to specific collectives, this was the first time the PP had subscribed to a proposition carrying a general message of moral recognition. The ruling party hoped, in this way, to end the battery of initiatives the opposition had been putting forward and close such debates once and for all, as the party representative explicitly stated. Coincidentally or not, this was just a few days after the UN Group on Enforced Disappearances, in response to the ARMH's request, issued a recommendation to the Spanish government on the investigation of disappearances (Cué 2002b). Although the media wrote 'The PP condemns Franco's coup' (Cué 2002c), more attentive observers have not failed to notice that what was in fact in the text of the motion was a general condemnation of 'totalitarian regimes opposed to the freedom and dignity of every citizen'. Moreover, the fact that this was approved in a Congress committee, rather than in a solemn act of the plenary, has been criticized for downgrading the importance of the act (Interview SP1).

This is all to say that the renewed willingness of the opposition to bring the past to the political debate is not only an outcome of the attempt to use it as a political weapon, but has to be understood in the context of mutable external dynamics that were putting the past under a new light in Spain's public sphere. Among those, the emergence of civil society initiatives was among the most remarkable and poignant. One could claim, based on social movement theory, that these initiatives would not have emerged in the first place if they had not benefited from a favorable political opportunity structure. While this is true for many of the associations that would emerge after the ARMH – especially those created after Zapatero's government released public funds to support exhumations – it is not entirely the case for pioneering organizations like AGE and ARMH. The question of why these organizations emerged at this specific moment in time is naturally puzzling and so far has not merited much attention. The next section seeks to start remedying this.

The 'late emergence' of civil society initiatives

The absence of longitudinal studies on the movement for historical memory in Spain complicates any attempt to delineate a precise map of the development of the associative scene. It is generally known, though, that there were few civil society initiatives before the ARMH and that there was an 'associative explosion' from the early 2000s onwards. While Gálvez Biesca (2006: 34) counted 30 associations at the end of 2003, there were over 100 in 2005, a phenomenon the author links both to the symbolic and media impact of the ARMH and to the public subsidies that would start being granted from 2005. At the end of 2017, the National Registry of Associations had listed over 300 associations dedicated to related themes.[14] The large majority of them are local associations dealing with related topics at the local level. The hegemonic state-wide ones are the ARMH and the *Foro por la Memoria*, both focused on exhumations (though with conflicting approaches on how and why they should be conducted) (Gálvez Biesca 2006: 35). Their predominance is visible in their local ramifications or in the local units that despite being independent, took their names from these associations.[15]

But while the creation of *Foro por la Memoria* was sponsored by the Communist Party at the end of 2002 – at a time when the ARMH had already put the exhumations issue on the agenda – the latter is a better example of a spontaneous civil society initiative, which rather than reacting to a favorable opportunity structure, contributed to opening it. By exposing an issue that had not been evident before and demonstrating the possibilities for action, it opened opportunities for other organizations to emerge (including *Foro por la Memoria* itself). The origins of the ARMH go back to 2000, when Emilio Silva, one of its founders and its president, put into motion the necessary process to exhume a mass grave where the remains of his grandfather lay, together with those of another dozen people. Silva was collecting stories from locals for a Civil War–related novel, in the small village where his father's family was from, when he learnt about the location of his grandfather's grave. At the same time as he established contact with the town hall authorities and the families of those believed to be in the same grave, Silva wrote a piece for the local newspaper *Crónica de León*, telling the story of his grandfather and stating his intention to exhume his grave (Silva himself was a journalist). This, in turn, made other people contact him – including various locals who approached the exhumation site to ask for help with locating/exhuming their family members – which impelled Silva and others to create the ARMH at the end of 2000 (Interview P3). While initially, the association did not have the intention of going beyond León, it gradually realized the magnitude of the issue, as media coverage prompted families from everywhere to contact the association (Interview SP3).

The story behind the formation of the ARMH testifies to the transformative role of incidental and contingent events. Had Emilio Silva decided not to collect locals' stories for a book he intended to write, and had he not met the person who told him about his grandfather, the ARMH would probably not have come to life (or at least not in the way it did). Encarnación (2014: 146) simplistically traces the associative movement back to the Pinochet affair. If it is true that ARMH founding members were perplexed by the attention given to the Pinochet case and the comparative lack of interest in Franco's crimes, it is a stretch to assume that this was what directly motivated them. Instead, it helped them realize that the so often referenced figure of the 'disappeared' in Latin America could be used in Spain too, which made the ARMH the first to speak of the 'Spanish disappeared' (Interview SP3). When speaking of their motivations, ARMH founding members refer instead to the inspiration taken from individuals who were at the time working with AGE on the rehabilitation of the guerrilla movement (Interview SP3). In his *Crónica de León* piece, Silva recounts how at the time he met an ex-guerrilla member, Francisco Martínez (known as Quico), who 'infected me with his immense struggle to recover memory' (Silva 2000).

If the social movement literature has shown that mobilization depends on grievances, organization, and political opportunities, it is true that the emergence of the ARMH benefited from a bit of all three, namely, the collaboration of local authorities in the first exhumation (*political opportunity*), the exceptional organizational and networking capacity of Emilio Silva (*organization*), and the emotional process of finding the grave of his grandfather, exhuming it, and receiving similar requests from other families (*grievance*). However, what is most revealing about the very early stages of the ARMH – and possibly of the entire movement on historical memory – is how the actions of a few early entrepreneurs can respond to and activate 'dormant grievances' and how these actions are often the result of contingent events. Rather than carry out a long-held plan to exhume his grandfather's grave, Emilio Silva stumbled upon information on it. Only then did he fully realize that the exhumation was a moral necessity (*grievance activation*), being helped in this process by individuals already engaged with the 'struggle to recover memory' and the realization that his grandfather was a 'disappeared', like the Latin American ones who were an object of attention in Spain at the time. His exceptional networking capacity and willingness to work on this issue brought his message to other families, who possibly went through a similar process of grievance activation and/or were provided with the opportunity to act upon that grievance by realizing that exhuming and reburying their relatives was a feasible endeavor.

The creation of AGE, three years before the ARMH, also tells us a great deal about contingency, the actions of a few early entrepreneurs, and the importance of their organizational and networking capacity. Its emergence can be traced back to the 1996 tribute to the International Brigades (the first mass coordinated effort to bring together disperse individuals or/and collectives), planned by some of the same people who then founded AGE. In the words of a founding member, 'now that we had dealt with the international brigades, I realized it was time to deal with all the other collectives' (Interview SP16). The mastermind behind the idea to organize the 1996 tribute seems to have been Adelina Kondratieva, a Russian brigadier who, after the collapse of the Soviet Union, visited Spain periodically – where she established contacts with numerous circles of people who had been part of the Republican army, ex-exiled, and ex-prisoners – and where she published her memoirs in 1994. Kondratieva was surprised by the absence of a tribute to the International Brigades, something that made her contact 'friends from clandestine times', with whom she established the Association of Friends of the International Brigades (Interview SP16). That the idea of organizing a tribute came from someone who had spent most of her lifetime outside Spain, in a country where official commemoration practices and the articulation of a wartime identity were encouraged, is perhaps not accidental.

AGE carries, in fact, the more extensive official name of *Association for the Creation of the Archive of the Civil War, the International Brigades, the War Children, the Resistance and the Spanish Exile*, though it has worked mostly on three fronts: archives; ex-guerrilla members; and 'war children'. The concern over these collectives was born out of the contacts AGE's founding members established with them. This was the case not only with the 'war children' an AGE founding member met in Russia when organizing the 1996 tribute to the International Brigades, but also with ex-guerrilla members. Quico (the same ex-guerrilla member who inspired Emilio Silva) was the one to ask AGE founding members if they would be willing to defend his cause (Interview SP16). In addition, AGE was partially born out of the aspiration to collect the disperse documentation on the Civil War defeated outside Spain. Its concern with the preservation of documentation abroad is, in turn, linked to the personal biographies of its founding members and the fact that they were interested in the preservation of personal memories that, due to advanced age, would soon disappear.

In fact, the sense of urgency over the preservation of testimonies and the remedying of situations considered unjust – which all the initiatives on 'historical memory' in one way or another attempt to do – has to be understood in a context where the Civil War generation was rapidly disappearing. The 1996 tribute to the International Brigades, for example, would not have been possible a couple of years later, given the advanced age of all those who participated. This is a point always underscored by those who put the associative movement into motion, who were keenly aware that it was becoming too late for some and the last opportunity for others (Interview SP3, SP16).

The definitive return of the past to Spanish politics (2004–2008)

If less attentive observers could have easily missed parliamentary discussions on the past prior to 2004, very few could have failed to note that Zapatero's first government (2004–2008) broke with former patterns, bringing the 'historical memory' issue to the front of the political debate. The early decision to create an Inter-Ministerial Commission for the Study of the Situation of Victims of the Civil War and Francoism, announced in July 2004, culminated in the approval of what became known as the Historical Memory Law – which in fact bears a much more extensive title: *Law 52/2007 of 26 December which recognizes and amplifies rights and establishes measures in favor of those who suffered persecution or violence during the civil war and the dictatorship*. In essence, this Commission was in charge of carrying out a study systematizing the rights of victims of the Civil War and dictatorship who had been so far recognized by fragmented pieces of legislation and, based on the identified gaps, draft a legislative proposal establishing the necessary measures to grant them appropriate 'recognition and moral satisfaction' (art. 2 §c, Real Decreto 1891/2004). The then vice-president of the government, Maria Teresa Fernández de la Vega, was designated as the head of the Commission, which was interpreted as a sign of its perceived importance. The fact that more than three years elapsed between the creation of the Commission and the approval of the final version of the law (at the end of Zapatero's first legislature in December 2007) already speaks volumes about the difficulties the PSOE faced both in drafting what turned out to be a more complex issue than anticipated and in negotiating it with its parliamentary allies.

Other significant initiatives taken by the central government at the time – some of them victim-centered and others which can be considered (timid) acknowledgment steps – included the allocation of public funds for exhumation projects (Orden PRE/3945/2005); the symbolic declaration of 2006 as the 'year of historical memory' (Law 24/2006 of 7 July), following a draft proposal by IU-ICV;[16] and the creation of a Documentation Centre on Historical Memory in Salamanca (Royal Decree 697/2007 of 1 June). Moreover, two pending issues deserved specific laws of their own: economic assistance to 'war children' (Law 3/2005 of 18 March); and the restitution to Catalonia of the documents confiscated from the Catalan government during the Civil War (Law 21/2005 of 17 November). This is an issue Catalan nationalist parties had insisted on for years, including ERC (Republican Left of Catalonia), a party that together with IU-ICV, constituted the parliamentary basis of support of Zapatero's minority government. Other issues were addressed through other types of measures throughout 2005 and 2006, sometimes following the recommendation of the Inter-Ministerial Commission, including an upgrade in Civil War pensions; the establishment of regulatory bases for awarding financial reparations; the authorization of expenses related to the removal of Francoist symbols; and a personal income tax exemption for reparations to victims of repression (Encarnación 2014: 164).

Law 52/2007 of 26 December, commonly known as the Historical Memory Law, was the most significant piece of legislation approved in Spain when it comes to the political treatment of the past, though its content is much less ambitious than its common designation would suggest. As Blakely puts it (2008: 324), symbolism triumphed over substance, since in legal–technical terms, the law was hardly necessary, as most of its aims could have been achieved through specific governmental decrees or by amending existing legislation. With a total of 22 articles, a long preamble, and a couple of additional dispositions, the bill touches on a wide range of issues, including: (1) a general moral recognition of those affected by any form of violence; (2) a declaration of illegitimacy of judicial condemnations dictated by political, ideological, or religious reasons; (3) improvement of compensation schemes and the creation of new ones for collectives previously uncovered; (4) assistance in the exhumation and identification of remains; (5) the withdrawal of Francoist symbols from the public space; (6) the prohibition of pro-Franco commemorations in the Valley of the Fallen (where Franco was buried); (7) a census on structures built with forced labor; (8) the amelioration of conditions for the extension of citizenship to the International Brigades; (9) measures on the acquisition and protection of documents as well as on the management of the General Archive of the Spanish Civil War; and (10) extension of citizenship to descendants of the Republican exile, among others.

Although this bill was highly contentious and criticized on almost every ground, it nonetheless constitutes a radical departure from the manner the past had been dealt with at the institutional level up to then. It was the first time that a government had granted visibility to this topic and made a commitment to address it, as well as the first time that reparatory and acknowledgment measures had been discussed as a whole (rather than through fragmented pieces of legislation on specific subjects) and as such, the first time they had been openly debated in the parliamentary plenary (rather than in less visible parliamentary committees). Whereas many have criticized Law 52/2007 on the grounds that its contents could have been addressed through less conflictual types of legislation, others argue that it was precisely this that made the law a privileged instrument of moral recognition and therefore, a public acknowledgment act in itself. As a PSOE representative has put it: 'A law has a symbolic meaning that is especially valuable and pertinent when the content of the norm is one of public reparation' (DSCD, Num. 296, 31 October 2007, p. 14632). To put it briefly, the law consolidates victim-centered types of measures (by ameliorating benefits and covering previously excluded groups) and improves Spain's record when it comes to public acknowledgment measures (condemning the dictatorship, recognizing victims, and dealing with public symbols), though there was certainly room to be more radical in this regard.

This law proved to be a contentious matter, coming under attack both from the right and from those to the left of the PSOE. The Popular Party and more conservative sectors of society ferociously opposed its existence on the simple grounds that it was revanchist, opening old wounds and threatening the spirit of the democratic transition. Civil society associations and parliamentary groups to the left of the PSOE were no less critical, considering that the law fell short of what was expected in many regards, namely, because: (1) it only declared political/ideological/religious sentences *illegitimate* (with no legal consequences), instead of *nullifying* the sentences issued by Francoist courts;[17] (2) the state did not take the lead in the exhumations process, limiting itself to providing assistance to civil society; (3) it put the Civil War and the dictatorship on a par with each other rather than disentangling them; (4) it excluded from the provision on the withdrawal of Francoist symbols those with artistic, architectonical, or religious value; (5) it spoke only of the right to the recovery of personal and family memory and granting an individual certificate of reparation and personal recognition (upon the victims' request), in this way 'privatizing memory'; and (6) it emphasized the centrality of the transition spirit and indirectly, was equidistant about the two sides in the Civil War, failing to recognize the Second Republic as a legitimate regime.

Accounting for the enactment of Law 52/2007 of 26 December

Despite its many detractors, the so-called Historical Memory Law broke with former memory patterns at the political level, including with the way the past had been dealt with under the PSOE's previous terms. To the question of why the PSOE was now ready to address an issue it had not tackled or even considered before, there are various possible answers, though there are good reasons to think some carry significantly more explanatory weight than others. Note that the factors mentioned in the following are meant to answer the question of why the PSOE was ready to put up with the symbolism of an overall law on 'historical memory' rather than simply address specific issues through separate and one-theme pieces of legislation (something that could have been expected, given the increasing pressures in this regard and the fact that some regional governments were already taking steps on related matters).

Aguilar (2008b) summarizes the different factors put forward in the already quite burgeoning literature, underlining five different explanatory lines: (1) generational changes within the PSOE itself, with the rise of a 'war grandchildren' generation, who had a different outlook on the past compared with the 'transition generation', including Zapatero himself; (2) the idea that the PSOE had to live up to the parliamentary initiatives that it had backed or proposed during the PP's tenure and similarly, honor the commitments assumed on the 20 November 2002 resolution, which had been left unfulfilled by the PP; (3) the fact that the PSOE's term in office coincided with highly significant anniversaries, such as the 70th anniversary of the start of the Civil War and the 30th anniversary of Franco's death; (4) the much-needed support of parliamentary partners on the left (given that the PSOE did not have an absolute majority), who were more strongly in favor of putting such issues on the political agenda; and finally, (5) civil society pressure, including groups that were also the outcome of generational changes and that secured the support of international organizations.

While all these factors are part of a propitious political environment, they differ greatly in their explanatory power. For example, the idea that the PSOE had to honor previous commitments assumed while in opposition offers little explanatory leverage when thinking of the usual gap in rhetoric versus behavior of parties that alternate between the opposition and the government. The fact that the PSOE had previously presented a legislative proposal requesting the annulment of politically motivated sentences under Franco, but later dropped this while in the government, is just one example of this. The same seems to hold true for the (un)importance of anniversaries. Evidence of that is the fact that the 50th and the 60th anniversary of the onset of the Civil War (1986 and 1996) did not prevent the absence of official commemorations.

A different factor one should be careful about emphasizing is the importance of generational changes and their different outlooks on the past. I consider that the emphasis should not be on generations *per se* but on the different political environments in which they grow up. Different generational outlooks are naturally endogenous and decisively shaped by the different contexts in which they are embedded. These provide inhibiting or facilitating conditions for the formulation of certain ideas and policies, and there is no doubt that the grandchildren generation grew up in an incomparably more favorable setting, free from the political constraints of the transition and at an age when the transitional justice norm had already reached a tipping point. However, by itself, this is not a sufficient condition, since political agents must have the motivation to transform an enabling environment into an actual policy. This is the more so in a setting where a measure/idea had not been previously advocated or formulated as such, and therefore, was not simply 'waiting in the oven' for the right political environment.

This is where the remaining two factors considered by Aguilar (2008b) come in. On the one hand, there are civil society initiatives that raise the salience of the issue and find their different pathways to the political sphere, eventually contributing – even if indirectly – to tipping the political balance in favor of policy implementation. In the case of the exhumations movement, to give an example, such pathways involved the Spanish Ombudsman (*Defensor del Pueblo*), which, after receiving several complaints, included a three-page section on the exhumations of mass graves in its 2003 report, something that did not go unnoticed in the parliamentary scene. In the plenary debate of 1 June 2004, the PNV representative notes:

> we have been witnessing over the last few years a healthy awakening of interest in the recovery of collective memory. Citizens do not stop exploring new ways of casting a critical eye on the past (…). Families and those affected do not stop presenting initiatives and complaints to public powers claiming their full recognition as well as symbolic and economic measures that make justice to them.
>
> (DSCD, Plenary Session, No. 13, 1 June 2004, p. 478)

There are, indeed, good reasons to think that Spain's recent past would not have become such a salient issue if it had not been for the associative scene at the time and in particular, the symbolically charged phenomenon of exhumations, which, as Figure 3.4 shows, registered a peak the year before

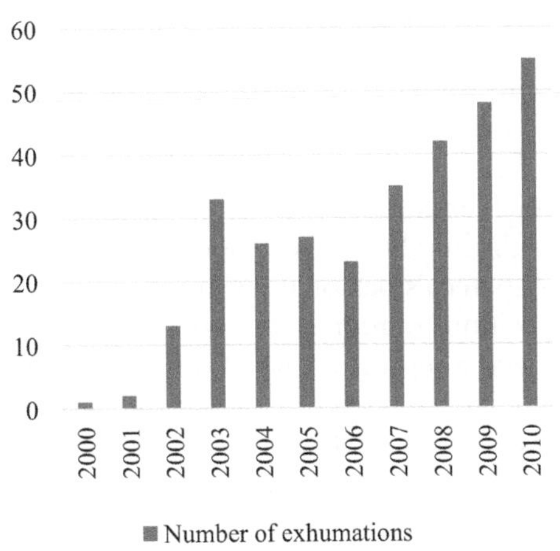

Figure 3.4 Evolution of the yearly number of exhumations (2000–2010). Source: Own elaboration based on data from Etxeberria (n.d.).

Zapatero took office. When thinking of such 'external sources of pressure', it is also relevant to highlight that the associative scene received the backing of international organizations, such as Amnesty International, which published three reports in 2005 and 2006 urging the Spanish government to fulfill its international obligations (Aguilar 2008b). Perhaps even more significant in this regard was the condemnation of the human rights violations committed by the Franco regime by the Council of Europe in March 2006, issuing a series of recommendations to the Spanish government.

However, if it is logical to think that Law 52/2007 would hardly have materialized without such external impulses, there are also powerful 'internal sources of pressure'. The PSOE's condition of minority government meant that it had to look for parliamentary allies to its left, among which were parties more strongly in favor of putting the 'historical memory' issue on the political agenda. The parliamentary support of ERC and IU-ICV was, in fact, a replication of the agreement achieved at the autonomous level in Catalonia in December 2003, when the so-called *Tripartito Catalán* took over. Though there is no mention of the issue in the latter's joint program, the Catalan government already had a plan to create a Committee on Historical Memory in early 2004. The support of these parties for this issue, however, did not come out of thin air, and external dynamics were certainly relevant in putting it in their agenda too (even if their motives went beyond satisfying a bottom-up demand), which reinforces the (indirect) importance of this factor.

An obvious rival explanation to these would be that the PSOE simply had a pre-established preference based on a well-anchored ideological sympathy. This goes in the direction of those who boil it down to a personal preference of Zapatero, who was the grandson of a Republic army officer executed during the war and therefore sensitive to such issues (Raimundo 2012: 97–98). The fact that Zapatero invoked his Republican grandfather during his investiture speech is often said to be proof of his intentions. Nevertheless, this reasoning is flawed, since Zapatero did not mention the 'historical memory' issue at all during his speech (despite its being brought up by ERC and ICV during the investiture debate), and the actual reference to his grandfather had little or nothing to do with it – 'my ideals are brief: an infinite craving for peace, love for the good, and social enhancement of the humble' (DSCD, Plenary Session, No. 2, 15 April 2004, p. 24). At best, Zapatero's personal sensibilities can be said to have created a positive predisposition to address this issue. The fact that Zapatero himself is from León and was a representative of this region for many years naturally made him familiar with the exhumations process and the civil society initiatives born there, including the ARMH (Interview SP9).

More importantly, explanations based on pre-established preferences can be ruled out with a good degree of certainty based on the absence of any indication that the PSOE would put forward a legislative piece of this type prior to its election. This is the more so when one takes into consideration that its 200-page-long electoral program became known as a 'catch-all program', covering a wide variety of issues, of which the 'historical memory' theme was not a part. Instead, the program made a brief reference to three separate issues – expansion of pensions to 'war children'; harmonization of pensions between Civil War mutilated and military officials; and the creation of a Centre for Documentation and Research on the Civil War and Francoism in the Salamanca Historical Archive – which suggests that prior to its election, the PSOE's intention was to continue to address specific issues through fragmented pieces of legislation rather than have a law with the degree of symbolism of Law 52/2007. The fact that the decision to create the Inter-Ministerial Commission for the Study of the Situation of Victims of the Civil War and Francoism was born out of a parliamentary initiative, presented less than two months after the investiture of Zapatero, further supports the proposition that the dynamics of parliamentary alliance-building in the context of a minority government were important in giving shape to the law under study.

Interviews with political representatives at the time partially confirm these assumptions. Among the PSOE representatives who were in some way involved with the topic, when asked where the idea of the law had come from, they pointed towards either (1) the demands of people and associations around them, (2) the fact that the law itself was an outcome of parliamentary initiatives, (3) the personal conviction of Zapatero, or (4) the dynamics of pact-making with parliamentary allies in order to get the needed parliamentary support (Interviews SP9, SP10, SP11, SP12). Note that the last point was spelled out by one high-profile PSOE representative in a very resolute way but was not confirmed by the others I interviewed. ERC deputies, on the other hand, are firmly convinced that the pressure of left-wing parties, and in particular ERC, obliged Zapatero to commit to a law he had not foreseen, as this was part of the conditions ERC had spelled out in order to support the PSOE's investiture (Interviews SP6, SP14, SP15).

It is unclear, however, whether this was indeed part of an exchange currency in the investiture agreement or whether Zapatero's government decided only later to respond to parliamentary initiatives and in this way please its parliamentary partners – while at the same time advancing a topic that fitted well with Zapatero's agenda of civic republicanism and protection of minorities.[18] Though both ERC and ICV mentioned the 'historical memory' issue during Zapatero's investiture, there is little indication in this debate that it was a major priority for these parties, and Zapatero, in his various responses, did not address it (DSCD, Plenary Session, No. 2, 15 April 2004). But in a similar vein to what was already taking place under the PP's rule, various parliamentary groups – CiU, ERC, GMX, IU-ICV, EAJ-PNV – started to put forward parliamentary initiatives on related measures as early as April 2004. Zapatero's government was quick to respond to them, endorsing a series of propositions on the recognition of victims in June 2004 and deciding on the creation of the Inter-Ministerial Commission for the Study of the Situation of Victims of the Civil War and Francoism at the end of July.

Although the law would be severely criticized by the PSOE's parliamentary allies for not being radical enough, the content and language of the norm would actually be importantly shaped by them, in particular by IU-ICV. Between the moment when a timid draft bill was introduced in parliament in September 2006 and its actual approval in October 2007, more than 350 amendments were introduced, some of which were responsible for the most significant (and most controversial) aspects of the law, such as the removal of Francoist symbols (Encarnación 2014: 171; Blakeley 2008: 319–323).

Paralysis and progress post-2007: why has Spain advanced so slowly?

If Law 52/2007 broke new grounds, it would take the Spanish central government more than a decade to take new steps meant to strengthen and widen the scope of this law. The 2008 economic crisis would dominate Zapatero's second turbulent term (2008–2011) and push other issues to the margins, while the consecutive governments of Mariano Rajoy's Popular Party (2011–2018) did nothing to improve Spain's record on transitional justice. If anything, the PP's governments constituted a setback. Though not officially repealing Law 52/2007, the PP followed on Rajoy's earlier promises not to allocate public money to this issue for most of its time in power, thus effectively ensuring that part of Law 52/2007 would become dead letter. This affected, for example, the capacity of families and associations to conduct exhumations, the total number of which would fall from an all-time high of 55 in 2010 to a low of 11 in 2013 (Etxeberria n.d.). Nevertheless, it was during the PP's years in the central government that some autonomous communities started to enact their own legislation, meant to complement or even expand Law 52/2007.[19]

The discourse of the PP has essentially remained the same over time and is very similar to the dominant narrative originating in the transition period: initiatives on the issue are equated with the attempt to 'open old wounds', 'generate tensions and divisions', and 'undermining reconciliation among Spaniards' (Humlebaek 2010; *ABC* 2014). Opposition parties are accused of 'oozing hatred', 'not letting the dead rest', and wanting to 'revive a distant past' (*La Vanguardia* 2014). In his mission to Spain in 2014, the UN Special Rapporteur on the promotion of Truth, Justice, Reparation, and Guarantees of Non-Recurrence, Pablo de Greiff, noted with some astonishment that several government representatives with whom he met tended to base discussions on the following proposition: 'either we all agree that we are fully reconciled, or the only alternative is the resurgence of underlying hatreds, which would entail too high a risk' (de Greiff 2014: 19). If this view does little justice to the strength of Spain's institutions and the absence of risk for the stability of the democratic order, as de Greiff himself notes, it shows the extent to which political representatives still use the same tropes as in the transition period.

To be fair, this is a view that is not exclusive to the PP. In fact, the PSOE itself has usually been careful to emphasize its endorsement of the transition's principles. This was visible in the 2007 Historical Memory Law itself, which starts its preamble by praising the spirit of reconciliation, mutual understanding, and respect for pluralism, which guided the democratic transition. Rather than questioning those principles, the measures in the law are framed as 'deepening the spirit of reunion and harmony of the transition'. The extent to which the PSOE was concerned with this matter is visible in the declarations of political representatives at the time. A member of parliament (who was often the PSOE's spokesperson on this matter) stated:

> Is it possible that Spanish society settles its debt with its history without breaking the basis of its current coexistence and the principles of reconciliation and pardoning that guided the democratic transition? – this is the central question produced by the debate on the so-called Historical Memory Law (...) The law goes as far as it can go without undermining the basis of coexistence; it settles the remaining debts with our history without reopening the wounds.
>
> (Jáuregui 2006)

While few people would take seriously the argument that questioning the transition pacts today would endanger coexistence, to speak of the transition's moral cop-out (that is, its continuities with the Franco regime and its oblivion of those who fought against it) is to put into question what became a quasi-'founding myth' of contemporary Spain. As one of the most significant and transformative historical periods in Spain's recent past – and unlike a long previous history of conflicts and dictatorships – the Spanish transition came to be regarded by the mainstream political elites and the general public as a highly successful moment. By breaking with past divisions and allowing the construction of the modern and European Spain that the PSOE became so keen on promoting, the transition is one of the very few historical moments most Spaniards are proud of, thus performing an important identitarian function. This is confirmed by a 2008 survey: when asked about Spain's most important historical event, 40% responded that it was the transition, and 74% confirmed that they took pride in Spain's transition process (CIS 2008). Though this number has decreased to 67% in 2018, it is still high (CIS 2018). Underlying the image of a successful transition is often the rejection of what is seen as a tragic and excessively confrontational past, in a demonstration of how the memory of a fratricidal civil war still weighs heavily over transitional justice debates. The testimony of a different PSOE representative substantiates this:

> I am not going to dishonor the generation of my parents, who made the transition, to honor the generation of my grandparents, who made the war. The generation of my grandparents was not better than the one of

> my parents, on the contrary. The generation of my grandparents was quite mad. And the generation of my parents sensible. To say they were cowards, or that they were afraid, is unjust and false. They learnt to overcome resentment and fear.
>
> (Interview SP11)

This is all to say that when it comes to understanding why Spain has progressed so little and so slowly on the transitional justice scale, the mainstream outlook on the merits of the transition – and the extent to which these are tied to the view that coexistence requires pardoning and forgetting – has to be considered. In other words, the endurance and predominance of views that made Spain's memory regime a consensual one in the past is an integral part of the reason why it struggles to take more robust TJ steps.

Nevertheless, Spain's memory regime today is no longer the same as the one prevalent at the time of approval of the 2007 Historical Memory Law. Firstly, one has to consider the extent to which this law in itself constituted a stepping stone, breaking new symbolic ground that contributed to the normalization of related issues. Speaking of exhumations or the withdrawal of Francoist symbols has become a less contentious issue than it was before. By changing the relationship of political institutions with the past and contributing to the normalization of certain themes, the law established a concrete basis that gave actors more room to make more ambitious claims from then onwards. This is important in understanding why TJ measures often seem to follow an incremental and stepwise fashion, as later measures can gradually expand the scope of earlier measures without provoking radical 'breaks'. To give a powerful example, removing the remains of Franco from the Valley of the Fallen would have been unimaginable prior to 2007. Nevertheless, it is what the socialist government of Pedro Sánchez did in 2019 after many years of debate regarding the so-called 'resignification' of the controversial Valley of the Fallen (a vast monument/mausoleum that houses the bodies of more than 30,000 Civil War victims in its subterranean crypts and where Franco's remains had pride of place inside the basilica). The 2007 law had already devoted one of its articles to this issue, which then led to the appointment of an Expert Commission for the Future of the Valley of the Fallen in 2011, whose recommendations included Franco's removal. This issue had been raised multiple times before parliament in subsequent years but had to wait for the left to return to power to be executed.

In addition, recent changes in Spain's memory regime have to be understood in the context of major transformations in Spain's political landscape in the mid-2010s, marked by growing fragmentation and polarization. The reasons for this can be traced back to the post-2008 economic meltdown and also to growing territorial tensions, corruption scandals, and a general crisis of political legitimacy, heavily affecting Spaniards' trust in politics and institutions (Vidal 2018). This translated into the rise of challenger parties, most notably the astounding emergence of the radical left *Podemos* (with 21% of the vote in 2015). Changes in the right-wing space have occurred later too, with the fast rise of the radical right *Vox* in 2019. The emergence of these parties (as well as the effect they produced on the positioning of mainstream parties) went hand in hand with high levels of polarization, and transitional justice/memory-related issues are only one of various topics affected by this dynamic. This is visible, for example, in the fact that *Podemos* adopted many of the claims of civil society associations, with its 2019 program going as far as to pledge to amend the amnesty law so that crimes against humanity could be prosecuted. The party explicitly incorporated the language of international human rights law and transitional justice principles into its programmatic documents, a trend that is also visible in PSOE's programs. Important in this regard is the fact that UN human rights bodies became more actively involved with the Spanish case throughout the 2010s – both the Working Group on Enforced or Involuntary Disappearances and the Special Rapporteur on the promotion of Truth, Justice, Reparation and Guarantees of Non-Recurrence paid (separate) visits to Spain in 2013 and 2014, issuing two reports with numerous recommendations. Left-wing parties have, from then on, regularly quoted them.

Also relevant is the fact that the rise of *Podemos*, as well as the massive anti-austerity mobilizations to which it responded, was accompanied by a discourse that questioned the legitimacy of the democratic transition and pointed towards its deficiencies in various respects, linking the (lack of) quality of Spain's current democratic system to the shortcomings of the transition. In its initial and most radical stage, *Podemos* characterized the Spanish political system as an 'oligarchical regime', which was forged by those at the top in pacts that were meant to secure the permanence and alternation in power of the same old elites (Franzé 2015). This was similar to claims coming from the anti-austerity movement, whose calls for 'real democracy' involved a negative judgment of the origins of the current regime. Though these views have not become hegemonic, their recent dissemination has created an environment where critical views of the transition period are no longer marginal. As Colom (2017) puts it,

> [a] changing social mindset has begun to alter the received narrative of the transition (…), [with] an increasing number of voices questioning the legacy of this consensus and blaming its original limitations for current social ailments, such as the lack of recognition of the former regime's victims, the non-accountability and self-reproductive tendencies of political elites, or the inability to stabilize the territorial model.

Indeed, the growing strength of such counter-discourses has reinforced the premise that Spain's democracy has paid insufficient attention to the victims of Francoism and the Civil War.

It is in this changing context that the Spanish central government has taken new measures to strengthen Law 52/2007 and take it further. Not coincidently, they were promoted by the PSOE-*Unidas Podemos* coalition government (a coalition that is nonetheless in a minority position and thus, reliant on regional nationalist parties in parliament). At the time of conclusion of this book, the Spanish parliament had just passed a new 'Democratic Memory Law' (Law 20/2022), which replaces Law 52/2007. Though the jury is still out on the interpretation of many of its (ambiguous) provisions and how much further it will take Spain on the transitional justice scale, there is no doubt that the language of this new law is far bolder than Law 52/2007 and its measures more ambitious. It is also a much more detailed and extensive text, with a total of 66 articles.

To start with, its preamble is visibly distinct from Law 52/2007 in that instead of adopting a somewhat equidistant position, it puts more emphasis on those who suffered or perished in the 'defence of democracy and freedom' and takes a much clearer condemnatory stance against the 1936 coup d'état and Franco's dictatorship and in favor of the country's democratic past, including the Second Republic. It also 'privatizes memory' to a lesser extent than Law 52/2007, in that it does not speak only of a right to 'personal and family memory' but also of the 'duty of public authorities to remember' and the importance of memory in the 'constitution of individual and collective identities'. Aside from this symbolic language, it partially meets some of the demands of the critics of the 2007 law, since (a) it declares the political convictions and sanctions imposed by Francoist courts null and void (rather than just *illegitimate*); and (b) it asserts greater state responsibility in the search for the disappeared (though it is unclear how this will differ from the previous assistance-based model). It also establishes an official register and census of victims and a national DNA bank to help identify remains. It goes further than Law 52/2007 in that it includes measures such as (a) the right to compensation for seized goods and economic sanctions; (b) sanctions against public acts involving the exaltation of the war and the dictatorship or the humiliation of the victims, also banning foundations or associations that engage in such activities; (c) the review and withdrawal of decorations, awards, recognitions, or distinctions that are incompatible with democratic values, as well as the abolishment of nobility titles awarded between 1948 and 1978; (d) the establishment of places of democratic memory; (e) and changes in the school curriculum, mandating the teaching of the war and dictatorship, including its repressive practices.

That said, the greatest novelty of this new law is the inroads it attempts to make in the field of justice. First, it creates a State Prosecutors' Office for Human Rights and Democratic Memory. Its functions are, however, only defined in terms of 'investigation of the facts that constitute violations of International Human Rights Law' and 'promoting the search for the victims', meaning that it is unclear whether it will have a criminal role or what the consequences or destination of its investigations will be. Secondly, the most controversial provision of this law states, in Art. 2 §3, that 'all laws of the Spanish State, including Law 46/1977 (...) on Amnesty, shall be interpreted and applied in accordance with international law and customary international law (...), according to which war crimes, crimes against humanity, genocide and torture are considered to be imprescriptible and not subject to amnesty'. Although this seems like a radical departure from the previous absence of challenges to the Amnesty Law, it is doubtful whether this provision can have any actual impact. Legal experts have pointed out that it constitutes a mere guideline on how laws should be interpreted (something that is hardly the legislator's function) and that it does not eliminate fundamental legal obstacles to the prosecution of Franco's crimes (something that an ordinary law like this one cannot do) (Lara and Ollé 2021; Rincón 2021). In fact, it is precisely because of the different interpretations of this provision's impact that it came to exist in the first place, since this was a concession from the PSOE to its allies – with *Unidas Podemos* believing that progressive legal actors can make use of it and PSOE representatives claiming that it carries no legal consequences (Cué and Casqueiro 2021). As others have pointed out, if the government had a real interest in the prosecution of such crimes and in the direct application of international law, it could have taken more unambiguous steps, such as modifying the Amnesty Law as well as the Criminal Code (Lara and Ollé 2021).

Underlying this debate is the fact that the Spanish judiciary has so far taken a traditionalist position when confronted with Franco's crimes. The most remarkable instance of that was the backlash against 'superjudge' Baltasar Garzón, who in response to petitions from victims' associations and families, launched a criminal investigation of Franco-era crimes in 2008, involving a total of 114,266 cases occurring between 1936 and 1951. In a bold and sweeping resolution, Garzón used a similar reasoning to the provision mentioned earlier (emulating what was being practiced elsewhere), arguing that the offenses under investigation constituted cases of enforced disappearances and crimes against humanity, which because of their ongoing (in the case of disappearances) and grave nature, should not be subject either to statutory limitations or to amnesty laws. As expected, this created much controversy in legal circles, as it was debatable whether Garzón had overstretched jurisdictional and procedural principles when claiming jurisdiction over hundreds of thousands of crimes committed 70 years before (Gil Gil 2012; Guarino 2010). This was the opinion of the Criminal Chamber of *Audiencia Nacional*, which ruled the court incompetent to pursue the case. Garzón would later face trial in Spain's Supreme Court for allegedly abusing his powers (crime of prevarication, i.e., knowingly issuing a decision contrary to the law) as a result of charges brought by far-right groups. Although the Supreme Court did not find him guilty in this case, it considered that Garzón was wrong to open such an investigation. In its long judgment (*Sentencia No. 101/2012*), it contested Garzón's reasoning on a number of different grounds and set the tone for the judiciary's (non-)relationship with Franco's crimes.

Though a lot could be said about the legal debate revolving around this issue, there are three fundamental aspects that come up time and again when discussing the legal obstacles to the judicialization of this issue, all of which were part of *Sentencia No. 101/2012*. The first and probably the most relevant has to do with the fundamental principle of legality and general prohibition against retroactive law, according to which no one can be held responsible for an offense that did not constitute a crime at the time it was committed. Because 'crimes against humanity' had not been clearly codified as such during the period of worst violations in the 1930s and early 1940s – neither in national nor in international law – the application of this typification is contested. What is more, the Spanish Supreme Court considers that a transposition into domestic law is needed (as the 'Spanish system does not contemplate the direct effectiveness of international norms'), and it was not until 2004 that crimes against humanity were incorporated into the Spanish Criminal Code. One way of circumventing this problem (as well as the hurdle of prescription) is to argue that for those crimes where the whereabouts of the victim are still unknown, the crime is 'continuous', i.e., continues up to this day. However, the extent to which this kind of argument can be used to circumvent issues of retroactivity is still a matter of debate, even in international legal circles (Guarino 2010: 77). For the Spanish Supreme Court, this argument amounts to a 'fiction contrary to legal logic', since 'it is not reasonable to argue that a person illegally detained in 1936, whose remains were not found in 2006, could rationally be thought to have continued to be detained beyond the statute of limitations of 20 years'. A second legal obstacle is precisely statutes of limitations or prescription periods. From the moment the Supreme Court rejected the application of international legal standards, it proceeded to argue that current criminal proceedings far exceed domestic statutory limitations and that international legal instruments declaring the imprescriptibility of certain crimes were signed by Spain only much later, therefore raising again the obstacle of retroactive (in)applicability. The third and final legal hindrance is, of course, the 1977 Amnesty Law, often invoked by Spanish courts as a barrier to judicial investigation. All of this is in addition to the more obvious fact that the majority of perpetrators are now deceased, thus preventing the realization of a regular trial.

Part of the Supreme Court's argumentation in defense of the 1977 Amnesty Law illustrates clearly why this law still enjoys a high degree of legitimacy in the eyes of many. The court speaks of the context of approval of the law and highlights that it was a 'patent vindication of the political forces ideologically opposed to Francoism' with an 'evident sense of reconciliation'. It also adds that it is 'precisely because the "transition" was the will of the Spanish people, articulated in a law, that no judge or court can in any way question the legitimacy of such a process'. If it is true that the theory that the law should be interpreted based on its original intentions at the time of the adoption ultimately reflects a conservative legal viewpoint, it is also the case that this argument is far from exclusive to the Supreme Court; it is often heard in non-conservative sectors too (Aguilar and Sánchez-Cuenca 2021). Regardless of the legal debate today, the origins of the Amnesty Law in Spain help us understand why it has a greater degree of legitimacy here than in contexts where amnesties are designed as a clear self-pardon (as in Uruguay or Chile). In Spain, questioning the Amnesty Law is a lot more controversial, not only because it was born out of a demand of the public and the democratic opposition, but also because this law is intimately linked to the idea of reconciliation and of a successful transition.

If it is still the case today that an idealized image of the transition poses obstacles to pro-accountability steps, it should also be noted how this went from a non-issue prior to Garzón's initiative to a debate that is at least taking place. Despite the setback produced by the failure of Garzón's initiative, it actually gave visibility to the pro-accountability cause and prompted the search for alternatives, the most remarkable being the so-called *Querella Argentina*, a complaint filed in Argentina in 2010 using the principle of universal jurisdiction. Although requests for extradition have been refused by Spain so far, the decision of an Argentinian judge to open a broad case on crimes against humanity committed in Spain between 1936 and 1977 has given further strength to the pro-accountability movement in Spain, with hundreds of other complaints added to the case since then and with new and old collectives uniting under a National Coordination Group in Support of the Argentinian Complaint. Moreover, by requesting the extradition of individuals linked to the last stages of the regime, this investigation is putting the abuses of this period under the spotlight too. This is a vivid example of how the consolidation of a transitional justice norm has opened up opportunities for domestic groups and helped individuals 'resignify' their experience as victims (Montoto Ugarte 2017).

Conclusion

Spain constitutes a prime example of what for a long time was a consensual memory regime, where neither political nor social voices made substantial demands for different forms of public reckoning with the past. In fact, Spain's memory regime during the transition period is characterized not only by the lack of demands but by a tacit elite agreement to avoid the politicization of past divisions and turn the page on a conflictual past. On the one hand, Spain's transition afforded few alternatives, given the balance of forces at the time and the particularly unstable transition context. Not only was there a fear of regime reversal by the military/hardline factions, but non-state political violence was giving substance to those fears. On the other hand, Spain's particular fratricidal past – having the obviously aggravating circumstance of having gone through a brutal civil war – made the emphasis on reconciliation and rejection of the past all the more pertinent in light of the ultimate goal of building a democratic and integrated polity. The 1981 coup d'état gave further substance to those fears, contributing to the prevention of possible bottom-up demands. The transition's premises of rejection of past divisions and 'forgetting' would become firmly entrenched over the following years, at the same time as elites embarked on a forward-looking project of democratic consolidation, modernization, and Europeanization, and at a time when the nascent transitional justice norm had not yet travelled to Spain.

As a result, Spain's transitional justice record is often characterized as 'too little, too late'. Even though reparatory measures were enacted before the so-called Law on Historical Memory in 2007, this point is still fair when considering that the first compensatory measure did not come until 1990. Moreover, the desire to avoid any sort of political engagement with the past was quite noticeable and only changed significantly from the moment the Popular Party took over (1996–2004) and new international and domestic dynamics were contributing to putting the past in the political agenda – namely, the controversy provoked by the Pinochet affair and growing societal interest in the Civil War and the dictatorship. That bottom-up initiatives engaged in such emotionally charged phenomena as exhumations helped in attracting much attention to their cause.

In accordance with the emergent visibility of the issue in the public and political scene – and importantly, with the concomitant interest of the radical left and regional nationalist parties in the issue – the PSOE of Zapatero decided to take a significant symbolic step by transforming a conglomerate of different issues into a law that despite all the controversy, denoted the will to morally engage with the recent past for the first time. If on the one hand, its measures are mostly victim-centered, it also took some timid acknowledgment steps. Though the change from a right-wing executive to a left-wing one is obviously important in understanding the timing of the so-called Historical Memory Law in Spain, it is most relevant that its approval cannot be understood outside the changes that the no-longer-so-consensual memory regime was undergoing in Spain. If on the one hand, this (timid) law has shown the extent to which mainstream political elites are still constrained by the idea that engaging with the past amounts to breaking the transition's ethos, on the other hand, it has clearly broken new symbolic ground that has helped create the room for further steps in a trajectory that – even though characterized by extreme delay – might not yet have ended.

Notes

1 Spain's transition period is usually considered to start shortly after Franco's death in November 1975. Its termination date is less consensual, with some pointing to the elections of June 1977 or to the approval of the new Constitution at the

end of December 1978, while others prefer to mark it with the February 1981 failed coup d'état or even with the 1982 general elections, in which a party with no links to Franco's regime won the elections for the first time.

2 The exception was the '*maquis*', a guerrilla-type movement constituted by a few thousand people who maintained clashes with the Civil Guard in mountain areas until their defeat in the late 1940s.

3 Comité Central del Partido Comunista de España. 1956. 'Declaración del Partido Comunista de España: Por la reconciliación nacional, por una solución democrática y pacífica del problema español.' Paris.

4 Examples of such measures are: Royal Law Decree 35/1978, on retirement pensions for Republican military or policemen (or widows/orphans) who were such before the start of the war; Law 5/1979 on pensions, social, and medical assistance to families of Spanish people who died as a consequence of the war; Royal Decree 391/1982, on integration of war mutilated into the general security scheme; Law 18/1984, on recognition of the years spent in prison as years of work, for social security purposes, for cases contemplated in the 1977 Amnesty Law; and others. For a more detailed list, see Aguilar (2008a).

5 This was a way to exclude (1) the 'nationalists' who had been arrested in Republican-held territory during the war (for less than three years) and who had already benefited from reparation measures and (2) those accused of terrorism in the late years of the dictatorship or the early days of the transition, who were younger than 65.

6 Most of the 41,162 rejected requests were due to the fact that the person concerned did not meet the requirement for three years in prison. Data available in: *Informe General de la Comisión Interministerial para el Estudio de la Situación de las Victimas de la Guerra Civil y del Franquismo*, 2006, p. 50.

7 BOCG, B-127-I, 9 May 1986 and BOCG, B-82-1, 12 September 1987.

8 By the time of the actual tribute, González had already lost the 1996 elections to the Popular Party, whose representatives were visibly uncomfortable and left the Congress of Deputies' tribute in the hands of the second vice-president of Congress, a PSOE deputy.

9 The general impact of the 1981 coup d'état is confirmed by a 1991 survey quoted by Aguilar (2006: 301), with 48.5% of respondents stating they feared something akin to a civil confrontation following the coup d'état (whereas only 18.5% said the same about the period following Franco's death).

10 *Interviú* was the only state-wide media vehicle that covered some of the exhumations, probably as a result of the fact that some of its (extreme-left-leaning) reporters had spent some time in prison and had links to the most radical opposition groups (Aguilar and Ferrándiz 2016).

11 The extent to which the PCE–PSOE general policy of reconciliation goes hand in hand with the absence of demands for TJ is also made clear by the fact that the only radical TJ initiative during the transition period came from a small group of people disenchanted with the moderation of the Communist Party. This was a symbolic attempt to create an 'international civil tribunal for the investigation of Francoist crimes' in 1978 in reaction to the official 'silence over the 40 years of terror' that was being 'masked as reconciliation' (Campelo 2013). This initiative was promoted by a small group of members of the Marxist-Leninist Communist Party (a splinter of the Communist Party, in favor of armed resistance to the dictatorship and associated with the armed group FRAP), with the inaugural gathering of its promoters ending with the intervention of the police.

12 About 8,000 Spanish citizens were sent to concentration camps, out of whom about 2,000 survived. The association *Amical de Mauthausen* in Spain raised

attention to these issues. Coincidentally or not, these parliamentary initiatives appeared shortly after the issue came under the spotlight on Spanish TV, thanks to a three-episode documentary on Spanish citizens sent to Mauthausen.

13 According to which courts may prosecute any individual (regardless of their nationality or where the crimes were committed) if the crimes under scrutiny are considered serious crimes in international law (such as crimes against humanity or genocide).

14 The list of associations (and search criteria used) can be requested from the author. The National Registry of Associations of the Ministry of Interior can be consulted here: https://sede.mir.gob.es/nfrontal/webasocia.html

15 There are more than 85 associations comprising 'recovery of historical memory' in their official denomination, though few of them have actual connections to the ARMH – an astonishing example of the capacity of 'early risers' to create 'master frames' and 'trigger a variety of processes of diffusion, extension, imitation and reaction' (Tarrow 2011). *Foro por la Memoria*, on the other hand, has about 20 local branches.

16 IU (*Izquierda Unida* [United Left]) and ICV (*Iniciativa per Catalunya Verds* [Initiative for Catalonia Greens]) formed a coalition in 2004–2008.

17 This was one of the major issues of contention. Though there is evidence that the PSOE studied this possibility, it did not do so because of the unforeseen financial and administrative consequences of opening hundreds of thousands of legal cases. This would not only create room for a large number of financial compensation claims but would also open the Pandora's box of property restitution (as the seizure of assets was often part of sentences) (Interviews SP3, SP4, SP10).

18 Note that Zapatero's term was known for its socially progressive policies, namely, when it comes to gender equality, liberalization of divorce, legalization of same-sex marriage, withdrawal of religious symbols from public spaces, etc.

19 An early example of this being Navarra, with *Regional Law 33/2013 of 26 December on the recognition and moral reparation to the victims of repression as a result of the 1936 military coup, of Navarra*. It is, however, from 2017 onwards that this trend accelerates, with another seven autonomous communities approving their own memory laws between 2017 and 2019.

References

ABC. 2014. 'El Vale de los Caídos sólo se modificará si hay "consenso político y social."' *ABC*, November 24, 2014.

Águila, Juan José del. 2001. *El TOP. La represión de la liberdad (1963–1977)*. Barcelona: Editorial Planeta.

Aguilar, Paloma. 2002. *Memory and Amnesia. The role of the Spanish Civil War in the Transition to Democracy*. United Kingdom: Berghahn Books.

Aguilar, Paloma. 2006. 'Presencia y ausencia de la guerra civil y del franquismo en la democracia española. Reflexiones en torno a la articulación y ruptura del "pacto del silencio".' In *Guerra civil. Mito y memoria*, edited by Julio Arostegui and François Godischeau, 245–293. Madrid: Marcial Pons.

Aguilar, Paloma. 2008a. *Políticas de la memoria y memorias de la política. El caso español en perspectiva comparada*. Madrid: Alianza Editorial.

Aguilar, Paloma. 2008b. 'Transitional or Post-transitional Justice? Recent Developments in the Spanish Case.' *South European Society and Politics* 13, no. 4: 417–433.

Aguilar, Paloma. 2017. 'Unwilling to Forget: Local Memory Initiatives in Post-Franco Spain.' *South European Society and Politics* 22, no. 4: 405–426.

Aguilar, Paloma and Ferrándiz, Francisco. 2016. 'Memory, media and spectacle: Interviú's portrayal of Civil War exhumations in the early years of Spanish democracy.' *Journal of Spanish Cultural Studies* 17, no. 1: 1–25.

Aguilar, Paloma and Ignacio Sánchez-Cuenca. 2021. 'Amnistía: ¿espíritu del legislador o espíritu de los tiempos?' *El País*, November 30, 2021.

Alonso, Gregorio and Muro, Diego, ed. 2011. *The Politics and Memory of the Transition: The Spanish Model*. New York: Routledge.

Balfour, Sebastian and Quiroga, Alejandro. 2007. *The Reinvention of Spain. National Identity since Democracy*. Oxford: Oxford University Press.

Barrutia, Gustavo Muñoz. 2006. 'La problemática del pasado y el discurso sobre la reconciliación nacional del socialismo español durante el franquismo y la primera parte de la transición: Su relación con la acción política del partido.' *Hispania Nova: Revista de Historia Contemporánea*, no. 6.

Blakeley, Georgina. 2005. 'Digging up Spain's past: Consequences of truth and reconciliation.' *Democratization* 12, no. 1: 44–59.

Blakeley, Georgina. 2008. 'Politics as Usual? The Trials and Tribulations of the Law of Historical Memory in Spain.' *Entelequia. Revista Interdisciplinar: Monográfico* 7: 315–330.

Boyd, Carolyn P. 2008. 'The Politics of History and Memory in Democratic Spain.' *The Annals of the American Academy of Political and Social Science* 617, no. 1: 133–148.

Campelo, Patricia. 2013. '*El Tribunal Internacional contra el franquismo trató de frenar una transición basada en el olvido*.' *Público*, December 2, 2013.

Casanova, Julián and Carlos Gil Andrés. 2014. *Twentieth-Century Spain: A History*. Cambridge: Cambridge University Press.

Casqueiro, Javier, and Anabel Díez. 2002. 'El PP acepta condenar el franquismo, pero rechaza indemnizar a los represaliados.' *El País*, February 20, 2002.

CIS. 2008. 'Memories de la Guerra Civil y el Franquismo.' *Estudio nº 2.760*, Abril 2008. https://www.cis.es/cis/export/sites/default/-Archivos/Marginales/2760_2779/2760/Es2760.pdf.

CIS. 2018. 'Barómetro de Septiembre 2018.' *Estudio nº 3223*, September 2018. http://datos.cis.es/pdf/Es3223mar_A.pdf.

Colom, Francisco. 2017. 'The Spanish Transition Forty Years later: Democracy, Devolution and Pluralism.' Global Center for Pluralism. https://www.pluralism.ca/wp-content/uploads/2017/10/Spain_FColom_Complete_Case_EN.pdf.

Cué, Carlos E. 2002a. 'La tierra devuelve a sus muertos.' *El País*, July 1, 2002.

Cué, Carlos E. 2002b. 'La ONU pide que se investigue dónde están enterrados republicanos fusilados tras la guerra.' *El País*, November 16, 2002.

Cué, Carlos E. 2002c. 'El PP condena el golpe de Franco y promete honrar a todas las víctimas de la Guerra Civil.' *El País*, November 21, 2002.

Cué, Carlos E. and Javier Casqueiro. 2021. 'La coalición choca por los efectos de la enmienda sobre la Ley de Amnistía.' *El País*, November 18, 2021.

Davis, Andrea. 2015. 'Enforcing the Transition: The Demobilization of Collective Memory in Spain, 1979–1982.' *Bullet of Hispanic Studies* 92, no. 6: 667–689.

Davis, Madeleine. 2005. 'Is Spain Recovering its Memory? Breaking the Pacto del Olvido.' *Human Rights Quarterly* 27, no. 3: 858–880.

de Greiff, Pablo. 2014. 'Report of the Special Rapporteur on the promotion of truth, justice, reparation and guarantees of non-recurrence, Pablo de Greiff. Mission to Spain.' UN Human Rights Council. https://digitallibrary.un.org/record/780680?ln=en.

Edles, Laura Desfor. 1998. *Symbol and Ritual in the New Spain: The Transition to Democracy after Franco*. New York: Cambridge University Press.

EFE. '65 años de historia escondida.' *El País*, July 29, 2002.

El País. 1998. 'España y Pinochet.' *El País*, October 20, 1998.

El País. 1999. 'Memoria civil del 36.' *El País*, September 16, 1999.

El País. 2002. 'Desaparecidos Nuestros.' *El País*, August 8, 2002.

El Socialista. 1974a. 'Olvidos que no se explican.' *El Socialista*, April 16, 1974.

El Socialista. 1974b. 'XIII Congreso - Resumen del Informe de la Comission Ejecutiva sobre la Situación Española y la Política del Partido.' *El Socialista*, December 1, 1974.

El Socialista. 1976. '14 de Abril.' *El Socialista*, April 10, 1976.

Encarnación, Omar. 2014. *Democracy without Justice in Spain: The Politics of Forgetting*. Philadelphia: University of Pennsylvania Press.

Etxeberria, Francisco. n.d. 'Exhumaciones llevadas a cabo em España desde el año 2000.' Sociedad de Ciencias Aranzadi and Universidad de País Vasco. Accessed May 24, 2018. https://politicasdelamemoria.org/wp-content/uploads/2015/09/Exhumaciones-desde-el-a%C3%B1o-2000-CSIC.pdf.

Faber, Sebastiaan. 2005. 'The Price of Peace: Historical Memory in Post-Franco Spain, a Review-Article.' *La Revista Hispánica Moderna* 58, no. 1–2: 205–219.

Ferrándiz Martín, Francisco. 2007. 'Exhumaciones y políticas de la memoria en la España Contemporánea.' *Hispania Nova: Revista de Historia Contemporánea*, no. 7.

Ferrándiz, Francisco. 2008. 'Cries and Whispers: Exhuming and Narrating Defeat in Spain Today.' *Journal of Spanish Cultural Studies* 9, no. 2: 177–192.

Fishman, Robert. 1989. *Labor and the Return of Democracy to Spain*. Working Paper 118. Notre Dame: Helen Kellogg Institute for International Studies.

Fishman, Robert. 2011. 'Democratic Practice after the Revolution: The Case of Portugal and Beyond.' *Politics & Society* 39, no. 2: 1–35.

Fox, Soledad. 2010. 'Franco's mass Graves and the History of Forgetting.' In *Unearthing Franco's Legacy: Mass Graves and the Recuperation of Historical Memory in Spain*, edited by Carlos Jerez Ferrán and Samuel Amago. Notre Dame: Notre Dame University Press.

Franzé, Javier. 2015. 'Podemos: ¿regeneración democrática o impugnación del orden? Transición, frontera política y democracia.' *Cahiers de civilisation espagnole contemporaine* 15. https://doi.org/10.4000/ccec.5988.

Gálvez Biesca, Sergio. 2006. 'El proceso de la recuperación de la "memoria histórica" en España: Una aproximación a los movimientos sociales por la memoria.' *International Journal of Iberian Studies* 19, no. 1: 25–51.

Gil Gil, Alicia. 2012. 'Spain as an Example of Total Oblivion with Partial Rehabilitation.' In *The Role of Courts in Transitional Justice. Voices from Latin America and Spain*, edited by Jessica Almqvist and Carlos Espósito. New York, Routledge.

Golob, Stephanie R. 2008. 'Volver: The Return of/ to Transitional Justice Politics in Spain.' *Journal of Spanish Cultural Studies* 9, no. 2: 127–141.

Golob, Stephanie R.. 2010. 'Evolution or Revolution? Transitional Justice Culture Across Borders.' Working paper, Instituto de Políticas y Bienes Públicos (IPP), CCHS-CSIC, no. 3.

González Márquez, Felipe. 2001. 'Chile, Argentina y las Comisiones de la Verdad.' *El País*, April 22, 2001.

Guarino, Angela M. 2010. 'Chasing Ghosts: Pursuing Retroactive Justice for Franco-Era Crimes Against Humanity.' *Boston College International and Comparative Law Review* 33, no. 1: 61–85.

Gunther, Richard. 2011. 'The Spanish Model Revisited.' In *The Politics and Memory of the Transition: The Spanish Model*, edited by Gregorio Alonso and Diego Muro, 17–40. New York: Routledge.

Higley, John and Gunther, Richard, eds. 1992. *Elites and Democratic Consolidation in Latin America and Southern Europe*. Cambridge: Cambridge University Press.

Humlebaek, Carsten. 2004. 'Uso políticos del pasado reciente durante los años de gobierno del PP.' *Historia del Presente* 3: 157–167.

Humlebæk, Carsten. 2010. 'Party Attitudes towards the Authoritarian Past in Spanish Democracy.' *South European Society and Politics* 15, no. 3: 413–428.

Ibárruri, Dolores, Manuel Azcárate, Luis Balaguer, Antonio Cordón, Irene Falcín, and José Sandoval. 1960. *Historia del Partido Comunista de España*. Paris: Éditions Sociales.

Igreja, Victor. 2008. 'Memories as Weapons: The Politics of Peace and Silence in Post-civil war Mozambique.' *Journal of Southern African Studies* 34, no. 3: 539–556.

Jáuregui, Ramón. 2006. 'Memoria, justicia y convivência.' *El País*, October 14, 2006.

Juliá, Santos. 1999. *Un siglo de España: Política y sociedad*. Madrid: Marcial Pons.

Juliá, Santos. 2006. 'Memoria, historia y política de un pasado de guerra y dictadura.' In *Memoria de la Guerra y del Franquismo*, edited by Santos Juliá, 27–77. Madrid: Taurus.

Juliá, Santos. 2007. 'De nuestras memorias y nuestras miserias.' *Hispania Nova: Revista de Historia Contemporánea*, no. 7.

Juliá, Santos. 2009. 'El Retorno del Pasado al Debate Parlamentario (1996–2003).' *Alcores. Revista de Historia Contemporánea* 7: 231–256.

Kovras, Iosif and Loizides, Neophytos. 2011. 'Delaying Truth Recovery for Missing Persons.' *Nations and Nationalism* 17, no. 3: 520–539.

La Vanguardia. 2014. 'El PP ampara el Valle de los Caídos.' *La Vanguardia*, December 17, 2014.

Labanyi, Jo. 2009. 'The Languages of Silence: Historical Memory, Generational Transmission and Witnessing in Contemprary Spain.' *Journal of Romance Studies* 9, no. 3: 23–35.

Lara, Jacinto and Manuel Ollé. 2021. 'Ley de Amnistía, principio de legalidade y prescripción.' *ElDiario.es*, November 22, 2021.

Lara, Luis Pérez, dir. 2013. *Entre la solidariedad y la memoria: Historia de la Asociación de Expresos y Represaliados Políticos*. Documentary. Madrid. https://www.youtube.com/watch?v=MB-wttuTI_M.

Linz, Juan J. and Stepan, Alfred. 1996. *Problems of Democratic Transition and Consolidation: Southern Europe, South America, and Post-Communist Europe*. Baltimore: John Hopkins University Press.

López Pintor, Rafael. 1981. 'El estado de la opinión pública española y la transición a la democrácia.' *Revista Española de Investigaciones Sociológicas* 13: 7–48.

Malamud, Carlos. 2003 'Spanish Public Opinion and the Pinochet Case.' In *The Pinochet Case: Origins, Progress and Implications*, edited by Madeleine Davis, 145–168. London: Institute of Latin American Studies.

Maraval, José María and Julián Santamaría. 1986. 'Political Change in Spain and the Prospects for Democracy.' In *Transitions from Authoritarian Rule: Southern Europe*, edited by Guillermo O'Donnell, Philippe C. Schmitter and Laurence Whitehead, 71–108. Baltimore: Johns Hopkins University Press.

Molinero Ruiz, Carme. 2006. '¿Memoria de la represión o memoria del Franquismo?' In *Memoria de la Guerra y del Franquismo*, edited by Santos Juliá, 219–246. Madrid: Taurus.

Molinero Ruiz, Carme. 2010. 'La transición y la "renuncia" a la recuperación de la "memoria democrática".' *Journal of Spanish Cultural Studies* 11, no. 1: 33–52.

Montoto Ugarte, Marina. 2017. 'Las víctimas del Franquismo en la "Querella Argentina": Luchas por el reconocimineto y nuevas desigualdades.' *Papeles del CEIC. International Journal on Collective Identity Research* 1, papel 164: 1–25.

Muro, Diego. 2008. *Ethnicity and Violence: The Case of Radical Basque Nationalism.* London: Routledge.

Nash, Elizabeth. 1983. 'The Spanish Socialist Party since Franco.' In *Democratic Politics in Spain: Spanish Politics after Franco*, edited by David S. Bell, 29–62. London: F. Printer.

Payne, Stanley. 2012. *The Spanish Civil War.* Cambridge: Cambridge University Press.

Pérez-Díaz, Víctor. 1990. *The Emergence of Democratic Spain and the 'invention' of a Democratic Tradition.* Working Paper 1. Madrid: Centro de Estudios Avanzados en Ciencias Sociales, Instituto Juan March de Estudios e Investigaciones.

Portal González, Almudena. 2014. 'Los muertos del Régimen de Franco entre 1952 y 1975.' Aportes: *Revista de historia contemporánea* 85: 7–50.

Powell, Charles. 2014. 'Revisiting Spain's Transition to Democracy.' In *The Arab Transitions in a Changing World. Building Democracies in Light of International Experiences*, edited by Senén Florensa, European Institute of the Mediterranean. Accessed October 20, 2017. https://charlespowell.eu/revisiting-spains-transition-to-democracy/.

Preston, Paul. 1986. *The Triumph of Democracy in Spain.* London: Methuen.

Preston, Paul. 2012. *The Spanish Holocaust: Inquisition and Extermination in Twentieth-Century Spain.* London: Harper Press.

Puerta, Gervasio. 2002. 'Puntualización.' *El País*, February 27, 2002.

Rincón, Reyes. 2021. 'Las dudas legales dificultan el intento del Gobierno de juzgar los crímenes del franquismo.' *El País*, November 18, 2021.

Río Sánchez, Angel del. 2008. 'La Memoria Histórica en escena. Demandas y movimientos sociales.' In *La recuperación de la memoria histórica. Una perspective transversal desde las ciencias sociales*, edited by Gonzalo Acosta Bono, Angel del Río Sánchez and José Mª Valcuende del Río, 103–116. Sevilla: Fundación Centro de Estudios Andaluces.

Serrano-Moreno, Juan E. 2012. 'Devenir un Descendant des Vaincus de la Guerre d'Espagne. Rupture Mémorielle et Rapport au Politique.' *Pôle Sud* 36: 87–106.

Share, Donald. 1985. 'Two transitions: Democratization and the evolution of the Spanish socialist left.' *West European Politics* 8, no. 1: 82–103.

Share, Donald. 1986. *The Making of Spanish Democracy*. New York: Praeger.
Silva, Emilio. 2000. 'Mi abuelo también fue un desaparecido.' *La Crónica de León*, October 8, 2000.
Soler, Mariano Sánchez. 2010. *La transición sangrienta: Una historia violenta del proceso democrático en España (1975–1983)*. Barcelona: Peninsula.
Sumalla, Josep María Tamarit. 2011. 'Transition, Historical Memory and Criminal Justice in Spain.' *Journal of International Criminal Justice* 9: 729–752.
Tarrow, Sidney. 2011. *Power in Movement. Social Movements and Contentious Politics*. Cambridge and New York: Cambridge University Press.
Vidal, Guillem. 2018. 'Challenging Business as Usual? The Rise of New Parties in Spain in Times of Crisis.' *West European Politics* 41, no. 1: 261–286.
Yáñez-Barnuevo, Luis. 1997. 'Habla, memoria, habla.' *El País*, December 3, 1997.
Zaguirre, Manuel. 2001. 'González afirma que no todos los implicados en el 23-F están condenados.' *El País*, February 24, 2001.

Chapter 4

Uruguay

From blockage to criminal accountability

Despite its distinctive history of almost uninterrupted democratic rule during the twentieth century, Uruguay did not escape the authoritarian tentacles that spread throughout Latin America during the Cold War. After an already tense decade during the 1960s, a civic–military dictatorship was effectively established in 1973, lasting for approximately 12 years (1973–1985). This period is commonly seen as an unfortunate interruption of an otherwise positive history of democratic rule, anchored on the values of citizenship, civism, political accommodation, strong institutions, and social peace (Roniger 2012: 53). This did not prevent an increasingly restless military from taking over politics in 1973 and cracking down on dissent. Left-wing sectors were the general target, with Uruguay becoming one of the countries with the highest rates of political incarceration, earning the infamous reputation of the 'torture chamber of Latin America'.

Unlike Spain and Brazil, but in line with its most immediate neighbor Argentina, the issue of justice for state-sponsored crimes emerged as a salient concern during the transition to democracy, becoming an object of political conflict. Human rights non-governmental organizations, victims, families, and their respective political circles were quick to place the issue on the public agenda, benefiting from a social movement scene that was receptive to the human rights discourse. However, the negotiated nature of the transition and the election of the moderate/conservative Colorado Party determined the hasty approval of the so-called Expiry Law, which would put an end to the criminal complaints families and victims had started presenting to courts. The issue gained even larger proportions when, not conforming with the approval of this law, families started a procedure for setting up a referendum. Even though the pro–Expiry Law vote would eventually triumph, and the topic would lose much importance for the years to come, Uruguay's conflictual memory regime during the transition period puts it on a different path from Brazil and Spain. If it is the case that political contingency also outplayed normative considerations, the bottom-up push for transitional justice (TJ) measures was, comparatively speaking, relentless. In this, some meso-level features of the Uruguayan case are important: rather than coming from an isolated group

DOI: 10.4324/9781003311607-7

of families, TJ-related claims were also espoused by human rights groups, the trade union confederation (PIT-CNT [*Plenario Intersindical de Trabajadores - Convención Nacional dé Trabajadores*]), as well as left-wing political figures.

With its members and basis of support being the main targets of repression, denunciations often came from left-wing political circles. Notwithstanding the divisions within the heterogeneous *Frente Amplio* (FA) – a coalition of left-wing parties formed in 1971 – the FA appeared committed to the language of human rights, opposing the Expiry Law and supporting the referendum intended to revoke it. This also set Uruguay on a different route from other cases, since it could be to an extent expected that as soon as the left reached power, advancements in TJ policies would follow. This was indeed the case from the moment the FA took office in 2005, though its path was not always smooth, consistent, or determined. Its TJ-related debates show that the rapport of apparently sympathetic parties with such policies is mediated both by strategic considerations and different views on how the past should be approached.

Nevertheless, and despite the fact that the left put forward more robust TJ measures, the first TJ initiative actually came from a member of the Colorado Party. The decision of President Jorge Batlle to create an investigative commission on the fate of the Uruguayan disappeared in the year 2000, in spite of appearing as a surprise to almost everyone, came after the issue resurfaced in the second half of the 1990s, with various new sources of pressure visibly bringing the topic back to the public scene. Since then, and particularly from the moment the left won the national elections at the end of 2004, the Uruguayan state has taken visible steps in terms of investigations, reparations, and more significantly, criminal prosecutions. Such steps, however, have been slow and incremental rather than fast and resolute. Uruguay has neither engaged in large-scale prosecutions, like Argentina, nor made use of international law (in order to circumvent amnesty laws and statutes of limitations). At first, the executive opted for a strategy of 'interpretative narrowing' of the Expiry Law – effectively excluding *some* cases from its application – and only at the end of 2011 did it manage to approve an 'interpretative law' that in practice did away with the Expiry Law. This gradual move created a Janus-faced situation whereby Uruguay is, on the one hand, one of the very few countries to have convicted two former heads of state and, on the other, a case where a slow, inefficient, and sometimes reluctant judiciary lacks enough state-sponsored resources, technical assistance, and information to deal with the hundreds of criminal cases still pending (Lessa and Skaar 2016).

Contextualization

After a relatively troubled nineteenth century, marked by independence from Spain, foreign intervention, and recurrent infighting between the two dominant political groups – the conservative rural *Blancos* and the liberal urbanized *Colorados* – a tradition of political negotiation/power-sharing was progressively forged, culminating in the creation of a Swiss-inspired collegial executive in 1917. The twentieth century's first three decades would inevitably become associated with one of the (if not *the*) most respected political figures in Uruguay's history, José Batlle y Ordóñez, responsible not only for the institutionalization of a consensus-based political model but also for major social and economic reforms that are said to be the basis of the modern Uruguayan state. These included the precocious creation of a modern welfare system, advanced labor rights protection, free education, nationalization of services and enterprises, and secularization of the state, among others (Caetano and Rilla 1994). As Weinstein (2007: 67) points out, Uruguay had free secular education before the British, an eight-hour workday before the Americans, and women enjoyed the right to vote before their French counterparts. The country was quite unique in the region, not only for its advanced social legislation but also for its high levels of urbanization and education, party identification and participation in politics, and high degree of civilian control over the military. Its democratic life, together with relatively high standards of socio-economic well-being, have earned Uruguay the nickname of 'Switzerland of Latin America'.

In large part as a result of this legacy, Uruguay's collective identity is said to have been forged around the values of citizenship, universal entitlements, strong institutions, and democracy itself (Roniger 2012: 53). The model of consensual resolution of political conflict lessened the tendencies towards political polarization and blurred ideological differences between political parties (Roniger and Sznajder 1999: 10). Nevertheless, the image of a 'civil and civilized' nation prevented neither a first authoritarian interlude (from 1933 to 1938) nor a period of growing social unrest throughout the 1950s and 1960s. Fueled by an economic downward spiral – including high inflation levels and declining income and living standards – social and political tensions arose. Growing labor and student mobilizations at the bottom, combined with mounting opposition to redistributionist policies and public spending by the economic elite at the top, contributed to a weakened and increasingly fragmented political system. The gradual loss of faith in the political system's representativeness and mounting ideological polarization gave birth to various left-wing manifestations, most prominently the unification of the labor movement into one large labor union in the mid-1960s – the CNT –and the parallel fusion of various left-wing groups and political sectors into one political group – the *Frente Amplio* – in 1971 (Barahona de Brito 1997: 40). It is quite unique in that it congregated diverse political groups, including Communists, Socialists, and Social Democrats.

Yet, the most radical manifestation of all was the emergence of a Marxist urban guerrilla movement in the 1960s – the *Movimiento de Liberación Nacional – Tupamaros* (MLN-T) – initially devoted to redistributive action (robbing banks and businesses and distributing stolen goods among the poor) and later turning to more violent forms of action, perceived as a legitimate means to dispossess the political and economic powerholders that upheld a capitalist, unequal, and dependent nation (rather than the desired socialist, egalitarian, and self-governing one) (Weinstein 2007: 70–71). Contrary to the small and socially isolated armed groups that emerged in Brazil during the dictatorship, the MLN-T had a significant social impact, with estimates placing the number of members between 4,000 and 5,000 (in a country that had a little more than 2.5 million people at the time) (Lessa 2003). But while it attracted some social sympathy during its first 'Robin Hood' stage, it lost much of its popular support when it turned to more violent actions at the end of the 1960s.

Uruguay took gradual but visible steps towards a non-democratic state from 1968 onwards, when in response to social agitation, the government enacted a limited form of martial law, suspending or restricting various civil rights and legal guarantees. This was followed by an escalating series of actions by the MLN-T (who benefited from a massive influx of new recruits) and the concomitant involvement of the military in increasingly repressive policies, not only towards the MLN-T but also against forms of social mobilization (Lessa 2013: 35). The process of 'militarization of the state' made a further qualitative leap, however, from the moment the military was put in complete charge of anti-subversion operations in 1971 after the mass escape of over 100 Tupamaros from prison (Barahona de Brito 1997: 40). From then onwards, the military – given carte blanche and unhampered by judicial constraints – went far beyond any previous administrations in the employment of brutal repressive techniques, applied in a systematic and sustained manner (Weinstein 2007: 72). This was at the same time as the MLN-T started to attack the armed forces directly, as the electoral defeat of the left in late 1971 convinced them that the armed struggle was the only way remaining (Rouquié 1987: 249). A state of 'internal war' was declared in April 1972, and what was left of individual liberties and constitutional guarantees suspended, with military courts being given jurisdiction over a wide range of civilian offenses (Lessa 2013: 35). This effectively meant that judicial protection and guarantees of due process were eliminated, with the judiciary and the parliament losing all control over arrests, making it virtually impossible to know who had been detained or where (Barahona de Brito 1997: 41–42). In the ensuing months, the army would successfully obliterate the guerrillas' infrastructure, capturing hundreds of active supporters and detaining thousands of others (Weinstein 2007: 72).

This slow-motion move towards authoritarianism was consummated in 1973 in two distinct occasions: the first in February, when President Bordaberry agreed to put the executive under the supervision of the newly established National Security Council (CONSENA), composed of commanders-in-chief of the armed forces and civilian ministers; the second when the same president decided to dissolve the parliament in June 1973 in response to its members' refusal to comply with the military's demand to strip one left-wing representative of parliamentary immunity (Lessa 2013: 35; Barahona de Brito 1997: 40). The labor union confederation (CNT) reacted with a two-week strike that culminated in a massive wave of arrests. Bordaberry would then proceed to dissolve the CNT, ban left-wing political organizations, continue to grant leeway to repressive measures, and place army officers at the head of the major state-owned enterprises (Roniger and Sznajder 1999: 13). It should be noted that even though inattentive observers sometimes assume that Bordaberry's *autogolpe* was a direct response to the Tupamaros' guerrilla activities, it is generally agreed historical knowledge that by June 1973, the military was already in control of the guerrilla movement (Roninger and Sznajder 1999: 25). The coup is seen essentially as a result of the pressure of the military for a greater political role in light of the high levels of social agitation and the perceived need to demobilize/depoliticize workers and reestablish 'order' (Caetano and Rilla 1987; Lessa 2013: 36). It was also not a coup d'état in the strict sense of the word (i.e., usurpation of civilian power by the military) but rather, what many have described as an *autogolpe*, given the connivance of the then ruling president (Rico 2015: 48).

About 15,000 former politicians were banned from engaging in any political activities via the 1976 Fourth Institutional Act. This covered anyone who had stood for office on the left as well as those *Colorados* and *Blancos* who had actually held office (Gillespie 1986: 177–178). While the left and the large majority of the *Blancos* opposed military rule, the position of the Colorado Party was more ambiguous. Its most conservative factions (the *Pachequistas*) promoted and participated in authoritarian rule, whereas other members made their opposition clear, though most of this party's members had no actual need to go into exile (Gillespie 1986: 178). Pro-democracy forces would, however, take over in the 1982 internal party elections, giving renewed credibility to the party.

Characteristics of repression

Having already defeated the most subversive enemy of all, Uruguay's armed forces used repression more as a means of control – rather than physical destruction – of political dissent, in contrast to Franco's first stage, but more in line with Brazil. As one of Roniger and Sznajder's (1999: 26) interviewees eloquently puts it, 'they operated as a social police force that, correcting, disciplining, and cutting the ill branches, are pruning the tree (…) They wanted a system in which the tree would not get infected anew, but basically they liked the tree they had'. In accordance with this, and as a way to discipline the ill branches, the regime would make widespread use of massive arrests, torture, and prolonged imprisonment as well as a system of complete 'invigilation of society'. Aided by the geography and demography of the country – with 50% of the fewer than 3 million inhabitants (2,788,429 in 1975) living in the capital, Montevideo – the monitoring and repressive apparatus of the state thoroughly and deeply penetrated society, to such an extent that many considered Uruguay to be the closest approximation to the Orwellian state

(Loveman 1998: 503). The best example of that was the classification of all citizens into an A, B, or C category according to levels of political reliability. For this, the state apparatus undertook an increase in police and military personnel, going from 42,000 to 64,000 individuals in the space of eight years (1970–1978) (Weinstein 1988: 51).

Uruguay is said to have had the highest concentration of political detainees in the world at some point during the dictatorship, gaining the dreadful reputation of the 'torture chamber of Latin America' due to its systematic application to all detainees; estimates reveal that about 2% of the population were detained and tortured, with about 5,000 to 6,000 people held as long-term political prisoners (Loveman 1998: 505; Lessa 2013: 39). This more or less coincides with the statistics put forward by *Servicio Paz y Justicia* (SERPAJ)'s *Nunca Más* report (1989), which calculates that about 18 in every 10,000 citizens were prosecuted by military justice and 31 in every 10,000 were incarcerated. The Lawyers Committee for International Human Rights goes as far as to estimate that one in every 47 Uruguayans suffered some form of repression, whether house arrest, torture, beatings, or a house raid (Loveman 1998: 505). Among those who were prosecuted by military justice, the majority came from two large detention waves: the first in 1972–1974, targeting mostly the MLN-T; and the second in 1975–1977, directed at left-wing political organizations (SERPAJ 1989). A survey confirms that repression was particularly targeted at politically engaged individuals, with 80% of the detainees declaring themselves to be active political militants (18% of whom occupied leadership positions) (SERPAJ 1989). Furthermore, this same survey confirms the extensiveness of the use of torture, with 99% of the prisoners interviewed stating they had been tortured. According to an ex-Navy member, torture was not only used as a means to extract confessions but was also widely perceived as a political instrument of ideological destruction of the opposition (SERPAJ 1989). In the words of Pion-Berlin (1994, 109–110), 'cycles of physical degradation and recuperation were purposefully and consistently applied with the objective of breaking the will of prisoners in order to acquire information' and 'send a chilling signal to all the political opposition'.

Uruguay had a fair share of 'disappeared' and secret executions, too. These were often a way to cover up deaths as a result of torture rather than a prime repressive method. Numbers are still debated, but the Human Rights Secretariat has recently updated official numbers to 123 politically motivated assassinations and 192 cases of forced disappearance (Lessa and Skaar 2016: 78). These numbers are greater than the ones put forward by the first state-sponsored investigative commission – the Peace Commission – which pointed to a total of 170 cases. Revealingly, only 26 of them were said to have occurred in Uruguayan territory, with the majority (128) having taken place in Argentina, the country with the largest number of Uruguayan exiles (Lessa 2013: 41). This was mainly a result of *Operación Condor*, a clandestine US-backed program that allowed the various Latin American security services to share information and coordinate their repressive activities. Sometimes transferred to Uruguay in secret flights, sometimes directly detained, disappeared, or assassinated in Argentina, political opposition groups were the evident target of these actions, with the *Partido por la Victoria del Pueblo* or People's Victory Party (PVP) and the *Grupos de Acción Unificadora* (GAU) registering the largest number of victims, concentrated in the period 1976–1978 (SERPAJ 1989). It should be noted that among those whose bodies appeared in Buenos Aires, there were some preeminent political figures who would become the most visible faces of repression for the decades to come. One was Senator Zelmar Michelini – a founding member of *Frente Amplio* who had already been a senator and a minister while in the *Partido Colorado* – and another was Héctor Gutiérrez Ruiz – a representative of the *Partido Nacional* (the second largest political party) who at the time of the coup was the president of the House of Representatives. They were both amongst the most vocal and respected voices against Uruguay's authoritarian drift.

Finally, a less severe but nonetheless highly impacting result of political repression that should be mentioned – in particular for its large proportions – is exile. Estimates vary from 28,000 to 62,000 exiles on the low end and go as high as 300,000 or 400,000 at the higher end (Skaar 2015: 76). Markarian's (2005: 68) comprehensive study on the ideas and actions of the exile estimates that between 1964 and 1981, almost 14% of the Uruguayan population left the country for either political or economic reasons, half of whom fled between 1973 and 1977, right after the coup. The community of political exiles was particularly active in denouncing the repressive situation in Uruguay abroad, in particular before Amnesty International and the US Congress (Markarian 2005). The latter suspended all military aid to Uruguay in September 1976, and Amnesty International launched an international campaign against the widespread use of torture in Uruguay that same year, classifying the country as 'one of the [world's] worst offenders of human rights' (AI 1977: 158). Although skeptical of the language of human rights at first – among other reasons, for its depoliticized focus on bodily harm rather than on the political experience or political goals of those harmed – the exiled community progressively adopted the human rights language as a means to mobilize the international community against the regime (Markarian 2005). They benefited from an increasingly favorable international environment, given the prominence that language was acquiring in international circles, with Amnesty International gaining the Nobel Peace Prize in 1977 for its campaign against torture and with Jimmy Carter making human rights a cornerstone of American foreign policy that same year.

The transition's political context

Uruguay's strong democratic tradition is likely part of the reason why the regime never entirely abandoned references to democracy and to Uruguay's traditional two-party system, which would supposedly be restored once subversion had been eliminated (Gillespie 1986: 177). Nowhere was this more visible than in June 1976 and November 1980. On the first occasion, President Bordaberry was removed from office after proposing a controversial constitutional project that foresaw the elimination of all political parties, to which the armed forces responded that they did not wish to share 'the historical responsibility of suppressing the traditional political parties' (Lessa 2013: 45). The second was when the regime started to look for means to legitimize itself, announcing as early as 1977 that a draft of a new constitution would be submitted to a national plebiscite. To be sure, there was nothing very democratic about the proposed constitution, but its submission to a referendum in November 1980 says something about the regime's desire to legitimize its institutionalization, in the same way as the lack of electoral fraud is possibly an indicator of its deference to voting procedures.

The rejection of the constitutional reform by 58% of the electorate constituted a major blow to the regime and took almost everyone by surprise (after an intense campaign period in which only the YES camp was given abundant visibility, portraying it as a vote for the 'orderly return of democracy'). Uruguayans sent a strong signal of rejection to the dictatorship and therefore initiated what is usually considered the start of the end of the regime – though it would take another four years and a round of failed negotiations for democratic elections to finally take place in November 1984. The military kept control of the transition process, announcing a three-year transition plan in July 1981 and bringing representatives of traditional political parties (the ones that had not been proscribed) to the negotiation table. These were allowed to resume their political activities in 1982, and internal party elections were scheduled for November 1982, with left-wing political parties remaining excluded. Once again, the regime would suffer a major blow via the electoral ballot, with the massive victory of the party sectors that opposed any type of continuity with military rule (Caetano and Rilla 1987: 104). This further strengthened opposition sectors, both inside traditional parties and within civil society.

A round of formal talks between the military and political party representatives would officially start in May 1983 at the Parque Hotel, at the same time as loosened restrictions on mobilizations allowed the labor union confederation – now called *Plenario Intersindical de Trabajadores* (PIT) – to organize a massive mobilization on 1 May, ten years after it had been banned (Caetano and Rilla 1987: 106). The Parque Hotel negotiations would eventually collapse by July 1983, as the military insisted on keeping the structures of the authoritarian state intact (in particular the National Security Council) while parties, backed by the results of the 1980 plebiscite, disagreed. A climate of confrontation at the top reflected and encouraged a climate of confrontation at the bottom. A new round of protest journeys – in which the PIT, the students' association, and human rights groups took the lead – started shortly after, culminating in the largest demonstration in the country's history on

27 November 1983 – the *Acto del Obelisco* – where an estimated 10% of the country's population were present (Caetano and Rilla 1987: 107; Barahona de Brito 1997: 70). This encouraged the various political parties (including members of the still illegal left) to form a united inter-party front – the *Multipartidaria* – which demanded an immediate reestablishment of civil and political rights as well as the lifting of all political proscriptions (Barahona de Brito 1997: 70).

Although at this point there seemed to be a possibility for Uruguay to move towards a *less negotiated* form of transition, as mobilization and radicalization intensified, several events would turn the game back in favor of the military and crucially shape the transition's architecture. To start with, the military never stopped showing signs of strength, intensifying press censorship or/and repression at certain times. Secondly, the conservative parties – *Partido Colorado* and the smaller *Unión Cívica* – were skeptical of popular mobilization and with it, maximalist demands that could jeopardize the transition. Wanting to keep a grip over the transition process and having always favored a conciliatory elite-led approach, these parties broke with the *Intersectorial* – an alliance of parties and social organizations to coordinate social mobilization – after the PIT organized a massive general strike in January 1984 without consulting the parties (Caetano and Rilla 1987: 114). Finally, and most importantly, mobilizations and the unification of the opposition in the *Multipartidaria* did have an important effect (though not exactly the intended one): pro-negotiating sectors within the armed forces, who feared the consequences of a growing factionalization of the military institution, started taking over the hardline sectors that had been dominant thus far (Barahona de Brito 1997: 72). In what was likely an intelligent move, the armed forces would progressively bring the *Frente Amplio* back to the scene and due to the latter's conciliatory stance, isolate the radical factions of the traditional *Partido Nacional* (also known as *Blancos*).

As the continued proscription of the *Frente Amplio* would likely entail a transfer of votes from the left to the *Partido Nacional* – as was the case in the 1982 internal party elections – both the military and the *Partido Colorado* (*Blancos*' largest rival and the military's favorite interlocutor) had an interest in avoiding this scenario. Enfranchising the first (or at least, its more moderate sectors) started to appear as the best possible way to avoid an electoral victory of the *Blancos*. Despite being a traditional conservative party, the *Blancos*' cherished and highly popular leader – Wilson Ferreira Aldunate – had become the number one enemy of the regime due to his radical populist–socialist posture as well as his highly critical and internationally visible stance on the dictatorship while in exile (where he escaped a regime-ordered murder attempt). There were grounds to believe that he would be the strongest presidential candidate if the military had agreed to de-proscribe him. It is thus not surprising that the *Blancos* favored a strategy of radical mobilizations against the regime as long as the armed forces would not accept bringing Ferreira

Aldunate back to the political scene. While for some time it was thought that the *Blancos* could count on the *Frente Amplio* for this – and therefore, more easily attract the support of the most mobilized sectors of society, associated with the latter – the fact is that the *Frente* showed a more conciliatory face from the moment the armed forces gave their first appeasing sign in March 1984: the release of its leader Líber Seregni (an ex-military officer himself) from his more than ten-year-long confinement. Despite internal divisions, the *Frente* would officially agree to join the negotiation table in June, to the surprise and outrage of the *Blancos*, effectively causing the *Multipartidaria* to break apart.

The ensuing Club Naval secret talks lasted for about one month (July–August 1984) and ensured a peaceful and negotiated transition to democracy, expected to culminate in the November 1984 elections and the transfer of power in March 1985. Despite the non-participation of the *Partido Nacional*, the presence of the *Colorados*, the *Frente Amplio*, and the *Unión Cívica* was enough to grant legitimacy to the so-called Club Naval Pact and to dictate the isolation of the *Blancos*' strategy. On the armed forces' side, the appointment of a new commander-in-chief, General Medina, seems to have greatly facilitated the process, as he was visibly more eager than his predecessor to find a way out. Rial (1990: 29–30) describes the Club Naval Pact as a simple restauration agreement in which the previous political, constitutional, and party systems (in place before the 1973 coup d'état) were recognized and expected to be restored after the elections. Among the transitory dispositions that served to provide some guarantees to the armed forces were: (a) the agreement to transform the National Security Council into an advisory body that could only be convened by the president (which in practice never happened); (b) the possibility for the president to declare a 'state of insurrection' in which military justice could take over regular justice (which also did not occur); and (c) the regulation of the system of military appointments in such a way that the military institution would keep control over it (Rial 1990: 28).

The armed forces would therefore drop their long-sought demand to have a National Security Council overlooking the actions of the executive, in the same way that they would accept the restriction of military jurisdiction to military representatives only in times of war (and not for common crimes committed in times of peace, as they had first demanded). This constitutes definite evidence that party representatives had a much greater leeway than at the Parque Hotel negotiations, in large part due to the shift in the ambitions of the military, who seemed much more interested in an exit solution than before. In turn, the parties also had to accept the continued proscription of both Ferreira Aldunate and Líber Seregni, who could not run in the November 1984 elections.[1] This paved the way for the victory of the *Partido Colorado*[2] and the election of the man who was considered the great architect of the Uruguayan transition – Julio M. Sanguinetti – for both his leading role during the negotiations and his apparent capacity to gain the trust of the military.

Uruguay's transition process is a vivid example of how transitions are not just a two-sided game between the incumbent camp and the democratic opposition camp, but rather, a more complex one where radical and moderate factions within a camp adapt their positions not only in light of the perceived power of the opposite sector but also as a result of strategic considerations relating to their relative positioning within the camp they belong to. That is, parties will move along the 'radical–moderate scale' not only according to the perceived strength of the opposition sector but also as a function of concerns with their own electoral outcomes and the parties' image. In the Uruguayan case, it is evident that the *Partido Colorado* had everything to gain from a pro-negotiation stance, while the *Partido Blanco* had everything to lose. The former was by far the military's favorite interlocutor and could therefore credibly stand behind an image of moderation and pragmatism that was promoted as the safest way to achieve a successful and peaceful transition to democracy. The residual power of the military was instrumental in overlooking the issue of political proscriptions, which conveniently kept the Colorado Party's biggest rival out of the political game. As convinced as the leader of the *Colorados* (Julio M. Sanguinetti) was about the negotiated/moderate approach being the best one possible, the fact is that it benefited the Colorado Party in more than one way: it boosted the party's image as a credible negotiator capable of achieving democracy via peaceful means; and it kept Ferreira Aldunate out of the political game, opening the way for Sanguinetti to be elected as Uruguay's next president. The *Blancos*, on the other hand, were obviously against proscriptions and therefore against a negotiated solution as long as these were not lifted. Wilson Ferreira Aldunate had already been the most voted-for candidate twice before, first in the 1971 general elections (not being elected due to Uruguay's peculiar electoral system[3]) and later in the 1982 internal party elections (which were open to the general public's vote); hence the *Blancos*' belief that if the military was forced to lift proscriptions, the way would be open for their party to finally be sworn into office.

The transition's course would therefore depend, ironically, on the *Frente Amplio*, the party most vilified during the dictatorship and the one that had suffered the most brutal consequences of repression by far. Knowing that their chances to win the national elections were meagre, FA's considerations had less to do with electoral calculations than with the impending balance of power and the internal and external image of the party. Líber Seregni's posture was from the start less radical than some would expect, though in agreement with the strategy he had already defended while in jail. 'Mobilization – Concertation – Negotiation' were the three axes of his policy, placing him somewhere between the *Partido Colorado*'s strategy of negotiation and the *Partido Nacional*'s mobilization one. Although there was a strong critical current inside the *Frente*, who believed that participating in the Club Naval talks would be equivalent to abdicating basic principles, Seregni's position would end up prevailing. This had to do, first and most obviously, with the desire to terminate the military's dictatorship once and for all, and the perception that the military was too strong and cohesive for this to happen in any other way than via a negotiated solution (Caetano and Rilla 1987: 126). Moreover, agreeing to negotiate with the military was the equivalent of seeing the *Frente Amplio* included in the formal political arena (De Sierra 1985 in Barahona de Brito 1997: 74). It was not until August that the *Frente* was officially legalized and given permission to participate in the November 1984 elections, a clear reward for its negotiating attitude. This was, in turn, crucial for its external and internal image: on the one hand, it allowed the *Frente* to acquire political respectability beyond radicalized left-wing sectors, after a long period in which the image of the left had been tainted by its association with violence and disorder; on the other, it gave space for the coalition to rebuild itself internally. Eleven years of exile, imprisonment, persecution, and clandestinity naturally raised concerns about the capacity of an already ideologically diverse coalition to rebuild itself, particularly in light of the fear that its electorate would move to the *Blancos*' radicalized sectors (Barahona de Brito 1997: 72).

The transition's conflictual memory regime

Unlike Spain or Brazil, where the absence of TJ measures provoked neither party contestation nor a visible and salient social demand, the topic would emerge in Uruguay throughout 1985 and 1986, culminating in the approval of an amnesty law for military actions in 1986 (the so-called Expiry Law) and more astonishingly, the submission of this law to a referendum in 1989. Families and human rights organizations would be the crucial actors behind this. Although their levels of activism, membership, and visibility did not reach anything even slightly resembling those of their Argentinian counterparts, they cleverly used Uruguayan institutions in a way that would create much trouble for the ruling Colorado Party. First, by submitting official charges against military officers as early as April 1985, they defied the military institution and created much tension between the military and civil judicial systems as well as between the armed forces and the government. This would turn military prosecution into a highly charged topic at the political level. Secondly, by making use of Uruguay's mechanisms of direct representation, a few family members launched a campaign to collect the signatures of 25% of the population in order to put the Expiry Law through a referendum, a campaign initiated in 1986 that would reach significant levels of support, culminating in the rejection of the families' claims at the ballot box in April 1989.

In understanding why, comparatively speaking, Uruguay's civil society had a mobilization impetus that Brazilian and Spanish ones did not have, there are not only structural differences in terms of democratic tradition and repression's characteristics (explored in Chapter 7) but also various meso-level differences worth taking into consideration. The first and most immediate one is that families benefited from a broader network of human rights organizations, which put them in contact with each other and provided spaces of organization, information, and legal support. In this, the influence of the Argentinian human rights movement is crucial, inspiring the creation of these organizations and groups and decisively influencing their organizational forms, repertoires of action, and discourses. Another fundamental aspect is the non-isolation of the human rights movement and the receptiveness of the broader social movement scene to human rights claims. This, in turn, helped open up political opportunities, as the *Frente Amplio* (and to a lesser extent, the *Partido Nacional*) echoed some of the human rights claims and brought related issues to parliament, something that is not independent of the *Frente*'s strong and embedded ties to its social constituencies.

In addition, families also benefited from a greater institutional opportunity structure, given that an amnesty law was not approved until December 1986, flooding the courts with legal complaints in 1985 and 1986 and later being able to make use of Uruguay's direct democracy mechanisms. Although they would not achieve any of their goals at the time, an overview of this period is essential in highlighting first, the salience that the issue had during Uruguay's transition period and second, its intimate connection to the Uruguayan left. This accounts for why the later reemergence of the topic in the public and political scene could, to an extent, be expected.

Furthermore, the comparatively higher salience of the issue in Uruguay – in contrast to Brazil and Spain – has to be understood in light of a background context that is fundamentally different in terms of civic and political culture and the concomitant (in)tolerance of political violence. As mentioned, Uruguay had been an institutionalized liberal democracy for most of the twentieth century, and the dictatorship was comparatively much shorter. The use of state violence had been an extremely unusual phenomenon before, which makes it plausible to assume that it constituted much more of a shock to Uruguayans. In addition, and as Roniger and Sznajder (1997) point out, political violence and impunity went very much against the country's self-image. Uruguay stands out not only for its high levels of citizenship participation and interest in politics (Moreira 2000) but also for the fact that Uruguayans take pride on a national identity based on principles of republicanism, democracy, and associated values. This has to be seen in the context of a country that had long been predominantly educated and urban.[4] This is not to say that Uruguayans are inherently more democratic, but that this rhetoric – consensually endorsed by all political forces – makes it more difficult to escape debates on justice and accountability. It is thus not surprising that the campaign against the Expiry Law portrayed this instrument as antithetical to the democratic ideals of the Uruguayan people, including justice, equality before the law, and civic consciousness (Roniger and Sznajder 1997: 67).

The human rights movement: Argentinian influence and networks of support

To start with, it is fairly impossible to ignore the exogenous influence of the Argentinian case in accounting for the emergence of the human rights movement in Uruguay (Interviews UR1 and UR2). As background, it should be noted that Argentina is perhaps the most cited textbook case in transitional justice for two main reasons: (1) the extent of transitional justice measures implemented right after civilians took office, including a state-sponsored investigative commission and judicial proceedings against the leaders of the military junta (greatly delegitimized after the Falkland debacle in 1982); and (2) an unusually strong and vocal human rights movement (with important links to transnational networks of human rights activism), something that is partially the result of the extraordinary extent of repression and the widespread use of disappearances as the main repressive method.

Besides Uruguayans following events in neighboring Argentina – a country that is very proximate to Uruguay in both cultural and geographical terms – almost as closely as their own, many Uruguayans experienced events themselves in Argentina. As mentioned, Argentina hosted the largest community of Uruguayan exiles,[5] to which the majority of the disappeared Uruguayans belonged. It is no coincidence that it was the Uruguayan community in exile that first made use of the human rights language, which proved an effective means of denunciation of the regime abroad. The first and most visible campaigns against the regime came from key political figures exiled in Argentina, like Senator Zelmar Michelini (who denounced the regime's violations before the Russell Tribunal in Rome in 1974) and Ferreira Aldunate (who testified at the US Congress in 1976) (Barahona de Brito 1997: 83). It was also on Argentinian soil that the first group of families (of those Uruguayans who had meanwhile disappeared in Argentina) started to coordinate, forming the group *Madres y Familiares de Uruguayos Desaparecidos en Argentina* between 1977 and 1979, in a similar fashion to the existing Argentinian family groups (Bucheli et al. 2005). It is telling that despite gathering various categories of relatives (wives, siblings, etc.), the group chose to follow the Argentinian emphasis on the *Madres* (mothers) (Alonso 2010: 32). An important moment in the consolidation of this group was the visit of the Inter-American Commission of Human Rights to Buenos Aires in September 1979, to whom they denounced all the cases of missing people they had recorded thus far (Bucheli et al. 2005: 29). The establishment of another relatives' group in Paris in 1978 – *Agrupación de Familiares de Uruguayos Desaparecidos* – was also intimately linked to the Argentinian experience, as it was formed by those whose family members had disappeared in Argentina and who themselves had meanwhile fled to Europe (Bucheli et al. 2005: 37).

The formation of the first – and most important – human rights organization in Uruguayan territory did not happen until 1981 and was also greatly inspired by events on the other side of the *La Plata* river. The ecumenical SERPAJ had already been active in Argentinian territory since 1974, assisting victims/ families and denouncing violations. The fact that one of its Argentinian founders won the Nobel Peace Prize in 1980 made SERPAJ known to a few Christian figures in Uruguay, who after establishing contact with SERPAJ in Argentina, decided to create a Uruguayan branch (Interview UR4). SERPAJ-Uruguay was in turn essential in the process of putting families in Uruguay in contact with each other and giving them spaces of reunion and information sharing. It therefore played an important role in the creation of the first family groups in Uruguayan territory, most notably the *Movimiento de Madres y Familiares de Procesados por la Justicia Militar* in 1982 and the *Madres y Familiares de Uruguayos Detenidos Desaparecidos* in 1983, informal and loosely organized groups that nonetheless became the most visible face of repression (Bucheli et al. 2005; Barahona de Brito 1997: 85). The latter would progressively incorporate the relatives' groups that had been established abroad, namely, the *Madres y Familiares* in Argentina. SERPAJ was also instrumental in establishing the *Instituto de Estudios Legales y Sociales* (IELSUR) in 1984, which, similarly to the Argentinian *Centro de Estudios Legales y Sociales*, provided legal representation and advice to families and victims. Significantly, IELSUR was composed by a group of lawyers who broke away from the Uruguayan Bar Association over disagreements on denunciations of disappearances and the defense of political prisoners (Bucheli et al. 2005: 43). IELSUR, in coordination with SERPAJ, began taking cases to court as early as 1984.

Although the Uruguayan human rights movement is usually considered to be much weaker than its Argentinian or Chilean counterparts (Barahona de Brito 1997; Alonso 2010), in part because of its comparatively late emergence, it decisively benefited from the fact that it was not born in isolation from the set of social forces that (re)emerged in 1983–1984 (Alonso 2010: 36). Not only did they emerge at the same time – and sometimes within the same clandestine spaces – but all major social forces incorporated the human rights claims themselves, judging in particular by the proliferation of 'human rights committees' inside all the major social movements' organizations, including the trade union confederation (PIT-CNT), the students' union (ASCEEP-FEUU), and the federation of housing cooperatives (FUCVAM). Though it is difficult to establish whether this was more the result of the influence of human rights organizations or of an inner sensibility towards human rights claims, the fact is that grassroots mobilizations were quick to associate the dictatorship with human rights violations, which became a *leitmotiv* of the fight against the regime (Bucheli et al. 2005: 46).

This, in turn, cannot be dissociated from what appeared to be a particularly cohesive social movement scene in 1983 and 1984, with all social forces congregating behind the ultimate goal of deposing the dictatorship. The human rights movement was part of this effort, particularly through SERPAJ, which enjoyed strong links to social organizations. This was most clear in the role it played in the first mass *cacerolada* against the regime (a form of protest based on banging of pots/pans) on 25 August 1983, when SERPAJ promoted a 'national reflection day' after a two-week hunger strike in reaction to the recrudescence of repression (following the failed Park Hotel talks). SERPAJ would concomitantly become part of the *Intersectorial* – a platform unifying parties and social movement organizations – together with the above-mentioned PIT-CNT, ASCEEP, and FUCVAM. Although this initiative was short-lived, it was responsible for the massive *Acto del Obelisco* in November 1983. Similarly, SERPAJ would be part of the *Concertación Nacional Programática* (CONAPRO) a year later, when parties made joint commitments to a vast number of policies ahead of the November 1984 elections. Thanks in large part to SERPAJ's efforts, the CONAPRO agreements included an explicit commitment to truth and justice policies, stating that 'state organs must seek to clear up events' and 'the judiciary must be provided with effective instruments to allow investigation' (Barahona de Brito 1997: 90). Though these agreements would quickly collapse, SERPAJ's achievement says something about the organization's non-isolation. This had also been made clear that year with the creation of the *Coordinadora de Entidades de Derechos Humanos* (CEDH), gathering all human rights organizations, key social movement organizations, and political parties' representatives (though Barahona de Brito [1997: 88] emphasizes that the latter reflected more individual than party commitments). The CEDH is said to have played a relevant role in promoting anti-government demonstrations in 1984 and early 1985 (Barahona de Brito 1997: 89).

It should be noted, however, that the notion of human rights was at the time most strongly linked to an unrestricted and general amnesty for political prisoners, a primary and unanimous demand within left-wing sectors and a constant presence in anti-regime demonstrations (de Giorgi 2014a; Bucheli et al. 2005: 46). Truth and justice appeared more as second-order demands in a period in which the situation of the large number of political prisoners, and the conditions under which they were detained, were more pressing and extensive concerns. It did not seem to be clear at first what was to be done about those who had disappeared, besides denouncing and asking for information (de Giorgi 2014a). Nonetheless, demands for justice and punishment would progressively appear throughout 1984 and would come to the front in 1985–1986 once elections took place and the question of political prisoners was solved. In bringing the situation of the disappeared to the public scene, the role of *Madres y Familiares* seems to be conspicuous. A member of the group recalls that many of those who were not directly affected did not know about the practice of disappearance until quite late and that it was only once *Familiares* started to show up more systematically in the public scene that the situation progressively changed. She recalls in particular the impact of the 1 May demonstrations in 1984 – where for the first time the group followed the Argentinian repertoire of bringing banners with photos of the disappeared – and their subsequent gatherings in Plaza Liberdad, in the center of Montevideo, every Friday (a clear replication of the Argentinian *Madres* weekly march at *Plaza de Mayo*) (Bucheli et al. 2005: 48–49).

In propagating their message, and similarly to what has been stated earlier, they counted on a network of support that went beyond those directly affected. The detailed testimonies of family groups collected by Bucheli et al. (2005: 49–52) confirm that they managed to at least publicize the situation of the disappeared among actively engaged political sectors in the months before democratic forces took over. They recall hundreds of information and denunciation 'public' talks hosted by workers' unions, neighborhood committees, and even political parties (the *Partido Nacional* and *Frente Amplio*) and speak of groups of young people who spontaneously approached them from the moment they started the weekly marches in Plaza Liberdad. In fact, one of their first events – the organization of the 'week of the detained disappeared' at the end of May 1984 – was endorsed by both students and workers' organizations. Though these organizations had meanwhile included disappeared-related demands in their platforms – namely '*aparición con vida de los desaparecidos*' (return of the disappeared alive), a frame imported from the Argentinian *Madres,* and '*juicio y castigo a los culpables*' (trial and punishment for the guilty) – it was only once elections took place that the theme of punishment for violations of human rights became conspicuous among social organizations (Demasi 2011: 87).

Political allies: accounting for the Frente Amplio's *commitment*

It is with the above-mentioned context in mind that one has to place the relationship of political parties to the human rights issue. Although the transition ended up being much of an elite affair, it was fairly impossible to ignore the topic, even if by omission. There is much speculation about a possible 'gentleman's agreement' between Sanguinetti and the military at the Club Naval talks, involving no prosecution guarantees, though there is no evidence this was the case. A renowned historian, who has done extensive research on this, thinks the issue was not touched upon at the Club Naval talks precisely 'because everyone knew there was no possible agreement on this theme' (Interview UR9). With the *Partido Nacional* excluded from the talks, the military and the *Colorados* could hardly afford to antagonize the left-wing *Frente Amplio* and risk the legitimacy of the pact. The *Frente*'s close links with the social movement scene meant that it echoed, to an extent, the grassroots commitment to the theme of human rights, and therefore, it would not accept anything short of a 'general and unrestricted' amnesty for political prisoners, in the same way that it would not agree on a general amnesty for military crimes. The overall conciliatory and negotiating posture of the *Frente* leaders was already at odds with a considerable part of its members and support basis, with Seregni having to constantly reassure them that the FA would not compromise on any basic principles (Barahona de Brito

1997: 79). In fact, it is said that General Medina was under pressure from the military to propose an amnesty at the talks but that Sanguinetti persuaded him not do so precisely because it would have forced the *Frente* to abandon the talks (Barahona de Brito 1997: 78).

The Uruguayan case is quite unique in that an amnesty for the military was not approved either before or right after the takeover of democratic forces. This is part of the reason why the human rights movement benefited from a greater opportunity structure at the institutional level when compared with cases where the immediate approval of an amnesty law made judicial prosecution unfeasible, as was the case in Brazil and Spain. In Uruguay, a small window of opportunity emerged in 1985 and 1986 (until the approval of the Expiry Law in December 1986), which allowed ordinary courts to claim jurisdiction over military offenses that had meanwhile been denounced by victims and families. Although these efforts would come to a halt with the Expiry Law, they should not be underestimated, first and foremost because they were responsible for making the topic of military prosecution a highly salient and debated one. Although this was of little consolation to the victims in the years to come, it was consequential in the very long run when the *Frente Amplio* came to power in 2005 and started finding loopholes in the Amnesty Law, something few questioned in light of what this issue had meant to the left in the 1980s. In other words, a conflictual memory regime during the transition can be said to have opened a window of opportunity for later treatment of the issue.

The backing of the *Frente Amplio* for what at the time were already defined as *human rights* claims was therefore crucial and sets the Uruguayan case apart. In spite of the general stance of the party being more moderate than that of the human rights movement, and sometimes ambiguous – varying greatly from sector to sector – the fact is that the FA was vital in bringing the topic to the political arena. First of all, and as just mentioned, it was largely because of its opposition to an amnesty for the military that such an agreement was not made at the Club Naval Pact. Secondly, it was the presence of the FA (and initially, the *Blancos*) in parliament that made the topic particularly contested at the political level, as it contributed to setting up parliamentary investigative commissions in 1985 and vehemently opposed the 1986 Expiry Law. Furthermore, the FA supported and mobilized its constituency to vote for the derogation of the Expiry Law in the 1989 referendum, which would in the process become a cause intimately associated with the Uruguayan left. Interestingly enough, and despite the overall defeat, the majority in the country's capital voted to revoke the law in the same year in which the *Frente* won the Montevideo municipal elections. Although it would take more than a decade for the *Frente* to achieve similar results at the national level, it could be generally expected that its earlier commitment to the topic would later translate into concrete measures if it were to achieve power. In understanding the overall commitment of the FA, there are two factors worth taking into consideration: (1) the fact that the large majority of the victims of repression were individuals with direct links to parties within the FA family; and (2) the extent to which the *Frente* echoed the grassroots commitment to the theme of human rights, given its close connections to the social movement scene. I am, however, of the opinion that the second factor is a greater determinant than the first, for the reasons outlined in the following.

Victimhood and TJ advocacy

While it is natural to think that those affected will be the ones demanding retribution – and demands, whenever existent, will certainly come from them – reality suggests that there is no automatic direct relationship between being a victim and making transitional justice claims. Prominent cases in this regard are presidents in Brazil and Uruguay (Dilma Rousseff and José Mujica), who were victims of torture but nonetheless did not seek to advance their country's transitional justice agenda (though the latter was eventually forced to). Within *Frente Amplio* itself, not every left-wing group/individual who was a target of violations supported transitional justice measures to the same extent, suggesting that there are other mediating factors in the relationship. This was clear, for example, in the different approaches between the small PVP (*Partido por la Victoria del Pueblo*) and the Uruguayan Communist Party, both of which were top targets of the dictatorship repressive apparatus. While the first was very active in denouncing violations and was intimately linked to *Familiares*, the second did not have a denunciation policy.

If some Communist Party members eventually presented legal complaints, they did it in their personal capacity and not under the guidance of the party. In fact, it was the commitment of specific individuals – who worked on convincing their peers to denounce the violations they had endured – that often made a difference. In the case of the Communist Party, the role of Senator Germán Araújo – a symbol of the fight against the dictatorship and one of the most outspoken voices for justice – seems to have been important in convincing others, as one testimony of a Communist Party member makes clear: 'Human rights were not important to us. We filed complaints, but only because Germán Araújo asked us to do so, otherwise we would have done nothing. The party would not tell you to denounce and therefore we did not question it' (in de Giorgi 2014a). One of the founders of *Frente Amplio* reports a similar dynamic, stating that it was in fact hard to convince many peers to denounce what they had endured:

> It was an internal process within the left to convince them they were victims. The traditional Uruguayan left that comes from the class struggle mentality and never considered the topic of human rights and human dignity as something important. What mattered was economic redistribution, equality, the class struggle, etc.
>
> (Interview UR5)

In attempting to account for group and individual-level variance in this regard, various sources coincide on the fact that the conception of 'heroic self-sacrifice' for what were important collective causes is at odds with a sense of victimization (Interview UR5; de Giorgi 2014a). This is said to be particularly extreme in the case of people associated with the MLN-T, 'who said they had done things voluntarily, considering themselves combatants to the same extent of the military (...), as if thinking otherwise would diminish the heroic Robin-Hood inspired legend they had built of themselves' (Interview UR5). Torture and long-term imprisonment were seen as part of the price paid for their revolutionary struggle (Roniger 2011: 697). This is largely coincident with Markarian's (2005) extensive inquiry on the adoption of the human rights language by the left-wing exile community and their initial reticence to do so. As this language focuses on the bodily harm to individuals rather than the political goals of groups, it appeared to be in conflict with calls for revolutionary action and sacrifice for the common cause. Adopting the human rights banner required revising the traditional heroic conceptions that made repression and abuses part of their expected political experience (Markarian 2005: 7). One should keep in mind that repression in Uruguay was targeted against active left-wing opposition groups, who could therefore, to some extent, expect reprisal. This is particularly the case for the most combative sectors, which saw the pre-dictatorship polarization period as an indicator of the 'radicalization of the class struggle' and therefore anticipated a strong reaction (Demasi 2011: 82).

All of this speaks to the importance of the perception of victimhood, that is, the extent to which individuals who were subjected to discretionary state violence perceive themselves as victims of something fundamentally unjust and, to an extent, unexpected. Interestingly, a founding member of the *Frente* who was active on the human rights front recounts how she was part of a Christian-inspired political group whose members had a greater sensibility towards the question of individual human dignity than those for whom collective political goals was all it mattered (Interview UR5). She adds that for many, 'the thinking very often went like: now that we are installed politically, let us focus our energies on doing all we can to change society'. This is similar to Markarian's (2005) point that many within the *Frente* preferred to focus on 'transitional politics', as that was what mattered at the moment. Although any conclusion on this topic is tentative, these cues suggest that politically engaged individuals – who saw their actions as part of a broader collective political struggle – might not automatically perceive what they endured in 'perpetrator versus victim' terms and might not look at the actions of state agents as regular crimes susceptible to individual criminal responsibility. Instead, because what they endured was part of a collective political struggle, the best form of retribution was the displacement of the dictatorship, the legalization of their respective political parties, and the possibility to participate in the political game (note how similar this is to what has been said for the Spanish case, with the crucial difference that in Uruguay, the human rights/transitional justice language was becoming available at a much earlier stage).

This is congruent with the fact that the most vocal claims recurrently came from family members with little or no political activity themselves, who were therefore 'victims *par excellence*'. This is the more so for those who were permanently deprived of a family member – by 'disappearance' or death – as this is the most brutal and unexpected type of repression and therefore, the one where the perception of injustice tends to be the most acute. A lawyer closely involved in this cause points out that 'the degree of acceptance of one's own situation matters' and that what was in fact 'the newest and most brutal and unexplainable phenomenon were disappearances' (Interview UR3). This provides one crude but nonetheless convincing indicator for why the degree of human rights activism was more significant in Argentina than anywhere else in the region, given the vastly greater number of disappearances. Importantly, one should take into account the particularly severe psychological strain that disappearances induce in families, given that the non-appearance of a body makes them carry, at least for some time, the hope that their family members can still be found alive. As Javier Miranda, a human rights lawyer who is himself a son of a disappeared parent, puts it, 'the detention-disappearance of a person leaves his or her loved ones in a state of permanent anxiety and uncertainty' (quoted in Skaar 2011: 154). This naturally makes denunciation and investigation most pressing in such cases.

Various indicators corroborate this. One is the number of judicial denunciations, which is greater for cases of enforced disappearance than for cases of torture. Although the available data does not cover every legal complaint presented in 1985–1986, out of the 37 cases where information on the type of crime is given, 21 refer to enforced disappearances, 7 to death, and 11 include torture (based on data compiled by *Observatorio Luz Ibarburu*). Another potential piece of evidence is the immediate dissolution of a group of family members of political prisoners – *Familiares de Procesados por la Justicia Militar* – as soon as these were released from prison, which suggests that families did not perceive further benefits from collective action besides the obvious primary goal of having their family members back. This contrasts with the *Madres y Familiares*, who have kept their activities going until today, similarly to the Argentinian *Madres* and *Abuelas de Plaza de Mayo*. It would not be until much later (2000) that an organization of political prisoners would be created (CRYSOL – *Asociación de Ex-Presos Políticos de Uruguay*).

The FA's grassroots' ties and its commitment to justice

In light of what has been said, the general endorsement of the *Frente Amplio* to human rights claims cannot be solely understood as a result of the direct links between the party and the subjects of repression. The *Frente*'s intimate connection to the social movement scene, the pressure of some of its most radical sectors, and the eagerness to appear as the 'true representative' of the victims of repression appear as more relevant factors. In addition, as the salience of the issue increased throughout 1985 and 1986 – in part as a result of the number of complaints that were flooding the courts – the higher the party's image-related incentives became, or the costlier it was to let down many of its constituents and members. According to de Giorgi (2013: 71), not engaging with this issue could carry high costs for the *Frente*, as this would disavow one of the main causes its militants were working on. In addition, it could prove costly for the internal unity of the party, since it became clear that its more radical sectors were not willing to accept anything short of full justice.[6]

Although it is hard, if not impossible, to quantify support for TJ within the FA in the initial stages of the transition, the general perception was that the actively engaged sectors were actually a minority (Interview UR2 and UR5). Mallinder (2009: 22) points out that even though some groups within the FA had long campaigned for investigations and punishment, the negotiating sectors (which were a majority) preferred to avoid a strong position on these matters out of fear of derailing the transition process and the desire to position the FA as a credible political option. Expectedly, those most vocal about human rights were also the sectors that did not support the negotiating posture of the *Frente* at the Club Naval talks (de Giorgi 2014a). To those, and to many among its basis of support (largely the same that had been taking up to the streets in the months previous to the elections), the *Frente* had to prove that participation in the talks was not a sign of softness with the dictatorship (Barahona de Brito 1997: 79). This is in a scenario where the *Blancos* profited from their non-negotiating posture to accuse the *Frente* of being accomplices to the impunity deal allegedly negotiated at the Club Naval.

An important background factor to have in mind here is that the *Frente* is the closest approximation in Latin America to the mass-organic type of party, with an exceptional grassroots presence, an active membership basis, and close and strong ties to various popular/social constituencies (Levitsky and Roberts 2011: 13–14). In fact, the embeddedness of the party (and its many branches) in social networks makes it sometimes difficult to point out where civil society ends and the party begins. Already before the first general election, and despite the fact that many on the left remained deprived of their political rights, the FA had a remarkable grassroots presence, with so-called base committees (with a minimum of 50 members) set up in each neighborhood or ward section, bringing together militants from every party within the FA (Gillespie 1991: 199). Although its social links are more obvious in the case of labor organizations, the links of human rights groups to certain FA minority sectors are also known – most notably the presence of Christian Democrats within SERPAJ and the close support given by the PVP to the groups of families (de Georgi 2014). In addition, as developed earlier, the human rights discourse went beyond single-issue groups concerned with this topic and became diffusely associated with the bottom-up opposition to the dictatorship. As one notable trade union leader explains, 'Uruguayan unionism has the unique characteristic of greatly transcending the world of work. Every union had a human rights group (...) and we always had an independent and advanced human rights policy' (Interview UR3). The involvement of the national confederation of trade unions (PIT-CNT) – the face of a remarkably strong and organized unionism – is both a symptom and a reflection of how intimately associated with the left the issue of justice was. This was visible, for instance, in the protest it staged outside the legislative palace in October 1986, gathering about 10,000 people, where a proposal on the punishment of human rights violations was being discussed (Barahona de Brito 1997: 139).

Despite justice for human rights violations not being a salient issue during the 1984 electoral campaign – with the *Frente* focusing instead on the release of political prisoners and the restauration of civil and political rights – the theme of justice was not entirely absent, and generic declarations on the moral duty to prosecute crimes could already be heard (Mallinder 2009: 25). The fact that its leading presidential candidates felt compelled to publicly commit themselves to bringing to justice those responsible for violations already tells us a great deal about the perceived expectations on this issue.

As the issue grew in salience throughout 1985 and 1986, so did popular endorsement of the cause. This was confirmed by survey data in mid-1986, when a poll covering the area of Montevideo showed that an overwhelming 78% agreed that justice should proceed (though most believed that realistically it would not), with 66% opposing an amnesty for the military (Barahona de Brito 1997: 208). It is, however, plausible to assume that at an initial stage (or at least before this survey was known), the *Frente*'s commitment had less to do with general electoral calculations than with not letting down its own constituents and its most radical sectors. This is substantiated by the fact that the party was actually trying to show a moderate face at the time – as the 1984 elections rewarded those sectors that had moved closest to the center, the party adopted a cooperative attitude, noticeable, for example, in its endorsement of a 'national accord' on economic policy in 1985 (and concomitant abandonment of some of its expected demands) (Gillespie 1991: 230). The fact that it was not able or willing to show the same degree of flexibility and moderation when it came to the issue of an amnesty for the military suggests that this was a more fundamental issue for the left.

It is, however, not possible to state with certainty that the FA would not have committed to the issue had it not been for its more radical sectors and connections to grassroots movements. The blurriness between the FA's parties and their constituents makes it difficult, if not impossible, to trace who influenced whom. That the families and human rights organizations were the first and most vocal groups can be well established. It is also the case that significant steps taken at the political level had already been preceded by related claims coming from the families. This is most notably the case of the establishment of two parliamentary investigative commissions,[7] a demand of families' organizations that the FA and the *Blancos* attended to in April 1985 (Alfaro 2016: 4). The fact that these parties took this step early on – following the intense March debates on the design of the amnesty law for political prisoners – attests, however, to their commitment. Bottom-up pressure was not so insurmountable at that point as to force into parliament an issue to which parties would have no sympathy, which is why rather than simply reacting to external and internal pressures, engaged political actors are better seen as part of the overall push that contributed to make this issue one of the most (if not *the most*) controversial and prominent topics in the Uruguayan public and political scene at the time.

Institutional opportunity structure: the Expiry Law and its discontents

In part thanks to the support of political actors and in part because of the availability of direct democracy mechanisms, families and human rights groups in Uruguay benefited from a relative window of opportunity at the institutional level. The first reason for this is that unlike in Brazil and Spain, there was no military amnesty provision in place during the early stages of the transition, meaning that judicial prosecution appeared at the time as a relatively more feasible possibility. Moreover, this was the case not only due to the absence of an amnesty law covering the military (up until December 1986) but also because of the existence of judicial networks of support – such as IELSUR – and what appeared to be a credible judicial apparatus, judging at least by the fact that all the Supreme Court judges who had served during the dictatorship were quickly replaced (Skaar 2011: 139). In addition, as a human rights activist and founding member of the *Frente* reveals, 'this is a small place, everyone knows everyone, we knew there were democratic-minded judges and, when making denunciations, we were waiting for certain judge's turn to come' (Interview UR5).

It is not entirely clear why the military did not push more forcefully for a self-amnesty. One interpretation is that there were many officers who simply did not regard their actions as crimes and who 'considered an amnesty an insult, given they had received orders to defeat the subversion' (Interview UR9). Note that the flood of judicial complaints had not yet started during the Club Naval negotiations, and the military might not have seen them coming. However, it is also known that there were sectors concerned about the issue and that General Medina was pressured not to leave the Club Naval talks without formal guarantees of no prosecution. Much speculation exists around a secret and possibly tacit 'gentleman's agreement' between General Medina and Sanguinetti, made during or shortly after the Club Naval talks, in which the latter gave guarantees to the former that trials would not occur (Barahona de Brito 1997: 78). This would explain why Sanguinetti ultimately proved to be against any form of justice and why Medina seemed to have been able to calm military ranks over the lack of guarantees. In any case, the fact that an amnesty covering military actions was neither explicitly agreed at the Club Naval nor incorporated into the amnesty law for political prisoners – unlike in Spain or Brazil – already tells us a great deal about the different status of this issue in Uruguay.

Both the apparent absence of this topic at the Club Naval and the exclusion of military and police officers from the first amnesty law can be traced back to the presence of political actors supportive of TJ who, explicitly or implicitly, obstructed such a deal. On the one hand, both Medina and Sanguinetti have made it clear that the issue was not discussed at the Club Naval because it would have constituted an obstacle to a successful negotiation, a reference to the presence of the *Frente* at the talks (Barahona de Brito 1997: 78). *Frente* representatives at the Club Naval talks similarly stated that the issue was never openly discussed, but that it was indirectly touched upon when the military proposed to keep military jurisdiction over all kinds of crimes committed by military men, a proposition that created much tension and that eventually did not pass – something that speaks for the strength of the opposition at the talks (Lessa 2009: 252). On the other hand, both the FA and the *Blancos* explicitly excluded the military and the police from their amnesty law proposals covering political prisoners, and they did have a considerable say in the formulation of what would become Law 15.737,[8] given their joint parliamentary majority (Bardazano 2013: 147).

It is in the context of intense political discussion surrounding the design of Law 15.737, the immediate release of all political prisoners in March 1985, and the press's extensive coverage of the abuses of the dictatorship that legal complaints started to clog Uruguayan courts, curiously at the same time as the Junta Trials were taking place in neighboring Argentina. Barahona de Brito (1997: 126) and Allier Montaño (2010: 54) estimate the number of cases that were being investigated in courts by the end of 1986 at more than 700, though neither of them states where those estimates come from. The *Observatorio Luz Ibarburu* – which has done the most extensive job in compiling information and following or sponsoring legal actions in recent years – registers a much more modest number of cases in those years. Regardless of the exact numbers, the fact is that these denunciations were sufficient to transform the topic of military prosecution into the most contested issue of the time and eventually culminate in the approval of an amnesty law covering the military in December 1986, known as the Expiry Law (Law 15.848). President Sanguinetti seems to have been caught by surprise, as he later declared that an amnesty for the military had not been approved before because

> it did not seem that denunciation of their crimes would become so important. There might be a few accusations, but it was not going to be

a big deal. Then things began to grow (...) Great numbers of accusations began rolling in, and we proposed an amnesty.

(Interview in Weschler 1990: 188)

The road to Law 15.848 was, however, far from straight. It was not until August 1986 that the Colorado Party first presented an amnesty proposal. Before, the ruling party had in fact been ambiguous about its position on the matter, though there were clear signs that the more denunciations started coming in, the warier the party became. This was visible as early as April 1985, when President Sanguinetti asserted that the military courts should have jurisdiction over the matter (Barahona de Brito 1997: 130).[9] In accounting for the wariness of the ruling party, there are various factors worth considering. First of all, it would be odd to see the Colorado Party take steps towards justice, given its partial connivance with the dictatorship. Although this is clearer for the conservative sectors than for Sanguinetti's party-wing, it would surely be uncomfortable to implicate some of its right-wing colleagues. Secondly, as mentioned earlier, it is widely believed that Sanguinetti made an explicit or implicit commitment to Medina. Thirdly, the threat of disobedience of some sectors within the military – with an officer declaring that they would not show up before civil courts – created a potentially unstable situation that further pushed Sanguinetti towards an amnesty. This is also the opinion of Barahona de Brito (1997: 136), who states that Sanguinetti feared that Medina would be unable to contain the insubordination of hard-line sectors, which had increased significantly as accusations proliferated in the press, the parliament, and the courts. Finally, this position was very much in line with the image of pragmatism Sanguinetti had always represented. His electoral campaign revolved around the desire for a '*cambio en paz*', a process of peaceful and orderly change in which avoiding confrontation was seen as an essential step or as a goal in itself. In line with the Spanish transition model – of which Sanguinetti showed a prodigious knowledge – Uruguay's president repeatedly stated that a climate of stability was essential and therefore, an amnesty was a legitimate means to deal with a destabilizing issue.[10]

The problem for the ruling party was that the absence of a parliamentary majority meant that a deal with one of the opposition parties would have to be struck. As the left appeared strongly committed to the issue, the *Partido Nacional* was the only viable option for President Sanguinetti. Nevertheless, this was far from an obvious endeavor at first, as the *Blancos* appeared only mildly committed to justice, in line with the party's strong opposition to the orchestrated transition and to the electoral prescription of its leader. On more than one occasion, representatives of the PN and the FA negotiated a project on a form of limited justice (restricting prosecution to certain cases), but the opposition of the most radical sectors within the *Frente* and the ambiguity of the *Blancos* – whose leader was found to be secretly negotiating with

Sanguinetti – prevented an agreement (which in any case could be met with a presidential veto). After having their first amnesty law proposal rejected in August 1986, the *Colorados* would manage to get most of the *Blancos* on board in December after intense behind-the-scenes negotiations and heated political debates. As military officers had threatened to disobey judicial summons, a climate of a looming institutional crisis (or for the most alarming voices, military insurrection) pushed a sufficient number of PN deputies to endorse an amnesty law for military and police crimes. Officially designated as Law on the Expiry of the Punitive Claims of the State (*Ley de Caducidad de la Pretensión Punitiva del Estado*), it was signed just hours before military officers were due to appear in court, on 22 December 1986.

Yet, this was not the end of the road for families and human rights activists. The second reason why they benefited from an institutional window of opportunity is that Uruguay's Constitution allows laws to be submitted to a referendum if 25% of the electorate requests it. In light of the prominence the debate had meanwhile acquired, a few family figures and ex-Tupamaros announced their intention of holding a referendum on the Expiry Law the day after it was approved, in what was the first attempt in the country's history to use this constitutional right to overturn a law. The FA announced its support for this initiative on 5 January 1987, shortly after all major social organizations had done so (PIT-CNT, ASCEEP-FEUU, FUCVAM, and SERPAJ) (Allier Montaño 2010: 72). Several *Blanco* politicians would also declare their support. Displaying an impressive organizational capacity, the organizers first set up an umbrella organization – the National Pro-Referendum Commission (CNR) – and then proceeded to create over 300 'neighborhood committees' in order to make the signature collection process feasible (Allier Montaño 2010: 74). This involved a great number of popular gatherings and door-to-door visits, a mass mobilization effort that once again put the issue at the center of public debates (Roniger and Sznajder 1999: 83).

The CNR was composed of many Uruguayan notables (such as Eduardo Galeano and Mario Benedetti) and led by three emblematic victims' relatives – Elisa Dellepiane (widow of Zelmar Michelini), Matilde Rodríguez (widow of Héctor Gutiérrez Ruiz), and María Ester Gatti (grandmother of a missing child). It did its best to appear non-partisan, focusing on ethics, truth, justice, and the reaffirmation of basic principles such as the people's right to decide and equality before the law (Roniger and Sznajder 1999: 84). While the FA kept a low profile in order to avoid politicizing the initiative, Buriano (2011: 177) is right to point out that its support, structures, and militant experience were fundamental in making this a viable endeavor. By December 1987, the CNR had submitted over 630,000 signatures to the Electoral Court, which after a long and dubious process of signature verification, eventually allowed the realization of the referendum in April 1989.

In the meantime, the association *Madres y Familiares* together with some legislators had also filed an unconstitutionality appeal against the Expiry Law, which the Supreme Court rejected in a split three–two sentence in

May 1988. SERPAJ was also active, most notably when putting into place a truth project with the goal of documenting the regime's repression in detail. Starting in March 1986, the *Nunca Más* project – inspired by similar reports in neighboring countries – used hundreds of testimonies and a survey of over 300 political prisoners to produce a report more than 300 pages long, released just before the referendum, in March 1989.

The referendum campaign was naturally met with much opposition, coming from the government, the military, and other conservative sectors. The initiative was often portrayed as a threat to stabilization and democratic consolidation, going against the spirit of pacification and reconciliation of the transition. President Sanguinetti adopted a 'moral equivalency' discourse, whereby the subversive elements that were allegedly behind the organization of the referendum had already been amnestied to the same extent as the military and were now leading a campaign motivated by rancor and revenge (Barahona de Brito 1997: 148–149; Roniger and Sznajder 1999: 85–87). General Medina warned shortly before the referendum that the vote would provoke 'bitter and unfortunate moments' and a 'strong confrontation' (Barahona de Brito 1997: 149).

Pragmatism and fear of destabilization would eventually win, with 56% of the voters deciding to retain the law. As devastating as these results were for the human rights movement, and despite symbolizing the defeat and end of a hard-fought battle, the referendum campaign stands out for being unique in the extent to which it used the wide mobilization of civil society and put impunity for dictatorship-sponsored crimes at the heart of the public sphere (Roniger and Sznajder 1999: 90). Although the *Frente Amplio* kept a low profile, the issue would inevitably become linked to the Uruguayan left, as most of the organizers of the referendum were members or supporters of the party, and its bases were deeply involved in the campaign process from its inception. Groups associated with the FA, such as the student union, were particularly active, in what constituted the first political mobilization experience for many among the youngest generations (Interview UR2). All of this is important because despite the negative results at the time, the salience and conflictual nature of the issue during this period – which contrasts enormously with its absence in Brazil and Spain – meant that its reappearance years later was not devoid of a previous history of mobilization, awareness, and familiarity with the topic and its framing in human rights terms.

From blockage to state acknowledgment

The post-referendum interregnum and the resurgence of civil society

The results of the 1989 referendum were at the time generally perceived as sealing the issue of accountability for the dictatorship's crimes. As citizens had spoken through the most democratic of means, the human rights movement naturally took time to recover, and civil society activity fell remarkably in the following years (Skaar 2011: 149). Though family groups would not disappear, their concerns faded from the public and political scene, and it would not be until 1996 that they would make a (remarkable) comeback. With the exception of marginal sectors within the left, related demands would also disappear from political parties' platforms. The only advancement produced in the first half of the 1990s would take place at the international level, when the Inter-American Commission of Human Rights responded to various petitions that had been filed by IELSUR, declaring in October 1992 that the Expiry Law was incompatible with Uruguay's international obligations to respect the victims' rights to a fair trial and judicial protection (Burt et al. 2013: 9). This position would be endorsed by the United Nations Human Rights Committee (UNHRC) too, but the fact is that this would have no concrete impact in Uruguay at the time. Uruguay's presidency had meanwhile changed to the *Partido Nacional*'s leader Luis Alberto Lacalle (1990–1995) – only to return to Sanguinetti in the following five years (1995–2000) – but the referendum results and the loss of salience of the topic during the first half of the 1990s meant that Lacalle did not have to deal with the issue.

Once more, events in Argentina would prove highly influential in changing the tide in Uruguay. In March 1995, the public confessions of an Argentinian retired navy officer, Adolfo Scilingo, would not only have a profound impact on the debate in Argentina but would also reverberate in Uruguay's public scene (Roniger and Sznajder 1999: 119). Scilingo became the first military man to acknowledge the existence of the so-called 'death flights', providing details on how the Argentinian armed forces dumped hundreds of victims from planes into the ocean after sedating them, usually following torture sessions. The commander-in-chief of the Argentinian army, General Balza, followed suit by recognizing for the first time the mistaken use of unjust and immoral means by the armed forces (Allier Montaño 2010: 150; Roniger and Sznajder 1999: 114–116). This naturally had strong repercussion in Uruguay, given that most of the Uruguayan disappeared had last been seen in Argentina.

This event prompted renewed calls for actions in Uruguay (Lessa 2013: 143). In a joint effort with *Familiares* and other human rights and social movement organizations, Senator Rafael Michelini called for the first *marcha del silencio* (march of silence) or *marcha por la verdad, memoria y nunca más* (march for truth, memory, and never again) on the anniversary of the four most emblematic murders, including that of Senator Michelini's father (Zelmar Michelini). On 20 May 1996, between 30,000 and 50,000 people flooded Montevideo's main streets in silent protest, carrying banners with photos of the disappeared (Skaar 2011: 150). Since then, the march has become a yearly tradition in Uruguay, drawing thousands of people and sending a powerful reminder of how unresolved this issue still is.

Importantly, these marches provided clear evidence of how demands had (strategically) shifted from justice to *truth*. The main mottos of the marches that followed would be 'We want the truth' (1997), 'Truth will set us free'

(1998), 'What is missing in our democracy? Truth!' (1999), 'Truth is possible and necessary' (2000) (Roniger 2012: 66). In light of the 1989 popular upholding of the Expiry Law, and because – in the words of a member of *Familiares* – 'we did not want people to repudiate the theme but rather to understand what had happened' (quoted in Allier Montaño 2010: 154–155), the main public demand shifted to investigation and acknowledgment in what is a clear case of strategic adaptation of civil society demands. Perhaps encouraged by this renewed activism, new victim organizations started popping up, including HIJOS in 1996 (formed by children of the disappeared), *Memoria para Armar* in 1997 (composed of female ex-political prisoners), CRYSOL in 2000 (an association of ex-political prisoners), and *Familiares de Asesinados por Razones Políticas* the same year (constituted by relatives of the victims) (Lessa 2013: 143). It is in this context that several proposals for the creation of an investigative commission were presented, coming from left-wing representatives, family members, and even a bishop who offered to act as mediator (Skaar 2011: 153–154; Allier Montaño 2010: 199). Civil society groups, with the support of the left, also did their best to activate foreign sources of pressure, from international institutions to foreign governments, with the Uruguayan government having to justify before the United States why it was not investigating cases of disappearances (Reuters 1998a; Reuters 1998b).

Another event that is unanimously agreed to have had an impact on discussions about the past in Uruguay is the so-called Gelman case, perhaps one of the most emblematic cases involving a missing child in the region (Allier Montaño 2010: 185–187; Skaar 2011: 155–156). It resurfaced at the end of the 1990s when the renowned Argentinian poet Juan Gelman made a request to President Sanguinetti to help him find his missing granddaughter after receiving indications that she had been handed to a policeman's family in Uruguay. Both the poet's son and his daughter-in-law had been kidnapped in Buenos Aires in 1976, with the latter having given birth to a child immediately before her disappearance. First met with a lack of response, Juan Gelman would then write an open letter and mount a worldwide campaign, as intellectuals from all over the world – including Günter Grass and José Saramago – joined in a petition to Sanguinetti, creating much embarrassment for the incumbent president and helping to reignite the national debate on the need to investigate past crimes. Sanguinetti would infamously declare that cases of disappeared children had never taken place in Uruguayan territory, only to be disproven a few months later when President Batlle took over and announced that Macarena Gelman had been found.

Batlle's acknowledgment policy (2000)

Despite being part of the same party as Sanguinetti, Jorge Batlle – president of Uruguay from 2000 to 2005 – was keen on differentiating himself from his predecessor when it came to the official recognition of the dictatorship's crimes. This was most clear at the very start of his mandate. Batlle took everyone by surprise when, on the day of his presidency's inauguration (1 March 2000), he waved to a group of *Familiares* during the presidential parade – the first time a president had acknowledged their presence – and spoke of 'sealing peace forever between Uruguayans' in his inauguration speech, in what was widely understood as a reference to the issue of the disappeared. Shortly after taking over, he met with a delegation of *Madres y Familiares* (April 2000) – an event of great symbolic importance, given that this was the first time a Uruguayan president had received them – after the group had sent the president an open letter in which they asked for a serious investigation that would answer four questions regarding the disappeared and the missing children: *when*, *where*, *how* and *why*?, leaving the *whom* aside (Allier Montaño 2010: 200). Batlle would take steps in this direction when deciding to create the so-called Peace Commission (*Comisión para la Paz*) – established by presidential Decree No. 858/2000 in August 2000 – with the task of gathering information on the disappearances and preparing a final report, which would include suggestions in terms of reparatory policies.

The Commission's mandate and ambitions were, however, quite restricted and conservative. It had limited powers and resources – relying on voluntary testimonies – and it failed to secure access to state archives (Lessa 2013: 146). Moreover, rather than producing a public accounting of the details of disappearances, it disclosed information to individual family members only (Burt et al. 2013: 10). In the preamble of Decree No. 858/2000, the focus was on national pacification – as the name of the Commission itself reveals – something that was criticized for falling into the assumption that there was ever a war or conflict rather than a top-down and unidirectional repressive apparatus. Batlle was clear in emphasizing that the commission was above all aimed at 'consolidating national pacification and sealing peace once and for all among Uruguayans', only aiming at a 'possible truth' (*Informe Final*, 10 April 2003). The Commission's exclusive focus on disappearances – and not on other crimes, such as torture and unjust imprisonment – also accounts for why its mandate was considered limited. In a more optimistic tone, Skaar (2011: 161) notes that the fact that sources of information were to be kept confidential encouraged some people to talk, including military men who volunteered important information on the *where* and *when* of disappearances, thus helping to clarify some cases. This nonetheless proved a double-edged sword, given that some information later turned out to be incorrect.

Composed of several notable political, religious, and civil society figures, the Peace Commission worked for almost three years, releasing its final report in April 2003. Out of the 299 cases denunciated, the Commission was able to corroborate the disappearance of 170 people (89 confirmed and 81 partially confirmed). Out of those, 26 were Uruguayan citizens who died in Uruguayan soil – mostly as a result of torture – while the vast majority

(128) were confirmed to have disappeared in Argentina (Comisión para la Paz 2003). Resolution 448/2003 adopted the Commission's conclusions and created a secretariat to continue its work (as there were still pending cases). Though the report's recommendations included compensations to relatives, Batlle's government would not follow through on this at a time when a financial crisis was absorbing most of the government's and the public's energy. Nonetheless, the Peace Commission had the merit of being the first ever official initiative to acknowledge that crimes had been committed by state agents during the dictatorship. Moreover, and contrary to the idea that there was a war or conflict during the dictatorship (as the name *Peace* Commission could suggest), the final report acknowledges that the vast majority of victims neither committed acts of violence nor participated in 'subversive organizations' and that their deaths had occurred after the insurrection groups had been disarticulated and defeated (Allier 2006: 90).

Accounting for the creation of the Peace Commission

In understanding why Jorge Batlle signaled his willingness to break with Sanguinetti's policy and acknowledge the issue of the disappeared, there are various factors worth taking into account, though they can all essentially be summed up in terms of the personal and political benefits Batlle could collect for himself. First of all, the recently inaugurated president would most likely not have taken up the issue if it had not been a salient topic on the public agenda in the years prior to his takeover, most notably because of the above-mentioned Marches of Silence and in particular, the Gelman case. The general public empathy towards the issue of the disappeared was well known, with various opinion polls from 1997 showing that between 54% and 59% of the respondents agreed that an investigation on the fate of the disappeared was imperative (Allier Montaño 2010: 199–200). The families, human rights organizations, the PIT-CNT, and specific legislators within the FA had been mounting pressure throughout Sanguinetti's legislature, not only on the streets but also in judicial forums outside and inside Uruguay.

Even if it was not a central issue during the electoral campaign – which was focused on economic issues, in light of the impending recession – it was an issue candidates responded to, with the FA most clearly committed to the topic, but also with Jorge Batlle already declaring that there was the possibility of opening up an investigation (Reuters 1999). The electoral program of the FA not only stated that an investigation on the fate of the disappeared was a priority for the party but also spoke of fighting impunity, quoting various international instruments on criminal accountability for human rights violations.[11] The fact that the FA was the strongest competitor in the 1999 elections – winning the first round of the presidential election – furthermore meant that the *Colorado* candidate could perceive potential benefits when addressing a topic that was most dear to the left-wing electorate. The attempt to establish cordial relations with the FA was visible at the start of Batlle's mandate, when he met with the FA leader to discuss the issue of the disappeared. At a time when the state of the economy and Batlle's staunch liberal solutions could have done much to erode the president's popularity, dealing with the human rights issue gave Batlle a human face that might very well have contributed to the high levels of public opinion approval registered in the first couple of months of his mandate (Allier Montaño 2010: 206).

Although Batlle's attitude constituted a marked break with Sanguinetti's policy, there are good reasons that account for his willingness to do so. The first is that Batlle probably had a different sensibility towards the dictatorship's crimes as a result of his different personal experience: he had been briefly imprisoned, barred from political activity (including in the 1984 elections), and lived in exile in Brazil during part of the dictatorship. The second is the well-known rivalry between Batlle and Sanguinetti, the two major figures of the Colorado Party. It seems to be accepted wisdom among Uruguayan circles that Batlle's acknowledgment policy had something to do with the attempt to distance himself from Sanguinetti or even use it as a 'political vendetta' against him (Lessa 2013: 146). The rivalry between the two is known to date back to the late 1980s, when Sanguinetti endorsed a different candidate for the presidency, and the party group to which they both belonged split in two as a result of related internal struggles (Sanguinetti creating the *Foro Batllista* and Batlle remaining within the *Lista 15*). They would both run for the 1994 presidential elections (when the electoral system still allowed various candidates from the same party), and in 1999, Sanguinetti would endorse a rival candidate. The fact that the Gelman case had contributed to tainting Sanguinetti's image right at the end of his presidential mandate, and that Batlle took less than one month to announce that Macarena Gelman had been found, is a strong indication that Batlle was keen on differentiating himself and was not at all deterred by the fact that this would create much embarrassment for his predecessor.

Challenges to the Expiry Law and criminal accountability

The approval of the Expiry Law and the results of the 1989 referendum naturally stalled judicial activity, including bottom-up demands for judicial investigation. Although judges could in theory open investigations in criminal cases without such demands, they generally relied on citizens to bring cases before them, and very few would be presented during the 1990s (Skaar 2011: 170).

Moreover, the Uruguayan Expiry Law has the particularity of putting much of the decision-making power in the hands of the executive, effectively undermining the principles of separation of powers and judicial independence. Indeed, Law 15.848 has been commonly considered an extremely controversial legal instrument, in large part because article 3 establishes that it is up to the executive to decide whether a case falls within the scope of the Expiry Law or not. Judges are required to send denunciations to the executive and to dismiss them if the latter considers they are covered by article 1, whereby the state relinquishes its punitive capacity for crimes committed until 1 March 1985 by military and police officials either for political reasons or in fulfilment of their functions. In practice, this meant that the Uruguayan president had considerable discretionary power to close down investigations at will. In addition, article 4 of the same law also placed the investigation of disappearances in the hands of the government, establishing that the court is to remit all testimony to the executive, which is responsible for launching an investigation and informing the plaintiffs of the results of these investigations (Mallinder 2009: 51–52).

According to Skaar (2011: 152), one of the first cases in which the judicial apparatus presented evidence to the executive – so that the latter could determine whether or not it was covered by the Expiry Law – was the so-called Zanahoria Case, presented by Senator Rafael Michelini in 1997 on the basis of new information regarding the clandestine burial site of the bodies of the disappeared. Although the responsible judge ordered an investigation and stated that its aim was only to return the bodies to the families (and not to instigate punitive action), his decision provoked much backlash. Military officials refused entry into military headquarters, the public prosecutor appealed the decision, and the Court of Appeals determined that the responsibility of investigation lay with the executive, which promptly proceeded to close down the case. Furthermore, the first-instance judge who opened the investigation was transferred to a civil court in what was perceived as a sanction for his actions (Mallinder 2009: 61–62).

The tide would start to change in the early 2000s, when victims and their lawyers followed strategies that had already been successfully employed in Argentina and Chile, seeking ways of circumventing the Expiry Law (Burt et al. 2013: 10). This was essentially done by finding loopholes in the text of the law, therefore excluding certain cases from its application. Since article 1 spoke only of military and police officials, one of the first innovative arguments was that the Amnesty Law did not apply to civilians, and so non-military state officials could be charged. This was one of the drivers behind the path-breaking case of Elena Quinteros, a schoolteacher who had been abducted from the Venezuelan embassy (where she had taken refuge) in 1976 and then disappeared. Quintero's mother and her lawyer (a PIT-CNT lawyer) requested the reopening of the criminal investigation in the year 2000 – after receiving new information on the case and facing much obstruction from the executive in the attempt to launch an investigation – subsequently bringing charges against the dictatorship's foreign minister and *Colorado* deputy Juan Carlos Blanco. In October 2002, a judge would accept this reasoning and charge Juan Carlos Blanco with Elena Quinteros' unlawful imprisonment in what constituted the first case of indictment for the dictatorship's human rights violations. The exclusion of civilians from the Amnesty Law would then be used as an argument to (re)open other cases – at the request of families and their networks of support at the political and civil society level – most notably against Juan María Bordaberry, head of state from 1972 to 1976 (Allier Montaño 2010: 234–236). In June 2005, Bordaberry and Juan Carlos Blanco would be charged with involvement in the infamous murders of legislators Michelini and Gutiérrez Ruiz and two other individuals (Amnesty International Report 2006).

It could be hypothesized that one of the reasons behind these first bold judicial steps had to do with the presence of an executive that appeared more sympathetic to transitional justice than the previous one. However, there is concrete evidence this was not the case under the Batlle administration. Although he was certainly more receptive than Sanguinetti, this was only when it came to demands for clarification of the facts and not for judicial prosecutions. This was visible in Batlle's endorsement of the Expiry Law as well as in the existence of counter-pressures coming from his government to make judges drop cases like the above-mentioned ones (Amnesty International Report 2004; Skaar 2011: 168). Though the indictment of Juan Carlos Blanco was an indication that there were judicial actors ready to challenge an unfavorable executive – which was supposedly the one responsible for launching investigations and deciding on the application of the Expiry Law – it is unclear whether the remaining judicial apparatus would follow these steps. This did not need to be the case, however, since the *Frente Amplio* was elected before any trials commenced, and the new executive would quickly proceed to give judges explicit authorization to exclude certain cases from the Expiry Law.

Transitional justice measures under the Frente Amplio's *first government*

The victory of the left in the October 2004 election was expected to bring changes in the executive's approach to transitional justice policies. This was already clear from the 2003 governmental program, where the FA spoke of its compromise to truth and justice in regard to the crimes against humanity perpetrated during the dictatorship. If, on the one hand, the program referred to the need to abide by article 4 of the Expiry Law – which suggested that the FA was not going to attempt to revoke the law – on the other hand, it also spoke of adapting domestic legislation to international human rights treaties, stating that 'impunity constitutes a real obstacle to democratic normalcy and to the overcoming of the traumas of the recent past'.[12] In fact, the internal debate on how to deal with the Expiry Law was known to divide the party. This was most clear in the 2003 Congress, when two opposing motions were debated, one from a representative of the PVP, advocating for the nullification of national norms that went against international law, and a rival one from a representative of the *Movimiento de Participación Popular*, arguing that this was not a strategically smart move from an electoral point of view. The latter position would win by 746 votes against 569 in what was perceived as yet another moderation step in the FA's attempt to win the presidency (de Giorgi 2014a).

The importance of this issue was clear from the very start, with the new president, Tabaré Vázquez, devoting the final paragraphs of his inauguration speech to the need to settle pending accounts on human rights. Emphasizing the various steps he intended to take towards the conduction of further investigations, Vázquez also made an explicit commitment towards a reparation policy in his first speech. Furthermore, he stated that the cases of Zelmar Michelini, Gutiérrez Ruiz, and Juan Gelman's daughter-in-law did not fall within the scope of the Expiry Law.[13] The exclusion of emblematic cases naturally raised the long-held criticism that there are different categories of victims in Uruguay, though Vázquez would later proceed to enlarge the scope of exceptions. Following a literal interpretation of article 1, the executive would allow judicial proceedings in cases that could be interpreted as falling outside the law's remit – crimes committed by civilians or by military/police high-ranking officers (given that the law spoke of those who followed orders), as well as offenses that took place outside Uruguay's territory or before the June 1973 coup. According to Amnesty International Report (2008), by the end of 2007, a total of 47 cases of human rights violations had been excluded from the Expiry Law by the Vázquez administration.

Despite these advancements, this approach was criticized by families and human rights groups. In the words of a preeminent human rights lawyer, it was based on aberrant ethical and juridical criteria (Interview UR10). For one of Vázquez's chief advisors, instead, it was the most pragmatic and quickest way of changing the interpretation of the law and producing significant advances on judicial proceedings without having to go through the political scandal that the law's derogation would create (Interview UR11). Indeed, Vázquez's conduct seems to have been guided, on the one hand, by the will to progress on the issue and on the other, by the desire not to stir up too much opposition. This was evident in November 2005, when the government sought to enact an Interpretative Law, which would code the exceptions to the law's applicability and transfer the decision-making power to the judicial realm, but ended up withdrawing the bill after facing much opposition from the military, opposition parties, and even human rights groups (who considered that the bill granted legitimacy to an illegitimate law) (Mallinder 2009: 65–67; Erradonea 2008: 29).

Regardless of ethical objections to the government's approach, the fact is that it allowed the unprecedented conviction of crimes perpetrated by agents of the dictatorship. These included high-profile figures of the regime, such as former President Juan María Bordaberry and former Foreign Minister

Juan Carlos Blanco – both arrested in November 2007 and sentenced to 30 and 20 years' imprisonment in 2010 – as well as former President General Gregorio Álvarez (1981–1985), arrested in 2007 and sentenced to 25 years in prison in October 2009. It should be mentioned that most judicial proceedings have not been this fast, though. In fact, the main challenge to criminal justice in Uruguay remains the slowness of judicial procedures. According to data compiled by the *Observatorio Luz Ibarburu*, the large majority of cases presented to the courts are still at the pre-indictment stage, and as of 2017, there were only a total of 13 convictions, involving 20 defendants. This same source points to a number of limitations in terms of available human and administrative resources, access to information, investigation drive, and lack of coordination of prosecutors' offices, among others.[14]

Other types of transitional justice steps were also taken during Vázquez's first presidential term in terms of both investigations and reparations. As far as the former is concerned, the executive ordered excavations at military sites in the search for human remains; requested the military to produce an investigation into the fate of the disappeared detainees, resulting in the military acknowledging the use of torture and the clandestine burial of 22 people; and officially released two publications elaborated by prestigious academics – one entitled *Historical Investigation on Disappeared-Detainees*, gathering a wealth of material on disappearances, and another entitled *Historical Investigation on the Dictatorship and State Terrorism in Uruguay (1973-1985)*, which dealt with executions, torture, political imprisonment, the repression of the left and the trade unions, and the general impact on society (Lessa 2013: 149–150).

When it comes to reparation-type policies, Uruguay has been particularly slow and irresolute. Law 18.033 (October 2006) significantly expanded the scope of Law 17.449 (January 2002), on the restauration of pension rights to those who for political reasons, could not work during the dictatorship (Erradonea 2008: 49). It granted a special reparatory pension for those who were imprisoned, but only in (the unlikely) cases where the beneficiaries did not already receive other pensions. In September 2009, Law 18.596 finally set up a special commission to pay compensations to victims, including political prisoners, minors born in detention, exiles, and torture victims (Lessa 2013: 150). According to a CRYSOL representative, the association congregating Uruguay's ex-political prisoners, these laws were fundamentally 'a conquest of CRYSOL', which found in the Vázquez's progressive executive a better interlocutor than 'the conservative and right-wing Batlle' (Interview UR13). It is curious to note that unlike Spain and Brazil, reparatory policies were not the first type of transitional justice measure enacted in Uruguay. Being the least confrontational, least visible, and most victim-centered kind of measure, they were the natural first step in contexts where the dictatorship's violations were not a salient public issue and where other kinds of measures appeared unthinkable at the time. In Uruguay, instead, the salience of criminal prosecution since the early stages of the transition – and the importance that this measure had for the families and support groups – overshadowed possible reparations policies.

Political and judicial challenges to the Expiry Law

Vázquez's 'perforation approach' to the Expiry Law was far from the only legal and political challenge this law would face after the takeover of the *Frente* over national politics. Unhappy with how partial and unequal the accountability policy was, some of the usual critics – human rights groups, PIT-CNT, the students' federation, and some FA legislators – created the National Coordinating Committee for the Nullification of the Expiry Law in November 2006. The goal was, once again, to launch a plebiscite initiative aimed at overturning the core articles of the law. In a sense, it was a more divisive campaign than the one in 1989, since it was not unanimously supported by left-wing sectors. Among other considerations, voting yet again on a law that had been previously confirmed by popular consultation was an obvious source of controversy. The pro-referendum committee argued, nonetheless, that the law continued to prevent justice in hundreds of cases and that it violated fundamental principles of constitutional and international law, not to mention the ethical duty towards families (Burt et al. 2013: 12). The strength of the pro-accountability movement was once again confirmed by its capacity to collect the necessary signatures for another plebiscite, due to take place in the same day as the October 2009 national elections. Once again, it fell short of the organizers' expectations, with 48% voting in favor. The unusual voting procedure – whereby those in favor had to include a 'yes' slip, while those opposed or undecided had to do nothing – is often partially blamed for the inability to reach the needed 50% quorum (Burt et al. 2013: 13).

Legal challenges to the Expiry Law were, nevertheless, moving forward at the same time. Just one week before the second referendum, the law was dealt a further blow when the Supreme Court issued a ruling declaring its unconstitutionality, following an appeal put forward by a public prosecutor in the *Nibia Sabalsagaray* case. This verdict allowed the prosecution of military officials, which had been previously covered by article 1 of the law, though the court can only declare a law's unconstitutionality on a case-by-case basis, and therefore, the above-mentioned verdict had limited applicability, even if it could serve as a precedent (Lessa 2013: 154). International legal challenges would also produce results less than two years later (February 2011), when the Inter-American Court of Human Rights (IACtHR) – following a complaint lodged by Juan Gelman and his granddaughter – issued a ruling declaring the incompatibility of the Expiry Law with the American Convention on Human Rights, ordering the Uruguayan state to guarantee that such a legal instrument would no longer constitute an obstacle to investigations and prosecutions (Burt et al. 2013: 14).

Despite the setback produced by the 2009 plebiscite, the IACtHR ruling in *Gelman vs. Uruguay* gave renewed strength to pro-accountability groups and had a visible impact on reopening the debate within the ruling party (de Giorgi 2013: 100; Interview UR7). Pro-accountability groups argued that the failure to overturn the law did not necessarily mean that people endorsed it and that in line with the ruling of the IACtHR, direct democracy instruments do not automatically make a law legitimate, not least from an international law point of view. In fact, the impact of the Gelman case on the Uruguayan government – led by José Mujica (2010–2015) – was noticeable even before the Court's decision was out. From the moment the Inter-American Commission of Human Rights sent the case to the Court in February 2010, the condemnatory decision was to be anticipated (in light of previous jurisprudence of the IACtHR on amnesty laws), propelling a handful of FA legislators, in alliance with civil society groups, to work on a draft bill proposing a new interpretation of the law, which in practice, would do away with it (Lessa 2013: 156).

Foreign Minister Luis Almagro was a key figure behind the initial impulse to promote this bill. He is said to have had a significant role in making his governmental peers sensitive towards the importance of avoiding the discredit that a condemnation by the Inter-American system would carry, emphasizing on various occasions that he was working towards a solution to offset the negative impact of the law on Uruguay's international image (Buriano 2011: 196). In addition to reputational concerns, Almagro highlighted that a condemnation by the IACtHR would include a compensation clause to the Gelman family that could be up to one million dollars (*La Nación* 2010). This debate occurred at the same time that Uruguay was preparing its candidacy to the presidency of the Human Rights Council of the United Nations (assumed in June 2011), something that perhaps contributed to further enhancing concerns vis-à-vis the country's international image. Declarations by an FA lawyer (who was part of the committee responsible for drafting the bill) went in the same direction, stressing the economic, political, ethical, and image-related consequences of the expected IACtHR condemnation. His remarks denote the apparent concern with the country's reputation at the international level:

> Uruguay is a country internationally respected for its democratic tradition and for its respect of human rights, with the exception of the dictatorship's period. For Uruguay, it affects us deeply to be condemned for the violation of a pact of which our country was one of the main promoters. Our jurists were the ones who carried forward and pushed for the acceptance of human rights guarantees. As for the political consequences, if we are condemned and do not act in accordance with the condemnation – which is to leave the Expiry law with no legal effect –, we would be incurring into permanent non-compliance and that could have consequences for our relationship with other countries.
>
> (Daoiz Uriarte in *Portal 180*, 2010)

However, this sort of concern did not prevent the bill from being an extremely controversial instrument, with political debates raging for months, and receiving much media coverage (Skaar 2015: 85). They painfully exposed the fissures the issue created within the *Frente* itself. The strongest objection was, expectedly, that it went against two popular pronouncements. The discomfort was such that three FA senators disregarded party discipline and refused to endorse the bill in late 2010. Mujica himself made his uneasiness obvious on several occasions, namely, when he interrupted a parliamentary debate to warn the FA parliamentarians of the political costs the bill could bring or when he declared that he had lost control over his foreign minister (Burt et al. 2013: 15; Lessa 2013: 156). After much discussion and modifications to the text of the draft law, and following the February condemnation by the IACtHR, the abstention of one FA deputy prevented the bill's parliamentary approval on 19 May 2011. This was one day before the annual March of Silence, which gathered about 100,000 people that year in another demonstration of the strength and transversality of the pro-accountability movement.

Despite being significantly weakened by this, the executive quickly proceeded to follow the recommendations of legal experts, who reasoned that the best and most practical way of dealing with the issue was for the executive to retrospectively revoke all the executive decisions that had used the Expiry Law to archive cases, on the grounds of the law's incompatibility with human rights treaties and international sentences. Executive Decree 33 did just that and was justified by the president's chief advisor as a result of the IACtHR's sentence, which in his words, 'obliged the Uruguayan state to leave the Expiry Law with no effect'.[15]

Nevertheless, there was still one major obstacle to the continuation of judicial proceedings: the looming statute of limitations. Crimes perpetrated during the dictatorship, if typified as common crimes, had a prescription period of 26 years and 8 months, meaning that judicial proceedings would have to come to a halt in November 2011. The Uruguayan judiciary had resisted the application of international human rights law in the way Chilean and Argentinian judges had done – which allowed the latter to bypass statutory limitations, either because the crimes were typified as crimes against humanity or because enforced disappearances were considered 'continuous crimes'. Although similar arguments had been tried in Uruguay, judges had mainly invoked national law and categorized disappearances as aggravated homicides. The July 2011 decision of the Supreme Court of Justice rejecting the use of the category of enforced disappearances – on the grounds that it had been incorporated into national legislation only in 2006 and could not be applied retroactively – generated further concern among human rights groups (Lessa 2013: 158).

In light of this, civil society organizations and various political groups within the *Frente Amplio* worked on ways to overcome the prescription obstacle. Various legislative proposals were presented and discussed within the FA's Special Committee on the Expiry Law. In late October 2011, Law 18.831 was ratified by parliament thanks to *Frente Amplio* votes. With only four articles, the law's stated aim is to reestablish the state's punitive capacity regarding the crimes of 'state terrorism' committed up until March 1985 (art. 1), which is the equivalent of effectively repealing the Expiry Law. It also establishes that the time elapsed between the approval of the Expiry Law and the approval of this law should not be computed in prescription periods (art. 2) and that said crimes are crimes against humanity (art. 3). This law also carried the implicit consequence that the judiciary now has full autonomy over what cases to open, no longer requiring executive approval (Soltman 2013: 837). When justifying this bill to the Senate, the *Frente* emphasized first and foremost that its purpose was to follow international norms, 'particularly those contained in the judgment of the Inter-American Court of Human Rights in the Gelman vs. Uruguay case'.[16] The fact that the *Frente* chose to quickly move forward with this proposal – despite previous hesitations, two negative referendums, heated accusations from opposition sectors, and credible doubts raised by well-known jurists about the actual need for and constitutionality of this bill – clearly shows the extent to which pro-accountability sectors managed to gain momentum within the party.

That said, it should be mentioned that the approval of this bill did not lead to the progress pro-accountability sectors hoped for. On the one hand, Law 18.831 has been challenged on various occasions, most notably in a 2013 Supreme Court ruling declaring articles 2 and 3 unconstitutional for violating the principles of legality and retroactivity of criminal law. In practice, this meant that in this case (as well as in others that followed), statutory limitations were invoked as an obstacle to prosecution. As the court can only decide on a case-by-case basis, its jurisprudence on this issue has been quite erratic, fluctuating according to the court's composition. On the other hand, and as mentioned earlier, judicial proceedings continue to suffer from serious delays and are hampered by a series of more practical obstacles.

Accounting for the FA's commitment

In understanding why the FA went against two referendums and took steps such as Law 18.831, various factors seem to be of obvious importance. The first is the sentence of the IACtHR and the fact that it strengthened the position of pro-accountability sectors. The Gelman ruling is commonly seen as the catalyst that brought about the eventual derogation of the amnesty law (Lessa and Skaar 2016: 82). This is the more so when considering that the second *Frente Amplio* government (2010–2015) was headed by ex-members of the MLN-T guerrillas (including Mujica himself), known for not being particularly keen to advance this agenda and for maintaining a resistance/combatant type of outlook (rather than perpetrator–victim) on past events

(Interviews UR5, UR9, and UR10; de Giorgi 2013: 90–91). Even opposition parties, which criticized the FA legislative initiatives, recognize the need to abide by at least part of the court's sentence. According to a high representative of the *Partido Nacional*, 'small countries are clinging to international law like no one else is and having a stain would weaken us when the time comes to claim our rights' (Gil 2011). This same point was made by other political figures on different occasions. In his defense of Law 18.831, Senator Michelini affirmed that 'if we did not comply with our international conventions, we would not be able to demand their compliance by other States, which is imperative for us due to our condition as a small country'.[17] These statements illustrate why international legal institutions seem to be taken particularly seriously in Uruguay.

But, if the Gelman sentence served as a catalyzing factor – together with the looming statute of limitations – it would have had little effect if it had not been for the strength of the pro-accountability movement and its presence within left-wing political sectors. This is the opinion of Burt et al. (2013: 17), who claim that 'key to getting this new legislation passed was the ability of civil society activists to connect with actors within the legislative and executive branches who themselves had long participated in civil society organizing against impunity'. Social movement studies have long pointed towards the importance of political allies in making the demands of the grassroots heard at the political level, and the anti-impunity movement in Uruguay is another example of that. However, I deem that the focus should not be simply on its capacity to establish connections with favorable political actors, but also on the extent to which the parties' social bases and certain political actors within the *Frente Amplio* have themselves been an integrative and constitutive part of this movement. Even if the theme is far from homogeneously endorsed by everyone on the left – and even though the presence of a human rights movement operating outside the FA is fundamental in explaining advancements – it is not far-fetched to state that this theme has become a part of the left's identity in Uruguay. The opposition to the Expiry Law was one of, if not the most, significant political battles of the left during the transition period and therefore, a constitutive part of the party's history at such a defining time.

The annual Marches of Silence – gathering thousands of people every year since 1996 – were a reminder of the capacity of this theme to mobilize broad sectors of society, including the same social movement organizations that are part of the social bases of the party. Indeed, part of the strength of the pro-accountability movement comes from the fact that it goes far beyond the families of the disappeared or the direct victims of repression. From the start, the strongest labor and social organizations in Uruguay – PIT-CNT, FUCVAM, and FEUU – have endorsed anti-impunity claims and offered their support to the families. A prominent example is PIT-CNT lawyer Pablo Chargoñia, who has been a key legal actor in bringing cases to court and who was behind the first judicial advancements produced in the early 2000s. Though these organizations are formally independent of the FA, the close links between them and the party are well known. Even if they are usually more radicalized and are said to have gained more autonomy in recent years, the extent to which they are still capable of shaping and influencing the party's agenda is part of the reason why the FA continues to be considered a primary example of a movement-based party in Latin America.

Although the exact bargaining process behind the above-mentioned legislative initiatives is not known, opposition parties were quick to brand these initiatives as another example of the FA succumbing to its more radical sectors. One deputy from the *Partido Nacional* goes as far as to state that 'the government has kept its promise to revoke the Expiry Law in exchange for having its most radical left-wing sectors – those who control social organizations as the PIT-CNT – accept its economic policies' (*La República* 2011a). Even though there is no concrete indication of such an agreement, it is obvious that there were internal pressures within the FA (as in any other policy matter).

Nevertheless, if the pressure of certain sectors was an important element, one should also recognize the party's willingness to produce advancements and go against two referendums. This would hardly be the case if this were not a topic which was important or at least, morally binding. As one Uruguayan political scientist puts it, 'besides internal pressures, the FA has the pressure of looking itself in the mirror and feeling uncomfortable for having a parliamentary majority and still abiding by a law that has always been experienced as a tragedy by the left' (Cibils 2010). An FA senator goes in the same direction, stating: 'I do not think there is a topic that generates more sensitivity for the left's identity than this one' (*La República* 2011b). Both testimonials point to the temporal longevity of the FA's relationship with this topic in an implicit reference to what this issue meant to the left at such a significant and constitutive moment as the democratic transition period. Then, as 20 years earlier, one has to place the FA's commitment in the context of a constant interplay between (a) the relentless struggle of the families and the human rights movement, (b) the support of broader social movement organizations, and (c) the party's grassroots embeddedness; with the difference that 20 years later, there was a previous and long history of engagement with the topic and two circumstantial events – the Gelman sentence and an upcoming statute of limitations – that provided opportunities and made the topic more urgent.

Conclusion

The case of Uruguay is particularly instructive for the purposes of this book, as it shows evidence that a negotiated transition to democracy does not necessarily have to be accompanied by a consensual memory regime. To be sure, the 1980 plebiscite and the results of the 1982 internal elections had already put the military in a more fragile position than in the other two country cases explored. The unwillingness of the *Partido Nacional* to sit at the negotiation table also speaks for a context of greater radicalization in Uruguay (though this had less to do with the perceived strength of the opposition camp than with its dissatisfaction over the proscription of its leader). Nevertheless, the key difference from other cases resides less in the way the transition was orchestrated than in the fact that social and political forces on the left were unwilling to give a *carte blanche* to the military, with everyone being well aware of that.

In understanding why social and political actors were sensitive towards this issue, there are various factors worth taking into account. At a macro/structural level, the geopolitical context is important, given that the influence of the Argentinian case is notorious, especially in the constitution and frames of reference of the human rights movement. The extent of political repression in a country that had been largely unused to violence before and had a strong democratic tradition also speaks for why many Uruguayans were not willing to let violations go unpunished. At the organizational or meso-level, the constitution of human rights and family groups, the receptiveness of a cohesive social movement scene to human rights claims, and the *Frente*'s strong and embedded ties to its social constituencies are important in understanding how the above-mentioned structural factors translated into actual demands and why the families of the victims did not find themselves isolated. Moreover, pro-accountability actors in Uruguay benefited from a few windows of opportunity at the institutional level. On the one hand, the absence of an amnesty for the military up until December 1986 allowed the opening of judicial investigations during 1985 and 1986, with apparent levels of trust in the judiciary translating into a flood of legal complaints. On the other hand, pro-accountability actors were able to make use of Uruguay's direct democracy mechanisms by promoting a referendum on the Expiry Law of December 1986.

Although the majority of Uruguay's population would vote to keep the law, the salience of this issue and the levels of conflict generated in this period make the transitional justice trajectory of Uruguay radically different from the two other country cases. As argued before, a conflictual memory regime offers greater opportunities than a consensual one for the later treatment of the topic. This is, first of all, because the theme became so intimately associated with the Uruguayan left that it could be expected that the *Frente* would take steps on the issue once in a position of power, either out of commitment and/or because of the pressure of pro-accountability sectors within and outside the party. Secondly, unlike consensual settings, where state actors will be careful not to produce radical breaks with the past, a conflictual memory regime makes the enactment of more robust measures less of a surprise (in light of a long history of social and political demands on the issue).

The fact that Uruguay's transitional justice trajectory starts off with the Peace Commission (rather than reparations, as in Spain and Brazil) and that this measure is enacted by a representative of the Colorado Party (rather than a left-wing politician) speaks for the peculiarity of Uruguay's TJ trajectory. This, I argue, is not independent of the comparatively higher levels of pressure in Uruguay and the concomitant public salience of the issue following the resurgence of the topic in the late 1990s – the Marches of Silence being the most visible face of this. The enactment of an acknowledgment type of policy that is more visible than reparations to victims – but that did not antagonize the military to a significant extent (in part because it was a timid one) – brought widely perceived reputational benefits to Batlle's administration. Moreover, the enactment of the first criminal accountability steps as soon as the *Frente* came to office speaks not only for the comparatively higher degree of commitment of this party but also for the different status of perpetrator-centered measures in Uruguay, with its early salience opening up the political space for its later treatment. This does not mean, however, that sources of pressure matter less in the case of a party that has a pre-established positive preference. This is, first of all, because the party's commitment comes in large part from its connection to the pro-accountability movement, but also because the move from the 'loophole approach' to Law 18.831 cannot be dissociated from the continuous pressure of the pro-accountability movement and their endorsement by the IACtHR ruling.

Notes

1 Despite the legalization of the *Frente* at the end of July, the armed forces never gave up on Seregni's proscription as well as the electoral ban of the most radical sectors of the *Frente*, such as the Communist Party, which nonetheless ran under another designation.

2 With about 41% of the national vote, the *Colorado* Party was followed by the *Blancos* with 35% and the *Frente* with 21%.

3 Uruguay had, until 1994, a double simultaneous voting system, which allowed each of the parties' sub-factions (well institutionalized in Uruguayan parties) to run with a different candidate. The votes for the factions were naturally counted as votes for the party to which they belonged. The party with the most votes would be the winning party and the presidency given to the candidate of the sub-faction of the winning party that had the most votes. Thus, even if a sub-faction had more votes than any other, it would win only if its party had been the most voted for.

4 By the early 1980s, the literacy rate was 96.3%, and urbanization stood at around 85% (Gillespie 1991: 17).

5 Argentina's military junta would not take over until 1976, three years after Uruguay's coup (1973). The effervescent political situation in Argentina previous to 1976 constituted an additional incentive for many of Uruguay's political exiles.

6 Ironically, it is in part because these sectors rejected any type of mid-way compromise on this issue that attempts to forge an inter-party agreement with the *Blancos* on a project establishing some form of limited justice repeatedly failed.

7 Two commissions were created: the Investigative Commission on the Situation of the Disappeared People and its Causes; and the Investigative Commission on the Kidnapping and Assassination of National Representatives Zelmar Michelini and Héctor Gutiérrez Ruiz. However, their mandate was severely hampered by

the lack of official support from the government as well as insufficient investigative powers, which is why they are not considered to fall into the category of truth mechanisms (Skaar 2011: 141). They nonetheless compiled relevant information that was meant to serve in future court proceedings.

8 Note that Law 15.737, though commonly regarded as an amnesty law, does not fully fall into this category, because it does not pardon 'blood crimes' but instead, establishes a system of commutation of sentences through which every day already spent in prison would count as three days. This, in practice, meant that all those condemned for 'blood crimes' were effectively released, as they all had already spent ten years in prison (and 30 was the maximum allowed in Uruguayan legislation) (Interview UR8). This was a means of reconciling the calls for a full-fledged amnesty coming from most of the opposition with the government's disapproval. In addition to this, Law 15.737 (March 1985) included provisions to facilitate the return and social reintegration of returning exiles, the restitution of confiscated property, and the restoration of public jobs to employees unfairly dismissed during the dictatorship (Lessa 2013: 135).

9 The Supreme Military Court would interpose a jurisdictional claim in August – at the same time as civil courts called for the arrest of three military officers – which would serve to held up judicial action for some months.

10 Interestingly, though, Sanguinetti's rhetoric on the justification of the Expiry Law would evolve over the years, as Álvaro de Giorgi (2014b) brilliantly demonstrates in a book entirely dedicated to this subject. If at first, the Expiry Law was framed as a 'sacrifice in the name of peace' – a lesser evil to avoid a military insurrection – it would later be put within the 'two demons' framework, that is, granting moral equivalency to the violence of the guerrillas and the repressive activities of the military. This allowed Sanguinetti to argue that the process of settling accounts for the military should involve settling accounts for the left too, as is visible in his interview with Weschler (1990: 188). De Giorgi's 2014 book subtly but clearly demonstrates that this is much more of an exercise in rhetoric than anything else, since Sanguinetti is well aware that (1) the guerrillas had been dismantled before the 1973 coup, (2) political prisoners is a more extensive category than guerrilla members, and (3) there was never an amnesty for the guerrillas, since instead, their sentences were commuted to one-third of the time.

11 *Grandes Lineas Programaticas y Propuestas de Planes de Gobierno. Aprobadas por el III Congreso Extraordinario del Frente Amplio 'Alfredo Zitarrosa'.* Montevideo, 20, 21, and 22 November 1998.

12 *Grandes Lineamentos Programaticos para el Gobierno 2005-2009.* IV Congreso Extraordinario del Frente Amplio. 20–21 December 2003. https://frenteamplio.uy/nuestra-voz/declaraciones-y-documentos/item/download/182_1c4cd23a669d80fcb96a9f03f112f164.

13 Speech by the President of the Republic, Tabaré Vázquez, in the Legislative Palace Act. March 1, 2005. http://archivo.presidencia.gub.uy/_web/noticias/2005/03/2005030111.htm.

14 *Observatorio Luz Ibarburu.* Accessed 2 March 2018. www.observatorioluzibarburu.org/acerca_de/.

15 Uruguay Government. 'Poder Ejecutivo revocará los actos administrativos incluidos en la Ley de Caducidad.' 27 June 2011. www.gub.uy/presidencia/comunicacion/noticias/poder-ejecutivo-revocara-actos-administrativos-incluidos-ley-caducidad.

16 Diario de Sesiones de la Cámara de Senadores, 45ª Sesión Extraordinaria, N° 115 – TOMO 488, 25 October 2011.

17 Ibid.

References

Alfaro, Raúl Olivera. 2016. 'Memoria, verdad y justicia en Uruguay: La gestión del pasado en un escenario de luces y sombras.' *ILCEA* 26. https://doi.org/10.4000/ilcea.3905.

Allier Montaño, Eugenia. 2006. 'The Peace Commission: A Consensus on the Recent Past in Uruguay?' *European Review of Latin American and Caribbean Studies* 81: 87–96.

Allier Montaño, Eugenia. 2010. *Batallas por la Memoria. Los usos políticos del pasado reciente em Uruguay*. Montevideo: Ediciones Trilce.

Alonso, Luciana. 2010. 'Defensa de los Derechos Humanos Frente a las Dictaduras Regresivas: Los casos de Argentina y Uruguay en Perspectiva Comparada.' *Studia Historica. Historia Contemporánea* 28: 23–50.

Amnesty International. 2004. 'Amnesty International Report 2004 – Uruguay.' London: Amnesty International. Accessed November 18, 2018. https://www.amnesty.org/en/documents/pol10/0004/2004/en/.

Amnesty International. 2006. 'Amnesty International Report 2006 – Uruguay.' London: Amnesty International. Accessed November 18, 2018. https://www.amnesty.org/en/documents/pol10/0001/2006/en/.

Amnesty International. 2008. 'Amnesty International Report 20084 – Uruguay.' London: Amnesty International. Accessed November 18, 2018. https://www.amnesty.org/en/documents/pol10/0004/2004/en/.

Barahona de Brito, Alexandra. 1997. *Human Rights and Democratization in Latin America: Uruguay and Chile*. New York: Oxford University Press.

Bardazano, Gianella. 2013. 'Los efectos de la ley. Entre la amistía en la tradición nacional y Núremberg en la conciencia de la huminadad.' In *Ley de Caducidad: Un Tema Inconcluso*, edited by Aldo Marchesi, Gianella Bardazano, Álvaro de Giorgi, Ana Laura de Giorgi and Diego Sempol. Montevideo: Ediciones Trilce.

Bucheli, Gabriela, Valentina, Curto and Valentina Sanguinetti. 2005. *Vivos los Llevaron: Historia de la Lucha de Madres y Familiares de uruguayos Detenidos Desaparecidos (1976–2005)*. Montevideo: Ediciones Trilce.

Buriano, Ana. 2011. 'Ley de Caducidad em Uruguay y esencia ético-política de la izquierda.' *Perfiles latino-americanos* 19, no. 38: 173–203.

Burt, Jo-Marie, Amilivia, Gabriela and Lessa, Francesca. 2013. 'Civil Society and the Resurgent Struggle against Impunity in Uruguay (1986–2012).' *The International Journal of Transitional Justice* 7, no. 2: 1–22.

Caetano, Gerardo and José Rilla. 1987. *Breve Historia de la Dictadura*. Motevideo: Ediciones de la Banda Oriental.

Caetano, Gerardo and José Rilla. 1994. *Historia Contemporánea del Uruguay: De la Colonia al MERCOSUR*. Montevideo: Editorial Fin de Siglo.

Cibils, Ana Inés. 2010. 'Polémica ley sobre juicios por violaciones a DDHH divide a Gobierno Uruguayo.' *Agence France Press*, October 26, 2010.

Comisión para la Paz. (2003). *Informe Final de la Comisión para la Paz*. Montevideo: Presidencia de la República.

de Giorgi, Ana Laura. 2013. 'El Frente Amplio y su laberinto. La izquierda uruguaya frente a la ley de caducidade.' In *Ley de Caducidad: Un Tema Inconcluso*, edited by Aldo Marchesi, Gianella Bardazano, Álvaro de Giorgi, Ana Laura de Giorgi and Diego Sempol. Montevideo: Ediciones Trilce.

de Giorgi, Ana Laura. 2014a. 'Democracia y derechos humanos: Claves de la reconfiguración de la izquierda uruguaya (1980–2014).' *Informe de Investigación CLACSO*. Buenos Aires: Latin American Council of Social Sciences.

de Giorgi, Álvaro. 2014b. *Sanguinetti. La otra historia del pasado reciente*. Montevideo: Fin de Siglo.

Demasi, Carlos. 2011. 'Conviviendo con la caducidad: Democracia, república y derechos humanos en Uruguay.' In *Luchas contra la impunidad: Uruguay 1985–2011*, edited by Gabriela Fried and Francesca Lessa. Montevideo: Ediciones Trilce.

Erradonea, Jorge. 2008. 'Justicia transicional em Uruguay.' *Revista IIDH* 47: 13–69.

Gil, Valeria. 2011. 'Caducidad: Acuerdan enviar proyecto sobre prescripción.' *El País - Uruguay*, October 13, 2011.

Gillespie, Charles. 1986. 'Uruguay's Transition from Collegial Military-Technocratic Rule.' In *Transitions from Authoritarian Rule: Latin America*, edited by Guillermo O'Donnell, Philippe C. Schmitter and Laurence Whitehead, 173–195. Baltimore: Johns Hopkins University Press.

Gillespie, Charles. 1991. *Negotiating Democracy: Politicians and Generals in Uruguay*. Cambridge: Cambridge University Press.

La Nación. 2010. 'Mujica sancionó al comandante em jefe del ejército.' *La Nación*, October 27, 2010.

La República. 2011a. 'Acuerdo Caducidad.' May 8, 2011.

La República. 2011b. 'DDHH: Fórmula "Miranda" no computa el período 1986–2011.' October 9, 2011.

Lessa, Alfonso. 2003. *La revolución imposible. Los tupamaros y el fracaso de la vía armada en el Uruguay del siglo XX*. Montevideo: Fin de Siglo.

Lessa, Alfonso. 2009. *La primera orden. Gregorio Alvarez, el militar y el dictador. Una historia de omnipotencia*. Motevideo: Sudamericana.

Lessa, Francesca. 2013. *Memory and Transitional Justice in Argentina and Uruguay: Against Impunity*. New York: Palgrave Macmillan.

Lessa, Francesca and Elin Skaar. 2016. 'Uruguay: Halfway towards accountability.' In *Transitional Justice in Latin America. The Uneven Road from Impunity towards Accountability*, edited by Elin Skaar, Jemima García-Godos and Cath Collins. Abingdon and New York: Routledge.

Lessa, Francesca, Tricia Olsen, Leigh Payne, Gabriela Pereira and Andrew Reiter. 2014. 'Overcoming Impunity: Pathways to Accountability in Latin America.' *The International Journal of Transitional Justice* 8: 75–98.

Levitsky, Steven and Kenneth M. Roberts. 2011. *The Resurgence of the Latin American Left*. Baltimore: Johns Hopkins University Press.

Loveman, Mara. 1998. 'High Risk Collective Action: Defending Human Rights in Chile, Uruguay, and Argentina' *American Journal of Sociology* 104, no. 2: 477–525.

Mallinder, Louise. 2009. 'Uruguay's Evolving Experience of Amnesty and Civil Society's Response.' Working Paper No. 4. *Beyond Legalism: Amnesties, Transition and Conflict Transformation*. Belfast: Institute of Criminology and Criminal Justice, Queen's University Belfast.

Markarian, Vania. 2005. *Left in Transformation. Uruguayan Exiles and the Latin American Human Rights Networks, 1967–1984*. New York: Routledge.

Moreira, Constanza. 2000. 'La izquierda en Uruguay y Brasil: Cultura política y desarollo político-partidario.' In *La Larga Espera. Itinerarios de las Izquierdas en Argentina, Brasil y Uruguay*, edited by Susana Mallo and Constanza Moreira. Montevideo. Ediciones de la Banda Oriental.

Portal 180. 2010. 'Más tiempo para derogar efectos de la ley de caducidad.' *Portal 180*, October 4, 2010.

Reuters. 1998a. 'Izquierda uruguaya planea nuevas acciones por desaparecidos.' Reuters, February 17, 1998.

Reuters. 1998b. 'Uruguay justifica ante EEUU no investigar desaparecidos.' Reuters, March 26, 1998.

Reuters. 1999. 'Sanguinetti deja un país saneado y reclamos por desaparecidos.' *Reuters*, October 30, 1999.

Rial, Juan. 1990. *Los partidos politicos Uruguayanos en el proceso de transición hacia la democracia*. Working Paper 145. Notre Dame: Helen Kellogg Institute for International Studies.

Rico, Álvaro. 2015. 'Revisiones sobre la caracterización del golpe y la dictadura en Uruguay.' In *Política y memoria: A cuarenta años de los golpes de Estado en Chile y Uruguay*, edited by Ana Buriano Castro, Silvia Dutrénit Bielous and Daniel Vázquez Valencia. México: FLACSO-México.

Roniger, Luis. 2012. 'La sacralizacón del Consenso Nacional y las Pugnas por la Memoria Histórica y la Justicia en el Uruguay Posdictatorial.' *América Latina Hoy* 61: 51–78.

Roniger, Luis and Mario Sznajder. 1997. 'The Legacy of Human Rights Violations and the Collective Identity of Redemocratized Uruguay.' *Human Rights Quarterly* 19, no. 1: 55–77.

Roniger, Luis and Mario Sznajder . 1999. *The Legacy of Human Rights Violations in the Southern Cone: Argentina, Chile, and Uruguay*. New York: Oxford University Press.

Rouquié, Alain. 1987. *The Military and the State in Latin America*. Berkeley: University of California Press.

SERPAJ (Servicio Paz y Justicia de Uruguay). 1989. *Nunca Más Uruguay: Informe sobre las violaciones a los derechos humanos, 1972–1985*. Montevideo: SERPAJ.

Skaar, Elin. 2011. *Judicial Independence and Human Rights in Latin America: Violations, Politics, and Prosecution*. New York: Palgrave Macmillan, 2011.

Skaar, Elin. 2015. 'Uruguay. Reconstructing peace and democracy through transitional justice.' In *After Violence: Transitional Justice, Peace and Democracy*, edited by Elin Slaar, Camila Gianella Malca and Trine Eide. New York: Routledge.

Soltman, Daniel. 2013. 'Applauding Uruguay's Quest for Justice: Dictatorship, Amnesty, and Repeal of Uruguay Law no. 15.848.' *Washington University Global Studies Law Review* 12, no. 4: 829–848.

Weinstein, Martin. 1988. *Uruguay Democracy at the Crossroads*. Boulder, Colorado: Westview Press.

Weinstein, Martin. 2007. 'The Left's Long Road to Power in Uruguay.' In *From Revolutionary Movements to Political Parties. Cases from Latin America and Africa*, edited by Kalowatie Deonandan, David Close and Gary Prevost. New York: Palgrave Macmillan.

Weschler, Lawrence. 1990. *A Miracle, A Universe. Settling Accounts with Torturers*. Chicago and London: The University of Chicago Press.

Chapter 5

Brazil

From a marginal issue to the 'right to truth'

When speaking of transitional justice (TJ) measures in the American Southern Cone, Brazil is often singled out as the country that lags furthest behind, in light of the absence of criminal accountability measures to this day. Its transitional justice trajectory has often been described as 'reparations-driven', given the emphasis on compensatory or reparatory measures (Abrão and Torelly 2012). This trend started under the Cardoso administration (1995–2002), which implemented a comprehensive reparations program covering both the families of the dead and disappeared and those who were subjected to various forms of political persecution. The creation of two organizations responsible for the administration of reparations – the Special Commission on Political Deaths and Disappearances and later, the Amnesty Commission – ended up performing a modest 'truth-collecting' function, as victims and their families told their stories in the process. This later facilitated the work of the National Truth Commission (2012–2014), an investigatory body that systematized the available information and produced a detailed and authoritative account of the repressive apparatus, naming both victims and perpetrators. This chapter constitutes, first and foremost, an effort at understanding what was behind the enactment of these measures, looking at the political context in which they were approved and identifying the relevant actions and actors. It also seeks explanations for the absence of criminal accountability measures, and places Brazil's transitional justice trajectory in the context of a highly top-down transition in which pro-TJ voices were few, weak, and isolated.

If it is true that Brazil's memory regime during the transition period appears to be much closer to the Spanish than the Uruguayan one when it comes to the absence of a salient demand for accountability, the degree of consensus is not as striking as in Spain. Despite their isolation, a few families made their demands heard within the amnesty movement and opened a few judicial cases. They faced, however, a very adverse political and institutional context, not only because they lacked the social and political basis of support the Uruguayan families enjoyed, but also because the military regime kept a very high degree of control over the transition process. Out of the three

DOI: 10.4324/9781003311607-8

country studies, Brazil's amnesty law was the one negotiated under the strictest conditions, approved by a parliament controlled by the regime in 1979, six years before the takeover by a civilian president. This meant not only that the amnesty law contained a hardly noticeable provision covering the crimes of state agents (just as in Spain) but also that it was not fully bilateral (as the opposition's 'blood crimes' were not covered). It is striking, though, that the amnesty law is still widely regarded as an achievement of the democratic opposition, since it followed a highly visible popular mobilization effort that had the amnesty demand at its core (as in Spain); besides the release of some political prisoners, this law was celebrated for allowing for the return of thousands who had been exiled and banished from their jobs and political life. It was, therefore, a major stepping stone in the process of 'slow, gradual, and careful' political liberalization that the regime itself had announced. The fact that the amnesty law covered state agents was not entirely unnoticed by the regime's opposition but was taken as an inevitable counterpart, given the balance of power at the time.

Thus, the lack of social and political support for accountability has to be put in the context of a particularly unfavorable political environment, which, as in Spain, precluded potentially relevant actors from even perceiving transitional justice measures as a possibility. But while in Spain there was a deliberate political commitment to reconciliation and moderation underlying the decision to leave the past behind, in Brazil there was no equivalent amnesty negotiation process. To the extent that 'pacts' were made, they were agreed upon by the political forces allowed by the regime, and the left was largely excluded from this process. Therefore, the absence of left-wing political support for accountability in Brazil should not be understood as a result of an implicit agreement but rather, of a social and political context in which accountability was neither perceived as possible nor taken as a priority.

In understanding this, there are a number of potentially relevant factors. The first has to do with the characteristics of repression. Because it produced fewer lethal victims (as a proportion of the population) and was more targeted at violent left-wing groups – which were small, fragmented, and largely isolated – the number of potential claimants (that is, victims and families) is comparatively smaller, and the degree of solidarity coming from external actors is perhaps less strong. In contrast to Uruguay, which had a stronger and significantly more unified left, Brazil's moribund left had been torn by divisions, and the moment of transition to democracy is not as much one of 'reorganization of the old' as 'creation of the new'. Although the newly founded Workers' Party attracted some of those who had been imprisoned and tortured, it emerged out of a 'new syndicalism' movement, which was different and keen on distinguishing itself from the 'old left'. Its focus was on the working class and the marginalized sectors of society, in an attempt to become the first mass-based party in Brazil. Similarly, an incipient human rights movement – which had been born in association with the defense of political prisoners throughout the 1970s – turned its attention to social and economic rights, in accordance with the growing mobilization of the working class and in response to Brazil's massive socio-economic inequalities.

The families of the hundreds who had died or disappeared for political reasons had, therefore, to wait for an administration that was sympathetic to their cause in order to have some of their demands heard. The approval of the first reparatory measures at the start of Cardoso's mandate (1995–2002) cannot be dissociated from the fact that he was the first president coming from the dictatorship's opposition circles, having among his key advisors people who had been active in the denunciation of state abuses back in the 1970s. However, credit has also to be granted to various sources of external pressure who played an agenda-setting role and who had their case strengthened by the discovery of a mass grave in São Paulo in the early 1990s.

The creation of the two reparatory commissions mentioned earlier (and their work over time), together with the establishment of a Special Secretariat for Human Rights during Cardoso's presidency, meant that the Brazilian state itself created institutions that would later serve to push for an advancement of the transitional justice agenda from within the state. The 'truth and memory' agenda would be explicitly adopted during Lula's second mandate (January 2007 to December 2010), shortly after Paulo Vannuchi took over the presidency of the Secretariat for Human Rights – an ex-prisoner and victim of torture known for his sensitivity towards the issue. Nevertheless, the decision to create a Truth Commission at the end of Lula's mandate also occurs after a period in which the families had expanded their circle of allies and some doors had been opened. Most significantly among those was – identically to Uruguay – the condemnation by the Inter-American Court of Human Rights (IACtHR) in the *Gomes Lund et al. v. Brazil* case in 2010.

Contextualization

If at the start of the twentieth century Brazil was predominantly rural and dominated by regional oligarchical elites, much of what came in the following decades resulted from efforts at centralization and the creation of a strong and paternalistic central state capable of regulating the economy and co-opting corporate interests. This was not without resistance (as with the Paulista war in 1932) and certainly not without the recurring interference in politics of the military, widely seen as a legitimate player of the political game. Its 'moderator' role is best described by Stepan (1971) as intervening in politics whenever part of the civilian elite deemed that an executive had to be removed or barred from taking over. If military officers had significantly contributed to putting an end to the *coronelismo* era (1889–1930) – characterized by the concentration of power in the hands of a few rural oligarchs – as well as to ousting Getúlio Vargas's dictatorship (1937–1945), they also did not hesitate to intervene repeatedly during Brazil's quasi-democratic experiment (1945–1964) whenever the conservative camp deemed that political representatives were going too far in their socio-economic reforms. This was the case in 1954, 1955, 1961, and finally with the coup d'état of 1964, when rather than a 'moderator' – which steps aside after securing a shift in power – the military became the agent of transformation itself and installed a military dictatorship that would last for over 20 years (1964–1985).

The social and political dynamics leading up to the 1964 coup fall neatly within a Cold War logic and are similar to the more renowned case of Chile, with a populist left-wing government raising the suspicion among part of the established elite that Brazil was on the road towards a socialist state. João Goulart's government (1961–1964) turned skeptics into die-hard enemies by proposing a comprehensive socio-economic plan that involved landholding reforms. Polarization was aggravated by a fragile economic situation as well as by Goulart's turn at the end of 1963 to radical left allies, whose strategy of collecting support through mass popular rallies further intensified the 'red scare' among the upper and middle classes. Goulart's endorsement of the unionization of enlisted men also inflamed tensions with the military hierarchy, which had long feared a left-wing infiltration among its lower-ranks, a fear substantiated five days before the coup when more than 2,000 low-rank sailors staged a mutiny in Rio. Skidmore (1988: 17) goes as far as to consider that the climate of social agitation came close to a 'proto civil war', with 'anti-communist paramilitary groups in S. Paulo terrorizing leftist student leaders, and with landowning elites paying gunmen to kill peasant organizers'.

The 1 April 1964 coup d'état and the bureaucratic authoritarian regime that followed are therefore commonly seen through a class-based lens, as a 'reaction to the extended political activation of the popular sector (…), perceived by other classes and sectors as a threat' (O'Donnell 1978: 7), as a way to 'arrest the shift of power to the urban working class' (Love 1970: 23), or as a result of the 'fear that a rising proletariat and an awakening peasantry would seize power and change the internal distribution of wealth' (Moreira Alves 1972 quoted in Flynn 1974: 322). This was in a context where rising literacy rates (literacy being a requirement for suffrage), together with rapid industrialization and urbanization, brought a new mass of voters to the political scene, disrupting the traditional patronage-based electoral deals. This happened at the same time that the Brazilian Labor Party (PTB) made significant electoral gains, and the working class became increasingly militant. It is worth noting, however, that the creation of the PTB in 1945 was an anticipatory elite-led move – rather than an effort from below – and was in part aimed at preventing a growing influence of the Communist Party and like-minded organizations (thus being radically distinct from what would later become the *Frente* in Uruguay). In fact, the dominant parties of the time, far from being anchored on social roots and cleavages, still operated largely within the logic of 'traditional politics', defined by Hagopian (1996: 16) as a system where 'political power is narrowly concentrated, access to decision making is restricted, channels of political representation are arranged hierarchically, and political competition is strictly regulated', with parties being 'vehicles of oligarchical control'.

The regulation of political competition is perhaps best evidenced by the fact that the Communist Party was outlawed as early as 1947, after a brief period of legality in 1945–1947, and following a decade (1935–1945) when it had been severely repressed. Militant anticommunism had already been at the origin of the Vargas dictatorship (1937–1945) after a rapidly suppressed 'Communist uprising' in 1935 (led by low-rank military men) and the discovery of an alleged Communist plot in 1937 (later proved to be false). The anticommunist imaginary was again at the origin of the 1964 coup – or at least, used as a rhetorical legitimizing tool – something sure to resonate well with public opinion, as surveys at the time revealed that over 60% of respondents in São Paulo considered it a danger, and as many as 80% supported the illegalization of the Communist Party (Sá Motta 2015: 9).

Besides forestalling the 'Communist conspiracy', the broad goals of the military involved sweeping economic and political change, including economic stabilization (i.e., control of inflation and attraction of foreign investment) and demobilization of the popular classes so as to control wage demands, on top of the eradication of political clientelism, corruption, and inefficient allocation of public resources (Hagopian 1996: 2). But while some military factions wanted to impose a hardline authoritarian rule, others sought to maintain some institutional characteristics of a restricted democracy as a means of obtaining popular support (Mainwaring 1995: 181). The moderate faction would prevail most of the time, and the Brazilian Congress would keep on functioning for most of the authoritarian period (after some of its members had been purged). Two parties were allowed: a pro-regime party (ARENA – National Renewal Alliance) and a party conglomerating the opposition, the Brazilian Democratic Movement (MDB). The Brazilian military dictatorship was therefore quite unique in the extent to which it welcomed the cooperation of right-wing civilian professional politicians and preserved an institutional framework in which political careers were maintained and a margin of dissent was allowed (Power 2016: 17). If the MDB struggled to survive in the first years, with outspoken critics risking their mandates, it gained traction (and votes) in the first half of the 1970s, benefiting from political liberalization and eventually contributing to the political dynamics leading to the restauration of democracy in 1985 (Mainwaring 1995: 183).

Characteristics of repression

In order to 'restore internal order', military leaders were quick to enact legislation expanding the power of the executive, including the power to suspend the political rights of any citizen, to cancel the mandate of legislators, and to suspend job stability for civil servants (Skidmore 1988: 20). According to Pereira (2005: 67), in the years between 1964 and 1973, about 517 people were deprived of the right to vote and to run for office, 541 elected officials were stripped of their mandates, 1,968 government workers were forced to retire, and another 1,815 were fired. This was part of 'Operation Clean-Up', aimed at rooting out alleged 'threats to national security'. In the immediate aftermath of the coup, between 10,000 and 50,000 people were detained, many of whom were released within days and most within weeks (Skidmore 1988: 25). This first wave of repression targeted supporters of the deposed government and left-leaning organizations, including Communists and their alleged collaborators in the civil service, universities, trade unions, state-owned firms, and the military itself (Pereira 2005: 67). Some of the detainees were picked up for torture – the kind of torture that in Brazil had been long used on ordinary criminal suspects – in order to extract information on 'Russian contacts' and the like (Skidmore 1988: 24).

Contrary to most dictatorships, in which the initial wave of repression tends to be more extensive and violent, Brazil's security apparatus would turn more ruthless from 1969 until the mid-1970s. As an armed left emerged at the time – though small, fragmented, and lacking any sort of mass base – this second wave of repression was more brutal, widespread, and centralized, targeted at 'shadowy groups within the armed left and their presumed support base, including students, academics, journalists, and clerics' (Pereira 2005: 20–21). While up until 1968 there is a record of 45 deaths at the hands of state agents and 4 disappearances, between 1969 and 1974 there is a total of 297 cases of deaths and disappearances (94 deaths and 203 disappearances), in accordance with the lists of victims provided by the recent report of the National Truth Commission (CNV 2014: 487–489, 577–582). In total, the Commission was able to gather information on 434 lethal victims of state violence (though it includes 11 cases that occurred before 1964). About 70 of those victims were killed or disappeared as a result of the annihilation of the Araguaia guerrilla – an armed movement formed by militants of the Communist Party of Brazil (PCdoB – a splinter group from the Brazilian Communist Party [PCB]) who had established themselves in a remote jungle-like region in preparation for what they hoped would be a focus of rural guerrilla activity. Their early discovery by the regime culminated in a brutal extermination campaign before they could gain any momentum.

The dictatorship's death toll indicates that widespread extrajudicial killings were not the regime's preferred repressive method. Repression in Brazil, as Pereira (2005) develops at length, was more judicialized and gradualist than in the rest of the Southern Cone, in the sense that the regime slowly modified aspects of traditional legality and subjected political dissent to the military legal system (which was not entirely isolated from the civil one), giving the process an appearance of legality. The *Brasil Nunca Mais* project (1985) – an impressive civil society initiative that clandestinely photocopied all the court proceedings of the Supreme Military Tribunal between 1964 and 1979 – documents in detail the cases of a total of 7,367 defendants. Out of the more than 11,000 criminal charges presented, more than half were due to membership in groups or movements opposed to the regime, and only 12.5% of all the charges referred to violent or armed action, in complete contrast to the claim that repression was a response to terrorist violence (*Brasil: Nunca Mais* 1988 quoted in Pereira 2005: 76–77). Pereira's (2005: 77) in-depth study on the judicialization of repression further reveals that one remarkable feature of political trials is the relatively high acquittal rates of military courts (over 50%), which, together with sentences that were relatively light, constitute evidence that the courts were not blindly sanctioning the regime's repression but following a conservative legalistic path.

Importantly, the *Nunca Mais* project became the best source of evidence on the widespread practice of torture by state agents. About 25% of the cases in the reviewed files included denunciations of torture, meaning that, at a minimum, 1,800 people were affected (Weschler 1990: 45). Note that this is surely only a fraction of those subject to torture, as it only encompasses those who were sent to court, who appealed to the Supreme Military Court, and who were courageous enough to denounce the practice while still under the custody of the repressive apparatus. The detailed description of multiple and horrifying instances of torture – with a wide variety of methods – reinforces the point made by the authors of the *Nunca Mais* book that despite the deep historical roots of the use of torture in Brazil, what happened after 1964 was of a different kind, in that torture was administered on a systematic basis and 'was an essential component of the semi-autonomous repressive system' (Weschlerm 1990: 58). More than half of the denunciations of torture occurred during the regime's most repressive stage (1968–1974), corresponding to the period in which military hardliners are said to have taken over and when the most infamous 'institutional act' was approved. Institutional Act Number 5 (AI-5, issued in December 1968), besides enacting various measures strengthening the executive's authoritarian power, eliminates basic constitutional guarantees (the right to *habeas corpus*) for 'national security crimes'. This is commonly considered the equivalent of 'institutionalizing the use of confessions extracted under torture as a basis for the repression and prosecution of opponents and dissidents' (Pereira 2005: 72). As restrictions on freedom of expression and reunion were severely tightened, and the executive was given greater arbitrary power (e.g., to sack public servants), the number of those forced into exile increased during this period, too. Though there are no precise estimates, it is usually considered that between 5,000 and 10,000 people left the country for political reasons.

In sum, if the recent report of the National Truth Commission updated the number of lethal victims to over 400, the work of the Amnesty Commission – created in 2002 to manage the attribution of economic and moral reparations to those who had suffered from non-lethal forms of political persecution – has recently estimated at 45,000 the number of cases that were reviewed positively (Torelly 2018: 6). To the best of my knowledge, there is no publicly available source discriminating this number according to the type of violations, but it includes not only torture and imprisonment but also due process violations and ill treatment, including job loss and forced retirement.

The transition's political context

The peculiarity of Brazil's top-down transition to democracy lies in its lengthy and protracted nature. In 1974, the then President Ernesto Geisel (1974–1979) announced the start of the so-called period of *distensão* (decompression) and *abertura* (opening), a 'slow, gradual and careful' process of political liberalization that would eventually lead to the return of a civilian government. This period of regime-led liberalization – involving loosening press censorship, decelerating repression, and the gradual revocation of draconian legal measures – would last as long as the dictatorship that had been in place by then. As the general intention of the military had been to 'restore order', the *raison d'être* of the regime had largely disappeared by 1974, when the most radical left-wing sectors had been annihilated and an 'economic miracle' performed. According to Mainwaring (1986: 153), the regime chose to liberalize 'not because of its weakness but because of its strength', as the good economic performance and the absence of a strong opposition fostered the regime's belief that it could withdraw at a minimal cost and liberalize at its own, controlled pace. Moreover, the author traces the liberalization impulse to the tensions between the military as an institution and the military as a government, as the politicization of the institution and concomitant internal divisions (especially during presidential successions) damaged its internal discipline and unity (Mainwaring 1986: 152–153). The growing autonomy of the security apparatus within the military establishment itself, together with the former's ideological radicalization, was also seen as dangerous by Geisel and his key advisors (Stepan 1988: 33). In addition, others highlight that the political opening was not independent of the loss of support of the bourgeoisie, as part of the business community started to criticize the preferential treatment given to state enterprises, Geisel's economic plan, and his centralized style of policymaking (Hagopian 1996: 11).

Geisel's time in office (1974–1979) was spent juggling the effort to contain an increasingly strong opposition, within the Congress and outside of it, and to placate the hardline opposition within the military (to whom he had to continuously demonstrate that he was in control of the opening process) (Bruneau 1992: 260). As the electoral performance of the MDB was significantly better than expected in 1974, electoral rules would be manipulatively changed ahead of the 1978 and 1982 elections in order to prevent the opposition party from controlling Congress and crucially, the electoral college. Civil society opposition would show renewed strength from 1978 onwards, with the appearance of various types of voluntary associations and social movements, such as neighboring groups, base ecclesial communities, women and black organizations, the environmentalist movement, etc. The Catholic Church, renowned associations of lawyers and journalists, and the student movement were also increasingly vocal. Particularly challenging was the reemergence of the labor movement, staging a wave of major strikes between 1978 and 1980 (mostly centered around wage demands) and launching the so-called 'new unionism', critical of government corporatist tutelage (Roett 1986: 375–376). The government would respond with a mix of 'repression, cooptation and concessions', including a wage policy reform in 1979 (Mainwaring 1986: 156). This was part of what Stepan (1988: 39) has described as a 'complex dialectic between regime concession and societal conquest', with the regime initially creating the conditions for civil society to sprout (with the Geisel administration intentionally using civil society to curb military hardliners, the author suggests), while at the same time allowing the opposition to be given a space that could force concessions in unanticipated directions. This was what happened with the 1979 Amnesty Law, which, as developed later, resulted from social mobilizations, though largely dictated in the regime's own terms. However, this first wave of popular mobilizations would not prove threatening to the regime and would decline after 1980. This is seen as a result of the regime's flexibility and capacity to use the traditional Brazilian system of (a) accommodation and cooptation of some parts and (b) control and exclusion of the most combative ones, using repression if needed (Viola and Mainwaring 1985: 205).

Apart from the 1979 Amnesty Law, the abolishment of Institutional Act Number 5, the 1979 reform of the party system (abolishing the existing two parties and allowing the creation of new ones), and the 1982 direct elections for state governors were visible and important steps in the process of opening up the political arena, despite the manipulative fashion in which they were enforced. Although the not-so-veiled intention of the 1979 party reform was the (successful) splitting of the opposition into various parties, it also had the unintended consequence of generating more opposition than anticipated, namely, with the creation of the Workers' Party (*Partido dos Trabalhadores* – PT) in 1980, born out of the 'new unionism' movement and challenging Brazil's tradition of elitist 'non-programmatic parties and pork-oriented politicians' (Nylen 2000: 127).

It was not until mid-1983 that the regime showed the first signs of political crisis and started to visibly lose its capacity to control the political process. This was first and foremost a result of divisions within the government's party, which, breaking with the previous pattern of submission to the executive and in the context of a deep economic crisis, had sectors clashing with the government over matters such as wage policy. With the president abdicating from coordinating the party campaign for the next presidential candidate, divisions over the choice of his successor were further exacerbated. It was in this context that the opposition-led campaign for direct presidential elections took over, demanding the elimination of the congressional electoral college (in which the government's party had an absolute majority) ahead of the 1985 presidential elections. The *diretas já!* movement swept Brazil's largest cities in the first months of 1984, in what was the largest wave of public demonstrations ever seen, in a rare (or perhaps unique) moment of unification of the various political and social opposition forces. Although the campaign would fail in its ultimate objective, it contributed to further eroding the legitimacy of the regime and to accentuating internal divisions (with members of the governing party supporting direct elections). The straw that broke the camel's back was the government party's endorsement of a presidential candidate despised by the more moderate party factions. These would defect and form the so-called *Liberal Front*, which would enter into an agreement with the largest party in the opposition – the successor to the MDB, now called PMDB (Brazilian Democratic Movement Party) – and support the opposition's presidential candidate, Tancredo Neves. In exchange, the defectors from the government's party would nominate the vice-president, José Sarney, and benefit from an 'equitable distribution' of government and administrative posts (Hagopian 1990: 158). This agreement was crucial in changing the correlation of forces within the electoral college, paving the way for the takeover of a civilian president in January 1985.

Note that Tancredo Neves was coming from the moderate opposition to the regime and was generally seen as a reasonable and flexible politician, gaining the support of most of the political spectrum and proving to be an acceptable candidate to a large part of the military hierarchy. He worked hard towards persuading the military not to intervene, namely, when it came to providing the assurance that there would be no persecution of military leaders (Mainwaring 1986: 168). This was one of the top concerns of the military at a time in which prosecutions had already been initiated in Argentina. Neves's commitment in this regard appears to have been enough to earn him the support of important military figures linked to ex-President Geisel as early as September 1984, including Geisel himself (Dimenstein 1985 quoted in Maciel 1999: 373). There are reports of various meetings between Tancredo and several military ministers in the months preceding the January 1985 electoral college, including the minister of the army, who took concrete steps to prevent a coup attempt when sidelining a few hardliners (*Veja*, 16 January 1985, quoted in Maciel 1999: 382). In a dramatic twist of events, Tancredo's death (due to illness) in April 1985 meant that his Vice-President José Sarney would take over, an unfortunate event for those who desired a greater break with the past, since in contrast to Tancredo, Sarney had been a supporter of the military regime and a member of the regime's party until 1984.

Linz and Stepan (1996: 168–169) are right to point out that the military organization was 'able to extract a high price for extrication', best visible in the fact that there were six military ministers in the cabinet of the first civilian president (1985–1990), and in the clear interference of the military on a whole range of issues at the time, for instance, playing a major role in the agrarian reform and unilaterally deciding whether military units were used to quell strikes. Moreover, the armed forces kept control over the Intelligence Service and defense issues, as well as autonomy in regulating their own affairs (Hagopian 1990: 155–156). Military influence over the 1987–1988

Constituent Assembly was also significant, succeeding in 'subverting most of the proposed constitutional clauses that would have curtailed military autonomy' and joining forces with President Sarney in preventing the move from presidentialism to a parliamentary or semi-parliamentary political system, in another sad demonstration of what a mix of 'pork-barrel payoffs and threats' can achieve in Brazil (Linz and Stepan 1996: 169). Fortunately for Brazil's democracy, and as Hunter (2000) develops at length, civilian authority over the military has increased considerably since the end of Sarney's presidency and throughout the 1990s, with President Cardoso in 1999 finally creating a unified and civilian-led Ministry of Defense. The armed forces' tutelage over Sarney's presidency is yet another reason to endorse the claim that the transition in Brazil was not complete until 1990, when the first directly elected president assumed office.

The transition's (mostly) unified memory regime

Brazil's memory regime during the transition period was neither as conflictual as the Uruguayan nor as consensual as the Spanish. If it definitely comes closer to the latter – given that accountability was far from a salient concern at both social and political levels – there were nonetheless a few dissenting voices (to a greater extent than in Spain). This was especially the case during the period of greater strength of the amnesty movement (1978–1979), prior to the adoption of the amnesty law (1979). Brazil's memory context was, however, shaped by the peculiarity of having an amnesty law approved at a much earlier point in time during the transition – when the military regime was still fully in control – and thus, the unfavorable balance of the time is clear in taking its toll on pro-accountability demands. This meant not only that there was little political space for dissenting voices, but that the subsequent dissolution of the amnesty movement left the remaining pro-accountability voices largely isolated. Both social and political actors moved on to focus on other business at a time when the democratic transition was not yet guaranteed and political parties were in a process of construction.

In understanding the social and political isolation of the few pro-accountability voices in Brazil, the highly top-down nature of the transition to democracy and the overall weakness and fragmentation of the left-wing opposition are the primary and most obvious factors, though not the only ones. Also relevant in accounting for the lack of social and political salience of the issue in Brazil are factors such as (a) the level of lethal repression, which was comparatively smaller in Brazil; (b) the targeted nature of the most brutal forms of repression, directed at radical left violent groups that furthermore suffered from (c) weakness, fragmentation, social isolation, and stigmatization; and finally, (d) the abundance of other serious human rights concerns that went far beyond political violence. These and other aspects are developed in the following.

The 1979 Amnesty Law

It was in the context of Brazil's 'slow, gradual, and careful' opening, and at a time when a variety of social movements and voluntary associations were emerging, that the amnesty movement appeared and took off. The timing of this movement, and of the 1979 Amnesty Law, is crucial in placing the debate over transitional justice in Brazil in context, because unlike in Uruguay and Spain, the amnesty bill would not be approved by a legitimately elected democratic parliament, and the amnesty movement would lose its strength long before the transition to a civilian presidency. The regime's leaders would get their way and approve a half-hearted amnesty law, from which those who had been convicted for 'blood crimes' were excluded, going against the amnesty movement's call for a 'broad, general, and unrestricted amnesty'. Moreover, the law included a clause that, despite the relatively ambiguous wording, provided a cover for the crimes of state agents, going against the movement's expressed desire for a non-reciprocal amnesty. Nonetheless, by allowing the return of thousands of persons who had been exiled – including preeminent politicians and intellectuals – the reintegration of those who had been banished, and the release of those condemned for non-violent political crimes, Law 6.683 (28 August 1979) was commemorated as a victory of the opposition and proved sufficient to produce a demobilization effect, in yet another example of how the 'dialectic between regime concession and societal conquest' has been used by Brazilian elites to accommodate *some* social demands and in this way, break or weaken a movement. The demands of the families of the dead or disappeared – which had been incorporated by the amnesty movement – were left unfulfilled, with the demobilization of the movement taking its toll on the families who still hoped for some form of *truth* and *justice*, leaving them feeling largely isolated.

Although the calls for amnesty were not entirely novel by then, the movement gained strength in the second half of the 1970s, initially motivated by the families of political prisoners. Pro-amnesty associations would start popping up throughout Brazil as well as in countries with a significant presence of the exiled community. Some events would contribute to making political repression a more salient issue at the time. The first was the brutal death of the then head of journalism of *TV Cultura*, Vladimir Herzog, at the end of 1975, a victim of torture. This created much public commotion, as it became clear that the official suicide story was a cover-up, leading to a week-long protest strike in the University of São Paulo (with more than 30,000 participants) and to an ecumenical service in São Paulo's cathedral attended by more than 8,000 people. The second was the international sources of condemnation of human rights violations in Brazil, most notably by the Carter administration in 1977.

It is in this context that amnesty claims become a commonly heard demand. In 1978, the Brazilian Amnesty Committees (CBA) were created with the intention of coordinating pro-amnesty actions in the various states where CBAs were formed. The First National Congress for Amnesty took place in November 1978, gathering 21 amnesty groups; by the time of their third national meeting in June 1979, there were a total of 45 regional entities (Greco 2003). The amnesty demand became highly visible, with public rallies, posters, banners, stickers, and pamphlets appearing in Brazil's streets and in highly visible places such as football stadiums (Mezarobba 2010: 10). Prisoners' hunger strikes would also be used to raise public attention and increase the pressure over the regime. Moreover, and importantly in giving the movement political access and visibility, it attracted the support of notable social and political segments, such as high-profile intellectuals and political figures – including the president of the MDB and various opposition representatives – as well as the National Conference of Bishops of Brazil, the Brazilian Press Association, the Brazilian Bar Association, and the Brazilian Society for the Advancement of Science (Mezarobba 2003: 21).

In fact, there is a visible class dimension associated with the amnesty struggle. In a country where fewer than 2% of young people had access to higher education at the time, estimates indicate that over half of political prisoners had a complete or incomplete university degree (Greco 2003). This is probably why the movement had a hard time connecting with more 'popular movements', whose demands were less political (Greco 2003). The testimony of Lula da Silva, at the time president of one of the most vocal Workers' Unions, is illuminating in this regard. Speaking of his first reaction to contact from a movement representative, he recalls saying: 'Amnesty does not fill the workers' bellies (...), that is not a priority for us' (quoted in Del Porto 2009). Lula furthermore recounts how he had previously thought the prisoners were common criminals, in accordance with the regime's rhetoric. Though his union would end up supporting the amnesty banner, Lula's reaction is indicative of the reasons why the amnesty movement did not penetrate the popular sectors to a greater extent.

As mentioned, the movement's recurring call was for a 'broad, general, and unrestricted amnesty': broad, meaning that it would cover all who had been punished by the repressive acts of the regime; general, in that it would be applied without examination of the merit of the crimes committed; and unrestricted, because it would not impose any conditions upon the beneficiaries (Ferreira 1979: 72 quoted in Schneider 2018: 19). Besides the release of political prisoners and the return and reintegration of those who had been banished or who had fled, the movement's demands gravitated around putting an end to the regime's repressive apparatus. This included the end of the use of torture and the revocation of the National Security Law, a banner that was intimately linked to the return of 'democratic freedoms', as the movement often claimed. Moreover, and when it comes to the specific cases of those who had died or disappeared at the hands of state agents, demands for (a) clarification of the circumstances under which they had occurred and (b) judicial accountability for such crimes were also part of the written resolutions and the 'minimum action program' of the movement's national congress (Greco 2003: 99). However, as these were the most maximalist demands and the ones that, pragmatically speaking, were the least likely to be considered, many within the amnesty movement – including those within the opposition party in Congress – were keen on dropping them in exchange for a compromise solution (Schneider 2010: 3; Fico 2010). Others were openly critical: a preeminent political prisoners' lawyer and MDB congressman was caught saying that 'one does not speak of a Nuremberg Tribunal while the Gestapo is in power' (Alves 1983: 186 quoted in Teles 2011: 443).

Unsurprisingly, the government's proposed bill, submitted to Congress at the end of June 1979, did not meet the main movement's call and had a clause specifically excluding those who were convicted for crimes of 'terrorism, robbery, kidnapping and physical attack' (Art.1 §2). President Figueiredo justified the amnesty's scope with the reasoning that terrorism is not a political crime, though at the same time declaring that ongoing judicial procedures for those same crimes would come to a halt. The initiative was framed by the president in a language of 'pacification', 'disarmament of spirits', and 'democratic coexistence' (Message No° 59 of 1979 in Congresso Nacional 1982: 21–23).

Moreover, article 1 of the proposed bill conceded an amnesty to 'political crimes or connected to them' (*crimes conexos*), defined as 'crimes of any nature related to political crimes or practiced for political motives' (art.1 §1). Although this formulation was ambiguous, attentive observers did not fail to notice that the veiled intent of this clause was to provide a cover for the crimes of state agents. Even though this was not the main focus of the debates at the time – which were, rather, centered on the inclusion or exclusion of the crimes mentioned in article 1 §2 – this was nonetheless an object of discussion at the time, most notably within the bi-partisan Amnesty Committee (*Comissão Mista sobre Anistia*), created in Congress to discuss and review the amnesty bill and the hundreds of proposed amendments submitted by members of Congress (Fico 2010; Schneider 2018).

Debates on who was to be included or excluded from the law originated a matrix of possible combinations, including: (1) a general amnesty for political prisoners, which was non-reciprocal, that is, which did not include state agents – the preferred outcome of the amnesty movement; (2) a general and reciprocal amnesty – which in the eyes of many in the opposition, would already be a great achievement given the political circumstances; (3) a partial amnesty for political prisoners (not covering 'blood crimes') in which state agents would not be covered either – a possibility that was considered but did not receive much support, given that the scope of the amnesty for political prisoners was the primary concern, more so than the inclusion or exclusion of state agents; (4) a partial amnesty for political prisoners that would cover state agents – the preferred option of the regime, and the one that would triumph. It is nonetheless quite remarkable that the Congress vote on two other options – one making amnesty general and non-reciprocal (option 1) and the other general and reciprocal (option 2) – came surprisingly close, with some ARENA deputies defecting (Schneider 2018: 30).

The discussions within the Congress's Amnesty Committee are one of the best sources when it comes to assessing the terms of the political debate at the time on the matters of concern here. Though there was much rhetorical emphasis on 'pardoning', 'pacification', 'disarming the spirits', and 'unifying Brazilians' (which was a rhetorically wise position in light of the opposition's desire to have all types of political crimes included), several MDB representatives were outraged not only at the exclusion of crimes of terrorism and others in art.1 §2, but also at the inclusion of the crimes of state agents. One of the boldest examples of that was the justification given to amendment no. 8, which was undersigned by a total of 19 congressmen:

> We defend an amnesty for every prisoner, pensioner, banished person (...), exiled, those who rebelled and reacted against the terrorism of repression. Before 1964 there was no terrorism in Brazil. This is a historical truth that will be studied in the future, the causes of what has been so often called subversive terrorism. (...) But the law aims to give to the executioners, the torturers, those who unleashed the storm, those who provoked despair and revolt – the sacred revolt of so many – an amnesty they do not deserve, and this would be a mockery of justice and human dignity. Those who should be sitting in the dock cannot be the judges. Amnesty has to be broad, general and unrestricted, for all the victims of the dictatorship and the crimes of repression.
>
> (Congresso Nacional 1982: 77)

It is striking to see a group of 19 congressmen undersigning this statement, which not only directly blamed the regime for the actions of the armed opposition but went as far as to suggest that those dictating the terms of the amnesty should be facing criminal justice. This was far from a majoritarian position, but it is illustrative of the fact that Brazil's memory regime was not as consensual as it appears on the surface. A few other representatives within the Congress's Amnesty Committee went in similar directions:

> Society has spoken on behalf of the investigation of those crimes. And not with an intent of revenge; not with an intent of torturing the torturer, murder the murderer, kidnap the kidnapper, or disappear the ones who it made disappear. But investigation of those crimes will allow society to, knowing the depth of such horrors, not permit their repetition ever again in our country.
>
> (Marcelo Cerqueira and Modesto Silveira in Congresso Nacional 1982: 134)

> To the error of wanting a half amnesty, (...) the government adds the one of not mentioning an explicit exclusion of torturers. It's an attack on peace and national reconciliation. How could it be allowed that those who persecuted, tortured, and killed coldly and perversely go unpunished? (...) National consciousness claims for the punishment of common criminals.
>
> (José Carlos Vasconcellos in Congresso Nacional 1982: 151)

A glimpse at the Brazilian press at the time suggests that this debate was not confined to the walls of Congress, and the media were openly covering it. Two leading figures of the MDB at the time openly stated, for example, that 'torture is a problem subject to common justice, amnesty for political crimes and impunity for common crimes should not be confounded' (Franco Montoro quoted in *Folha de S. Paulo* 1979a) or that 'torturers are public agents who committed abuses, there is no political motive in their actions' (Ulysses Guimarães quoted in *Folha de S. Paulo* 1979b).

Nevertheless, given the balance of power at the time, everyone was realistically aware that the government would get its way when approving the amnesty bill, despite the intensification of the pressure of the amnesty movement in August 1979. Representatives of the MDB had said themselves that, realistically speaking, a partial amnesty would already be a great achievement (Greco 2003: 121). Even those actively engaged in civil society initiatives dealing with the denunciation of repression and the protection of human rights were ready to accept concessions in exchange for a greater good:

> We knew it would be inevitable to accept limitations and admit that criminals within the government, or protected by it, escaped the punishment they justly deserved, but we considered that it was convenient to accept this, given the ensuing benefits for the political prosecuted and their families and the fact that we would have back our companions.
>
> (Dalmo Dallari – member of the Justice and Peace Commission – quoted in Fico 2010: 332)

Despite a highly heated debate in Congress (with both military men and pro-amnesty activists in the audience), most MDB representatives would end up voting in favor of the government's amnesty proposal – thus contributing to the perceived legitimacy of this law and, in the words of Fico (2010: 333), 'sealing the foundational pact of the transition'. MDB representatives underlined, nonetheless, that they would keep on fighting for a general, broad, and unrestricted amnesty. The topic would indeed remain on the agenda for some time, though it would inevitably die out as the revision of the National Security Law the year before, together with presidential pardons (*indultos*) in November and December 1979, would end up benefiting those who had been punished for the gravest crimes, too (Mezarobba 2003: 46). As President Figueiredo himself announced, his project 'reopen[ed] the field of political action', allowing the return of political militants to political life – including major figures of the opposition – in line with the announced party reform (and with the regime's self-interested intent of fragmenting the opposition). For this reason, many would surely share the opinion, written in the editorial page of *Folha de S. Paulo* (1979c) after the law's approval, that 'a cold and unpassionate analysis shows an overall positive balance, with the reintegration of new national forces in the political bodies deciding the future of the country. In this sense, popular pressure (...) had a highly constructive impact.'

The families of the dead and disappeared: an isolated and marginal struggle

Although the Amnesty movement would still organize a National Congress in November 1979 – in which, among other things, there were talks of creating a tribunal for denouncing the crimes of the dictatorship – there were already signs and concern over what would quickly become a reality: the demobilization and 'atomization' of the movement. There was for many a sense that their mission had been largely accomplished. Those who did not feel that this was the case – in essence, some of the families of those who had died or disappeared (hereafter referred to as 'families') – complained, in one of the last amnesty meetings in 1980, that the issue of 'crimes of the dictatorship and their direct executioners has been treated, at the very least, in a careless manner by the amnesty movement' (Greco 2003: 349). The blow the Amnesty Law caused to the families is visible when looking at the emotive reaction of Suzana Lisbôa in Congress on the day of the law's approval, when she defiantly shouted that she wanted the body of her husband back (Mezarobba 2003: 64). As Lisbôa herself recounts: 'the impact of the amnesty law on the cause of the families was very strong. (...) A lot of people demobilized. (...) We felt very abandoned at the time' (Interview quoted in Gallo 2012: 334). Similar feelings were conveyed by another family member:

> In 1979, with the amnesty, the exiled come back, some prisoners are released (...) and the amnesty movement is over, because the only people that did not come back were the disappeared. We [the families] kept on fighting, but without an organization that would allow us to go after information. In the meantime, we were 'shooting in every direction', but without an organization.
>
> (Interview BR1)

Although some families would still count on the support of CBAs and members of the Catholic Church to organize a first expedition to the Araguaia region in 1980 – in search of the bodies of the disappeared there – most other doors seemed closed at the time. Not only did they lack a unified organization that would speak for their cause – at least, up until the constitution of the group *Tortura Nunca Mais* in 1985[1] – but it was also unclear what could be done besides claiming the right to an investigation, given the political context of the time.

Letters to Figueiredo's administration were invariably left without an answer. Families of the Araguaia guerrilla would open a legal case against the Federal Union in 1982 – to locate the bodies, clarify the circumstances, and provide access to information held by the armed forces – but the first (negative) verdict would not come out until 1989, and after various stages of appeal, the families would have to wait until 2003 for a first favorable verdict (Santos 2010). One family member recounts how at the time she wanted to open a legal action against one specific torturer, but that she could not find a lawyer who would support her case because 'they all said we would lose, it would be a waste of time'; she further recalls that a different lawyer refused to take up her case, accusing her of being a 'terrorist' (Interview BR18). In a testimony to the National Truth Commission, a former judge who was interrogated about judicial inertia similarly stated: 'do you genuinely believe there was any possibility of trying to open a legal case against a police or military authority at the time?' (CNV 2014: 949). Besides the early approval of the Amnesty Law, families were faced with other legal barriers. Suzana Lisbôa describes how lawyers pointed out to her that the prescription period for illicit acts committed while on public duty was of five years only (quoted in Mezarobba 2007: 343).

It is, however, striking to note that not all judicial doors were closed during the dictatorship – a few families and their lawyers, aware of the impossibility of conducting criminal processes, opted instead for filing civil declaratory actions of responsibility of the Federal Union. The first instance in which a judge was bold enough to rule in favor of a family was in 1978 in a case opened by the Herzog family, who sought to disconfirm the official version of suicide and hold the Federal Union responsible for Herzog's illegal imprisonment, torture, and death, with the concomitant recognition of the duty to provide reparation to the family (CNV 2014: 950). This was, however, not enough to create a wave of denunciations or judicial proceedings that could have caused great embarrassment to the regime. The fact that the Amnesty Law came as early as 1979 meant that judicial doors were closed before any realistic attempt at opening criminal processes could be made, in contrast to what happened in Uruguay.

Moreover, families of the dead and disappeared in Brazil did not benefit from close connections with an emerging network of human rights activism. Although church-based groups were initially engaged in helping out the families and political prisoners during the harshest repressive period, this did not translate into support for accountability demands later on. While in Uruguay and Argentina the human rights banner became intimately associated with the issue of the dead and disappeared, the same did not happen in Brazil, where a growing and diversified human rights network took advantage of the climate of political liberalization in the early 1980s to bring other human rights concerns to the fore, especially focused on the most marginalized sectors of society. This has naturally to be put in the context of a country with a hugely inegalitarian economic system, where large segments of the population did not enjoy the most basic social and economic rights. Poverty, rising crime and police violence, treatment of common prisoners, basic sanitation, housing, and health care were among the many concerns of the existing and emerging human rights groups. Note that the human rights agenda in Brazil accompanied, to an extent, the existing waves of mobilization. While the amnesty movement was in line with the existing concern over the situation of political prisoners and the recovery of civil and political liberties, the demobilization of this movement in 1979 occurred at the same time as a growing working-class movement put an emphasis on economic and social rights instead.

This shift was noticeable not only at a general level but also within the church-based groups that had engaged in the defense of political prisoners. The Justice and Peace Commission of the S. Paulo Archdiocese had been the most active in this regard, created in 1972 by Archbishop Dom Paulo Evaristo Arns – one of the most outspoken critics of repression – to give a response to the growing numbers of families and friends who sought his help. Recording testimonies, denouncing abuses in the press, and assisting the families in a number of ways (such as helping locate prisoners or offering legal advice) were the Commission's main activities (Pope 1985: 436). As Amanda Pope (1985: 441) recounts in detail, from 1978 onwards, 'the Justice and Peace Commission felt compelled to reorient its dialogue and scope of activity' in light of a changing sociopolitical context, the growing working-class movement, and an expanding network of human rights activism in which church or church-affiliated entities that focused on the marginalized sectors became more prominent. In this context, the Justice and Peace Commission said it would 'give special emphasis to working with the periphery and the base communities' and assumed as its most urgent task the 'verticalization of the *abertura*, in the sense of extending its gains to the marginalized sectors also' (quoted in Pope 1985: 444). Despite this, it is worth noting that the S. Paulo Archdiocese was behind the most significant investigative effort at the time – the *Brasil Nunca Mais* (Brazil Never Again) report, published in 1985.[2]

The lack of engagement of the human rights community with the issue of investigation and accountability for the crimes of the dictatorship has, therefore, to be understood both in light of a weak family/victims' movement whose demands appeared unrealistic at the time and the prominence of other major human rights concerns. Note that torture in police stations, maltreatment of common prisoners, and police violence towards the most marginalized sectors of society were common and widespread practices in Brazil.

Moreover, the general social isolation of the families in Brazil – in comparison to other Latin American contexts – cannot be dissociated from the characteristics of repression as well as the characteristics of the radical left groups most affected by lethal repression, namely, their weakness, fragmentation, and social isolation. To begin with, severe forms of repression were highly selective and in part judicialized, which meant that in a country of continental dimensions, such as Brazil, the killings and disappearances of a few hundred were not enough either to prompt a large and unified family movement or to attract the sympathy of large social segments. The fact that non-lethal violations were vastly greater in number than lethal ones meant that the early approval of the Amnesty Law – with its release of prisoners and reintegration of those banished or in exile – resulted in the demobilization of most sectors who had come together to denounce the repressive apparatus and demand an amnesty law. As in other cases where disappearances were used as a repressive tool, the families of the disappeared were the ones who attempted to keep the issue alive, as 'back in the early 1980s, many families still carried hopes a disappeared person could be found alive' (Interview BR12). However, the fact that the number of disappearances revolved around 200 precludes from the start the appearance of a strong and unified family movement, on top of a political and social context that was entirely unfavorable.

In addition, apart from a few cases that attracted more attention and created greater embarrassment for the regime, such as the one of Vladimir Herzog, a large portion of the remaining lethal victims were associated with radical and violent left-wing groups – catalogued by the regime as terrorists – who were themselves highly fragmented and socially isolated. Rather than one large guerrilla group (such as the Tupamaros in Uruguay or the Montoneros in Argentina), the leftist guerrilla movement in Brazil was 'composed of dozens of revolutionary groups, the majority being small organizations with a few hundred militants with no real firepower' (Napolitano 2018). These were mostly splinter groups from the Brazilian Communist Party (PCB), which had decided against using violent tactics. They had a very meager social basis of support, largely 'concentrated in the more radical segments of the student movement' and with little or no support among the workers and peasants they aimed to speak for (Napolitano 2018). This is to say that most lethal victims came from a minority of young, urban, middle-class Brazilians, whose social revolutionary aims never enjoyed much popular sympathy (Reis 2004 quoted in Schneider 2011: 46). The consequence of this is not only that they lacked a significant social and political basis of support that would vindicate their memory later on, but also that their families would have to deal with the social stigma associated with the armed struggle.

> Many people within the left itself thought in the way the military did: 'blood crimes' are absurd, those who engaged in the armed struggle are terrorists. Repression separated between terrorists and subversive.
>
> (Interview BR1)

A paradigmatic case in this regard was that of the Araguaia guerrilla, the most significant attempt at armed struggle in Brazil (led by the PCdoB, which had earlier split with the PCB) and the group that holds the most significant share of those who disappeared. Its (literal) isolation meant that the families would first of all have trouble in proving the guerrilla actually existed; and second, that the 'families of the Araguaia' appeared very often as a separate group rather than part of a broader and unified family movement. In the words of one of them, when referring to her time as a militant of the amnesty movement:

> No one believed there had been a guerrilla in Araguaia, we were very isolated, it seemed like a conversation of fools (...) The left did not know there was an Araguaia, they thought we were crazy. I had all my companions dead and missing.
>
> (Interview BR18)

Political isolation

The isolation of the families of the dead and disappeared from political organizations – including the ones they or their family members had once fought for – cannot be dissociated from the unfavorable political context at the time. Not only was it entirely unrealistic to make accountability demands, but the opposition was too busy reorganizing itself. An emerging 'new left' was in a process of creation – and was keen on distinguishing itself from the 'old left' – whereas the surviving left-wing political groups were weak and fragmented, and seemed eager to avoid the stigma associated with armed action and social revolutionary goals. The fact that existing radical left groups were small, fragmented, and socially isolated – in contrast to a stronger, unified, and socially rooted left-wing movement in Uruguay – meant that the dictatorship was largely successful in eliminating or disarticulating many of them. This was not the case for the two Communist parties, but they too remained divided and weak, having to deal with the decimation of part of their ranks and continuous clandestine activity up until 1985. The period of transition to democracy in Brazil was for them a period of soul-searching and identity crisis, as their ideological and social isolation became evident. Their strategy was, rather, one of moderation, institutionalization, and integration into political life, and those who had engaged in armed struggle – such as the PCdoB in Araguaia – were keen on avoiding the social stigmatization that came with it at a time in which social revolutionary ideas were in crisis (Greco 2003: 382). Even those who had not engaged in violent tactics, such as the PCB, positioned themselves against 'revanchism', which, in the words of the party's leader at the time, 'would complicate the democratic process' (Maciel 1999: 373). In the words of one family member:

> The party which we fought for [*Partido Comunista do Brasil* – PCdoB] changed its politics completely – they wanted to ignore what they had done, they did not want to discuss their participation in the armed struggle, they were already trying to articulate themselves in order to participate in political life and get elected.
>
> (Interview BR18)

The social isolation and identity crisis of the 'old left' (to which many ex-political prisoners refer in Teles's [2011: 447] oral history project) is visible and perhaps further aggravated in the drain of intellectuals and militants to other party formations, including the newly founded Workers' Party (PT), to which the Communist parties were largely antagonistic. Note that even though the PT attracted and incorporated some of the old left-wing militants, it was born out of a vacant political space within the labor movement and was keen on creating its own new brand of politics. The reason why the PT attracted considerable attention at the time was not so much because of its initial results (electing 16 out of 559 federal representatives in 1986) as because it was such an anomaly in Brazilian politics, being born out of union activism and focusing on a 'democratic socialist' approach to bring the excluded to a highly elitist political scene. The popular sectors the PT was coming from, and whom it intended to represent, were in turn distant from the social revolutionary/middle-class left most affected by repression during the dictatorship. Though it is possible to spot a reference to the 'investigation of torture, political persecutions and police arbitrariness, and punishment of those responsible' in one of its founding documents, this appears to be an isolated demand.[3] Its focus on the working class and the marginalized sectors of society meant that when speaking of the dictatorship's oppressive treatment, its emphasis was on the violations of workers' rights (related to strikes, wages, labor conditions, unions' freedoms, etc.) and their concomitant social and economic exploitation by the business classes in alliance with the military dictatorship.[4]

Moreover, whereas in other countries the transition to a democratic regime brought back the same old party formations – which had kept some form of organization during the clandestine times and already had strong identities and social ties before – the same cannot be said about Brazil. Brazil's tradition had been one of underdeveloped parties, mostly created from above, and with weak and malleable identities (Mainwaring 1988). Partially as a consequence of this, and of the maintenance of a restricted party system during the dictatorship, the major players of the transition were essentially those who had either been an integral part of the dictatorial regime or had been allowed by it. This also means that the transition period was a time of creation and definition of party identities, namely, for the left, which was still dealing with the same old problems of fragmentation and weakness and was focused on becoming a relevant player of the political game.

As Keck (2010) notes, the transition period was one of ambiguity and lack of clear political projects, characterized by a state of flux in which there were no well-defined organizational agents, who, more than occupying a political space, had to actually create it. Writing in 1988, Mainwaring (1988: 98–99) was still apprehensive about whether truly competitive parties 'can and are being constructed' in Brazil, noting that the rapid growth of a party like the PT is hindered by

> Brazil's highly elitist political culture, the difficulties of the labor movement in overcoming corporatist mechanisms (...), the fact that the industrial labor force is a smaller percentage of the economically active population than was the case in the European countries during the formation of mass labor parties, and the profoundly conservative nature of Brazil's transition to democracy.

Though his concerns would later prove mostly unwarranted, the fact is that conditions in the 1980s were not propitious to the cause of the families. This is, first of all, because of the more obvious facts that the families were few and political players were not interested in adopting a confrontational position towards the military at a delicate time, but also because the left was weak and in a process of construction. Its priorities were (re)organization, integration into political life, and the establishment of social ties with constituencies for whom the dictatorship's repressive apparatus was far from being a concern.

> Left wing forces were focused on trying to re-organize themselves, a lot of us were involved in forming the Workers' Party at the time. We did not speak much about punishment for the armed forces, it was a bit of a forgotten issue.
>
> (Interview BR4)

> The left went to take care of its business, organize political parties. No political party ever dared to raise the issue of the disappeared, it's an 'indigestible' issue because it involves directly the military.
>
> (Interview BR1)

It is nonetheless relevant to point out that Tancredo Neves, the indirectly elected president who would die before taking office, had shown some sympathy towards the families' cause and had in fact received a delegation of the Araguaia families in his office in 1984. During the amnesty discussions, he had already presented one amendment to the amnesty bill in which a police investigation on the disappearances was proposed (Mezarobba 2003: 63). Although it is unclear how much margin of maneuver he would actually have had, the families naturally considered his death and replacement by Sarney an unfortunate event. In an interview by Mezarobba (2007: 337), Sarney would state:

> I can assure you that the transition negotiated by Dr. Tancredo (...) was very careful in not allowing for any type of revanchism – either on the left or on the right. (...) Tancredo would surely not take any radical position, he was very afraid of a reversal.

When asked about his administration's stance, Sarney states that 'it was not an issue on the political agenda', though he also mentions that 'it would not be prudent at the moment' and that the 'military hid the issue, there was no information' (Mezarobba 2007: 337–338).

From bones to reparations

It often takes an external and accidental event to bring an issue onto the public and political agenda and/or to give interested sectors the necessary impulse to force an issue (back) into the public scene. This is the more so if it is an emotionally charged event. In the case of the disappeared and their relatives, the recovery of bodies is definitely such an event. This is what happened in Brazil, where the discovery of a mass grave in September 1990 would contribute to the first (timid) investigative steps both at the local level and in the National Congress, where the families were able to find and count on the support of a few key political allies. The initial impulse came from a journalistic investigation on police violence in the city of São Paulo, when a reporter found out about a clandestine mass grave dating back to the 1970s in a cemetery in São Paulo's periphery (Perus), where a few political prisoners had been buried together with thousands of indigents. In the words of a family member, 'there was a political advancement with the opening of the Perus grave; people started to believe that our claims were true, that there were indeed political disappearances' (Interview BR18). The discovery attracted media attention, and the then mayor of the city of São Paulo, a PT representative – Luiza Erundina – showed critical support for the families, creating a Special Commission for the Investigation of the Remains together with a Commission of Inquiry, stimulating similar investigations in other cemeteries and cities (Cano and Ferreira 2006: 107–108; Gallo 2012: 337). The group *Tortura Nunca Mais* would be behind similar efforts to open other clandestine graves, leading to the discovery of another 14 bodies of political prisoners in a cemetery in Rio and 6 in Recife (Mezarobba 2003: 74). It was in the sequence of these events that a PT representative in Congress, deputy Nilmário Miranda (who had himself been a political prisoner for over three years), proposed the creation of an External Commission for the Search of the Disappeared. Its goal was to follow the ongoing investigations and help the families in their search for information. This commission would function from 1991 until 1994, and despite lacking binding powers, it would carry out investigations that allowed the discovery of the fate of a few of the disappeared. It also managed to get hold of documents from the armed forces that led to the first official recognition of the existence of the Araguaia guerrilla group (Cano and Ferreira 2006: 107).

The opening of the Perus grave also prompted the families to exercise greater pressure towards the opening of military and police archives, a request they made directly to the president at the time, Fernando Collor (Teles 2001: 170). He would follow up on his promise and order the transfer of the archives of the extinct Department of Political and Social Order (the main repressive agency of the dictatorship) to the respective state governments, where they would then become public. This would be the most significant step taken by Collor's government (1990–1992) – from whom the families did not expect much, given his conservative past (namely, as a member of the military regime's party up until 1985) – in what was otherwise a very eventful presidency, marked by radical measures to fight Brazil's chronic hyperinflation crisis and ridden by corruption scandals that would lead to Collor's impeachment. He would be replaced in 1993 and 1994 by his vice-president, Itamar Franco, who would put in place a grand stabilization plan (*Plano Real*) that in 1994 would finally put an end to the hyperinflation crisis.

In 1993, the families – now officially organized in the *Comissão de Familiares de Mortos e Desaparecidos Políticos* (CFMDP), simply known as *Familiares* – together with human rights groups and the External Commission for the Search of the Disappeared, held a national meeting in which they drafted a bill proposing the creation of a commission to study the deaths and disappearances on a case-by-case basis (Teles 2001: 180). The proposal seems to have been accepted by the then minister of justice but did not obtain an answer from President Itamar Franco. Nilmário Miranda would try to renegotiate a different law with the executive, providing for the payment of pensions to the victims' relatives. The president conceded at first, only to go back on his word after facing some resistance on the part of the military (Mezarobba 2003: 78). The fact that his successor, Fernando Henrique Cardoso, showed greater openness towards the cause and a greater determination to go against an unfavorable opinion coming from military agents shows (once again) that political representatives do matter. His past as an opponent of the dictatorial regime and renowned social sciences academic – who had been banished from teaching in Brazil and who had spent time in exile – also placed greater expectations on him than on any previous president. The families and other external sources of pressure would, once again, make sure the issue was part of his agenda.

The reparations program and its antecedents

Nothing in Cardoso's electoral program could have enabled one to foresee what would become informally known as the Law on the Dead and Disappeared (Law 9.140/95), establishing a reparations program for their relatives. Though Cardoso would later give assurance that he was personally committed to the question, there were also a series of events in early 1995 (before the first announcement that the government was studying a draft bill, made at the end of May) that sent Cardoso constant reminders about this issue and in all likelihood, played an important agenda-setting role. To begin with, the families made sure that presidential candidates would not forget about them during the electoral campaign, delivering a 'letter of intent' (*Carta Compromisso*) in which they asked for some of the same things they and Nilmário Miranda had already proposed to Itamar Franco, namely, the official recognition of the state's responsibility for the imprisonment, death, and disappearance of political opponents and the creation of a special investigative and reparatory commission (Mezarobba 2007: 48). The first sign of encouragement came in August 1994, when a representative of the president signed the families' letter. Secondly, pressure would also come from the newly created Permanent Commission of Human Rights in the Chamber of Deputies, presided over by Nilmário Miranda. Miranda himself recounts how in their second meeting, on 8 March 1995, they met the then minister of justice, Nelson Jobim (who had himself been a part of the External Commission for the Search of the Disappeared), and presented a human rights agenda, in which the recognition of the state responsibility for the political deaths and disappearances was the top issue (Miranda 2006). By the beginning of April, the press was already announcing that the Human Rights Commission was preparing a draft bill (*Folha de S. Paulo* 1995).

Thirdly, Cardoso would be confronted with international pressures in at least two other instances. One was at the end of March when meeting the president of Amnesty International, Pierre Sané, who declared himself 'extremely disappointed' with the attitude of the president on the issue of the disappeared, adding that Cardoso did not show 'enthusiasm' when declaring the issue 'too complicated' (Souza 1995). Sané also stated that 'one cannot declare to have a compromise with an issue and not attempt to resolve it'. These declarations suggest that at that point, Cardoso did not yet have a clear policy plan, though it is also possible that Sané was referring to the position of the president on the issue of criminal responsibility for the perpetrators, which was a top demand of Amnesty International. The Office of the President promptly replied to these declarations, saying that Cardoso had been misunderstood by Sané, perhaps because of a language issue (doubtful in light of Cardoso's reputation in English-speaking academic circles) (Souza 1995). The fact that the president was clearly irritated by Sané's declarations shows he was not indifferent to the issue, though.

Another instance causing embarrassment to Cardoso was in a meeting with intellectuals and academics in Washington, when later in April, a Brazilian professor at George Mason University confronted him with the case of her disappeared brother, asking emotionally about the whereabouts of his body and the circumstances of his death. Cardoso replied that relatives had the right to information and compensation, but that such information was not in his hands, though he would try to investigate her brother's case (Silva 1995). A new family/human rights campaign would start just a few weeks later (Neri 1995a), on the same day that the well-known writer/journalist Marcelo Rubens Paiva – son of a disappeared congressman who had been a personal friend of Cardoso – published an article in a widely circulated magazine (*Veja*), which is said to have struck a chord with Cardoso (Mezarobba 2007: 54). In this article, he questioned the president's apparent lack of commitment and recalled the fond words of the 'friend, professor and sociologist Fernando Henrique Cardoso', who had written about Rubens Paiva in 1981, in a text in which he made a plea to 'never forget'. The fact that Rubens Paiva's widow was the one family member chosen to be present in his cabinet on the day of the approval of Law 9.140/95 is perhaps not a coincidence.

It was after these events that on 23 May 1995, the minister of justice received a delegation of the families, who handed him a publication they had just edited, compiling all the information gathered over the years on cases of deaths and disappearances. In addition, they presented a project for a draft bill, inspired by the steps the Chilean government had taken, proposing the official acknowledgment of the disappeared and the creation of a special commission of investigation and reparation. On that same day, the press reported that the government 'agreed to recognize the list of the disappeared, though there is still resistance concerning reparations and official acknowledgement of the responsibility of the state' (Neri 1995b). The day after, though, it was announced that the Ministry of Justice was studying a compensation scheme for the families, as this was a 'reasonable solution' that would 'not go against the military', said one representative (Nogueira and Secco 1995). Note also that this issue was being discussed at the same time that the first 'National Human Rights Plan' was being prepared under the coordination of the Ministry of Justice's chief of staff (José Gregori), who was also the one in charge of drafting the bill on the dead and disappeared. In an interview, Gregori recalls how he pointed out to the president that 'the credibility of the human rights plan needed a solution for the historical question of the disappeared, something the President agreed with' (quoted in Mezarobba 2007: 59). It is worth mentioning that José Gregori had himself been a preeminent lawyer for political prisoners during the dictatorship, integrating the church-based groups engaged in denouncing human rights abuses. His sensitivity to this question was well known, as well as his close links with Cardoso.

Cardoso would later write in his political biography: 'my life story prompts me to repair, in one of my first governmental acts, what I always considered unjust: the lack of recognition of the Brazilian state for the death and disappearance of political prisoners' (Cardoso 2006: 548–549). He also narrates in detail that, being aware of how delicate the question was, he had had a frank conversation over dinner with his military ministers, at the beginning of his legislature, in which he told them about his intention to grant reparations for the regime's worst violations. On that occasion, he disclosed his personal story of imprisonment and intimidation and how he clearly saw signs of torture in some of his prison-mates, also recalling the times when he met with security forces to protest against the imprisonment and physical mistreatment of fellow academics (Cardoso 2006: 254–256). Unfortunately, no information is provided on the exact date of the dinner Cardoso refers to, and therefore, it is not possible to know how it fits chronologically with the events mentioned earlier. In an interview with Mezarobba (2007: 54), Cardoso insists: 'there was a lot of pressure, it is true, but there was an intimate motivation, mine and from the people around me. It was my experience, with or without pressure we would have done it'.

Law 9.140/95, approved in December 1995, officially recognized the death of 136 people who had disappeared after having been detained by state agents for their alleged participation in political activities (art. 1) and established a monetary compensation scheme for the relatives of the dead and disappeared (art. 10), which in no circumstance was to be less than R$ 100,000 per case[5] (art. 11 §1). Moreover, the law created a Special Commission on Political Deaths and Disappearances (CEMDP) that would decide on the incorporation of other cases and be responsible for the management of petitions for compensation, on top of making its best efforts to locate the bodies of the disappeared in cases where there was an indication of their possible location (art. 4). Although this commission had no termination date, it was during the first few years that it worked more intensively so as to process the hundreds of requests it received. The most militant families were important in this regard, encouraging other relatives to present their petitions. In total, the Special Commission reviewed 475 cases. On top of the 136 people already recognized as dead–disappeared in Law 9.140/95, it reviewed the cases of another 221 people positively, based on testimonies and documents the relatives themselves would present (CEMDP 2007: 48).

Despite being an active part of the process – with one representative in the CEMDP – the families criticized the law on several grounds, including: (1) the fact that the burden of proof lay with them; (2) the inability to access all possible sources of information, as certain documents/archives remained secret; (3) the exclusion of cases due to the lack of evidence; (4) the inability of the CEMDP to uncover the circumstances of many deaths, as well as to find the bodies of the disappeared; and (5) the fact that only the families could request the acknowledgment of the deaths or disappearances, which made it a private rather than a public issue (Gallo 2012: 340; Mezarobba 2010: 13). Nonetheless, the final and overall evaluation of Law 9.140/95 and the work of the CEMDP has been perceived as quite positive. Despite its limitations, the whole process of submission, discussion, and approval of cases in the Commission ended up serving a truth-telling purpose and performing a symbolic reparative function the families did not quite anticipate at the beginning. In the words of Cano and Ferreira (2006: 134), who have done extensive research on this issue,

> the work of the Commission was able to prove that most of the official versions given at the time of the deaths were false and most victims were either summarily executed or died as a result of brutal tortures. This recognition enabled the relatives to vindicate the memory of their loved ones and to deny the claim that they had been criminals or that they had simply run away from home.

In sum, the families' version of the repressive past (radically opposed to the version of the military) was, for the first time, recognized officially as legitimate, though there are doubts as to the extent that this message was effectively carried beyond interested circles.

It was also under the government of Fernando Henrique Cardoso that non-lethal victims of the regime's discretionary power managed to further their demands for compensation. The 1979 Amnesty Law had been extremely limited in terms of restitution provisions for those who had lost their jobs or whose professional status had been affected for political reasons. Since then, many had been trying to regulate their situation, be it in terms of reintegration into active service or recognition of the time affected as years of work, for job promotion and retirement purposes. A series of constitutional amendments, decrees, and other types of measures had been enacted in this regard, but in a disorderly, fragmented, and partial fashion. Demands for compensation had been discussed, too, but it was not until 1991, under Collor's government, that a law regulating social security benefits (Law 8.213) provided a 'special retirement pension' for those covered by the Amnesty Law. The situation was, however, far from clearly regulated, because there were still many cases pending the recognition of the status of amnesty recipient. Under Cardoso's government, the initial decision to revise these pensions (in light of denunciations relative to frauds and excessive amounts), and the slowness in the procedures regarding the recognition of amnesty recipients, led to increasing contestation and pressure coming from civil society organizations representing those affected, including labor unions. It was during the 20th anniversary of the 1979 Amnesty Law that their demands were discussed in Congress and that the president received a committee of representatives, though it would take until 2001 for a bill to be finalized and sent to Congress, and until 2002 for it to be transformed into law (Mezarobba 2007: 124–132).

Law 10.559/2002 is the first to deal comprehensively with reparation measures – including financial compensation – directed at those affected by torture, arbitrary arrests, dismissals and transfers for political reasons, kidnapping, forced exile, banishment, student purges, and illegal monitoring (Abrão and Torelly 2012: 154). Besides the right to financial compensation, the law secured other restitution rights, such as (1) recognition as valid, for all purposes, of the period in which the individual was forced to stop working; (2) the right to job reinstatement for public employees; (3) the right to conclude unfinished education; and (4) the recognition of foreign university diplomas (Chapter I). Among other things, law 10.559/2002 specified in detail who could be declared an amnesty recipient (*anistiado politico*) (Chapter II) and established an 'Amnesty Commission' within the Ministry of Justice to review and evaluate requests for political amnesty and reparations (Chapter IV). Up until 2009, the Amnesty Commission received almost 65,000 requests; out of the almost 48,000 assessed by then, about 31,000 were reviewed positively – that is, recognized as amnesty recipients – 10,578 of whom were granted economic compensation (Abrão et al. 2009: 17). The criteria for determining the type and amount of compensation varied, depending not only on how long the punishment had lasted but also on whether or not it had involved job loss, as in this case, the individuals (or their dependents in the case of death) were to be retroactively compensated according to what their earnings would have been if they had kept their job, also taking into account hypothetical job promotions. The focus on the professional consequences of repression, rather than on how intense it had been, has received a fair amount of criticism (namely, because many who were professionally affected ended up with compensations superior to those received by the families of the dead and disappeared). This is possibly related to the fact that the pressure for the enactment of Law 10.559/2002 came mostly from labor unions (Interview BR16).

From the 'right to truth and memory' to the National Truth Commission

Although there were legitimate reasons to place great expectations on a government led by the Workers' Party, it would take until its second mandate for the topic of 'truth and memory' to appear on its agenda, and until the third one for the National Truth Commission (CNV – *Comissão Nacional de Verdade*) to be installed. This is surely not independent of the fact that the normative environment had changed between 2003, when Lula first took office, and 2010, when the bill on the creation of the CNV began to be drafted. By 2010, the topic had expanded beyond the families and had become a concern within other circles (often activated by the families), such as a few members of the Federal Public Prosecutor's Office, the Brazilian Bar Association, and perhaps most notably, the Inter-American System of Human Rights. It is worth noting, however, that these are relatively small 'epistemic circles' and that Brazil contrasts with Spain and Uruguay in that the topic never attracted much public attention prior to the creation of the National Truth Commission. Moreover, it is a case in which individual governmental agents themselves played a role in pushing for the TJ agenda *from within* the state, judging by the importance that the head of the Special Secretariat for Human Rights, Paulo Vannuchi, is said to have played.

The recognition of the 'right to truth and memory'

It is not entirely clear why the Workers' Party 2002 electoral program was silent on the issue, while the 2006 one has a passage dedicated to 'furthering the work on the Right to Truth and Memory and the official reparation by the Brazilian state to the dead and disappeared'. One possible reason has to do with Vannuchi himself, who took over as human rights minister in late December 2005. His sensitivity towards the topic was well- known, as he was one of the heads and authors of *Brasil Nunca Mais*. Shot and imprisoned at the age of 20 for his involvement in an opposition armed group, he spent five years in jail, where he was a victim of abuses and torture. The fact that the Special Secretariat for Human Rights took various initiatives on the theme of 'Truth and Memory' during Vannuchi's mandate (2006--2010) is hardly independent of his figure. However, it is said that Lula was not happy with the treatment given to the topic, explicitly asking Vannuchi to work on it when nominating him head of the Special Secretariat for Human Rights (Interview BR15). Other sources similarly reported that Lula told Vannuchi 'he did not want to be remembered by history as someone who suppressed the military past' (Pimentel 2008 quoted in Schneider 2010: 11).

Sending reminders to Lula's government during his first mandate was again an action moved by the families, this time thanks to a favorable judicial decision. The legal case opened by the families of the Araguaia guerrilla against the Federal Union in 1982 had finally resulted in a favorable verdict in July 2003(!), with a federal judge ordering the disclosure of all secret military information regarding the military operations against the Araguaia guerrilla and the handover of the remains of the victims to the relatives, together with information on the circumstances of the deaths (Santos 2010). This decision came two years after the families had found allies within the Public Prosecutor's Office, who opened inquiries and public civil actions related to the Araguaia case and organized a visit to the region in 2001, carrying out excavations and collecting testimonies from locals, discovering, among other things, that the army still monitored the region. A public prosecutor in charge at the time recalls, however, the setbacks and retaliation suffered because, in his words, 'there was a complete lack of support, coming from the government, the defense ministry, the federal attorney general's office, etc., which made me step back on this issue for a while' (Interview BR16).

Although the 2003 verdict did not make federal institutions go as far as the families wished for, it nonetheless obliged the government to take concrete steps (at the same time that the Federal Attorney General's Office [*Adovacia Geral da União* – AGU] appealed against parts of the decision). An inter-ministerial commission was created to work on the identification of the disappeared in Araguaia, and an expedition to the region was organized by the Secretariat for Human Rights in 2004, but with no results. Furthermore, the issue of information secrecy became a topic of contention, with the government sanctioning a new law establishing the rules for accessing secret documents in May 2005 (Law 11.111) and ordering the transfer of some of the archives under the control of the Brazilian Intelligence Agency to the National Archives that same year. The army would, however, insist that all of its documents related to the Araguaia guerrilla had been destroyed, something that many did not believe.

In addition, Lula's first government showed some goodwill towards the families' demands when reformulating the 1995 Law on the Dead and Disappeared in June 2004 (Law 10.875) so as to expand the scope of application beyond those who had died under custody and include deaths during public demonstrations and armed conflict with public agents, as well as those whose suicide could have been linked to the psychological damages caused by repression (Cano and Ferreira 2006: 141). This led to the reactivation of the CEMDP, whose work of reviewing the cases eligible for compensation lasted until 2006. In spite of the idea of producing a publication documenting the work and findings of this body having already been suggested in 2004 by Nilmário Miranda (the then head of the Special Secretariat for Human Rights), it was his successor, Paulo Vannuchi, who gave this project a definitive impetus as early as during Lula's second mandate.

In accordance with the above-mentioned electoral promise, the 500-page book/report *Direito à Memória e à Verdade* (Right to Memory and Truth) was released in August 2007 in an official ceremony in the presidential palace. The publication was a sort of updated version of *Brasil Nunca Mais*, documenting in detail the case of every victim that went through the CEMDP, with the significant difference that it was now an official state publication, produced by the Special Secretariat for Human Rights together with the CEMDP.[6] Strikingly enough, the report adopted a position and language unlike any other official document before, speaking of 'state terror' and accusing the repressive apparatus of imprisoning, torturing, and killing its opponents (thus going against the thesis of a few 'rotten apples' that had escaped the regime's control[7]). Furthermore, and even more surprisingly, a critique of the Amnesty Law could be spotted when the report made reference to the 'continuous crime thesis', stating that 'to the extent a state agent knows where the bodies were taken and does not reveal anything, the crime of concealment continues to be practiced up to this day' (CEMDP 2007,: 50). Vannuchi, together with the president of the CEMDP, was nonetheless keen on emphasizing that there was 'no spirit of revanchism' and that the release of the book signaled 'the search for agreement, the sentiment of reconciliation, and the humanitarian goals that drove the 11 years of work of the Special Commission' (CEMDP 2007: 8). The report, together with a warning by the minister of defense against possible negative reactions, created some tensions with the armed forces, who made clear that they did not accept a revision of the Amnesty Law (Cantanhêde 2007).

Together with this publication, the Human Rights Secretariat took other parallel initiatives aimed at fulfilling its mandate on 'truth and memory', namely, the promotion of a touring photographic exhibition entitled 'The Dictatorship in Brazil 1964–1985' and the inauguration of various monuments/memorials honoring the 'Indispensable People' victimized by the regime (Mezarobba 2010: 20; Schneider 2010: 9). In the same vein, in May 2009, the executive launched the project *Memórias Reveladas* (Revealed Memories), also known as the Reference Centre on Political Struggles (1964–1985), so as to store and make available online a variety of archives and documents from multiple sources in a network supervised by the National Archives. The task of promoting 'truth and memory' with a broader educational purpose was also assumed by the Amnesty Commission, materialized through the so-called 'Amnesty Caravans', which toured the country beginning in April 2008. Besides taking the appreciation of amnesty requests beyond the walls of the Ministry of Justice, these itinerant public sessions put an emphasis on victims' testimonies and public tributes, in an attempt to perform an acknowledgment function. This transformation within the Amnesty Commission is often credited to the figures of Tarso Genro (minister of justice from 2007) and Paulo Abrão (head of the Amnesty Commission from 2007), both of whom showed great receptiveness to the nascent debate on (criminal) accountability.

The antecedents of the National Truth Commission

The above-mentioned steps suggest that the proposal for creating a 'truth commission' – which first appeared in the Third National Human Rights Program, signed by Lula in December 2009 – did not come out of nowhere. Concrete steps in terms of the 'truth' and 'acknowledgment' functions a 'truth commission' is supposed to perform were already being taken, though in a significantly more modest and piecemeal fashion. Up until December 2009, these various steps, besides being easy to miss by less attentive observers, could be interpreted as isolated actions by the few bodies that were sympathetic to the cause – in essence, the Secretariat for Human Rights and the Ministry of Justice (where the Amnesty Commission was located). The extent to which these bodies were themselves autonomous actors, who contributed to opening up the debate on transitional justice from *within* the state and to channeling some of the demands from civil society, attests to the non-monolithic character of Brazilian governmental institutions and thus adds another layer of complexity to this case-study. In understanding the apparent heterogeneity of the Brazilian government – and perhaps, the reluctance of the Workers' Party to take more decisive TJ steps – it should be underlined that, unlike the legislative majorities of the *Frente Amplio* in Uruguay, Brazil's presidents invariably have to rely on multiparty coalitions (in a scenario of extreme party fragmentation in Congress).

Proof that the debate on transitional justice was also being furthered from *within* the state is the fact that the Ministry of Justice organized a public hearing in July 2008 on the 'Limits and Possibilities for Judicial Accountability of the Agents who violated Human Rights during Brazil's State of Exception'. During this event, individuals such as the minister of justice (Tarso Genro), the head of the Human Rights' Secretariat (Paulo Vannuchi), and the president of the Amnesty Commission (Paulo Abrão) were critical of the Amnesty Law and its application to crimes such as torture, a position that the Brazilian government would surely not dare to take officially (Ferraz 2008; Scolese 2008).

This event was not the first to bring attention to (the lack of) accountability for the crimes of the dictatorship, though. Two years before that, a judge had accepted a family's plea to put Colonel Carlos Alberto Brilhante Ustra on trial for the crimes of kidnapping and torture back when he was the head of São Paulo's most notorious repressive body, using the innovative legal argument that such crimes are not subject to a prescription period. Though this was a civil suit (*ação civil declaratória*) – asking solely for the recognition of moral and physical damages – it was nonetheless relevant in reigniting the debate on impunity for such crimes (Magalhães 2006). While this trial was under way, a few public prosecutors became involved in this debate and in May 2008, opened an additional public civil action against Ustra and another former top military chief (Audir Maciel), this time speaking for 64 victims (Vasconcelos 2008).

The activation of a few allies within the Federal Public Prosecutor's Office at this specific time had to do not only with the actions of the families but crucially, with the consolidation of a transitional justice norm elsewhere. As a leading public prosecutor reveals, he was influenced by legal changes occurring elsewhere in Latin America, with the Argentine Supreme Court declaring the unconstitutionality of the country's amnesty laws in 2005 and the IACtHR deciding in the *Almonacid-Arellano et al. v. Chile* case in 2006 that amnesties are unlawful when used to protect crimes against humanity (Interview BR16). Two public prosecutors who were among the first to become involved with this issue recall how they only became acquainted with the field of Transitional Justice at this time and how they helped promote a seminar in 2007 – with the support of the Human Rights Secretariat and other institutions – where the International Center for Transitional Justice was first invited to Brazil and where legal innovations on human rights accountability were discussed (Interviews BR8 and BR16).

These same public prosecutors were part of the above-mentioned public hearing of July 2008, which was in part motivated by the legal actions they had opened. This public hearing, in turn, motivated the Brazilian Bar Association to file a motion with the Supreme Court that same year (the so-called ADPF 153), questioning the application of the Amnesty Law to public agents who had engaged in grave common crimes. As the Federal Attorney General's Office (AGU) was due to take a position in this case, the tensions and distinct positions within Lula's government became more visible than ever, with the AGU opting to endorse the application of the Amnesty Law, but with five other governmental ministries submitting their own briefs (the Ministries of Defense and Foreign Relations in favor of the Amnesty Law, while the Ministry of Justice, the Special Secretariat for Human Rights, and the chief of staff positioned themselves against) (Cavallaro and Delgado 2012: 98). Virtually at the same time, in October 2008, a court in São Paulo issued a ruling favorable to the Almeida Teles family, 'morally' and symbolically condemning Carlos Alberto Brilhante Ustra for kidnapping and torture.

This is all to say that by the time the government decided on the creation of a 'truth commission', at the very end of Lula's third and final mandate, the debate on how to address the crimes of the past and the collection of actors who supported forceful measures had been amplified. A high government official stated that the report *Direito à Memória e à Verdade* was an initial step in 'unblocking the issue (…), in a correlation of forces that advanced significantly until 2010', with the Human Rights Secretariat gaining the support of the Ministry of Justice and the chief of staff (Interview BR15). The same source points out, though, that the original proposal for the creation of a 'truth commission' came from family requests put forward during the human rights conferences that were at the basis of the Third National Human Rights Program (*Programa Nacional de Direitos Humanos* – PNDH-3). This is one of the main instruments of human rights policy in Brazil, which in the case of this third edition, was known for having been built through a participatory process involving civil society. The same government representative adds that although the idea of creating a 'truth commission' was not new,

> as a state agent, as part of a coalition in which there are right-wing members, I have to take certain precautions the families do not and should not have. When civil society proposals start to appear in the regional and national human rights conferences, that's when the best scenario starts to be configured.
>
> (Interview BR15)

Such conferences are one of the various participatory mechanisms the Workers' Party had been keen on developing at the national level and which, for our purposes, can be considered as an institutional channel opening up the opportunity structure for civil society participation, including the families. These conferences are described by Pogrebinschi and Tanscheit (2017) as 'multi-level deliberative processes' dealing with specific policy areas, gathering 'ordinary citizens, civil society organizations, private stakeholders, elected representatives, public administrators, and other social and political actors', and culminating with a final set of policy recommendations voted for by the participants. Before the final national conference, meetings at the local and state level were organized in preparation for the former. In the specific case at hand, the intention of updating the last PNDH (dating back to Cardoso's presidency) was announced by Lula at the beginning of 2008, with a series of local and state conferences being organized and culminating in a final national conference on human rights in Brasília in December 2008. Gathering more than 1,000 participants, a wide range of human rights issues were discussed and integrated into 7 broad 'thematic axes', the last one referring to the 'right to truth and memory'. Note that the other six thematic axes were already part of a proposal put forward by the conference's executive secretariat in April 2008, before the state-level conferences. The incorporation of the 'right to truth and memory' axis occurs only later. This was a result of the families' mobilization in the state conference of Minas Gerais (and the subsequent endorsement of their proposals by most participants) (Interviews BR1, BR18), though others also point to the important role played by Vannuchi himself in encouraging the creation of a specific thematic group on 'truth and memory' (Interview BR5). The establishment of a 'National Truth and Justice Commission' was among the various proposals presented, with the others referring mostly to issues such as the opening of archives and access to information, educative and cultural type of initiatives, and the naming or renaming of public spaces.[8] The PNDH-3, elaborated by the Human Rights Secretariat, is faithful to the thematic axes of the National Conference and incorporates many of its proposals, though often taming them down. This is clear in the case of the National Truth Commission itself, as the initial proposal was for a Truth and *Justice* Commission, capable of forwarding its findings to the competent judicial organs, a prerogative that was quickly withdrawn.

The first version of the PNDH-3, approved by President Lula in December 2009, would, however, be subjected to revisions, resulting in a newly updated and more moderate version in May 2010. This was a consequence of the intense *negative* pressure the government was subjected to after the PNDH-3 was first signed. On top of the tensions provoked by the proposal to create a 'truth commission', the PNDH-3 touched upon a number of other controversial issues that infuriated some of the most powerful lobbies in Brazil. This was the case with the church and agro-business, as the initial version of the PNDH-3 supported the decriminalization of abortion, same-sex civil union and adoption rights, the withdrawal of religious symbols from public spaces, new forms of mediation of land conflicts, etc. (Adorno 2010). The government would end up taking a step back on some of these issues, to the dismay of the human rights community. As for the axis on 'truth and memory', among the various revisions, the most significant was the withdrawal of the proposal to outlaw the naming of public spaces after people who had committed human rights violations, in a clear concession to the irritation this provision provoked among military circles. It is nonetheless significant that the government remained keen on maintaining the 'truth commission' proposal, despite the crisis it created within Lula's cabinet (not to mention the ferocious attacks from segments of Brazil's mainstream media, known for its conservatism). Once again, Vannuchi seems to have been a key governmental player. As the defense minister and three leading military officials threatened to resign – alleging that the text of the PNDH-3 was 'insulting, aggressive and revanchist' – Vannuchi responded in the same way, suggesting that he would leave his post if major concessions were made (Cantanhêde and Iglesias 2009). Lula managed to pacify the situation after a crisis meeting in which a few revisions to the original text of the PNDH-3 were agreed upon. Meanwhile, proceedings for the instauration of a National Truth Commission (hereafter CNV) started to be taken, with a law proposal reaching the Chamber of Deputies as early as May 2010.

Besides the role played by the PNDH-3 and the conferences that backed it, there was an additional source of pressure looming over the head of the Brazilian government – the anticipation of a condemnation by the IACtHR in the case *Gomes Lund et al. v. Brazil* (also known as the Araguaia guerrilla case). For some within the pro-accountability movement, the sudden determination of the Brazilian government to implement the CNV was a strategic response to the impending condemnation, in an attempt either to prevent it altogether or to save face and demonstrate that the Brazilian state was taking concrete transitional justice steps (Interview BR16). The timing of events suggests this is indeed a credible hypothesis. Though the case had been submitted to the Inter-American Commission on Human Rights back in 1995 and admitted in 2001, it was not until October 2008 that the Commission produced the Report on the Merits No. 91/08[9] (in which it considered Brazil to be in violation of a series of human rights), submitting the case to the Inter-American Court in March 2009. Based on that report and on the court's previous case law, the condemnation of the Brazilian state could be anticipated with a good degree of certainty by the time the PNDH-3 was being drafted and signed, even if it would take until November 2010 for the court to issue its ruling (this is similar to Uruguay, where the anticipation of a condemnation, previous to the actual ruling, was enough to get the government moving). One possible indicator that the creation of the CNV is not independent of proceedings in the Inter-American System of Human Rights is the fact that the decision to create it was used by the Brazilian state as evidence before the Court that it was taking transitional justice steps. The Court itself notes this in the verdict, stating that in its defense, 'Brazil highlighted the future constitution of a National Truth Commission', but making it clear that 'the activities and information that this commission will eventually obtain do not substitute the obligation of the State to (...) ensure the legal determination of individual responsibility by means of criminal legal procedures'.[10]

Some families and their allies correctly point out that the Brazilian government had not shown the willingness to create a 'truth commission' until the IACtHR condemnation was looming on the horizon. They point, for example, to the astonishing coincidence that the project to create the commission was sent to Congress on the same day that they were at an IACtHR court hearing (Interview BR1, BR18). However, it is possible that as direct litigants in the case, they overstate its causal impact. A slightly different but plausible line of reasoning is that the IACtHR ruling (together with the PNDH-3 conferences) – rather than pushing the government to do something it would otherwise not wish to do – created an opportunity for certain governmental agents to push for and justify a policy that was already somewhat aligned with the governmental agenda. This is plausible not only because there had already been concrete governmental steps in the field of 'truth and memory' before, but also because other court cases (most notably the rift caused by the Belo Monte dam case in 2011) show that decisions by the Inter-American System that go against governmental interests are met with a backlash rather than a change in policy. In either case, the anticipation of the IACtHR condemnation was most likely important, either in directly pressing the government or in reinforcing the position of pro-TJ sectors within it.

Although the bill predicting the establishment of the CNV reached the Congress in May 2010, it would take until November 2011 to be converted into Law 12.528, and until May 2012 to be formally installed in an official ceremony, where President Dilma Rousseff (2011–2016) designated the CNV's seven independent commissioners in the presence of an audience that included all of Brazil's ex-presidents since 1985. Law 12.528 established the CNV with the aim of 'examining and shedding light on the grave human rights violations' perpetrated in the period between 1946 and 1988, 'in order to ensure the right to memory and historical truth and promote national reconciliation' (art. 1). Unlike previous bodies, which ended up serving a fact-finding function as a result of an extensive reparations policy (the CEMDP and the Amnesty Commission), the CNV was allowed greater powers, such as the prerogatives to request classified documents, convene witnesses and testimonies, hold secret hearings, ask for witness protection, or request technical exams, not to mention the capacity to name individuals and institutions responsible for human rights violations and to make official recommendations (Torelly 2018: 10).

Its loose mandate, however, meant that its first year of work was characterized by much tension and conflicting pressures, resulting in its virtual paralysis. Many of the broader conflicts related to what the CNV should represent and aim for were present within the Commission itself, including opposing views on whether it was meant to 'close the books' on the past (conciliatory approach) or be an additional stepping stone in the process of furthering historical and legal accountability (conflictual approach). Its links to civil society were also an object of debate. Though the CNV opted to work mostly behind closed doors, the unexpected dissemination of local independent commissions (set up by local governments, civil society groups, universities, etc.) meant that some of the CNV's members would end up liaising with these (Torelly 2018: 14). This connection, together with the refusal of the military to cooperate with the CNV, helped tip the balance towards a non-conciliatory approach, which became evident in its final report, released in December 2014. Although families and activists were highly critical of the CNV – for its size, duration, lack of grassroots connection, closed-door policy, and importantly, for not adding much in terms of what was already known – they welcomed its official acknowledgment function as well as some of its most provocative recommendations (Interview BR1).

Indeed, the CNV's main accomplishment seems to be not so much in terms of reporting new facts but rather, of assembling them in a systematic way, 'thickening the narrative with testimonial evidence', and making a strong case for the fact that violations did not take place in an isolated way (as the military has always claimed) but were coordinated and performed with the knowledge of high-ranking officers (Torelly 2018: 18). As such, the CNV's (2014: 964) first recommendation was the acknowledgment by the armed forces of its institutional responsibility in the serious violations of human rights that took place during the military dictatorship. Its three-volume report, with over 3,000 pages, constitutes an updated, detailed, and authoritative account of the repressive apparatus, its functioning, and consequences. Besides updating the number of deaths and disappearances from the 357 recognized by the 2007 CEMDP's report to 434 cases, the CNV was bold enough to name 337 public officials responsible for serious violations of human rights, based not only on direct authorship but also on the 'political-institutional responsibility' of the chains of command (CNV 2014: 846–931). Moreover, it extended the range of research themes beyond the traditional ones and dedicated its second volume to previously neglected thematic issues such as the violations practiced against peasants, indigenous communities, LGBT, and others. Though the report opts to put an emphasis only on those who died for strict political reasons, it is striking that it indicates that more than 8,000 indigenous people were killed during military rule. Among its 29 recommendations, the most controversial one was surely its stance on criminal accountability, adopting the view that the scale and systematic manner in which crimes were committed amounted to crimes against humanity, which in accordance with international jurisprudence, should not be subject to statute of limitations and to the application of amnesty laws (CNV 2014: 965).

Despite this, President Dilma Rousseff was keen on emphasizing, during the ceremony in which she received the CNV's final report, that democracy was built 'through pacts and national agreements' and that 'truth does not mean revanchism; truth should not be a reason for hatred or for the settling of accounts' (Haubert et al. 2014). Though Rousseff's personal preference for the revision of the Amnesty Law had actually been made clear before (she had been a victim of torture herself), she is said to have adopted this posture in order to avoid problems with the armed forces (Haubert et al. 2014). Indeed, to understand Rousseff's conflict-avoidance posture, it is important to highlight the extent to which the implementation of the CNV itself put the relationship of the government with the military under strain. As Vitelli (2021) describes, there were various episodes during Rousseff's administration that significantly increased the levels of tension between the executive and the armed forces, the CNV being perhaps the most relevant one. Not only there is plenty of evidence that the armed forces sabotaged the work of the CNV (preventing its access to information), but criticism coming from military figures was made public (Torelly 2018; Vitelli 2021). As example, an association of retired officers (the Military Club) described the CNV's report as 'absurd', a 'collection of half-truths, slander and whole lies, packed with pieces of truth' (Salomão 2014).

What is more, this is in a context where the Ministry of Defense acted as an intermediary but often came across as a simple spokesperson of the armed forces. Tensions with the Ministry of Defense were thus part of the daily routine of the CNV (Torelly 2018: 15). This is one of various episodes raising warranted doubts about the extent of civilian control over the armed forces in Brazil, or to put it differently, whether the Ministry of Defense is a representative of the government to the armed forces or rather, a representative of the armed forces within the executive. Such doubts are further strengthened by the fact that the response to conflict with the military invariably tends to be one of appeasement rather than reprimand (Vitelli 2021).

Note also that the CNV's report came at a time in which the deterioration of the political situation in Brazil was already perceptible as a result of an economic crisis, social unrest, and a major corruption scandal ('Operation Car Wash') affecting a vast swath of the political class and tarnishing the reputation of Dilma Rousseff's party in particular. Rousseff was in a weak position from the very start of her short second mandate, after a general election (October 2014) that had been the most disputed and polarized in Brazilian democracy at that point. The year 2015 was characterized by massive anti-government/anti-corruption protests, with conservative forces taking advantage of the situation to question the legitimacy of Rousseff's government and push for her impeachment, something that eventually materialized in 2016. It is hard to overstate the extent of this institutional crisis and the degradation of Brazil's political life throughout the mid- and late 2010s. The election of far-right candidate Jair Bolsonaro in 2018 – a former army captain known for his professed fondness for the military dictatorship – was an obvious symptom of that. It is thus unsurprising that the recommendations of the CNV were largely ignored, and that the TJ agenda has vanished from the political scene.

The lack of criminal accountability

Rousseff's view on the negotiated nature of Brazilian democracy, and the implicit acknowledgment that such pacts prevent(ed) any form of account settling, did not entirely come as a surprise. Although her main motivation was surely averting a backlash from conservative sectors and the military, she was also aware that there was a widespread perception in Brazil that the Amnesty Law was a major stepping stone in the process of democratization in Brazil – commonly seen as 'the birthplace of Brazilian democracy, the moment in which a new order is found' (Interview BR12). Take the editorial of the newspaper of record *Folha de S. Paulo* (2014) following the release of the CNV's report:

> The period of political violence needs to be known and debated, but it was the amnesty that enabled [the country] to overcome it. (...) The unrestricted amnesty given by the Brazilian dictatorship in 1979 was a decisive step for peacefully overcoming the nefarious situation (...) [and] it is one of the pillars on which Brazilian democracy is based. It was its acceptance by political forces that broke the cycle of retaliations inaugurated in 1964. It is neither reasonable nor desirable that international commitments, determining that torture is an imprescriptible crime, override juridical national sovereignty.

It is noteworthy that the text speaks of an 'unrestricted amnesty', something that is factually incorrect but often perceived as true. Moreover, it seems to equate 'unrestricted' with 'bilateral', subverting the reason why the amnesty movement spoke of an 'unrestricted amnesty' back in the late 1970s. The 'two-demons' narrative is also somewhat present (and it is often what justifies pro-amnesty positions). Even though the editorial recognizes that military repression was 'disproportional and abusive', it speaks of a 'cycle of retaliations' and of 'right and left-wing factions that recurred to violence and that led to the collapse of democratic regimes in various countries, including Brazil'. The assertions that left- and right-wing violence led to the 1964 coup d'état and that the amnesty law put an end to a 'cycle of retaliations' (when the small armed left-wing opposition appeared only after 1964 and had been destroyed long before the Amnesty Law) are not rigorous from a historiographical point of view, but once again, reflect the dominant perception in Brazil. In fact, a commonly held critique against the CNV – which is far from coming only from military circles – was that it did not investigate 'both sides', silencing the violence and political project of the radical left.

Similar views on the historical significance of the Amnesty Law had been espoused by the judges of the Federal Supreme Court (*Supremo Tribunal Federal* – STF) back in April 2010 when responding to the challenges posed by the Brazilian Bar Association in ADPF 153.[11] By a vote of seven to two, the STF decided to uphold the Amnesty Law. Similarly to the Supreme Court in Spain, the STF justified its position based on the historical context of the law's approval. It argued that, rather than a regime-imposed self-amnesty,

> the amnesty law resulted from a political agreement generally supported by Brazilian civil society (...) being recognized as a necessary and desired measure for a peaceful transition to the rule of law, (...) a fundamental underpinning for the current democratic constitutional order.[12]

On a more technical note, the STF argued that the Amnesty Law is part of Brazil's constitutional order via constitutional amendment no. 26/1985, which besides calling for the Constitutional Assembly responsible for the 1988 Constitution, reiterated the Amnesty Law provisions. This is important, not only because it shows a perceived connection between the amnesty law and the birth of the democratic constitutional order, but because it gives this norm constitutional protection. The STF notes, however, that its duty is purely to interpret the law and that changes to its wording fall within the competence of the organ that enacted the law in the first place, that is, the legislative power.[13]

Interestingly (and perhaps not coincidentally), the STF decision came only a few months before the ruling of the IACtHR in the *Gomes Lund et al. v Brazil* case (conveniently shielding the STF from engaging with the IACtHR ruling). In its defense before the IACtHR, the Brazilian state similarly emphasized that 'to understand the merits of the amnesty law it is necessary to take into account that this law functions in a broad and gradual process of political change and redemocratization of the country', further highlighting that the 'the amnesty was preceded by a public debate' and was commonly considered 'an important step in the national reconciliation process.'[14] The IACtHR, instead, argued that regardless of the type of amnesty or historical circumstances, Brazil's Amnesty Law was not compatible with the American Convention on Human Rights or with the court's jurisprudence on instruments that restrict the duty to investigate and sanction grave violations of human rights. Thus, it held the Brazilian state 'responsible for the forced disappearance of 62 people between the years 1972 and 1974 in the Araguaia region', using the doctrine of continuous violations to justify its say over events that had occurred prior to Brazil's recognition of the court's jurisdiction (Cavallaro and Delgado 2012: 99–100). The apparent incompatibility of these two decisions puts Brazil in a legal conundrum, as the relationship between the domestic constitutional order and international obligations has not been clearly defined. Though there are sound legal arguments that can be made to overcome this challenge (as in Tang 2015), the highest judicial authorities in Brazil have so far maintained a 'sovereigntist' view of judicial matters, privileging domestic decisions over international ones.

This was, at least, the point of view of some of the STF's judges on the aftermath of the IACtHR ruling, publicly stating that 'the decision can have moral effects, but does not imply an annulment of the STF's decision' or that despite international embarrassment, 'the decision of the STF prevails over the IACtHR's ruling' (*Estadão*, 15 December 2010). The minister of defense similarly stated that 'the decision would not produce any legal effects', as the Brazilian Supreme Court's decision 'was the final word on the matter' (Cavallaro and Delgado 2012: 100). Though federal prosecutors have opened a series of criminal lawsuits since the IACtHR's ruling – which was fundamental in changing the power balance within the MPF (as pro-accountability prosecutors are no longer a minority) – the Brazilian judiciary has continued to close all doors (Bernardi 2017). Either the lawsuits are struck down from the start, as judges invoke the Amnesty Law and the STF decision, or they are later blocked by the STF, as the defendant can file a 'complaint' to the STF when its authority is deemed to be under challenge (Interview BR16). However, the STF will be forced to reanalyze its view on the matter, as other legal challenges have been presented since the IACtHR ruling, namely, a 'clarification motion' (*embargo de declaração*) regarding ADPF 153 and an additional ADPF (ADPF 320), using some of the IACtHR's arguments and defending the ruling's binding nature. The STF has been awfully slow in responding to these challenges, though, perhaps as a result of the legal conundrum in which it finds itself.

If much can be said about the conservative nature of the higher echelons of Brazil's judiciary, the lack of training and receptiveness towards international law, or the dominance of a formalistic/positivist legal culture (which in fact, seem to be common characteristics of the judiciary of all countries under analysis), it should also be noted that judicial activism on this matter is a relatively recent phenomenon in Brazil. It wasn't until the IACtHR ruling, and the subsequent change of heart within the MPF, that one could speak of judicial activism regarding the crimes of the dictatorship. Either because of the previous lack of allies and/or the perception that the judiciary's doors were closed, the fact is that the families in Brazil did not or could not mount a sustained litigation effort before, as family movements in other parts of Latin America had done.

Finally, and on a different note, the absence of criminal accountability for the crimes of the dictatorship comes as no surprise if one zooms out of the issue of political crimes under the dictatorship and looks at Brazil's broader and deeply problematic relationship between top-down violence and impunity, and low regard for human rights in general. If a transition from an authoritarian to a democratic regime is generally expected to be accompanied by basic guarantees involving the protection from arbitrary violence from the state and equal and fair treatment under the law, the fact is that Brazil is still a very 'ugly democracy' in this regard (Pereira 2000). Although targets have changed from political opponents, and the state no longer deliberately perpetrates violent abuses, the fact is that the sharp increase in crime rates during the 1980s and 1990s was accompanied by growing violence from the security forces, be it in the form of torture of suspects, maltreatment of prisoners, deliberate executions, or death squads in which state officials are active participants (Pinheiro 1998). Public support for brutal policing methods is high and often comes in combination with the rejection of human rights discourse and practice, which in Brazil is commonly associated with the 'rights of criminals' and with policies that allegedly cripple the effort to fight crime (Cavallaro and Delgado 2012: 93–94). This, together with the fact that those victimized almost always come from the poorest and most marginalized sectors of society, contributes to widespread impunity for the abuses committed by state officials. In his impressive comparative study on judicial responses to police killings throughout the 1990s, Daniel Brinks (2008) depicts the grimmest picture for the two Brazilian cities he includes in his study – São Paulo and Salvador – where conviction rates for police officers are well below 5%, compared with 20% in Buenos Aires and 50% in Uruguay.

This is all to say that apart from the most obvious political and legal barriers to accountability for the crimes of the dictatorship, pro-accountability actors operate in a broader social and normative environment that is not favorable to their cause, given the widespread *normalization* of violence and impunity in Brazilian society. Note that the point here is not to draw unwarranted causal relationships between the lack of accountability for past violations and present ones (as many tend to do). It is simply to state that families and their allies face an additional obstacle in Brazil – in comparison to settings where accountability is the norm and violence is overwhelmingly rejected as a tool of social control – in essence because this scenario inevitably reduces the visibility of their claims and their pool of support. It is no coincidence that they are commonly accused of being 'fixated on the past' rather than on the all too pressing current human rights situation (Interview BR15).

Conclusion

Brazil is a textbook case when it comes to the impact of a highly top-down transition to democracy on transitional justice trajectories. Besides precluding the treatment and general interest in the topic during the transition period, it meant that potentially favorable state agents would take careful and progressive steps, going from the most victim-centered and least confrontational type of measure – monetary reparations – to those that occupy a middle space in the 'transitional justice scale' – investigative and acknowledgment measures – without yet daring to take further steps. Its largely consensual memory regime during the transition period, and the fact that there had been no sustained litigation effort until recently, complicates the task of challenging the country's Amnesty Law. The idea that this law was a concession to the regime's opposition and part of a successful move towards democracy is still widespread and can be mobilized both by conservative sectors and by governmental actors who do not wish to generate conflict with the armed forces. Though families have come a long way in gaining support for their cause over time – as the transitional justice agenda has become more established internationally and progressive legal actors in Brazil formed an 'epistemic community' on this issue – the lack of accountability for the crimes of the past does not appear all too surprising in a country where violence and impunity are still widespread.

Moreover, and when it comes to accounting for the implementation of TJ steps, Brazil's case largely confirms the initial expectations regarding the combined effect of favorable political actors and positive sources of external pressure. To begin with, the first appear indispensable in a setting where demands come from a small and isolated group, as was the case in Brazil during the 1990s. If they surely played an agenda-setting role by sending constant reminders to political actors, the early decision of the Cardoso administration to give a response to the families of the dead and disappeared says something about a positive predisposition that Cardoso himself insists he had. The choice of a reparations policy is in accordance with the perceived need to attend to a small group on an issue that was salient only for them, with the added benefit that reparations are the least conflictual type of measure (as the recognition of the existence of victims leaves the thesis of a 'few rotten apples' within the military largely unchallenged). By the time the PT decided to take a bigger TJ step, with the implementation of the National Truth Commission, the situation for the families had changed, benefiting from a wider network of support, some institutional opportunities (e.g., participation in the national human rights conference), a few judicial advancements (e.g., Ustra's condemnation), and importantly, a favorable decision of the IACtHR. If it is true that a few key governmental agents appeared fundamental in pushing for an advancement of the TJ agenda from within the state, those same agents recognized that a policy of that type – surely more visible and conflictual than reparations – could only be implemented if there were external demands to back them.

Notes

1 In 1985, the group *Tortura Nunca Mais* (Torture Never Again) was founded in Rio de Janeiro by a group of families and ex-prisoners. It was brought together by the desire to identify the agents of the dictatorship who had practiced or been directly involved in repression and who now occupied publicly visible positions, using typical strategies of 'naming and shaming' in the press (Coimbra, 1996: 168). They succeeded in removing or preventing the nomination of a few individuals, as well as in suspending the medical license of a few medical practitioners denounced for their collaboration in torture sessions (Mezarobba 2003: 67–68). Similar groups would be created in other cities, too.

2 This large and impressive project was the result of several years of clandestine work, with Dom Paulo Evaristo Arns and the Presbyterian pastor Jaime Wright putting together a team who secretly photocopied more than one million pages of court proceedings of the Supreme Military Tribunal (for a fascinating account on this, see Weschler 1990). This resulted in an extensive and detailed publication, which came out right after the 1985 election, listing, among other things, the names of the 17,420 individuals who had faced the military justice system, the 1,843 cases of those who had the courage to denounce the use of torture, the 144 times someone testified for the death of an activist or political prisoner, as well as a list of 125 disappearances (Mezarobba 2003: 57–58).

3 *Partido dos Trabalhadores*. Programa (1980). Available at: https://fpabramo.org.br/csbh/wp-content/uploads/sites/3/2017/04/02-programa_0.pdf (accessed 10 October 2018).
4 See, for instance, its national electoral platform (1982). Available at: https://fpabramo.org.br/csbh/wp-content/uploads/sites/3/2017/04/02-plataformaeleitoral.pdf (accessed 10 October 2018).
5 This was about US$100,000 at the time, 1,250 times the national minimum wage (Cano and Ferreira 2006: 152).
6 Note that this report, together with the work of the Special Commission, holds some similarities to the work performed by 'Truth Commissions', and thus, depending on how loose the definition adopted is, it could already be considered as such. Here, I chose to side with Schneider (2013: 152) in considering that the work of the Special Commission falls short of what is usually expected from such investigatory organs, in essence because rather than a pro-active investigatory stance, the burden of proof was placed upon the families, not to mention that its sessions were kept private and had little to no public visibility.
7 This point of view was defended, for example, by General Oswaldo Pereira Gomes – the armed forces' representative within the CEMDP – who wrote a piece for *Folha de S. Paulo* (Gomes 1998) stating that 'the revanchists are wisely taking advantage of the running sore left by a small minority who, going against the tradition of the armed forces and without the support of military commanders, yielded to the temptation of torture, in order to obtain faster and more effective results'; he defends the armed forces' tradition in Brazilian politics as one of 'strong social orientation, respect for national sovereignty and, above all, moralization of public life'.
8 *Resoluções Aprovadas na 11ª Conferência Nacional de Direitos Humanos*. Available at: www.ipea.gov.br/participacao/images/pdfs/conferencias/Direitos_humanos_XI/deliberacoes_11_conferencia_direitos_humanos.pdf (accessed 20 August 2018).
9 The Commission produced this report shortly after organizing a debate (or 'thematic audience') on 'the amnesty law as an obstacle to justice in Brazil', which, not coincidentally, took place shortly after (and with some of the same participants as) the public hearing on judicial accountability organized by the Ministry of Justice in July 2008.
10 *Gomes-Lund et al. ('Guerrilha do Araguaia') v. Brazil*, Preliminary Objections, Merits, Reparations, and Costs, Judgement, Inter-Am. Ct. H.R. (ser. C) No. 219, ¶¶ 295–297 (24 November 2010).
11 ADPF (*Arguição de Descumprimento de Preceito Fundamental* – Claim of Breach of Fundamental Percept), a mechanism of 'constitutionality control'.
12 Case ADPF No. 153/DF, Supremo Tribunal Federal, Relator Min. Eros Grau (April 2010) quoted. in Tang 2015: 262–263.
13 Case ADPF No. 153/DF, Supremo Tribunal Federal, Relator Min. Eros Grau (April 2010).
14 *Gomes-Lund et al. ('Guerrilha do Araguaia') v. Brazil*, Preliminary Objections, Merits, Reparations, and Costs, Judgement, Inter-Am. Ct. H.R. (ser. C) No. 219, ¶¶ 130–133 (24 November 2010).

References

Abrão, Paulo and Marcelo Torelly. 2012. 'Resistance to Change: Brazil's Persistent Amnesty and Its Alternatives for Truth and Justice.' In *Amnesty in the Age of*

Human Rights Accountability: Comparative and International Perspectives, edited by Francesca Lessa and Leigh A. Payne, 152–181. New York: Cambridge University Press.

Abrão, Paulo, Marcelo D. Torelly, Sueli Aparecida Bellato and Roberto Vieira Alvarenga. 2009. 'Justiça de Transição no Brasil: O papel da Comissão de Anistia do Ministério da Justiça.' *Revista Anistia Política e Justiça de Transição* 1: 12–21.

Adorno, Sérgio. 2010. 'História e desventura: o 3° Programa Nacional de Direitos Humanos.' *Novos Estudos CEBRAP* 86: 5–20.

Bernardi, Bruno Boti. 2017. 'Fighting Against Impunity: The Federal Prosecution Service and the Gomes Lund Case.' *Revista Brasileira de Política Internacional* 60, no. 1: 1–21

Brinks, Daniel M. 2008. *The Judicial Responses to Police Killings in Latin America*. New York: Cambridge University Press.

Bruneau, Thomas. 1992. 'Brazil's Political Transition.' In *Elites and Democratic Consolidation in Latin America and Southern Europe*, edited by John Higley and Richard Gunther, 257–281. Cambridge: Cambridge University Press.

Cano, Ignacio and Patrícia Salvão Ferreira. 2006. 'The Reparations Program in Brazil.' In *The Handbook of Reparations*, edited by Pable de Greiff. New York: Oxford University Press.

Cantanhêde, Eliane. 2007. 'Jobim e militares abortam crise sobre tortura.' *Folha de S. Paulo*, September 2, 2007.

Cantanhêde, Eliane and Simone Iglesias. 2009. Contra "Comissão de Verdade", comandantes ameaçam sair.' *Folha de S. Paulo*, December 30, 2009.

Cardoso, Fernando Henrique. 2006. *A arte da política: A história que vivi*. Rio de Janeiro: Civilização Brasileira.

Cavallaro, James L. and Fernando Delgado. 2012. 'The Paradox of Accountability in Brazil.' In *After Oppression. Transitional Justice in Eastern Europe and Latin America*, edited by Vesselin Popovski and Monica Serrano. Tokyo: UN University Press.

Coimbra, Cecília. 1996. 'Tortura: Nunca Mais.' Interview by Ângela de Castro Gomes e Virgínia Fontes. *Tempo* 1, April 30, 1996.

CEMDP (Comissão Especial sobre Mortos e Desaparecidos Políticos). 2007. *Direito à Memória e à Verdade*. Brasília: Secretaria Especial dos Direitos Humanos da Presidência da República.

CNV (Comissão Nacional da Verdade). 2014. *Report of Brazil's National Truth Commission*. Brasília. http://www.cnv.gov.br/

Congresso Nacional. 1982. *Anistia. Comissão Mista sobre Anistia. Vol. I and II*. Brasília: Centro Gráfico do Senado Federal.

Del Porto, Fabíola Brigante. 2009. 'A luta pela anistia no regime militar brasileiro: A constituição da sociedade civil e a construção da cidadania.' *Revista Perseu* 3, no. 3: 44–72.

Estadão . 2010. 'STF defende Lei da Anistia após decisão sobre Araguaia.' *Estadão*, December 15, 2010.

Ferraz, Lucas. 2008. 'Governo abre debate sobre punição à tortura.' *Folha de S. Paulo*, July 31, 2008.

Fico, Carlos. 2010. 'A negociação parlamentar da Anistia de 1979 e o chamado "Perdão aos Torturadores".' *Revista Anistia e Política e Justiça de Transição* 4: 318–333.

Flynn, Peter. 'Brazil: Authoritarianism and Class Control.' *Journal of Latin American Studies* 6, no. 2 (1974): 315–333.

Folha de S. Paulo. 1979a. 'MDB divulga amanhã o substitutivo da anistia.' *Folha de S. Paulo*, August 6, 1979.

Folha de S. Paulo. 1979b. 'Para Ulisses, tortura não é ação política.' *Folha de S. Paulo*, August 7, 1979.

Folha de S. Paulo. 1979c. 'Agora, a nova lei.' *Folha de S. Paulo*, August 24, 1979.

Folha de S. Paulo. 1995. 'União pode pagar famílias de desaparecidos.' *Folha de S. Paulo*, April 5, 1995.

Folha de S. Paulo. 2014. 'Página virada.' *Folha de S. Paulo*, December 12, 2014.

Gallo, Carlos Artur. 2012. 'Do luto à luta: Um estudo sobre a Comissão de Familiares de Mortos e Desaparecidos Políticos no Brasil.' *Anos 90* 19, no. 35: 329–361.

Gomes, Oswaldo Pereira. 1998. 'O revanchismo e a lei dos desaparecidos.' *Folha de S. Paulo*, March 26, 1998.

Greco, Heloisa Amélia. 2003. 'Dimensões fundacionais da luta pela amnistia.' PhD diss. Universidade Federal de Minas Gerais.

Hagopian, Frances. 1990. 'Democracy by Undemocratic Means?: Elites, Political Pacts, and Regime Transition in Brazil.' *Comparative Political Studies* 23, no. 2: 147–170.

Hagopian, Frances. 1996. *Traditional Politics and Regime Change in Brazil.* Cambridge: Cambridge University Press.

Haubert, Mariana, Natuza Nery and João Carlos Magalhães. 2014. 'Dilma chora e diz que documento não pode servir para "revanchismo."' *Folha de S. Paulo*, December 11, 2014.

Hunter, Wendy. 2000. 'Assessing Civil-Military Relations in Post-authoritarian Brazil.' In *Democratic Brazil. Actors, Institutions, and Processes*, edited by Peter R. Kingstone and Timothy J. Power, 101–125. Pittsburgh: University of Pittsburgh Press.

Keck, Margaret E. 2010. 'A lógica da diferença: O partido dos trabalhadores na construção da democracia brasileira.' In *A transição brasileira para a democracia*, 37–63. Rio de Janeiro: Centro Edelstrein de Pesquisas Sociais.

Linz, Juan J. and Alfred Stepan. 1996. *Problems of Democratic Transition and Consolidation: Southern Europe, South America, and Post-Communist Europe.* Baltimore: John Hopkins University Press.

Love, Joseph L. 1970. 'Political Participation in Brazil, 1881–1969.' *Luso-Brazilian Review* 7, no. 2: 3–24.

Maciel, David. 1999. 'Democratização e Manutenção da Ordem na Transição da Ditadura Militar à Nova República (1974–1985).' MA diss. Universidade Federal de Goiás.

Magalhães, Mário. 2006. 'Militar vira réu em processo por tortura durante a ditadura.' *Folha de S. Paulo*, September 10, 2006.

Mainwaring, Scott. 1986. 'The Transition to Democracy in Brazil.' *Journal of Interamerican Studies and World Affairs* 28, no. 1: 149–179.

Mainwaring, Scott. 1988. 'Political Parties and Democratization in Brazil and the Southern Cone.' *Comparative Politics* 21, no. 1: 91–120.

Mainwaring, Scott. 1995. 'Review: Political Parties and Democratization in Brazil.' *Latin American Research Review* 30, no. 3: 177–187.

Mezarobba, Glenda. 2003. 'Um acerto de contas com o futuro. A anistia e as suas consequências - Um estudo do caso brasileiro.' MA diss. Universidade de São Paulo.

Mezarobba, Glenda. 2007. 'O preço do esquecimento: As reparações pagas às vítimas do regime militar (uma comparação entre Brasil, Argentina e Chile).' PhD diss. Universidade de São Paulo.

Mezarobba, Glenda. 2010. 'Between Reparations, Half Truths and Impunity: The Difficult Break with the Legacy of the Dictatorship in Brazil.' *SUR* 7, no. 13: 7–25.

Miranda, Nilmário. 2006. *Por que Direitos Humanos*. Belo Horizonte: Autêntica Editora.

Napolitano, Marcos. 2018. 'The Brazilian Military Regime, 1964–1985.' In *Oxford Research Encyclopedia of Latin American History*, edited by William Beezley. New York: Oxford University Press.

Neri, Emanuel. 1995a. 'Campanha pede que FHC reconheça mortos.' *Folha de S. Paulo*, May 10, 1995.

Neri, Emanuel. 1995b. 'Familiares levam lista de mortos ao governo.' *Folha de S. Paulo*, May 23, 1995.

Nogueira, Rui and Alexandre Secco. 1995. 'Governo estuda uma indenização às famílias.' *Folha de S. Paulo*, May 24, 1995.

Nylen, William R. 2000. 'The Making of a Loyal Opposition: The Workers' Party (PT) and the Consolidation of Democracy in Brazil.' In *Democratic Brazil. Actors, Institutions, and Processes*, edited by Peter R. Kingstone and Timothy J. Power, 126–143. Pittsburgh: University of Pittsburgh Press.

O'Donnell, Guillermo. 1978. 'Reflections on the Patterns of Change in the Bureaucratic-Authoritarian State.' *Latin American Research Review* 13, no. 1: 3–38.

Pereira, Anthony. 2000. 'An Ugly Democracy? State Violence and the Rule of Law in Postauthrotarian Brazil' In *Democratic Brazil. Actors, Institutions, and Processes*, edited by Peter R. Kingstone and Timothy J. Power, 126–143. Pittsburgh: University of Pittsburgh Press.

Pereira, Anthony. 2005. *Political (In)Justice: Authoritarianism and the Rule of Law in Brazil, Chile and Argentina*. Pittsburgh, PA: University of Pittsburgh Press.

Pinheiro, Paulo Sérgio. 1998. *Democratic Consolidation and Human Rights in Brazil*. Working Paper 256. Notre Dame: Helen Kellogg Institute for International Studies.

Pogrebinschi, Thamy and Tanscheit, Talita. 2017. 'Moving Backwards: What Happened to Citizen Participation in Brazil?' *Open Democracy*, November 30.

Pope, Clara Amanda. 1985. 'Human Rights and the Catholic Church in Brazil, 1970–1983: The Pontifical Justice and Peace Commission of the Sao Paulo Archiodiocese.' *Journal of Church and State* 27: 429–452.

Power, Timothy. 2016. 'The Brazilian Military Regime of 1964–1985: Legacies for Contemporary Democracy.' *Iberoamericana* 16, no. 62: 13–26.

Roett, Riordan. 1986. 'The Transition to Democratic Government in Brazil.' *World Politics* 38, no. 2: 371–382.

Sá Motta, Rodrigo Pato. 2015. 'The 1964 Coup and Dictatorship in Opinion Polls.' *Tempo* 20: 1–21.

Salomão, Lucas. 2014. 'Clube Militar vê coleção de 'calúnias' em relatório da Comissão da Verdade.' *G1*, December 10, 2014.

Santos, Cecília MacDowell. 2010. 'Memória na Justiça: A mobilização dos direitos humanos e a construção da memória da ditadura no Brasil.' *Revista Crítica de Ciências Sociais* 88: 127–154.
Schneider, Nina. 2010. 'Breaking the 'Silence' of the Military Regime: New Politics of Memory in Brazil.' *Bulletin of Latin American Research* 30, no. 2: 198–212.
Schneider, Nina. 2011. 'Impunity in Post-authoritarian Brazil: The Supreme Court's Recent Veredict on the Amnesty Law.' *European Review of Latin American and Caribbean Studies* 90: 39–54.
Schneider, Nina. 2013. "Too little, too late' or 'Premature'? The Brazilian Truth Commission and the Question of "Best Timing".' *Journal of Iberian and Latin American Research* 19, no. 1: 149–162.
Schneider, Nina. 2018. 'Legislative Efforts against Impunity in the 1979 Amnesty Debate in Brazil.' *Bulletin of Latin American Research* 37, no. 1: 18–32.
Scolese, Eduardo. 2008. 'Tarso defende punição para quem torturou na ditadura.' *Folha de S. Paulo*, August 1, 2008.
Silva, Carlos Eduardo Lins da. 1995. 'Professora pede "justiça."' *Folha de S. Paulo*, April 22, 1995.
Skidmore, Thomas. 1988. *The Politics of Military Rule in Brazil, 1964–85*. New York: Oxford University Press.
Souza, Carlos Alberto de. 1995. 'Dirigente mundial da Anistia critica FHC.' *Folha de S. Paulo*, April 12, 1995.
Stepan, Alfred. 1971. *The Military in Politics: Changing Patterns in Brazil*. Princeton: Princeton University Press.
Stepan, Alfred. 1988. *Rethinking Military Politics: Brazil and the Southern Cone*. Princeton: Princeton University Press.
Tang, Yi Shin. 2015. 'International Justice through Domestic Courts: Challenges in Brazil's Judicial Review of the Amnesty Law.' *International Journal of Transitional Justice* 9: 259–277.
Teles, Janaina de Almeida. 2001. 'Mortos e Desaparecidos Políticos: Um resgate da memória brasileira.' In *Mortos e Desaparecidos Políticos: Reparação ou Impunidade?*, edited by Janaina Teles. São Paulo: Universidade de São Paulo.
Teles, Janaina de Almeida. 2011. 'Memórias dos cárceres da ditadura: Os testemunhos e as lutas dos presos políticos no Brasil.' PhD diss. Universidade de São Paulo.
Torelly, Marcelo. 2018. 'Assessing a Late Truth Commission: Challenges and Achievements of the Brazilian Truth Commission.' *The International Journal of Transitional Justice* 12, no. 2: 1–22.
Vasconcelos, Frederico. 2008. 'Procuradoria acusa ex-chefes do DOI-Codi.' May 16, 2008.
Viola, Eduardo and Mainwaring, Scott. 1985. 'Transitions to Democracy: Brazil and Argentina in the 1980s.' *Journal of International Affairs* 38, no. 2: 193–219.
Vitelli, Marina. 2021. 'Back to Basics: Assessing Military Involvement in Politics in Contemporary Brazil.' *Brasiliana: Journal for Brazilian Studies* 10, no. 2: 10–28.
Weschler, Lawrence. 1990. *A Miracle, A Universe. Settling Accounts with Torturers*. Chicago and London: The University of Chicago Press.

Part III

Comparative analysis

Chapter 6

Making sense of the timing of transitional justice

One of the main goals of this study, and of the in-depth case-study analysis conducted in the previous chapters, was to understand what confluence of factors leads to the implementation of transitional justice (TJ) measures at specific moments in time in contexts of *delayed transitional justice*. In all three cases, it is evident that the political environment became gradually more favorable over the years after a delicate transition period in which the negotiated nature of the political transformation process and the concomitant balance of power contributed to either preventing TJ steps or making them altogether unthinkable. However, if a more favorable political environment might be seen as a 'necessary condition' to understand *delayed* TJ steps in such settings, it is insufficient by itself. Shaping the timing of the decision to implement them, and the kind of policy chosen, are also more proximate contextual factors, including the actions and preferences of social and political actors with an intentional TJ-related project. I explore in particular the interplay between the preferences of policy-making actors and the existence of sources of demand/pressure so as to assess under what configuration of the two TJ policies are enacted and what they can say about the specific policies implemented.

In what follows, I summarize the main empirical findings for each of the main TJ policies under study. For the sake of clarity, I synthetize my findings at the end of each section in a table where I attribute a rough qualitative score to the two main dimensions under consideration – (a) the executive's preferences and (b) sources of pressure – and provide a justification for why that is so. To be clear, 'preference scores' are based on previous postures, party programs, and the quality of the measure itself. 'Pressure scores' are obviously related to the level of demand but also to how powerful that pressure is deemed to be on policymakers. The available evidence is also used to postulate which factor or type of change best accounts for timing (in accordance with the three scenarios anticipated in the theoretical framework). These scenarios are put under a comparative light in a second stage, where I draw some conclusions about the timing of TJ policies, the overall importance of the confluence of favorable supply and demand factors, and also what

DOI: 10.4324/9781003311607-10

these can tell us about the choices of specific TJ policy instruments and their sequencing.

Spain 1 (SP1). Reparations (Law 4/1990)

The 18th additional provision of the State General Budget Law of 1990 (Law 4/1990) established a financial compensation scheme for those imprisoned 'as a consequence of the circumstances contemplated in the Amnesty Law 46/1977' or to their spouse in case of death (though with two caveats: it only applied to those who had spent more than three years in prison and to cases where the recipient was more than 65 years old by the end of 1990).[1] Out of all the TJ policies under study, this was the least politicized and the one that had enjoyed the least visibility, thus complicating the task of tracing the factors behind its implementation. The language of the law was strikingly apolitical, its text did not carry anything resembling a moral or symbolic recognition of the unjust character of the imprisonments it made reference to, and the issue did not even deserve a law of its own, appearing instead as a provision in the State General Budget Law.

The reticence of the ruling party to approve this measure was evident, given that parliamentary proposals for reparatory measures of this type had already been put forward before but had been either ignored or outright rejected by the ruling Socialist Party (PSOE). Various small left-wing parliamentary groups had been responsible for such proposals in 1986, 1987, and then again at the beginning of 1990. The fact that the PSOE had ruled with absolute majorities since 1982 and that it took until 1990 to approve a law foreseeing reparations is another solid indicator of the unimportance of this topic. It is striking that parties to the right of the PSOE (first the Social and Democratic Center and later the Popular Party) had shown their support for such measures – parties whose origins in the authoritarian regime could have made them averse to such measures – suggesting that the political costs of implementing them were low. The benefits were, however, also not entirely evident, given that this was a low-key issue that seemed to concern only the small parliamentary groups that put forward proposals on this issue, possibly motivated by the collective of ex-prisoners they had connections to. The financial and administrative burden of a measure that was likely to affect tens of thousands of people is possibly what deterred the PSOE for some time, together with the fact that there was no visible demand on this issue.

It is not clear what led the Socialist Party to change its mind in June 1990, when incorporating a monetary compensation scheme into the yearly State Budget Law, but the fact that this took place shortly after another parliamentary proposal by IU-IC (United Left-Initiative for Catalonia) in February 1990 suggests that these parliamentary groups played an agenda-setting role. It is possible that by repeatedly raising the issue of the financial needs of ex-political prisoners, these groups influenced the ruling party's considerations

Table 6.1 Qualitative scores of SP1

SP1	*Score*	*Evidence*
Supply/Preferences	**Low**	The same government had rejected similar proposals before. This was a 'timid' measure, carrying no symbolic recognition.
Demand/Pressures	**Low**	The few legislative initiatives presented by small left-wing parliamentary groups are the only evidence of sources of pressure.
Type of change (reason behind timing)	**Cannot be assessed.** There was neither a change in executive nor a visible change in sources of demand (since left-wing groups had already presented similar legislative initiatives before).	

on the appropriateness of this type of measure. Another plausible hypothesis is that having almost lost their absolute majority in 1989, the PSOE was trying to please possible future parliamentary allies (in light of the IU's good results in 1989). The choice of a victim-centered measure (rather than a more conflictual type of TJ policy) is obvious in a context where the consensual memory regime of the transition was still in place and where providing forms of reparation to the victims was an acceptable and expected practice, but morally engaging with the past was not.

Spain 2 (SP2). Historical Memory Law (Law 52/2007)

Law 52/2007, which became popularly known as the 'Historical Memory Law', carries in fact the more extensive title 'Law 52/2007 of 26 December recognizing and amplifying rights and establishing measures in favor of those who suffered persecution or violence during the civil war and the dictatorship'. This is already a good reflection of the controversies surrounding the formulation of this law, with quite a symbolic breadth, on the one hand, but being mostly victim-centered, on the other. Thinking in terms of the transitional justice scale, however, I consider that this law performs somewhat of an (limited) acknowledgment function, given that it goes beyond typical victim-centered measures, touching upon issues such as the withdrawal of Francoist symbols from public spaces. The law in itself, by conglomerating a vast number of issues, performed an acknowledgment function, even if it was more timid than many of its advocates had wished for. This is the more so if one considers the extent to which it broke with previous patterns of political (dis)engagement with the recent past.

In accounting for the timing of implementation of this measure, it seems clear that this law would not have been conceived in the first place if there had not been a break with Spain's consensual memory regime in the years preceding the PSOE's takeover in 2004. As has been developed at length, Spain's treatment of its recent past was being questioned at the political and societal level during the Popular Party's (PP) second mandate (2000–2004) in a way it had not been before. In other words, a series of pressures at the international and national level – including the Pinochet case and new civil society initiatives – were placing the topic on the public and political agenda. Discussions on the Spanish past permeated the media and cultural life at a much more visible pace than before. The emergence of a social movement for the 'recovery of historical memory', which engaged in the emotionally charged process of exhumations, powerfully illustrated the extent to which Spain had not dealt with its past, using the symbolic capital of dead bodies. The fact that the issue could, moreover, be used as a political (de)legitimation tool, at a time when the right was particularly strong, created incentives for the parliamentary opposition to bring the issue to the political scene. This new memory context is in great contrast to the one of Law 4/1990, and it is thus essential in understanding why the PSOE of 2004 was ready to take more controversial and visible steps than the PSOE of 1990.

If it is logical to think that this context would hardly have had an effect without a positive predisposition on the side of Zapatero's government, there are good indicators that the executive's preference would not have been 'activated' in the first place if it had not been for the external sources of pressure placing the issue on the agenda. The most immediate one was the PSOE's parliamentary allies, who brought up the issue of 'historical memory' during Zapatero's investiture debate and, given the PSOE's condition of minority government, enjoyed some leverage. The fact that Law 52/2007 had not been foreseen in the PSOE's electoral program – and that this particular program became known as a 'catch-all' program, touching upon all sorts of controversial progressive social policies – is the best piece of evidence that the law responded to other considerations besides the executive's preferences. In turn, the commitment of small left-wing and regional nationalist groups cannot be understood outside the broader dynamics that were putting the issue on the public agenda.

As seen in detail, there was a conjuncture of different types of events in the late 1990s and early 2000s that contributed to increasing the overall interest in Spain's past. At the supranational level, the Pinochet affair created embarrassing parallels with Spain's way of dealing with its past. At the domestic political level, the rule of the PP generated incentives for the left-wing opposition to use the past as a political weapon. At the civil society level, nascent initiatives were pointing towards 'forgotten issues', most poignantly the one of mass graves. Thinking in counterfactual terms, it is highly unlikely that Zapatero's parliamentary allies and Zapatero's own government would have nurtured an interest in the topic had it not been for this changing context.

Table 6.2 Qualitative scores of SP2

SP2	*Score*	*Evidence*
Supply/Preferences	**Medium**	The PSOE had presented legislative initiatives on related issues during the previous legislature while in opposition; however, it did not foresee this specific measure in its electoral program.
Demand/Pressures	**Medium**	The minority government condition of the executive gave some leverage to its parliamentary allies, keen on putting this topic on the agenda. This was shortly after the emergence of a social movement for the 'recovery of historical memory', focused on exhumations.
Type of change (reason behind timing)	**Change in supply and demand.** A shift in the executive from the PP to the PSOE was necessary, but evidence suggests the PSOE would not have taken this step (at least not in this form) without pressure from its parliamentary allies.	

Therefore, while the change from the PP to the PSOE government was necessary for Law 52/2007 to come about, it is reductionist to focus on a change in party colors. The contrast between the PSOE of González (1982–1996) and that of Zapatero shows that, more than a matter of different preferences, they operated in radically different memory environments. While in the 1980s almost no one would question the legitimacy of Spain's way of dealing with the past, the same did not happen in the early 2000s, when the transitional justice norm was starting to become more readily available and when beliefs about the appropriate way of dealing with the past were undergoing change and contestation.

Brazil 1 (BR1). Reparations (Law 9.140/1995)

Law 9.140/95 established one of the most generous compensation schemes in Latin America and created a Special Commission on Political Deaths and Disappearances, responsible for the management of reparatory petitions. To begin with, it is clear that the timing of implementation of this law cannot be dissociated from the figure of Fernando Henrique Cardoso. He was the first president of Brazil to come from the social democratic opposition to the dictatorship, and his profile as a highly renowned academic who had spent part of the dictatorship in exile placed greater expectations on him. Cardoso himself has since stated that he was personally committed to the issue and that he would have taken measures in that respect regardless of sources of pressure (interview with Mezarobba 2007). In his political biography, he states: 'my life story prompts me to repair, in one of my first governmental acts, what I always considered unjust: the lack of recognition of the Brazilian State for the death and disappearance of political prisoners' (Cardoso 2006: 548–549). The fact that he had previously signed a 'compromise letter' with the families and the 'quality' of the reparations program that was implemented speak for the executive's preferences in this regard.

On the other hand, Cardoso was subject to agenda-setting pressures that the PSOE of Felipe González was not. Though these were not so strong as to force Cardoso to take a step he would not have wished to take, they surely played an agenda-setting role and were resilient enough to create 'embarrassment' if Cardoso did not address this issue. As developed at length in the chapter on Brazil's case, these include a small family movement, a few political allies, and organizations like Amnesty International. A series of small circumstantial pressure-building events in early 1995 sent constant reminders about the issue (before the government announced in May that it was studying a bill), and thus, the 'pressure' side of the coin deserves an emphasis in this case too.

Although the families' demands went beyond reparations and focused on the creation of an investigative commission and acknowledgment of the state's responsibility, the choice of the executive to focus on a victim-centered compensation scheme is obviously not independent of the attempt to keep it a low-conflict issue, as the declarations of one government representative made clear: it was a 'reasonable solution' that would 'not go against the military' (Nogueira and Secco 1995). The fact that this was an issue that had not gained much visibility outside the directly interested circles explains why the government did not find the necessary incentives to go beyond

Table 6.3 Qualitative scores of BR1

BR1	*Score*	*Evidence*
Supply/Preferences	**Low–Medium**	Though this measure was not foreseen in Cardoso's electoral program, he had previously signed a 'compromise letter' with the families. The quality of this measure adds to the executive's commitment.
Demand/Pressures	**Low–Medium**	There were various (relatively small) sources of pressure, which seemed to have played an agenda-setting role.
Type of change (reason behind timing)	**Change in supply and demand.** At first sight, this case might be a case of a 'supply change', given the shift in executive and quick implementation. However, a detailed look at the months that preceded this measure shows that the government seemed initially reticent and that agenda-setting pressures were present, even if their capacity to strike a chord with this particular executive speaks for the 'supply' side too.	

victim-centered measures. The establishment of an Amnesty Commission later on – broadening the governmental reparatory program to all of those affected by other types of repression, such as torture, arbitrary arrests, dismissals/transfers for political reasons, etc. – also seems to be an outcome of the demands of interested circles.

Brazil 2 (BR2). National Truth Commission (Law 12.528)

The fact that the proposal to create the CNV (*Comissão Nacional de Verdade*) did not appear until the end of the Workers' Party's second mandate is a strong indicator that this measure was not purely a result of a positive preference of the executive. However, the fact that a positive preference is a *necessary* condition is clearly in evidence in this case, given that despite the backlash coming from the military and the minister of defense himself, the government decided to keep the proposal, unlike some of the other controversial issues that had also been put forward by the PNDH-3 (Third National Human Rights Program, December 2009). Moreover, it was a governmental institution itself that created the necessary institutional opportunities for civil society to shape the human rights agenda through the establishment of multilevel participatory mechanisms (the local and national human rights conferences). The initiatives that had been put forward before by the Human Rights Secretariat (a ministry-like institution) on the field of 'truth and memory' show, furthermore, that this institution was not indifferent to the issue and demonstrate how state institutions themselves can play a role in furthering the transitional justice agenda from within the state.

The fact that the government found the necessary resolve to put forward the proposal to create the CNV in 2010 and not before is surely not independent of the changes that occurred between the moment the Workers' Party took over in 2003 and the end of its second mandate, most notably the expansion of the concern for TJ measures beyond a small and largely isolated group of families. On the one hand, the families benefited from the first favorable judicial (non-criminal) decisions – most notably the one issuing a moral condemnation of the practice of torture by Coronel Ustra in 2008 – and the activation of a few 'epistemic circles', such as public prosecutors within the Federal Public Prosecutor's Office, who at the time became aware of the discrepancy between Brazil's transitional justice record and what was done elsewhere in Latin America. On the other hand, this resonated with favorable political actors, such as the minister of justice, responsible for organizing a public hearing to discuss judicial accountability for the crimes of the dictatorship in July 2008, and giving further visibility to the question. The Inter-American Commission on Human Rights would join this debate in the same year, producing a Report on the Merits of the *Gomes Lund* case in October 2008 and submitting the case to the Inter-American Court of Human Rights (IACtHR) in March 2009. The anticipation of an

Table 6.4 Qualitative scores of BR2

BR2	*Score*	*Evidence*
Supply/Preferences	**Medium**	Initiatives on 'truth and memory' had been put forward before, but a 'Truth Commission' could not be anticipated. The fact that this measure created an internal governmental crisis shows the executive was deeply divided.
Demand/Pressures	**Medium**	The anticipation of the IACtHR condemnation was a source of pressure. The families gained some new allies. Some governmental figures played a role in pushing the TJ agenda 'from within'.
Type of change (reason behind timing)	**Change in demand.** It is the expansion of the circles of pressure that best explains *timing*, because the ruling party had been in power before. However, the fact that sources of pressure can come from *within* the state, too, complicates the distinction between top-down preferences and bottom-up pressures.	

international condemnation is, in turn, said to have influenced the decision of the government to move forward with the Truth Commission proposal, either in an attempt to avoid the IACtHR condemnation altogether or by providing an opportunity for favorable governmental agents to push for the creation of the CNV.

In sum, *internal* and *external* sources of pressure became more vocal, thus encouraging the government to stand up to the conflict that this would create with the military and conservative circles. In understanding why they became more vocal at the time, the consolidation of the transitional justice norm at the transnational level is one important factor, most visible in the consolidation of the IACtHR jurisprudence on the matter, but also influencing epistemic groups in Brazil as well as the language of the family movement.

Uruguay 1 (UR1). Peace Commission (Presidential Resolution, August 2000)

The decision of President Batlle to create an investigative commission came as a surprise to many, since Batlle was coming from a party with an ambiguous relationship with the dictatorship (though he was not part of the most conservative faction and had in fact been temporarily arrested, living for a large part of the dictatorship in exile). Out of the various TJ measures under study, this is the only one that did not come from a party whose colors denoted a possible positive ideological predisposition towards the issue. This, together with the choice of an acknowledgment-type mechanism, cannot be dissociated from the peculiar salience of the issue in Uruguay (when compared with first-time TJ measures in Brazil and Spain). If in the theoretical framework I predicted that TJ would remain a key concern only for the victims and families and therefore did not provide obvious political incentives to political circles outside the typical sympathetic ones, the Uruguayan case demonstrates that in fact, the issue can enjoy a higher salience than anticipated, thus bringing potential political benefits, be they reputational or even electoral.

Whereas in Spain and Brazil, the first TJ measures came at a time in which the memory regime was still largely consensual – and thus, the choice of victim-centered measures made the most sense – Uruguay's transitional justice trajectory was, as we have seen, conflictual from the start. Though it is the case that the issue lost much of its salience after the 1989 referendum, there were a series of events in the second half of the 1990s that would put the issue back on the public agenda and reactivate internal and external pressures. The first was military confessions in Argentina in 1995 (where many Uruguayans had disappeared) revealing the existence of the so-called 'death flights' (bodies thrown into *La Plata* river). This had an impact on the families and their allies in Uruguay, who organized the first March of Silence in 1996, one of the largest civil mobilization moments, gathering between 30,000 and 50,000 people in the streets of Montevideo, and which became a yearly event. An additional event was the international campaign led by renowned poet Juan Gelman in search of his missing granddaughter in Uruguay in 1998–1999. The president at the time, Sanguinetti, was known for his antagonism towards the issue (having been the main orchestrator of the transition pacts), which explains why it was necessary to wait until a different president's takeover to see a response to the families' claims, now focused on investigation and search for the bodies of the disappeared.

The salience of this issue is proven not only by the yearly holding of the Marches of Silence, drawing thousands of people every time, but also by the fact that polling agencies actually cared to ask the electorate about this issue, showing that the majority of the respondents were in favor of investigating the whereabouts of the disappeared (Allier 2006: 89). The public image benefits proved to be genuine, as the good ratings of President Batlle at the start of his administration were largely attributed to this issue (Zuasnabar 2018). In light of the public salience of the issue, and because the families' demands were focused on truth, it made more sense for the Batlle administration to opt for an acknowledgment-type mechanism than victim-centered policies. Moreover, because the Peace Commission had, in fact, limited investigatory powers and the rhetorical focus was on 'national pacification' and 'sealing peace once and for all', it did not prove costly for civil–military relations.

Table 6.5 Qualitative scores of UR1

UR1	*Score*	*Evidence*
Supply/Preferences	**Low–Medium**	There is little evidence that Uruguay's president had held preferences in this regard before. However, pundits assume he had a politically motivated preference (to shame Sanguinetti). The limited mandate and powers of the Commission add to this.
Demand/Pressures	**High**	The 'Marches of Silence' drew thousands of people. The international campaign led by Juan Gelman was a source of embarrassment. It was a salient issue in the public scene.
Type of change (reason behind timing)	**Change in supply and demand.** A shift in the executive was necessary, but the absence of previous commitment and the considerable levels of pressure speak for the role of the latter.	

Uruguay 2. (UR2) 'Loophole approach' to the Expiry Law (2005)

Out of the parties under study, the *Frente Amplio* (FA) was the only one to take a favorable stance on criminal accountability from early on, decisively contributing to making the Uruguayan memory regime a conflictual one from the start. The 1989 referendum on the validity of the Expiry Law, and the preceding signature collection process and campaign, was one of the most significant political events of that time and as such, became intimately associated with the Uruguayan left, both the party and grassroots left-wing groups. The annual Marches of Silence – congregating families, their supporters, and political representatives, most often from the FA –provide evidence that this was not a forgotten or resolved issue. The party programs for the 1999 and 2004 elections reflected this, with the FA making specific references to 'truth and justice' for the crimes of the dictatorship. Consequently, if there is one case where a new executive's preference comes close to a sufficient condition for the implementation of TJ measures, it is this one. This is the more so if one considers that challenging the results of the 1989 referendum was considered costly from an electoral point of view, as the debate in the 2003 Congress demonstrated. This is why the first FA executive initially opted for a 'loophole approach' to the Expiry Law rather than its outright revocation.

However, commitment does not come out of nowhere; it has to be understood in light of a party that comes closest to the mass-organic ideal type of political party, with the most interested circles – families and the various

Table 6.6 Qualitative scores of UR2

UR2	*Score*	*Evidence*
Supply/Preferences	**High**	The historical support for this issue and the party programs speak for this, together with its quick implementation.
Demand/Pressures	**High**	Civil society groups continued to exert pressure in this regard, namely, when it came to seeking new ways of circumventing the Expiry Law in courts.
Type of change (reason behind timing)	**Change in supply.** The shift to a left-wing executive was the decisive factor behind the timing of implementation of the 'loophole approach' to the Expiry Law, which the executive adopted from the start.	

social organizations that support them – being part of the party's constituencies and membership basis (and with a few of them actually being FA representatives). Moreover, the decision to adopt perpetrator-centered measures – the most conflictual option on the TJ scale – has to be placed in a context where the amnesty law had always been the object of contention *par excellence*, being already under challenge in courts by the time the FA took over, based on a 'loophole approach' imported from neighboring countries. That is, while in Spain or Brazil it would come as a shock to see the executive challenging the country's amnesty law, in Uruguay it could be expected that the FA would take steps in this regard once/if in office.

Uruguay 3 (UR3). Law 18.831 (2011)

If at first the FA executive decided to abide by the text of the Amnesty Law, following a 'loophole approach' – certainly in the hope of satisfying pro-accountability sectors while not going against the 1989 popular pronouncement – the former objective was far from met. The pro-accountability movement gained new resolve, and even though they were faced with another setback in a second referendum, the IACtHR ruling of 2011 and the upcoming statute of limitations in the same year were used to put further pressure upon the FA to do away with the Expiry Law. The movement showed its strength in the annual March of Silence of 2011, gathering about 100,000 people, at the same time as debates were raging within the FA on how to comply with the IACtHR ruling, seen as damaging to the country's good international reputation. Sources of pressure seem therefore to have been decisive in pushing the FA to approve Law 18.831 in October 2011, going against the Expiry Law and reestablishing the state's punitive capacity.

Table 6.7 Qualitative scores of UR3

UR3	*Score*	*Evidence*
Supply/Preferences	**Medium**	The ruling party was deeply divided on this issue.
Demand/Pressures	**High**	Judging by the IACtHR condemnation, the looming statute of limitations, and the pressure of pro-accountability sectors.
Type of change (reason behind timing)	**Change in demand.** New sources of pressure (e.g., IACtHR) best explain *timing*, given that the ruling party could have taken such steps before.	

Comparative conclusions

Based on all of this, and thinking firstly about the most immediate changes propelling the implementation of TJ measures at specific moments in time, the cases at hand can be grouped under the three scenarios identified in the theoretical framework.

1. **Change in supply:** Interestingly, only one case fits neatly into this scenario (UR2). Here, the most significant event in explaining the timing of a TJ measure is a change in power from a non-favorable executive to a favorable one, whose preferences on TJ policies had already been demonstrated before. Not coincidentally, this happens only in the Uruguayan case, where a conflictual memory regime had existed before, meaning that more significant TJ steps were only dependent on a more favorable opportunity structure at the political level. The coming to power of the left, for the first time since Uruguay's transition to democracy, largely explains why the country's amnesty law was challenged at this particular time, allowing some significant criminal convictions from this moment onwards.
2. **Change in demand:** In scenario 2, the most significant event prior to policy implementation is new sources of pressure (which arise in a context where there was no change in executive). This was possibly the case for SP1 and most clearly the case of BR2 and UR3, which curiously coincide in the fact that the condemnation of the IACtHR was among the main sources of pressure. This speaks clearly for the importance of the consolidation of the TJ norm at the transnational level and in particular, in the Latin American context – where the IACtHR (and countries like Argentina) have been at the forefront of efforts to develop an innovative jurisprudence in the field of transitional justice.
3. **Change in supply and demand:** The cases of UR1 and SP2 fall most obviously in here (and perhaps BR1 too). In this scenario, a shift in

decision-making actors is necessary to open up the opportunity structure for TJ measures, as the previous incumbent was largely opposed (e.g., President Sanguinetti in Uruguay and the PP in Spain). However, it is different from the first scenario in that rather than being in line with a previous commitment, policy implementation cannot be dissociated from agenda-setting pressures and with them, the increasing salience of the issue in the public scene. This was the case of the pressure of parliamentary allies upon the PSOE of Zapatero in Spain – propelled by the preceding change in memory context that the 'movement for the recovery of historical memory' had helped to create – and the Marches of Silence and the Gelman case in Uruguay before Batlle's election in 1999. While in the Spanish case, these events/pressures helped create an issue that was simply not perceived as a political issue before the early 2000s, in the Uruguayan case, they contributed to the renewed salience of an issue that had almost disappeared from the public agenda in the early 1990s.

In summary, out of seven cases of TJ policy implementation, four benefited from a shift to a more favorable executive (UR2, UR1, SP2, BR1). But while all were implemented by parties or leaders who stood in opposition to the dictatorship, only in one case can we speak of an executive that had an established preference on TJ policies before. In all the remaining six cases, there is evidence of new sources of pressure setting the agenda and providing policymakers with the necessary incentives to take TJ steps.

That being said, the most relevant conclusion to draw from the preceding analysis is that regardless of which factor is most relevant in understanding *timing*, both demand- and supply-side factors are necessary to account for the implementation of TJ measures, and no story is complete without taking both into the equation. Even in the case of UR2 (the only one to fall into the first scenario), it is not possible to detach the preferences of the *Frente Amplio* from the fact that it has been so intimately linked to the pro-accountability movement and that families and their networks of support have remained active over the years, including some members/allies within the party itself. Similarly, in cases where external pressures deserve a particular emphasis (as in BR2 and UR3), it is quite evident that they would not have had the same influence if they had not had a receptive interlocutor in power. Thinking counterfactually, it is clear that no conservative government would have implemented a Truth Commission in Brazil or that any party other than the *Frente Amplio* would have effectively revoked the country's amnesty law, judging by the high degree of opposition these measures invariably aroused within conservative sectors.

The only measure to go against the initial prediction that TJ policies are usually enacted by the same political sectors that congregate those who were part of the opposition to the dictatorship (that is, the left, in the case of right-wing dictatorships) was the Peace Commission in Uruguay (UR1). However, the president's personal trajectory was one of opposition to the dictatorship, and his decision to take a TJ step is not independent of a context where there were more significant sources of pressure than in other contexts, with the issue enjoying significant public visibility, meaning that strategic incentives certainly existed. Aside from this one instance, all the remaining cases fall into the proposition that TJ measures for right-wing dictatorships, when implemented, come at the hands of left-wing parties.[2] The 'left wave' that swept Latin America in the 2000s – with the Workers' Party in Brazil and the *Frente Amplio* taking over for the first time – and the 'left turn' of the PSOE of Zapatero (whose first legislature became known for its progressive policies on various fronts) is thus one additional dimension to take into consideration when accounting for the (delayed) *timing* of TJ policies.

These, however, were rarely implemented without a previous history of civil society activism. The strength of family movements and their allies does not necessarily come from numbers (the exception being the Uruguayan case) but from the fact that they engage with emotionally charged topics (e.g., past violence, exhumations) and make basic moral claims about what today are considered fundamental rights (e.g., right to justice and truth, right to recover the body of a relative, etc.). In this, they have been helped by the consolidation of the transitional justice norm at the transnational level. It is relevant to note once again that the three countries under study transitioned to democracy when this norm was not yet available and implemented *delayed* TJ measures at the same time as it became consolidated. Directly or indirectly, this norm impacted all three countries and is thus relevant in understanding *delayed* TJ implementation. This is most obviously the case for UR3 and BR2, where sources of pressure increased thanks to the rulings of the IACtHR, whose jurisprudence has been at the forefront of the promotion and definition of the TJ norm. It is, however, visible in several other instances. The fact that a Spanish judge was the one to initiate what is the probably the most emblematic case of transnational prosecution, i.e., Augusto Pinochet's indictment in 1998, was not without domestic repercussions, contributing to bringing the past back to the political and public scene in Spain. This was the same judge who in 2008 would launch a controversial criminal investigation into Franco's crimes, importing legal arguments that were being used in the Latin American continent. If it is true that the doors of the Spanish judiciary have been closed, the pro-accountability movement has been growing since then and has attempted to make use of transnational opportunities (through the so-called *Querella Argentina*), not coincidentally lodged in a country that has been a champion of transitional justice.

Although this work has focused more on proximate factors and their 'form' – that is, the relevant actors and actions rather than the content and substance of their discourse – it is clear across all cases that the consolidation of a transitional justice norm and its specific language have contributed to empowering domestic movements. The ways in which this norm has shaped their discourses and actions – and importantly, contributed to attracting new allies – is an aspect that deserves more research. In Spain, for example, a founding member of the Association for the Recovery of Historical Memory (*Asociación para la Recuperación de la Memoria Histórica* [ARMH]) recounts how there was a learning process involved in using the language of human rights for the cases of civil war exhumations, something the ARMH only became acquainted with when it submitted Spain's case to the UN group on enforced disappearances in 2002 (Interview SP3). The importance of this language in helping the affected sectors resignify their experience as *victim* and its previous unavailability should, indeed, not be underestimated when looking at *delayed* social initiatives in Spain. The same holds true for Brazil when thinking of the previous isolation of the families and the fact that they gained new allies over time, including lawyers in tune with international legal developments in the field. This was clear in the case of a few public prosecutors who started to endorse their cause from 2006–2007 onwards, an 'epistemic circle' that has in fact grown afterwards (in particular since the IACtHR ruling) and which may still contribute to future challenges to the country's impunity record. Uruguay, instead, stands out for having been exposed to the core ideas underlying the transitional justice norm from an earlier moment in time. Legal strategies in use in Argentina or Chile had been tried there since at least the early 2000s, including the famous 'loophole approach' to the amnesty law, which would eventually allow criminal convictions in Uruguay.

If all that has been said so far is important in understanding the *timing* of TJ policies, the study of supply and demand dynamics can also shed much light on the *kind* and *sequencing* of TJ policies being implemented. In contexts where the 'memory regime' was still largely consensual, i.e., where the issue did not generate a great deal of pressure – being a demand of only a small group of directly interested people – and where the executive had not previously exhibited a visible preference for TJ policies, decision-makers opted for a 'low-cost measure', that is, a largely victim-centered measure that allowed them to respond to a circumscribed demand while keeping conflict low or non-existent. This was most obviously the case in SP1 and BR1. In both instances, these reparation-type steps kept the consensual memory regime largely intact, as they did not attract a good deal of attention and did not require a significant degree of symbolic engagement with the violations of the past. This is especially true for SP1, and less so for BR1, given that Brazil's reparation program was more robust and comprehensive, performing a limited acknowledgment function. This is perhaps not independent of the fact that pressures from the families, as well as signs of sympathy from the executive, are more visible in the Brazilian case than in the Spanish one.

On the other hand, acknowledgment measures (UR1, SP2, BR2) were enacted at a moment in which TJ measures were not (or no longer were) a concern of a small and isolated group only. In SP2, the 'memory regime' was clearly undergoing changes previous to the takeover of the PSOE in 2004, and the 'historical memory' issue was gaining an unprecedented salience at the social and political level, which explains why the ruling party, and its parliamentary allies in particular, were keen on putting it in the agenda. In Brazil (BR2), the families were no longer entirely isolated, and epistemic circles *within* and *outside* the state were pushing forward the TJ agenda, in a scenario where the ruling party had already shown an interest in the 'truth and memory' agenda and where the anticipation of the IACtHR condemnation created further pressures and opportunities.

However, neither Brazil nor Spain has ever experienced levels of activism on the TJ issue comparable to those in Uruguay, in the same way as neither of the two countries has a party with a historical commitment to the issue like the *Frente Amplio*. It is no coincidence that the most conflictual type of TJ policy – criminal accountability measures – has only been enacted in this context (UR2 and UR3), where the issue of justice for the crimes of the dictatorship had been politicized from early on and where the pro-accountability movement continued to exert pressure in this direction over the years. This is not to say that criminal accountability measures are unthinkable in the Spanish or Brazilian context, but it is relevant that in both cases, judicial activism on this issue is a more recent phenomenon than it is in Uruguay.

The observation of the development of these dynamics also suggests that there is a particular *sequencing* to the evolution of TJ trajectories in contexts like the ones under study. It is true for all three cases that they have progressively (even if very slowly) moved from more innocuous measures first to more robust and more conflictual ones later. Even in the least favorable case, Spain, there has been an obvious evolution between a compensation scheme that involved no form of symbolic engagement with the past (Law 4/1990), a law that timidly performs an acknowledgment function by putting the victims of past persecution under the public eye in an official manner for the first time (Law 52/2007), and the recently approved 'Democratic Memory Law' (Law 20/2022), which takes a more clear symbolic stance on the past and expands the scope of previous measures. This evolution is also visible in the expansion of civil society demands, which in the early 2000s were very much focused on the less contentious issue of exhumations and now include criminal accountability measures.

But if it is true that in all cases, less robust measures preceded more robust/conflictual ones, the first steps were not the same everywhere. The fact that Uruguay started its trajectory with an investigatory commission, and that the other two countries opted for a reparations program instead, is certainly not independent of the different memory regimes. As mentioned, reparation programs allow policy actors to respond to a small and circumscribed demand without fundamentally challenging a consensual memory regime, as these are largely victim-centered measures attracting little public attention.

Instead, in conflictual regimes like the Uruguayan one, responding to more visible and less circumscribed demands (largely focused on 'truth' and 'justice') with reparations would surely be more easily interpreted as 'silence money', affecting the reputation of political decision-makers. Small wonder that Uruguay actually took longer than Spain and Brazil to develop its reparations program (and that this was only part of a broader 'TJ package' under the FA government).

Regardless of this difference, it is still true that broadly speaking, the evolution of TJ trajectories seemed to follow an incremental and stepwise logic. In understanding why is this so, supply and demand considerations are naturally important, as decision-makers are usually risk-averse, and civil society movements tend to adjust their expectations to what they perceive is possible at a specific moment in time. It is natural that decision-makers prefer to avoid radical breaks with past patterns and will thus opt for less conflictual steps first, particularly when it comes to sensitive issues like the one under study, where there are relevant sources of opposition (most obviously, the military). Following this logic, it is thus relevant to consider how earlier measures can open up opportunities for later, more robust ones. In other words, if TJ measures (and demands) are a response to the dominant 'memory environment' and work with what is perceived to be possible at each time, these measures in themselves help shape and modify the memory regime in such a way that further steps will not be perceived as an impossibility but as a more realistic development of previous steps.

To give some concrete examples, think of Franco's exhumation from the Valley of the Fallen as late as 2019 and how Law 52/2007 helped build the momentum that eventually made this measure a realistic one. Similarly, if it is true that Brazil's Truth Commission was a major step forward, it does not appear as such a radical break with past patterns when considering the preceding work of the Brazilian government on the issue, particularly the 2007 publication of a 500-page book/report *Direito à Memória e à Verdade* (Right to Memory and Truth). In turn, this report was only possible because it built on the work of the Special Commission on Political Deaths and Disappearances (CEMDP), an organization created in 1995 to manage Brazil's reparations program. Even in Uruguay, where the memory regime was the most favorable, a left-wing executive first opted for a 'loophole approach' to the Expiry Law (excluding some emblematic cases from the law first) and only took steps to effectively revoke this law several years later.

None of this means that TJ trajectories are linear and automatic. On the one hand, setbacks are possible and in these case-studies at least, usually happen when a right-wing executive takes over, as the existing TJ mechanisms can be 'emptied out' (think of the PP's non-allocation of public funds to the provisions of Law 52/2007, for example, or more recently, Bolsonaro's extinction of the CEMDP in Brazil in 2022). On the other hand, further steps are not automatic, and no significant measure is taken without a confluence of favorable factors, including a good deal of mobilization capacity and the presence of favorable and influential political allies.

Notes

1 Complementary legislation to the 1977 Amnesty Law had already been approved on various occasions by different governments, but I do not qualify it here as falling under the category of 'reparations', as their aim was to overcome discriminatory situations established under Franco, integrating all the affected as equal citizens. In other words, they were more of a rehabilitation procedure – intending to provide the affected with what they would normally have had if they had not been affected – rather than a compensation/recognition of the damages.

2 This proposition could be contested in the case of BR1, given the ideological heterogeneity within Cardoso's party, the Brazilian Social Democracy Party (PSDB). However, its origins go back to the (moderate) opposition to the dictatorship and to center–left positions.

References

Allier, Eugenia. 2006. 'The Peace Commission: A Consensus on the Recent Past in Uruguay?' *European Review of Latin American and Caribbean Studies* 81: 87–96.

Cardoso, Fernando Henrique. 2006. *A arte da política: A história que vivi*. Rio de Janeiro: Civilização Brasileira.

Mezarobba, Glenda. 2007. 'O preço do esquecimento: As reparações pagas às vítimas do regime militar (uma comparação entre Brasil, Argentina e Chile).' PhD diss. Universidade de São Paulo.

Nogueira, Rui and Alexandre Secco. 1995. 'Governo estuda uma indenização às famílias.' *Folha de S. Paulo*, May 24, 1995.

Zuasnabar, Ignacio. 2018. *Treinta años de opinión pública en el Uruguay*. Montevideo: Konrad Adenauer Stiftung.

Chapter 7

Making sense of differences in countries' trajectories

Other than the drivers behind the specific timing of implementation of transitional justice (TJ) policies, this work also has the ambition to contribute to the comparative literature on TJ policies, asking why the countries under study differ from each other in the extent to which they have implemented TJ policies. Making use of the TJ scale developed in Part I, this chapter specifically asks why Uruguay went the furthest (to the point of putting former heads of state in jail), why TJ policies were more timid in Spain (largely victim-centered), and why, roughly speaking, Brazil stands mid-way between the two (having established an important 'public acknowledgment' type of initiative). All that has been said in the previous chapter already sheds some light on this question, given that levels of demand and decision-makers' preferences are uneven across cases and correlate fairly well with the country's TJ record. However, a focus on actors and the proximate factors influencing the timing of TJ implementation does not tell us much about where the different levels of demand and supply come from, that is, the more structural factors affecting perceptions, preferences, and behavior.

It has hopefully become apparent that political and social actors across the different countries did not start from the same baseline and that features of their specific historical, normative, and cultural context matter in understanding the country's relationship with the political treatment of past crimes (something which is true both for the transition period and for the periods in which TJ steps were taken). This is why each country-chapter started with a historical contextualization. Particular attention was given to the transition period and to the way the past was approached back then – what I call the 'memory regime' – both because this was the 'moment zero' of the country's relationship with past crimes and because the more structural factors that help account for TJ outcomes (and for the shape of the memory regime itself) include important transition-related variables. In the following, I develop why and in which ways the type of memory regime forged during the transition period is a useful analytical tool in understanding TJ outcomes later on, that is, in accounting for cross-country differences in how far each went on the TJ scale. In a second part, I highlight the most relevant structural factors

DOI: 10.4324/9781003311607-11

that contribute to accounting for both the type of memory regime and TJ outcomes, and which are therefore relevant in understanding cross-country differences.

Type of memory regime

In the theoretical framework, I argued that it makes sense to think analytically about TJ as part of an overall 'TJ trajectory' that follows a path-dependent pattern, meaning that TJ trajectories later on are conditioned by prior approaches towards the treatment of the past. In line with the importance that path-dependence theories attribute to initial conditions, the moment of regime transition is deemed to be particularly important in shaping the type of 'memory regime' – that is, the dominant pattern of how society and institutions approach their recent past – as this will place the country on a specific path-dependent course that will influence the actors' perceived room for action and expectations later on. This is not to say that actors are forever locked into a deterministic path and that there is no room for (re)action or (r)evolution, but that these will occur relative to what was there before and will be shaped by it. Drastic breaks are, however, not expected, given that political actors tend to be conflict-averse. For the sake of simplicity, I distinguished between unified and conflictual regimes depending on whether relevant political and social actors have a consensual or a non-consensual approach towards the treatment of the past. If non-consensual or conflictual, the past is an object of visible political contention, as there is a significant group of actors pushing for TJ measures. If consensual or unified, and in the context of negotiated transitions, the past is left largely unpoliticized.

As seen in detail, Uruguay had a clearly conflictual memory regime from early on, in total contrast to Spain and to some extent, Brazil, where there was a conscious or unconscious political consensus not to address past crimes in order not to destabilize the present. In Uruguay, the efforts of the families and human rights groups and the support of broader segments of society, including a large part of the social movement scene and the *Frente Amplio*, transformed the issue of criminal accountability for the violations perpetrated during the dictatorship into one (if not the most) controversial topic of the time, to the point of being subject to a referendum in 1989. Although the negative result of the referendum would take its toll on the pro-accountability movement, the issue became a defining political battle of those years, and for a large segment of society, the Expiry Law would forever become shamefully associated with impunity for grave human rights violations.

This is in complete contrast to the Spanish case, the archetype of what a consensual memory regime looks like. Not only were there no political and social voices making demands for forms of public reckoning with the past, but there is actually the aggravating circumstance that there was a tacit elite agreement to avoid the politicization of past divisions and turn the page on a conflictual past. Brazil's memory regime comes closer to the Spanish one – in the sense that TJ measures were not a salient issue, either at the political or at the social level – but with some important differences. The first is that there were more dissenting voices in Brazil, coming in particular from families of those who had died or disappeared. They were a small but noticeable part of the amnesty movement, opening a few legal cases and gaining some political interlocutors during the amnesty debates. Unlike the Uruguayan families, however, they ended up significantly more isolated at the social and political level, especially after the dissolution of the amnesty movement. This difference is important, because as soon as political opportunities arose later on – with the opening of a mass grave in São Paulo in the early 1990s and the arrival of Cardoso to the presidency in 1995 – the group of families already had their networks established, and the issue was known to Cardoso. The second notable difference from the Spanish case is that there was no tacit elite agreement to avoid politicizing the past in overall terms (an agreement the left was keen on embracing in Spain). To the extent that there was a 'transition pact' in Brazil, it referred to criminal prosecutions only. This is why in Spain, any TJ measure that goes beyond the most victim-centered ones is met with accusations of violating the transition spirit, while the same cannot be said of Brazil. In Brazil, the highly top-down transition most obviously dictated the terms of the amnesty debate, and the provision to extend the law to state agents was a pragmatic result of that, rather than the result of a broad and consensual agreement to 'leave the past behind'.

But, how exactly do these differences in memory regimes during the transition period have an impact years or even decades later, and how can they help account for cross-country differences in TJ outcomes overall? Simply put, I deem that it is no coincidence that the only country with a conflictual memory regime during the transition period is the only one where perpetrator-focused measures were enacted – thus, being the one that went furthest on the TJ scale – in the same way as it is no accident that the country with the most consensual regime is the one that lags furthest behind.

The impact of the transition's memory regime is perhaps most evident in Spain, where political actors have shown themselves to be decisively constrained by the view that the decision to 'leave the past behind' was one of the crucial anchors that made the highly cherished transition to democracy a successful endeavor. This was clear in the text of Law 52/2007 – popularly known as the 'Historical Memory Law' – where the praise for the transition's 'spirit of reconciliation and consensus' is revealing of the extent to which its drafters felt they were walking on eggshells. This is the more so when one considers that this law was mostly victim-centered and only took timid acknowledgment steps, which nevertheless, were met with widespread accusations of breaking the transition's consensus, something that the ruling party constantly tried to refute. The Spanish case is evidence that the extent to which actors are constrained by the transition's memory regime has to do not only with the weight of past postures *per se* but with the perceived benefits of this posture to a higher good – a functioning and widely praised democracy. This is why I deem that it is no coincidence that the recent discussion of new TJ steps comes at the same time (and often from the same circles) as the legitimacy of the transition's pacts is put into question.

Brazil is somewhat similar to Spain in the way the transition's agreements are used to justify the absence of TJ steps, though this is more clearly the case for criminal accountability measures only. Its amnesty law – which actually found inspiration in the Spanish one – is similarly perceived as a major stepping stone on the road to democracy and continues to be used today to preclude prosecutorial attempts. This does not mean that political actors genuinely empathize with this view – as opposed to using it as a rhetorical device to avoid conflictual steps – but the fact that left-wing actors themselves invoke the transition's pacts tells us much about the perceived memory environment in which they operate. However, Brazil is different from Spain in that the left was not in practice a part of the transition deals and that Brazil's transition was the one most strictly conducted from above. This, together with the difference that Brazil's military is more vocal even today, is the reason why I suspect the unwillingness of the Brazilian left to challenge the amnesty has less to do with the law's symbolism than with the desire to avoid conflict.

Finally, I argued that Uruguay's conflictual memory regime during the transition period put Uruguay on a transitional justice path-dependent trajectory that is entirely distinct from that of the other two cases. This is first of all because the theme became intimately associated with the Uruguayan left – to the point of having been the defining political battle of the transition period – and thus, the *Frente Amplio* was bound to take steps on the issue when/if it had the opportunity to do so. Secondly, the fact that it had previously been a highly conflictual issue actually opened up the political space of opportunity for its later treatment, in the sense that TJ measures could to an extent be expected. They will come as less of a surprise to sectors that opposed them while being a legitimate expectation of at least part of the party's constituency. This has also to be understood in an entirely different discursive environment, which is in part shaped by the transition's memory regime, too. In Uruguay, the issue of criminal accountability for the dictatorship's crimes has always been framed as a human rights issue, and the Expiry Law has been widely perceived as an impunity instrument, very much in contrast to the other two countries under study.

Factors conditioning the type of memory regime and TJ outcomes

The fact that relevant social and political actors in Uruguay found the means and motives to 'enact' a conflictual memory regime and that the same did not occur in Spain and Brazil is a puzzle that begs for an answer. Why did victims/families in Uruguay find the means to mobilize, and why did the left endorse their claims, whereas the same did not occur in Spain and Brazil during the transition period? While a significant amount of detail has been given on the intricacies of each transition context in the case-study chapters, the goal here is to zoom out and highlight the cross-country 'structural' differences that can facilitate or hinder the position of social and political actors in putting forward TJ claims.

As stated in Chapter 2, the existing comparative literature on TJ outcomes has pointed to various potentially relevant variables. While these variables are meant to account for cross-country differences in *outcomes*, in practice, they can help account for both *memory regimes* and *outcomes*, because for a TJ outcome to happen, social and political actors necessarily have to make TJ a politicized and salient issue, that is, enact a 'conflictual memory regime'. In this sense, the variables outlined in the following should be taken not only as factors that are relevant in understanding memory postures during the transition period but also as features that play a role in accounting for cross-country differences in TJ outcomes. In Chapter 2, I set out to use the list of factors provided by Olsen et al. (2010) in their large-n study, slightly adjusting them to the cases at hand. Compiling them into variables that are proximate to one another, I arrive at a list of four sets of relevant variables: authoritarian regime duration and history of a democratic past; characteristics of repression; the transition's political context; and international influence. In the following, I develop how and in what ways they can help account for cross-country differences in memory regimes and TJ outcomes.

Regime duration and democratic past

While Olsen et al. (2010) do not find a correlation between regime duration and the implementation of TJ measures, they do find one as far as the 'democratic past' is concerned. In practice, these two variables can be approached jointly in the cases at hand because the countries with the longest authoritarian regimes are the ones that have the least previous democratic experience, and vice versa. Uruguay is the only one of the three countries that had a solid democratic tradition prior to the dictatorship, and it is also the country that has experienced the shortest dictatorship (around 12 years). Spain, on the other hand, has had the longest authoritarian regime (around 38 years) and the shortest-lived democratic experiences. Brazil stands in the middle, with a dictatorship that lasted for about 21 years and a previous democratic experience that although longer than Spanish one, was also characterized by instability (and low democratic quality). Variation in regime duration and democratic past does correlate neatly with memory regimes and TJ outcomes, but why exactly is this so?

One important dimension is that Uruguay had a much easier time restoring its political and legal system as well as some of the civil society organizations that were active before. Unlike Spain and Brazil, it was sufficient for

Uruguay to restore the democratic apparatus that had been in place before the dictatorship – namely, the 1967 Constitution – rather than going through the process of drafting a new constitution and building a new political and legal system. Political challenges were especially acute in Spain, where a number of historically highly divisive cleavages had to be addressed (e.g., form of governance, the model of territorial organization, state–church relations, etc.). Uruguay's political parties were also the same as before, in great contrast to Brazil – where the whole party system was *in the making* and where the left was busy rebuilding itself almost from scratch – and unlike the Spanish right-wing spectrum, where new parties were formed by elites coming from the dictatorial regime's ruling circles.

In fact, while in Spain political elites agreed that it was best to find solutions that were different from past ones, the inverse happened in Uruguay. Rial (1990: 25) notes that the search for a 'better yesterday', in line with the myth of the old 'happy Uruguay' – seen as superior to other developing countries in its political culture, life quality, and the civic and cultural capital of the population – was at the basis of a social imaginary pushing for 'restoration'. That is, while Uruguayans looked with deference to their democratic past, the opposite was true in Spain. The short-lived Second Republic was associated with the instability that gave birth to the Spanish Civil War, which further contributed to increasing the posture of moderation and risk-aversion during the Spanish transition.

The concrete implication of this is that the absence of great renovation challenges in Uruguay – in contrast to both Brazil and Spain – freed up space for other concerns, namely, human rights violations during the dictatorship. In addition, the greater confidence in Uruguay's democratic vocation and 'civic credentials' probably made social and political forces less risk-averse than in Spain and thus, less accommodative of outgoing forces.

Characteristics of repression

Levels of repression tend to be considered an important variable in accounting for transitional justice choices, in great part because they can have a direct impact on the level of demand for transitional justice policies, often coming from victims. The general expectation is that 'a higher number of abuses will increase the likelihood that the state will adopt transitional justice mechanisms' (Reiter et al. 2013: 144). However, empirical findings from statistical studies are contradictory. Focusing on contexts of war, Reiter et al. (2013: 164) find supporting evidence that 'post-conflict cases with higher battle deaths are indeed more likely to prosecute state agents and hold truth commissions.' Binningsbø et al. (2012: 737), on the other hand, make use of a different dataset, which shows that trial processes are more common in cases of low-intensity conflicts (with fewer than 1,000 battle-related deaths) than in full-blown civil wars. Referring to authoritarian regimes only, Olsen et al. (2010: 53) find little correlation between the level of repression and the use of various TJ mechanisms.

Our cases show no clear-cut correlation between the severity of violence and TJ outcomes, given the much higher number of deaths of Spain, not only during the Civil War but also in its aftermath. However, I think this variable should not be easily dismissed, since on the one hand, it can help account for variation between Uruguay and Brazil, and on the other hand, there are good reasons to set the Spanish case apart from the other two. This is, first of all, because of the civil war context and the concomitant two-sided nature of violence. As argued before, the context of civil war (as opposed to a context of dictatorship only) complicates the identification of victims and perpetrators, meaning that it contributes to precluding the demand and employment of TJ measures. This context propels arguments of 'shared responsibilities' and 'collective madness', often used to defend the position that 'the past should be left behind'. This is in line with Kovras's (2017) finding that the *type of violence* matters, as TJ measures are more often enacted in post-authoritarian settings than in post-conflict ones. Moreover, as shown in detail before, Spain has the aggravating circumstance of having a regime that was much lengthier than the other two and in which the peak of repression was concentrated at the start. What this means is that the victims of the worst period – associated with the Republican side – grew old and got used to a regime of stigma, silence, and fear. Unlike the families of the 'disappeared' in Uruguay and Brazil – who could have a remnant of hope that the 'disappeared' would be found alive – the same did not happen in Spain (given how long it had been since the worst repressive period and because the repressive methods of the Franco's regime did not involve disappearances later on). Moreover, because the transition period in Spain involved high levels of separatist violence, this further complicates the issue of liability for state agents at this stage.

In contexts where violence is more restricted, and perpetrators and victims can be more easily identified – as in Brazil and Uruguay – differences in the heavy-handedness of top-down repression can indeed be thought to affect the mobilization capacity of the families and the recruitment of allies. The fact that Uruguayans experienced more heavy-handed repression than Brazilians on a per capita basis (an estimated 2% of Uruguay's population was imprisoned and tortured!) meant that a greater number of people could relate to the cause of the families. In Brazil, instead, the fact that the most violent forms of repression were relatively more targeted at small and isolated political groups had an impact in their social isolation later on. This, together with the important fact that the geography of Uruguay helps with establishing networks and creating a cohesive social movement scene – very much in contrast to Brazil – should be taken into account when comparing the mobilization capacity of families in Uruguay and Brazil.

In addition to the relative intensity of repression, the comparative analysis of Brazil and Uruguay also begs for an emphasis on a different repression-related variable: the history of state repression and its perpetuation over time, and the concomitant (lack of) expectation in terms of fair treatment from the state and respect for human rights. It is logical to think that the social and political reaction to repression will depend on *how used* people are to state violence, that is, on how much of a *shock* it is to see state agents employ repressive tactics. Though the lack of concrete data leaves me with little empirical basis of support, it seems to be widely accepted that the use of state violence was a very unusual phenomenon in Uruguay before the dictatorship, in line with the widespread image of a 'civil and civilized' nation (Roniger and Sznajder 1999,: 58). This is very much in contrast with Brazil and its long history of top-down violence. Pinheiro (1998) speaks of 'the serious human rights violations that occurred during the democratic periods before 1964' in Brazil and the 'lengthy tradition of the authoritarian practices of elites against "nonelites" and class interactions', which account for the long history of endemic violence in Brazil. Pereira (2005: 41) similarly notes that 'the practice of judicial repression of political opposition is to some extent a feature not just of the 1964–1985 regime, but of the Brazilian state'. In fact, when speaking of repression in Brazil, it is common to go as far as to point to Brazil's history of slaveholding on a grand scale (abolished in 1988) and how this translated into a highly hierarchical society (Pereira 2005: 41). Furthermore, and as highlighted before, violence coming from state security forces continued to be heavily practiced during and after the transition (especially against the most marginalized sectors of society), and impunity continues to be the norm. This clear-cut contrast between Uruguay and Brazil is surely an important background factor in understanding why families in Uruguay attracted the sympathy of larger social segments – which certainly had much higher expectations in terms of fair treatment from the state and respect for human rights – whereas those in Brazil remained largely isolated.

The transition's political context and impact on the amnesty laws

The detailed description of each country's transition context has made it clear that despite the negotiated nature of all three, there were actually visible cross-country differences in their respective political contexts, namely, in terms of the correlation of forces (or 'balance of power') and risk-aversion postures. Out of the three, the Uruguayan transition appears as the one that was controlled least strongly by the outgoing forces. Whereas it was no different from the other two in that it was initially led from above, the defeat of the regime in the 1980 plebiscite and the results of the 1982 internal party elections put the military and the most conservative sectors in a more fragile position than outgoing forces in Brazil and Spain. The unwillingness of one of Uruguay's major mainstream parties to sit at the negotiation table (the

Partido Nacional) speaks of a context of greater radicalization in Uruguay, possibly contributing inadvertently to putting the *Frente Amplio* in a position of greater strength, given that it became an indispensable actor at the Club Naval talks.

Importantly, the relatively greater strength of a unified left at the negotiation table in Uruguay meant that outgoing elites did not leave with an unequivocal amnesty deal. As spelled out in detail in the chapter on Uruguay, this opened a small window of opportunity for the families and support groups, who had a realist opportunity to submit charges in Uruguayan courts throughout 1985 and 1986, thus amplifying the issue. The fact that the enactment of the Expiry Law came as a reaction to this situation makes the amnesty issue unequivocally different in Uruguay. This contrasts heavily with the Brazilian case, where the amnesty law was approved six years before the first civilian took office and ten years before the first direct presidential election, under the terms imposed by the regime. The fact that Brazil had the most unfavorable correlation of forces at the time of definition of its memory regime contributed to leaving pro-accountability voices largely isolated – as their demands appeared unrealistic at a time in which Brazil still had plenty of major political challenges ahead.

In fact, looking at each country's amnesty laws and the different contexts in which they were approved not only tells a great deal about the correlation of forces and different perceptions of what was possible, but also speaks directly to the reasons behind the different memory regimes back then and cross-country variation in criminal accountability outcomes. Uruguay is the only country out of the three that had separate amnesty laws for political prisoners (Law 15.737) and for the military and policemen (Law 15.848, the so-called Expiry Law). This was once again a result of a more favorable balance of power, given the joint parliamentary majority of the FA and the *Blancos* when the first law was approved and their opposition to the inclusion of the military and the police in this law. This separation meant that the Expiry Law would explicitly be associated with impunity for military and police crimes. The first law, in contrast, could hardly be characterized as a law of impunity, given that 'blood crimes' by political prisoners were not forgiven, having their sentences reduced instead by one-third of jail time.

In Spain and Brazil, on the other hand, the above-mentioned distinction was not made, and laws, which focused almost exclusively on political prisoners, had one provision that either explicitly (Spain) or implicitly (Brazil) covered state agents. In both cases, this provision was largely taken as a natural counterpart to an agreement or political situation that afforded no other alternative. In Brazil, this was most obviously the result of an entirely unfavorable correlation of forces, given that the law was approved very early on in the transition process, in a parliamentary setting where the party sponsored by the regime held a majority, and the military was still firmly in control. While this could in principle have negatively affected its legitimacy, this was hardly the case, as it was widely endorsed by the opposition and seen as the result of a bottom-up demand, on top of being a crucial signal of the 'opening' of the regime. In Spain, instead, the 1977 Amnesty Law was approved by a newly inaugurated democratic parliament that was keen on making it a symbol of the end of past divisions – in line with the transition's spirit of consensus – though this specific law was actually linked to a delicate bargaining context whereby the violent crimes committed shortly before its enactment (most notably by the separatist group ETA) were included, too. Political violence during the transition period (including separatist violence) and the concomitant military agitation in Spain made for a more unstable transition context than in the other two countries, thus contributing to the general risk-aversion posture.

These different contexts had/have a number of important consequences. The most obvious is that in both Spain and Brazil, these laws were celebrated for the concrete benefits they brought to political prisoners and for constituting a symbolic stepping stone in the path towards a democratic and integrated polity. This was especially the case in Spain, where there was a consensual political effort to make this law the quintessential symbol of reconciliation (for reasons particular to the Spanish context), coming most notably from left-wing sectors. It occurred to hardly anyone to challenge these laws until several decades later, when successful challenges elsewhere resonated with domestic actors in Brazil and Spain. Besides the legal difficulties involved in challenging these laws at this point in time, these initiatives are met with accusations of subverting the historical context in which they were approved, the intention of the legislators, and the backing of the amnesty movements that pushed for amnesty laws in these countries. If it is true that in Uruguay there was also a major obstacle – the referendum results on the Expiry Law –, the fact is that it still continued to be seen as a contentious legal instrument, which had no other explicit goal than to protect former state agents. In line with its different context, legal challenges started earlier in Uruguay, and the design of the law itself allowed the executive to decide what fell within its scope.

International influence

While international advocacy networks were far from developed at the incipient stages of these countries' processes of regime change, there is important variation in how the TJ norm has travelled across time and space. The greater extent to which the Uruguayan case was influenced by its Argentinian neighbor since the early stages can hardly be overstated. As Sikkink (2011) has argued, Argentina is a key case in the early instigation of an accountability norm, starting in the first half of the 1980s. As highlighted before, not only is it the case that Uruguay shares strong geographical and cultural bonds with Argentina, but most of the Uruguayan 'disappeared' were actually abducted in Argentina, where the largest share of the Uruguayan exiled community resided. It is no surprise that families and human rights groups drew inspiration from their counterparts in Argentina and that the trials of the Junta in 1985 resonated loudly across the border, possibly encouraging families and victims to follow the same patterns of legal mobilization.

It is, in fact, striking to see how developments in Uruguay tend to follow those in Argentina in temporal terms: the Expiry Law was enacted at virtually the same time as the Full Stop Law (*Ley de punto final*) in Argentina; the military confessions in Argentina in 1995 produced an impact in Uruguay too; the so-called 'truth trials' (*juicios por la verdad*) started in Argentina in 1998, at the same time as *truth* became a more salient demand in Uruguay, impacting on the creation of the Peace Commission in 2000; the Argentinian amnesty laws were declared null by Congress in 2003, and the first trials started in 2006, while in Uruguay, the 'loophole approach' to the Expiry Law was enacted from 2005. Moreover, it is no coincidence that the issue of criminal accountability for grave violations became immediately framed as a human rights issue in Uruguay, following the same language used by a strong pro-accountability scene in Argentina. Although political actors in Uruguay tend to be somewhat dismissive of the influence Argentina plays (the negotiating and democratic vocation of Uruguayans is said to contrast with the quick temperament and confrontational nature of Argentinians [Interview UR8]), the fact is that it is impossible to miss the parallels.

This is in great contrast to Spain, where in line with the absence of political or social initiatives on the matter, there was no widespread perception that there was a pending human rights issue when it came to the victims of the Civil War and the dictatorship. It was not until the Association for the Recovery of Historical Memory (*Asociación para la Recuperación de la Memoria Histórica* [ARMH]) made exhumations a contentious issue that the recovery of the bodies of family members started to be publicly articulated as a *human right*, and in this, the ARMH visibly borrowed from the language associated with the Latin American disappeared. Before the Pinochet case in 1998, there are no signs that other countries' experiences regarding accountability for past crimes had any publicly visible impact in Spain. It is telling that it was not until 2002 that the Spanish case was submitted to the United Nations Working Group on Enforced or Involuntary Disappearances, an organization that had already denounced disappearances in Uruguay and Brazil throughout the 1980s. The same is true for Amnesty International, which was more active in Latin America during this period and only drew attention to Francoist crimes after the appearance of the 'historical memory movement' in Spain. The fact that the TJ norm did not travel to Spain until the late 1990s/early 2000s is important because, as I highlighted before, the 'TJ culture' has provided a normative framework that has helped those who suffered from state violence construct a sense of victimhood and develop and affirm a feeling of entitlement to certain rights as a result.

Different geopolitical neighborhoods can also say something about why Brazil is somewhere between the two. On the one hand, Brazil is not as culturally proximate to Argentina as Uruguay is, and it took longer to adhere to international human rights standards. This is visible, for example, in the fact that it did not sign the American Convention on Human Rights until 1992 and did not recognize the jurisdiction of the Inter-American Court of Human Rights (IACtHR) until 1998 (Uruguay had done so in 1985). However, its (late) insertion into the Inter-American human rights system made it more exposed to the TJ norm than Spain. As highlighted before, the IACtHR has played a pioneering role in the development of transitional justice–related jurisprudence, not only when it comes to judicial remedies and the lack of validity of amnesty laws, but also in terms of the 'right to truth' and comprehensive reparation policies. Besides the alleged role of the 2010 condemnation in the decision to create the National Truth Commission, this same ruling has quantitatively and qualitatively strengthened the pro-accountability movement in Brazil. Moreover, Brazil's geopolitical environment is different from the Spanish one in that by 2010, Brazil was one of the very few countries in Latin America that did not have an investigation commission of this type. If it is true that developments in Latin America are far from unknown in Spain, the European geopolitical and legal orbit does not exert the same kind of influence in the matters of concern here. Even though a few complaints have been brought to the European Court of Human Rights after the backlash against Garzón in 2008, they have been ruled inadmissible (on the basis that the applicants took too long to present them).

Conclusion

Despite exhibiting an apparent similarity in the type of transition and the concomitant absence of TJ measures at this stage, a zoom into the transition period provides evidence that the way the violations of the past regime were approached was not the same everywhere. In line with path-dependence theories, I argued that the moment of transition from dictatorship to democracy was key in defining a country's 'memory regime' – that is, how the violations of the predecessor regime are approached from a political perspective – because this is an issue that will be explicitly or implicitly present at this stage and because the *time zero* of any regime is naturally important in setting the tone. Assuming that initial conditions leave an imprint that shapes perceptions and discourses, and facilitates or complicates choices, I argued that later cross-country differences in the political treatment of the past are not independent of the 'memory regimes' in which actors are embedded.

To put it bluntly, the fact that social and political actors in Uruguay found the means and the motives to make the past a highly salient and conflictual issue during the transition period facilitated the perpetuation of conflictual patterns over time and the enactment of robust TJ measures later on. The politicization of the accountability issue during the transition, its early framing as a human rights issue, and the widespread endorsement of progressive sectors meant that social and political actors needed only to wait for an 'opportunity window' to reintroduce the topic on the agenda. Instead, in Spain, and to a lesser extent in Brazil, a consensual memory regime and its perpetuation over the years meant that (new) interested circles were faced with the harder task of breaking with a past pattern of (active) silence. This is especially the case if the transition's agreements were widely endorsed at the time and seen as an important feature in the creation of a democratic and integrated polity. Although this is, to an extent, true for both, it is especially the case in Spain, where there was a broader and more consensual agreement across the political spectrum and where the seriousness of past divisions contrasted more neatly with the achievements of the transition period. This, as argued, is not independent of the greater difficulties that political actors in Spain have in dealing with transitional justice measures nowadays.

Explanations based on different types of memory regimes naturally beg for answers regarding the structural factors that shape the type of memory regime, that is, the country-specific features that condition the posture of social and political actors in the first place. The factors that I choose to emphasize were a combination of variables highlighted in the literature with those that inductively appeared as the most relevant when comparing the three country cases. While relative differences in the correlation of political forces during the transition is one of such factors – which could put into question the initial assumption that we are dealing with the same type of transition to democracy (not *exactly* the same after all) – this is not the only factor that explains the existence of a conflictual memory regime in Uruguay, besides failing to account for the subtler differences between the memory regimes of Spain and Brazil (considering that the Brazilian amnesty law was the one approved under the most unfavorable correlation of forces, but Spain is the country with the most consensual regime).

In Uruguay, the favorable geopolitical environment, its democratic history, and the levels of repression in a society that was unused to state violence are important factors too, not to mention the institutional opportunities and the meso-level factors that were highlighted in the chapter on this specific case. Spain, instead, distinguishes itself from the other two not so much because the correlation of political forces was more critical (at least not in comparison to Brazil) but because of (1) the context of a ferocious civil war at the onset of a long dictatorial regime, (2) the challenging transition context in terms of violence and construction of a radically new polity, and (3) the lack of a previously stable democratic experience. Brazil, on the other hand, stands out for its highly top-down transition and for the relatively lower levels of repression, in the context of a society that has an ambiguous and historically entrenched relationship with violence and (the lack of) accountability for state agents.

While the transnational diffusion and consolidation of a transitional justice norm is undoubtedly contributing to the creation of more cross-country convergence over time, the fact is that most of these domestic-specific factors continue to play out in one way or another and are thus essential in understanding differences in where the three countries stand today.

References

Binningsbø, Helga Malmin, Cyanne E. Loyle, Scott Gates, and Jon Elster. 2012. 'Armed Conflict and Post-conflict Justice, 1946–2006: A Dataset.' *Journal of Peace Research* 49, no. 5: 731–740.

Kovras, Iosif. 2017. *Grassroots Activism and the Evolution of Transitional Justice. The families of the Disappeared.* Cambridge: Cambridge University Press.

Olsen, Tricia D., Leigh A. Payne, and Andrew G. Reiter. 2010. *Transitional Justice in Balance: Comparing Processes, Weighing Efficacy.* Washington, DC: United States Institute of Peace Press.

Pereira, Anthony. 2005. *Political (In)Justice: Authoritarianism and the Rule of Law in Brazil, Chile and Argentina.* Pittsburgh: University of Pittsburgh Press.

Pinheiro, Paulo Sérgio. 1998. *Democratic Consolidation and Human Rights in Brazil.* Working Paper 256. Notre Dame, IN: Helen Kellogg Institute for International Studies.

Reiter, Andrew G., Tricia Olsen and Leigh A. Payne. 2013. 'Transitional Justice and Civil War: Exploring New Pathways, Challenging Old Guideposts.' *Transitional Justice Review* 1, no. 1: 137–169.

Rial, Juan. 1990. *Los partidos politicos Uruguayanos en el proceso de transición hacia la democracia.* Working Paper 145. Notre Dame: Helen Kellogg Institute for International Studies.

Roniger, Luis and Sznajder, Mario. 1999. *The Legacy of Human Rights Violations in the Southern Cone: Argentina, Chile, and Uruguay.* New York: Oxford University Press.

Sikkink, Kathryn. 2011. *The Justice Cascade: How Human Rights Prosecutions are Changing World Politics.* New York: W. W. Norton.

Conclusion

Unlike what the term *transitional* justice (TJ) could otherwise suggest, this manuscript started by pointing to the plethora of empirical examples showing that TJ measures are far from being a *transitional* affair. Despite the passage of time – and the obvious difficulties that might bring in terms of investigation and recollection of events – we often see TJ measures being implemented several decades after the abuses they refer to. This prompted me to ask two main sets of questions: what explains the timing of such delayed measures, and why do countries with similar types of transition to democracy follow different TJ trajectories in a post-transition setting? Almost inevitably, this also led me to explore follow-up questions related to the kind of TJ policies chosen and the sequence in which they are implemented. The existing transitional justice literature has started to explore these aspects only recently, and this is the reason why Kovras (2017: 238) has made a plea for scholars to expand the temporal scope of the study of TJ and provide a more dynamic picture and theory of TJ capable of capturing not only *the why* but also *the when* and *how* of TJ outcomes.

Narrowing it down to contexts that similarly initiated their TJ path under 'constraining' conditions, that is, under a negotiated transition to democracy, I argued that while the transition's balance of power is an important part of the answer to why TJ measures could not be implemented at that time, this alone does not provide a satisfactory answer for why these measures are enacted at certain points in time or for why countries diverge in their TJ outcomes later on. In what follows, I summarize the main findings of this research in the form of four main takeaways.

Takeaway 1. The timing of TJ is better understood by a favorable confluence of grassroots activism and influential political allies

In contrast to approaches that privilege either the importance of grassroots activism or the strategic and ideological considerations of political actors and decision-makers, this work has made the case that a confluence of both

DOI: 10.4324/9781003311607-12

is necessary to account for the implementation of TJ measures. On the one hand, it has demonstrated that there is no one unique path to TJ implementation and that proximate changes in either of these two dimensions (or in both at the same time) can account for the timing of TJ implementation. As an example, the change to a favorable executive in Uruguay in 2005 – with the left-wing *Frente Amplio* (FA) being elected for the time in the country's history – best explains the timing of the adoption of the so-called 'loophole approach' to the amnesty law that same year, allowing Uruguay to take the first criminal accountability steps. In contrast, there are other contexts where TJ measures were implemented by executives that had been sitting in power for years, and their timing is best explained by renewed sources of pressure. Uruguay is again a good example, as the FA's decision to finally take steps to revoke the amnesty law in 2011 is not independent of the condemnation of the Inter-American Court of Human Rights (IACtHR) that same year, as well as renewed pressure from pro-accountability actors. The same can be said about the implementation of the National Truth Commission in Brazil in 2011 despite the fact that the Workers' Party had been in power since 2003.

On the other hand, it is perhaps most relevant to highlight that none of these changes took place without the other 'necessary condition' being present already. This is to say that a change to a favorable executive in Uruguay in 2005 is insufficient to fully explain the steps taken then without taking into consideration the strength of the pro-accountability movement, the presence of allies of the movement within the FA, and the fact that pro-accountability actors were already testing 'loophole approaches' in Uruguayan courts by then, inspired by similar actions across the border. Similarly, renewed sources of pressure would hardly have any effect in other contexts if they did not have a favorable interlocutor in power. This is best proven by the counterfactual that conservative sectors in all three cases would surely not have responded to renewed sources of pressure, judging by their high degree of opposition to such measures and the fact that when in power, no TJ steps are taken (or reversals happen).

While the cases under study here show that party colors matter, this does not mean that this will always be the case. The work of Monika Nalepa (2010) in Eastern Europe, for example, shows that factions coming from the previous authoritarian regime can have their own strategic incentives to implement TJ measures (such as preventing the passage of more severe TJ steps in the future). Future research could benefit from studying the conditions under which party colors matter and those in which they do not. My hunch is that party colors will matter less in settings where TJ is a highly salient and politicized issue, and vice versa. The case of the 2001 Peace Commission in Uruguay, approved by a president coming from a conservative party, is perhaps instructive, as there were surely strategic incentives to take such steps in light of the greater salience and visibility of the issue in this setting.

Takeaway 2. A 'path dependence' lens is well suited to the study of transitional justice trajectories

While it is surely a truism to highlight that the past shapes the present or that the present is best understood in light of the past, it is no less true that a path-dependency analytical lens has helped me shed much light on the reasons why the countries under study differ in their TJ trajectories and outcomes. Borrowing the notion of 'memory regimes' from Bernhard and Kubik (2014), I argued that the dominant patterns of memory politics in reference to the past regime's violence during early stages has an enduring influence over future approaches towards the same issue. This is in line with the importance that path-dependence/historical institutionalist approaches attribute to initial conditions in shaping the development of follow-up processes and is part of the reason why I focused in particular on the transition period, the moment in which the memory regime is first defined.

I leveraged the fact that despite a similar type of negotiated transition to democracy, the countries under study differed considerably in the way social and political actors approached the issue back then. In contrast to Spain and Brazil, Uruguay had a 'conflictual memory regime' from early on, meaning that accountability for the crimes of stage agents was one (if not *the* most) salient and contentious issue of the transition period. Significant political and social actors mobilized around this issue to the point that it was submitted to a referendum in 1989. Despite its negative results for the pro-accountability movement, it is still the case that for a significant share of Uruguayans, and for the left in particular, the country's amnesty law became forever perceived as an instrument of impunity for serious human rights violations and thus, a shameful stain on the otherwise good reputation of the country. The opposite is largely true for Spain and Brazil, where the issue of past violations was left unpoliticized and where the transition pacts, and in particular their respective amnesty laws, were largely perceived as an instrument of pacification and reconciliation, and thus, an important stepping stone on the road towards a successful process of regime transformation. Unlike Uruguay, there were no political or social voices (or only very isolated ones) pushing for accountability for the past crimes of state agents, because this was seen as either unrealistic or simply unconceivable. This is the more so in the Spanish case, where the past was an object of political attention only in so far as there was a consensual approach not to politicize it as part of a broader effort at creating a clean slate for a newly integrated polity.

The fact that still today, mainstream political (and judicial) actors in Spain and Brazil show a great deal of reverence for the countries' amnesty laws and for the 'pacts of the transition' – invoked to justify the absence of criminal accountability steps – is the best piece of evidence that the transition's memory regime has an enduring impact. This is particularly evident in Spain, where political actors have shown themselves to be decisively constrained by the view that the decision to 'leave the past behind' was one of the crucial anchors that made the highly cherished transition to democracy a successful endeavor. That Uruguay was the only country out of the three where the amnesty law was later challenged and where a left-wing executive took steps to undermine it is much less surprising in light of the obvious difference in its memory regime.

What this also implies is that memory regimes are useful in understanding the *kind* of TJ steps that are taken later on. In conflictual memory regimes, more conflictual measures can be expected, and vice versa. It is noteworthy that in Spain and Brazil, the first significant TJ steps were largely victim-centered, in the form of compensation schemes. These are among the least conflictual and visible types of TJ measures, allowing political actors to respond to a circumscribed demand without significantly 'rocking the boat'. In both cases, it was only many years later, once the memory regime started to change – with an expansion in the number and visibility of TJ norm entrepreneurs and allies – that slightly more robust measures were taken. Even though none of the two countries have (yet) gone as far as Uruguay in implementing criminal accountability steps, it is still noteworthy that the memory regime has been under transformation and that judicial accountability has gone from an almost non-issue to a recurrent demand of grassroots activists.

Takeaway 3. Transitional justice trajectories often follow a stepwise logic

Although this manuscript started with few theoretical pretensions when it comes to the sequencing of TJ measures, all that has been said earlier about the path-dependent nature of TJ trajectories and the empirical results of the research itself suggests that there is a particular sequential/incremental logic to the evolution of TJ trajectories in contexts that similarly started under very constraining conditions. As mentioned before, all three cases have progressively (even if very slowly) moved from more innocuous measures first to more robust/conflictual ones later – confirming that the Transitional Justice Scale introduced in Chapter 1 is not only useful in categorizing TJ measures but can also be a decent representation of reality. Despite the differences between Uruguay and the other two countries in the kind of measures that were implemented (something best explained by its memory regime), it is still the case that, broadly speaking, even Uruguay proceeded in a stepwise fashion.

These observations are similar to Kovras's (2017) phase-based theoretical framework. Studying four different countries (Chile, Lebanon, South Africa, and Cyprus) that also went through negotiated transitions, Kovras arrives at a similar conclusion, making the case that there is an incremental logic to the process of truth recovery for the disappeared. After a phase of institutionalized silence, he argues that most families privilege a form of 'forensic truth' (exhumations), which might or might not lead to a stage of 'broader truth' later, depending on other factors. Though this work has been less focused than his on the importance of forensics, I have similarly observed that grassroots activists adapt their demands to the political context and have gradually expanded their claims over time (something that the social movement literature on 'political opportunity structures' has long observed).

In understanding this, it is of course important to have in mind that the political conditions preventing the implementation of TJ measures in the transition period did not disappear all of a sudden and that relevant sources of opposition (most obviously the military) remained. As decision-makers are usually risk-averse and prefer to avoid radical breaks with past patterns (and as the demands from civil society will adjust to this), it makes sense that less antagonistic TJ steps are taken first. Even in the Uruguayan case, it is noticeable how prior to the implementation of the 2001 Peace Commission, families' demands were more focused on 'truth' than on 'justice'.

It is also relevant that once certain measures are in place, new demands for further steps can then more realistically be made, building on the progress (and shortcomings) of previous steps. If TJ policies are usually a response to undergoing transformations in the memory regime, it is also fascinating to consider how these steps are in themselves important in opening the space of opportunity for further changes. This is not only because earlier steps factually facilitate later ones – for example, investigatory steps might uncover evidence that is later of use in criminal proceedings – but also because earlier measures will gradually shape and modify the memory regime in such a way that further/more robust steps will be, at least, perceived as conceivable. Think, for example, of how unthinkable Franco's exhumation from the Valley of the Fallen would have been prior to the so-called Historical Memory Law of 2007 in Spain and how its occurrence in 2019 came as little surprise after years of discussion on the matter.

There is nothing automatic about this process, however, and as family movements know all too well, it takes an enormous deal of effort and time to produce any advancements, which will be invariably criticized by them as 'too little, too late'. Still, once one zooms out and adopts a broad longitudinal lens, it is virtually impossible to miss the incremental/stepwise fashion in which TJ policies are often implemented in contexts of negotiated transitions.

Takeaway 4. The diffusion and consolidation of the transitional justice norm is important in understanding TJ trajectories and recent changes

Although the empirical chapters have made it clear that there are factors specific to each country's domestic context that should be considered when understanding delayed TJ steps, and that they cannot be properly understood outside their specific historical circumstances, there is little doubt that recent changes in the memory regime of all three countries have been influenced by the diffusion and consolidation of a transitional justice norm at the transnational level. The morally compelling idea that states ought to confront a violent past and provide redress to the victims is, in world-historical terms, quite recent and has undoubtedly gained ground in the last two decades. It has, however, not travelled to every country at the same time, and the fact that Argentina was an early instigator of this norm, and that Uruguay has been influenced by its closest neighbor from the start, is part of the reason why the latter stands out in terms of the commitment of left-wing political actors, the strength of the pro-accountability movement, and the overall salience of the topic when compared with the other two case-studies.

In Spain and Brazil, instead, the late appearance of the 'historical memory movement' in the first, and the expansion of the pro-accountability movement in the second, occurred at the same time as their ideas and discourses were being shaped by what international institutions, advocacy networks, and activists in other countries were saying in terms of the 'right to justice, truth, redress, and memory'. It is relevant that it was not until the founder of the Association for the Recovery of Historical Memory (*Asociación para la Recuperación de la Memoria Histórica* [ARMH]) in Spain submitted the case to the UN Working Group on Enforced or Involuntary Disappearances in 2002 that exhumations were reframed as a *human right* and that families started redefining themselves and their deceased family members as *victims* rather than casualties or even martyrs (a point also underscored by Kovras 2017: 234). As stated before, the way in which the transitional justice norm empowered domestic movements and provided a framework that has helped those affected construct a sense of victimhood – and develop and articulate a sense of entitlement to certain rights as a result – is an aspect that deserves more research.

Most importantly for the purposes of this manuscript, some of the sources of pressure that were highlighted are the ultimate and most direct manifestation of the transitional justice norm – most notably the impact of the IACtHR condemnations on delayed TJ initiatives in the cases of Brazil (2010) and Uruguay (2011), but also the alleged impact of the Pinochet affair in bringing the past back to Spanish politics in the late 1990s. If at the time transitional justice was simply not an issue in Spain, it is remarkable to see Spanish left-wing parties today directly quoting the recommendations of the UN Special Rapporteur on the promotion of Truth, Justice, Reparation, and Guarantees of Non-Recurrence.

One broader implication of the diffusion and consolidation of a transitional justice norm at the international/transnational level is that negotiated transitions to democracy occurring today are subject to a substantially different normative environment than those that occurred during the so-called third wave of democratization. In other words, the TJ framework will more be readily available, and TJ expectations are or will be placed upon transitioning states, perhaps contributing to preventing altogether the type of 'unified memory regimes' that Spain and Brazil had.

References

Bernhard, Michael and Jan Kubik, eds. 2014. *Twenty Years After Communism. The Politics of Memory and Commemoration*. New York: Oxford University Press.

Kovras, Iosif. 2017. *Grassroots Activism and the Evolution of Transitional Justice. The Families of the Disappeared*. Cambridge: Cambridge University Press.

Nalepa, Monika. 2010. *Skeletons in the Closet. Transitional Justice in Post-Communist Europe*. Cambridge: Cambridge University Press.

Annex

List of interviewees (2015–2018)

Country Code	*Category*
Spain	
SP1	Academic expert
SP2	Academic expert
SP3	Civil society – ARMH
SP4	Academic expert
SP5	Academic expert/expert consulted by the government
SP6	Political actor – ERC
SP7	Academic expert
SP8	Academic expert
SP9	Political actor – PSOE
SP10	Political actor – PSOE
SP11	Political actor – PSOE
SP12	Political actor – PSOE
SP13	Political actor – PNV
SP14	Political actor – ERC
SP15	Political actor – ERC
SP16	Civil society – AGE
Uruguay	
UR1	Academic expert
UR2	Academic expert
UR3	Civil society – PIT-CNT/lawyer
UR4	Civil society – SERPAJ
UR5	Political actor – FA
UR6	Academic expert
UR7	Political actor – FA
UR8	Political actor – *Partido Colorado*
UR9	Academic expert
UR10	Civil society – PIT-CNT / lawyer
UR11	Political actor – FA
UR12	Political actor – FA
UR13	Civil society – CRYSOL

Country Code	*Category*
Brazil	
BR1	Civil society – *Familiares*
BR2	Academic expert
BR3	Civil society – *Levante Popular da Juventude*
BR4	Civil society/advisory role at the Special Secretariat for Human Rights
BR5	Civil society/advisory role at the Special Secretariat for Human Rights
BR6	Amnesty commission/academic expert
BR7	Human rights lawyer
BR8	Public prosecutor/Special Commission on Political Deaths and Disappearances (CEMDP)
BR9	Amnesty Commission
BR10	Civil society/advisory role at the Special Secretariat for Human Rights
BR11	Public prosecutor
BR12	Academic expert/civil society – *Familiares*
BR13	Civil society/Amnesty Commission
BR14	Lawyer – Brazilian Bar Association
BR15	Political actor – PT
BR16	Public prosecutor
BR17	Academic expert
BR18	Civil society – *Familiares*
BR19	Academic expert

Index

Note: Page numbers in *italics* indicate figures, **bold** indicate tables in the text

Abrão, Paulo 191–192
Acto del Obelisco 118, 125
ADPF 153, 192, 199, 201
Aldunate, Wilson Ferreira 118–120, 123
Almagro, Luis 148
Álvarez, Gregorio 146
American Convention on Human Rights 147, 200, 240
Amnesty Commission 159, 165, 188, 191–192, 196, 217
Amnesty International 29, 92, 116, 184, 216, 239
Araguaia guerrilla 164, 176, 179, 183, 189–190, 195
Archive, War and Exile Association (AGE) 81–82, 84–87
Asociación de Ex-Presos Políticos de Uruguay (CRYSOL) 130, 139, 146
Association for the Recovery of Historical Memory (ARMH) 70, 92; creation/impact 74, 81–86; exhumations as a *human right* 225, 239, 248
Association of Anti-Francoist Ex-Prisoners and Politically Persecuted (AERPA) 65–66, 82
Association of Friends of the International Brigades (AABI) 66, 86
Aznar, José María 80

Basque Nationalist Party (PNV) 75, 77, 80–82, 91, 93
Batlle, Jorge 111, 144, 146, 154, 223; acknowledgment policy 139–142, 219
Blanco, Juan Carlos 143–144, 146
Bolsonaro, Jair 198, 227
Bordaberry, Juan María 113–114, 117, 144–145
Brasil Nunca Mais 164–165, 177, 189–190
Brazilian Bar Association 171, 188, 192, 199
Brazilian Communist Party (PCB) 162–164, 178–179; *see also* Communist Party of Brazil (PCdoB)
Brazilian Democratic Movement (MDB) 163, 166, 168, 171–174

Cardoso, Fernando Henrique 159, 161, 169, 203, 231; reparations (Law 9.140/1995) 183–187, 215–217
Carter, Jimmy 29, 116, 170
Club Naval 119–120, 126–127, 131, 133–134
Collor, Fernando 183, 187
Communist Party of Brazil (PCdoB) 164, 179–180
Communist Party of Spain (PCE) 48, 50, 65, 74–75, 84; transition period 52, 54–56, 61; *see also* United Left
Communist Party of Uruguay 112, 128
Council of Europe 92
Coup d'état: 1936 (Spain) 48, 59, 77–78, 84, 98; 1964 (Brazil) 162–164, 199; 1973 (Uruguay) 114, 116, 119, 145; 1981 (Spain) 27, 56, 64, 67, 70–71, 102
crimes against humanity 97, 99–101, 144, 149–150, 192, 197
criminal accountability: Brazil 159, 191, 197–198, 201; comparative analysis 226, 230, 232, 237, 239, 244–246;

theoretical framework 22–23, 28, 33, 36; transitional justice definition 14, 16, *18*; **Uruguay** 110, 141–142, 154, 219–220

'Democratic Memory Law' 98, 226
diffusion (norm) 22–24, 26, 28, **41**, 242, 247–248
Direito à Memória e à Verdade (publication) 190, 193, 227

Elena Quinteros case 143
ETA (terrorist group) 51, 52, 56, 58, 76, 80
European Court of Human Rights 240
External Commission for the Search of the Disappeared 182–184

Familiares (Uruguay) *see Madres y Familiares de Uruguayos Detenidos Desaparecidos*
Federal Public Prosecutor's Office 188–189, 192, 217
Federal Supreme Court (STF) 199–201
Figueiredo, João 172, 175–176
Franco, Itamar 183–184

Garzón, Baltasar 76, 99–101, 240
Geisel, Ernesto 166–168
Gelman: case 139, 141–142, 148, 223; *Gelman vs. Uruguay* 148, 150; Juan 139, 145, 147, 219, **220**; Macarena 139, 142; sentence 151–152
Genro, Tarso 191–192
Gomes Lund et al. v. Brazil case 161, 195, 200, 217
González, Felipe 64, 66–68, 215–216
Gutiérrez Ruiz, Héctor 116, 136, 144–145

Herzog, Vladimir 170, 176, 178
human rights movement (Uruguay) 122–124, 127, 137, 151–153; *see also* pro-accountability movement

Initiative for Catalonia Greens (ICV) 74, 88, 92–94
Instituto de Estudios Legales y Sociales (IELSUR) 124, 133, 138
Inter-American Commission of Human Rights 123, 138, 148, 195, 217
Inter-American Court of Human Rights (IACtHR): Brazil 161, 192, 195–196, 200–201, 203, 217–218, **218**; comparative analysis 221–226, 240, 244, 248; Uruguay 147–150, 154, 221, **222**
Inter-American System of Human Rights 188, 195
Inter-Ministerial Commission for the Study of the Situation of Victims of the Civil War and Francoism 87–88, 93
International Brigades 66, 81, 86–88
International Criminal Court (ICC) 23, 28
international human rights: law 34, 97, 106, 149; norms 73; standards 240; treaties 34, 144, 149
Intersectorial 118, 125

Justice and Peace Commission (S. Paulo's Archdiocese) 177
'justice cascade' **23**, 28

King Juan Carlos 54, 56

Lacalle, Luis Alberto 138
Law 4/1990 (reparations) 64–65, 82, 212, 214, 226
Law 18.831 (re-establishing the state's punitive capacity) 150–151, 154, 221–222
Law on Historical Memory (Law 52/2007) 45, 47, 74, 87–88; accounting for enactment 89–94, 213–215; comparative analysis 226–227, 231; post-2007 94, 98
Law on the Dead and Disappeared (Law 9.140/95) 183, 185–186, 190, 215–217
legality principle 34, 100, 150
Lula da Silva, Luiz Inácio 161, 171, 188–191, 193–195
lustration 1, 16, 23

Madres y Familiares de Uruguayos Detenidos Desaparecidos (*Madres y Familiares*) 124–125, 128, 130, 136, 138–140
March(es) of Silence 138, 141, 149, 151, 154, **220**, 220–223
Michelini, Rafael 138, 143, 151
Michelini, Zelmar 116, 123, 136, 138, 144–145
military confessions 31, 219, 239; *see also* Scilingo, Adolfo

Miranda, Nilmário 182–184, 190
Mujica, José 128, 148–150
Multipartidaria 118–119

National Renewal Alliance (ARENA) 163, 173
National Security Council 113, 117, 119
National Truth Commission (CNV) 159, 176, 217–218; comparative analysis 223, 227, 240, 244; creation/antecedents 188, 191–198; report 164–165, 199
Neves, Tancredo 168, 181–182
norm entrepreneurs 24–25, 37, 246
Nunca Más report (Uruguay) 115, 137

Observatorio Luz Ibarburu 130, 134, 146

'pact of forgetting' 57, 68, 73
'pact of silence' 45–46, 57
Parque Hotel negotiations 117, 119
Peace Commission 115, 153; comparative analysis 223, 239, 244, 247; creation 140–141, 218–220
People's Alliance 56, 63
People's Victory Party (PVP) 116, 128, 131, 144
Perus grave 182–183
Pinochet, Augusto 1, 28, 224, 239, 248; affair (Spain) 76–81, 85, 102, 214, 248
PIT-CNT (Plenario Intersindical de Trabajadores-Convención Nacional de Trabajadores) 111, 124–125, 132, 136, 141, 147, 151–152
Podemos 97–99
pro-accountability movement: Argentina 34–35, 239; Brazil 195; comparative analysis 223–224, 226, 230, 244–245, 248; Spain 101; Uruguay 147, 149, 151, 154, 221

Querella Argentina 101, 224

Rajoy, Mariano 94
Republican Left of Catalonia (ERC) 75, 88, 92–93
Rousseff, Dilma 128, 196–198

Sanchéz, Pedro 96
Sanguinetti, Julio M. 144, **220**, 219, 223; second presidency (1995–2000) 138–139, 141–142; transition period 119–120, 126–127, 133–137
Sarney, José 168–169, 181–182
Scilingo, Adolfo 138
Seregni, Líber 119, 120, 126
SERPAJ (*Servicio Paz y Justicia*) 115, 124–125, 131, 136–137
Special Commission on Political Deaths and Disappearances (CEMDP) 159, 186, 190, 196–197, 215, 227
Special Rapporteur on the promotion of Truth, Justice, Reparation and Guarantees of Non-Recurrence 94, 97, 248
Special Secretariat for Human Rights 161, 189–190, 193
statute of limitations 34; Brazil 197; Spain 62, 99–100; Uruguay 111, 149–152, 221, 222
Suárez, Adolfo 54–56, 61, 64
Supreme Court: Spain 99–101; Uruguay 133, 136, 147, 149–150; *see also* Federal Supreme Court

Third National Human Rights Program (PNDH-3) 191, 193, 217
third wave of democratization 2, 4, 26–27, 29, **41**, 248
Tortura Nunca Mais 176, 182
'transitional justice culture' 28, 72–73, 239
'transitional justice spectrum' (Grodsky) 19
Tuparamos (MLN-T) 112–115, 129, 136, 150, 178

Unión Cívica 118–119
Union of the Democratic Center (UCD) 55–56, 64, 67
United Left (IU) 65–66, 74, *75*, 78, 81–82, 212; United Left-Initiative for Catalonia Greens (IU-ICV) 88, 92–94
United Nations Working Group on Enforced or Involuntary Disappearances 83, 97, 225, 239, 248
universal jurisdiction 28, 76, 101
US Congress 116, 123
Ustra, Carlos Alberto Brilhante 192–193, 203, 217

Valley of the Fallen 88, 96, 227, 247

Vannuchi, Paulo 161, 189–190, 192, 194–195
Vázquez, Tabaré 145–147
vetting *see* lustration

'war children' 75, 81, 86, 88, 93

Zapatero, José Luis Rodríguez 82, 84, 87–88, 90–94, 214, 223–224